On Pagans,
Jews, and
Christians

Also by Arnaldo Momigliano

La composizione della storia di Tucidide (1929)

Prime linee di storia della tradizione maccabaica (1931)

L'opera dell'imperatore Claudio (1932)

Filippo il Macedone (1934)

Contributo alla storia degli studi classici e del mondo antico (1955–1987)

Secondo contributo alla storia degli studi classici (1960)

The Conflict Between Paganism and Christianity in the Fourth Century (ed.) (1963)

Terzo contributo alla storia degli studi classici (1966)

Studies in Historiography (1966)

Quarto contributo alla storia degli studi classici (1969)

The Development of Greek Biography (1971)

Quinto contributo alla storia degli studi classici (1975)

Alien Wisdom (1975)

Essays in Ancient and Modern Historiography (1977)

Sesto contributo alla storia degli studi classici (1980)

Storiografia Greca (1982)

New Paths of Classicism in the Nineteenth Century (1982)

Problèmes d'historiographie ancienne et moderne (1983)

Sui fondamenti della storia antica (1984)

Settimo contributo alla storia degli studi classici (1984)

Arnaldo Momigliano

On Pagans, Jews, and Christians

WESLEYAN UNIVERSITY PRESS

Middletown, Connecticut

Published by Wesleyan University Press
Middletown, CT 06459
All rights reserved

Printed in the United States of America   10   9   8   7

LIBRARY OF CONGRESS CATALOGING-IN-PUBLICATION DATA
Momigliano, Arnaldo.
    On Pagans, Jews, and Christians.
    Bibliography: p.
    Includes index.
    1. Rome—Religion.   2. Judaism.   3. Historiography.
I. Title.
BL810.M66   1987   291'.0937   87-24264
ISBN 0-8195-5173-2
ISBN 0-8195-6218-1 (pbk.)

For Professor Karl Christ

CONTENTS

I hope that these papers speak for themselves. They are a selection from the more recent volumes of my *Contributo alla storia degli studi classici e del mondo antica* (Rome, Edizioni di Storia e Letteratura, 1955–1987) and form a continuation of the *Essays in Ancient and Modern Historiography* published by Wesleyan University Press in 1977. The title, *On Pagans, Jews, and Christians*, defines the present choice more precisely and perhaps indicates what has been my main interest in historical research. The treble tradition—Jewish, Classical, and Christian—that I have inherited as a Jew and as an Italian invited exploration and clarification, but did not carry inside it the seeds of any dramatic conflict. The spirit of the Risorgimento is still active in Italy. The conflicts in which I have been involved during my life—and the resulting cruelties—have other origins.

A.M.
December 1986
University of Chicago
Scuola Normale Superiore Pisa

LIST OF ABBREVIATIONS

ACD	*Acta Classica Universitatis Scientiarum Debreceniensis*
ANRW	*Aufstieg und Niedergang der Römischen Welt*
BICS	*Bulletin of the Institute of Classical Studies*
Bull. Com. Arch.	*Bulletino della Commissione archaeologica communale in Roma*
CIL	*Corpus Inscriptionum Latinarum*
CJ	*Classical Journal*
Corp. Pap. Jud.	*Corpus Papyrorum Judaicarum*
CPhil	*Classical Philology*
CQ	*Classical Quarterly*
CRAcad. Inscr.	*Comptes rendus de l'Académie des Inscriptions et Belles-Lettres*
Degrassi ILLRP	A. Degrassi, *Inscriptiones Latinae Liberae Rei Publicae*
Ditt.³	W. Dittenberger, *Sylloge Inscriptionum Graecarum* ³
FGrH	F. Jacoby, *Fragmente der griechischen Historiker*
ICS	*Illinois Classical Studies*
ILS	H. Dessau, *Inscriptiones Latinae Selectae*
JHS	*Journal of Hellenic Studies*
JRS	*Journal of Roman Studies*
Pap. Soc. It.	*Papiri greci e latini* (Pubblicazioni della Società italiana per la ricerca dei papiri greci e latini in Egitto)
PG	J. P. Migne, *Patrologiae Cursus, series Graeca*
PL	J. P. Migne, *Patrologiae Cursus, series Latina*
PP	*La Parola del Passato,* Naples
P.-W.	Pauly-Wissowa, *Real-Encyclopädie der classischen Altertumswissenschaft*
REL	*Revue des Études Latines*
Rend. Linc.	*Rendiconti della Accademia Nazionale dei Lincei*
Rend. Pont.	*Rendiconti della Pontificia Accademia Romana di Archeologia*

Rev. Ét. Aug.	*Revue des Études Augustiniennes*
Rev. Ét. Grec.	*Revue des Études Grecaues*
Rh. Mus.	*Rheinisches Museum für Philologie*
Riv. Fil. Class.	*Rivista di Filologia e di Istruzione Classica*
TLS	*Times Literary Supplement*

On Pagans,
Jews, and
Christians

I

Biblical Studies and Classical Studies: Simple Reflections upon Historical Method

PRINCIPLES OF HISTORICAL research need not be different from criteria of common sense. And common sense teaches that outsiders must not tell insiders what they should do. I shall therefore not discuss directly what biblical scholars are doing. They are the insiders.

What I can perhaps do usefully is to emphasize as briefly as possible three closely interrelated points of my experience as a classical scholar who is on speaking terms with biblical scholars:

1) our common experience in historical research;
2) the serious problems we all have to face because of the current devaluation of the notion of evidence and of the corresponding overappreciation of rhetoric and ideology as instruments for the analysis of the literary sources;
3) what seems to me the most fruitful field of collaboration between classical and biblical scholars.

Let me admit from the start that I am rather impervious to any claim that sacred history poses problems which are not those of

An address to the section on method of the Centennial Meeting of the Society of Biblical Literature in Dallas, Texas, November 6, 1980. *Annali della Scuola Normale Superiore di Pisa*, Serie III, vol. XI, fasc. 1, 1981, pp. 25–32.

profane history. As a man trained from early days to read the Bible
in Hebrew, Livy in Latin, and Herodotus in Greek, I have never
found the task of interpreting the Bible any more or any less complex than that of interpreting Livy or Herodotus. Livy is of course
less self-assured about the truth of what he tells us about Romulus than the Pentateuch is about Abraham. But the basic elements
of a sacred history are in Livy as much as in the Pentateuch. It so
happens that the Romans entrusted their priests with the task of
registering events; and in one way or another the priestly code of
Rome contributed to the later annals written by senators or by
professional writers. It is unnecessary to add at this eleventh hour
that the problems about understanding the texts, guessing their
sources, and determining the truth of their information are basically the same in Roman as in Hebrew history. The similarity extends to the means and methods of supplementing and checking
our literary sources by archaeology, epigraphy, numismatics, and
what not. Whether biblical or classical historians, we have also
learned that archaeology and epigraphy cannot take the place of
the living tradition of a nation as transmitted by its literary texts.
At the same time, we have been cured of early delusions that the
reliability of historical traditions can be easily demonstrated by
the spade of the archaeologists. A nice example was provided two
years ago by the discovery, by now famous, of an archaic Latin
inscription in the town of Satricum. What is now known as the
Lapis Satricanus is a simple dedication to Mars (Mamars) by the
companions (sodales) of Publius Valerius. This is the text, on two
lines with something missing at the beginning:

. . . ei steterai Popliosio Valesiosio
suodales Mamartei

The date of the inscription is unlikely to be earlier than 530 B.C.
or later than 480 B.C. Roman tradition tells us of a Roman consul
Publius Valerius Poplicola for the first year of the Republic (traditionally 509 B.C.); but the reality of this consul had been doubted,
for good and for bad reasons. Are we now to regard the Publius Valerius who has appeared in Satricum as identical with the Roman
consul of 509 B.C.? And can we claim this identification as a vin-
dication of traditionalism? Biblical scholars are used to such
problems.

On the other hand, we have learned that archaeology allows us to pose problems which the literary tradition does not even suggest. When we catalogue the furniture of the tombs of eighth-century-B.C. Latium we are by implication asking questions about the material culture of Iron-Age Latium, its relations to Etruria, to Greece, etc., which are simply outside the literary tradition. But of course there is a difference between asking intelligent questions and producing plausible answers. We have to learn to live with a disproportion between the intelligent questions we can ask and the plausible answers we can give. This is the only consolation I can offer to my biblical colleagues who have not yet found a plausible answer to their intelligent questions about Genesis chapter 14 and who do not delude themselves that the Ebla tablets are going to oblige in this respect. The most dangerous type of researcher in any historical field is the man who, because he is intelligent enough to ask a good question, believes that he is good enough to give a satisfactory answer.

If I said there is no basic difference between writing biblical history and writing any other history, it is because I wanted to introduce what to my mind is the really serious problem about writing any history today. There is a widespread tendency both inside and outside the historical profession to treat historiography as another genre of fiction. The reduction of historiography to fiction takes various forms and is justified with varying degrees of intellectual sophistication. It is sometimes presented in the simple form of reducing any literary product (including historiography) to the expression of ideological points of view; that is, of explicit or concealed class interests. It is also offered, with greater sophistication, as an analysis of historical works in terms of rhetorical postures; and, finally, it is elaborated by combining ideological and rhetorical analysis with the purpose of proving that any historical account is characterized by a rhetorical posture which in its turn indicates a social and political bias. The conclusion is in all cases the same: there is no way of distinguishing between fiction and historiography.

I shall not speak about the specific forms this rhetorical analysis takes in biblical studies. At present, the most eminent representative in this country of the combination of the rhetorical with the ideological approach in order to dissolve historiography into fiction is my friend Hayden White. He is a dominating influence in the two periodicals *History and Theory* and *New Literary History* and, remarkably enough, has found strong support in Peter Munz's recent book *The Shape of Time: A New Look at the Philosophy of History*, published in 1977. This support is particularly remarkable because Peter Munz by origin and formation represents German historicism filtered through English analytical philosophy. Needless to say, Hayden White's main work is *Metahistory*, 1973. His volume *Topics of Discourse: Essays in Cultural Criticism* collects important papers which are partly earlier and partly later than *Metahistory*. Among his most recent papers I note his discussion of Droysen's *Historik* in *History and Theory*, 1980, No. 1, and the essay on *Literary and Social Action* in *New Literary History*, Winter 1980, No. 2.

In his earlier work Hayden White emphasized the rhetorical postures of the historians. Going back to Giambattista Vico, he tried to reduce all historiography to four basic attitudes, expressed or perhaps rather symbolized by the rhetorical figures of metaphor, metonymy, synecdoche, and irony. Metaphor, according to White, prevailed in the sixteenth and seventeenth centuries, metonymy in the eighteenth century, synecdoche in the early nineteenth century, irony in the late nineteenth century, followed up by the present-day irony about irony. The book on *Metahistory*, however, proved that these chronological distinctions had little importance for White, as he showed there that all four rhetorical modes were vital and competitive in the nineteenth century, when Ranke stood for synecdoche, Michelet for metaphor, Tocqueville for metonymy, and Burckhardt for irony. Nor is it clear that these figures of speech really represent different political and social attitudes, for three conservatives like Ranke, Tocqueville, and Burckhardt wrote in different rhetorical keys.

More recently White gave me the impression of attributing less importance to rhetorical categories. He has been treating literature (including historiography) as a commodity which comes into the market with the peculiarity of being able to speak about the conditions of its own production. He has also stated that in the nineteenth century historiographies of whatever kind served to defend the status quo, which may cause some surprise in regard to Karl Marx.

Now, all this may be right or wrong, but is irrelevant to the fundamental fact about history—that it must be based on evidence as a *conditio sine qua non*, whereas other forms of literature are not compelled to be so based, though of course nothing prevents a novel or an epic poem from being pedantically founded upon authentic archival documents. One is almost embarrassed to have to say that any statement a historian makes must be supported by evidence which, according to ordinary criteria of human judgment, is adequate to prove the reality of the statement itself. This has three consequences. First, historians must be prepared to admit in any given case that they are unable to reach safe conclusions because the evidence is insufficient; like judges, historians must be ready to say: "not proven." Secondly, the methods used to ascertain the value of the evidence must continually be scrutinized and perfected, because they are essential to historical research. Thirdly, the historians themselves must be judged according to their ability to establish facts. The form of exposition they choose for their presentation of the facts is a secondary consideration. I have of course nothing to object in principle to the present multiplication in methods of rhetorical analysis of historical texts. You may have as much rhetorical analysis as you consider necessary, provided it leads to the establishment of the truth—or to the admission that truth is regretfully out of reach in a given case. But it must be clear once for all that Judges and Acts, Herodotus and Tacitus are historical texts to be examined with the purpose of recovering the truth of the past. Hence the interesting conclusion that the notion of forgery has a different meaning in historiography than it has in other branches of literature or of art. A creative writer or artist perpetrates a forgery every time he intends to mislead his public about the date and authorship of his own work. But only a historian can be guilty of forging evidence or of knowingly using forged evidence in order to support his own historical discourse. One is never simple-minded enough about the condemnation of forgeries. Pious frauds are frauds, for which one must show no piety—and no pity.

I shall only add that I have purposely confined my remarks to rhetorical analysis and refrained from any generalization about form-criticism, of which rhetorical analysis is only a variety. I am very conscious that at least in men like Hermann Gunkel form-

criticism has been a powerful instrument for historical understanding, not a sign of helplessness before realities.

To conclude, I will ask myself where a classical scholar can
help biblical scholars most usefully. My answer would be that in
the field of political, social, and religious history differences are
more important than similarities—and therefore knowledge of
Greco-Roman history can be useful only for differential comparison. Hence the failure in the attempt of importing the Greek notion of amphictyony into the far more complex history of the
Hebrew tribes.

But Jewish historiography developed at least from the fifth century B.C. in conditions shared by Greek historiography. Both had
constantly to refer to the reality of the Persian Empire. More specifically, there are questions of dependence of later Jewish historiography on Greek historiography which have seldom been
formulated with the necessary clarity. I shall give two examples.
The idea of the succession of the universal empires is to be found
first in Greek historians from Herodotus to Dionysius of Halicarnassus, passing through Ctesias, Polybius, and that strange Roman
disciple of the Greeks, Aemilius Sura, probably an elder contemporary of Polybius. It is a notion dependent on the basic Greek discovery of political history. Outside Greek historical thought, the
idea of a succession of empires appears first in the Book of Daniel,
chapter 2, if we date this chapter, as I believe we must, about 250
B.C. I must state explicitly that no theory of universal succession
of empires is to be found in the Book of Tobit, chapter 14, whatever may be its date.

The idea of the succession of reigns with different degrees of
perfection is of course familiar to Iranian thought, but only with
reference to the Iranian state. On the other hand, the Babylonians
of the Hellenistic age registered in their chronicles (or so-called
prophetic chronicles) the succession of rulers of different nation-
ality in Babylonia. Neither in Iran nor in Babylonia have we so far
discovered the notion of a succession of universal empires, as Daniel knew it. The only proper comparison is with the Greeks. Daniel has much in common with Iranian and Babylonian texts, but
not about the succession of universal empires. We must therefore
ask the question whether the author or, rather, authors of Daniel—beginning with the author of chapter 2—got the idea from

the Greco-Macedonians who ruled the East after Alexander. Personally, I answer this question in the affirmative. Until evidence to the contrary is provided, I take it that about 250 B.C. a Jew, either in Mesopotamia or in Palestine, got hold of the Greek idea of succession of universal empires and transformed it.

I am less positive about another question of this kind. In Herodotus Book VII, Part II, the military scene is dominated by the defense of the pass of the Thermopylae. The ideological scene is dominated by the conversation between Xerxes and the Spartan Demaratus, who explains to Xerxes why the Greeks, and especially the Spartans, will not yield to the Persians: they do not obey individual men, but the Law. In the Book of Judith, before Judith herself appears on the scene, our interest is concentrated, on the military side, on the Jewish Thermopylae, the mysterious place Bethulia, while the ideological background is filled by the conversation between Holophernes and Achior, who is not a Jew, but unpredictably (because he is an Ammonite) will become one. Achior explains to Holophernes that the Jews will not yield so long as they obey their Law.

When Judith appears, she presents herself to the Assyrians as the person who can reveal the secret path through the mountains, exactly as the traitor Ephialtes does in Herodotus.

The structure of the second part of Herodotus VII and of the first section of the Book of Judith is articulated on the same sequence of an ideological dialogue and of a peculiar military situation. We must ask ourselves whether the author of the original Hebrew Judith knew Herodotus directly or indirectly. Here, as I have said, I am less sure about my answer, but my inclination to give again a positive answer is reinforced by another, better known, coincidence between the Book of Judith and a Greek historical text. It has long been recognized that the five days the thirsty Jews besieged in Bethulia give themselves before surrendering have their exact counterpart in the five days the thirsty Greeks besieged by the Persians in Lindos give themselves before surrendering: the Greek story is contained in the Chronicle of Lindos, a compilation from previous sources written in 99 B.C.

Whatever his date, the author of the original Hebrew text of Judith seems to have been acquainted with stories reported by Greek historians about the wars of the Greeks against Persia. If there was anything which conceivably could interest the Jews, it was what the Greek historians thought about oriental empires and especially about Persia. *Daniel* and *Judith* may perhaps be defined as texts which in Hellenistic times and under Greek influence tried to present an image of the Jews as subjects of the previous universal empires: this image was of course very relevant to what the Jews could do or could hope for under the Greco-Macedonian universal empire.

Notwithstanding the example provided by Eduard Meyer, classical historians have been slow in understanding what Persia meant to the other nations. But we are now beginning to make some progress. This is my favorite field for exchange of information between classical and biblical historians.

2

Historiography of Religion: Western Views

WITHIN THE JEWISH and Christian traditions, the origin of philosophical and historical examinations of religion lies in the works
of the ancient Greeks. This is equivalent to saying that the point
of departure for these traditions' philosophical and historical self-
examination is Greek thought. Other attitudes toward the development of religion are undoubtedly to be found in Egypt, Mesopotamia, India, and China before Greek thought intervened, but
these attitudes will remain outside my present consideration. I
shall here be concerned basically with the examination of religion
within the Hellenic tradition. Even within this tradition, I shall
concentrate my attention on Christian writers.

HISTORICAL AND PHILOSOPHICAL DICHOTOMY

A significant distinction was imposed by the very nature of the
Greek perspective: philosophical examination and historical examination of religion became two distinct branches of knowledge.
Indeed, it is characteristic of Greek thought to distinguish in general (at least from the fifth century B.C. onward) between philoso-

phy and history. No doubt philosophical criticism operates inside a historical or antiquarian examination of religion, and, reciprocally, the empirical knowledge of cults and myths collected by historians or antiquarians assists philosophical criticism of religion. But the two subjects—philosophical and historical evaluations of religion—are seldom fused or, at least, seldom confused.

To indicate the depth of this dichotomy in Western thought, it is enough to mention David Hume, who was one of the most radical eighteenth-century thinkers about religion—perhaps one of the most radical thinkers about religion of modern times. Hume approached religion from both the historical and the philosophical points of view. In his *Natural History of Religion* (1757), in which he treats religion in historical terms, he states, "As far as writing of history reaches, mankind, in ancient times, appear universally to have been polytheists." Findings about modern tribes only confirm for him the facts adduced by the ancients about the original polytheism of mankind. In the *Dialogues concerning Natural Religion,* which appeared three years after his death, in 1779, Hume discusses religion from a philosophical point of view. His concern is not the evolution of religion but the validity of religion. He contends that the argument from design for the existence of God is of doubtful value. It is generally recognized that Hume took Cicero's *On the Nature of the Gods* as a formal model for his *Dialogues concerning Natural Religion.* There is no obvious ancient model for his *Natural History of Religion,* but he must have carefully considered Diodorus Siculus's *Historical Library,* Book 1 (of the first century B.C.) and was familiar with the work of Herodotus and Lucian.

THE ANCIENT GREEKS

After Herodotus (fifth century B.C.), history in Greece tended to be confined to what we would call political and constitutional history, although doctors like Galen use the word *historia* to mean a compilation of medical reports in literature. Other aspects of the past such as religious ceremonies, festivals, or sacrifices, were more frequently examined in monographs that were sometimes generically designated *archaiologia* (in Latin, *antiquitates*). Biography was a separate literary genre: if the subject of a biography was a religious personality (a religious reformer, a priest, a holy man, or even a superstitious politician), biography was a contribution to the history of religion. Within Christianity such biographies were written to recount the lives of saints.

Poetry

Two well-known features of Greek Archaic poetry had consequences for the study of religion. The poetry of Hesiod, especially his *Theogony*, shows a marked tendency to treat the world of the gods as a historical world. In Hesiod's poetry there is a succession of generations of gods in which older gods, without necessarily dying, lose their power in confrontations with younger gods. The society of gods is perceived as a society to which new members are added and in which members gain or lose power. There is not only a change of human attitudes toward gods, but there is also a change in the attitudes of the gods themselves. In Hesiod, myth already incorporates the notion of a succession of leading gods: myths are presented as a sort of history of religion. Another important feature of Greek Archaic poetry is its openness to criticism of the gods. Such criticism often radically repudiated commonly held views about the gods. For example, Xenophanes (fl. 500 B.C.) remarked that just as the Ethiopians imagine their gods to be similar to themselves, so horses, if they could paint, would paint their gods as horses.

Philosophy

The critical opinions about the gods in Greek Archaic poetry encouraged and inspired philosophical critiques of religion and historical research on the diversity of religions among the nations. Philosophers tended to separate God from man to the point of making God almost unintelligible except as the first mover or as a celestial body. The Stoics used allegorical interpretation (which had been current in explaining away embarassing episodes of the *Iliad*) to turn mythology into a confirmation of their pantheistic materialism. In the handbook *Theologiae graecae compendium* by Cornutus (c. A.D. 50), one finds a systematic summary of Stoic allegory with some interesting statements about the religious attitudes of primitive man. Only Epicurus (341–270 B.C.) insisted on believing in the existence of the traditional gods; his position did not allow the gods to exercise any influence on men, and he found in their happiness a model for the happiness of philosophically minded men. It is surprising how few references are made to the gods in the extant works of Aristotle; passages about them are almost marginal remarks (*On the Heavens* 2. 1. 284a; *Metaphysics* 1. 2. 982b, 11. 8. 1074b). Hence, in later Greek thought, especially among Neoplatonists, mystical practices were introduced to supplement the scanty information about gods in the discussions of the philosophic masters.

Historical Research

Supported by visits to sanctuaries and by travels to foreign countries and remote localities, historical research provided both the raw material and the guiding principles for alternative historical interpretation. As a keen traveler and as one adept in the comparative method (which contemporary doctors used to explain climatic differences), Herodotus provided a model for research on religion. He explained similarities between Greek and Egyptian gods by claiming that the Greeks had derived their gods from Egypt. His account of the Scythians shows his awareness of the difference between reporting and believing. Even more telling of this awareness is his conclusion of the story of Salmoxis: "Whether there was a man called Salmoxis, or this be a name among the Getae for a god of their country, I have done with him" (4. 95–96). Herodotus influenced Greek, and later, Roman writers who explored the customs of foreign countries and who also, as natives, explained to Greeks and Romans the characteristic features of their own countries. Accounts by non-Greeks became particularly frequent after Alexander the Great. These non-Greeks, who had adopted the Greek language, include Manetho (fl. third century B.C.), Berossus (fl. 290 B.C.), and later Flavius Josephus (c. A.D. 37–100). Incidentally, Josephus's writings on the Jews comprise the only complete ancient account of a "barbarian" religion by a native to be preserved—although they were preserved through Christian, not through Jewish, tradition. Posidonius (c. 135–

51 B.C.) of Apamea in Syria deserves special note insofar as he was both a Stoic philosopher of somewhat mystical inclinations and a universal historian who purported to be a continuator of Polybius; he was, however, more anthropologically oriented than his predecessor.

Greek and Roman historians tended to ignore religion, especially when they dealt with Greek and Roman history. The most obvious exception is represented by the registration in Roman annals of unfavorable divine signs observed by, or testified before, Roman magistrates. Consequently, most of what we know about Greek and Roman cults is derived from specific monographs on religious subjects (e.g., Plutarch on the Delphic oracle and Lucian on the Syrian goddess), accounts by travelers and geographers (e.g., Strabo and Pausanias), or, finally, works by Christian polemicists (e.g., Lactantius and Augustine).

Books on religion during the Hellenistic and Roman period reflect contemporary perspectives and interests. In the third century B.C., the ruler cults were developed by Alexander's immediate successors. Ruler cults had, of course, existed before in and outside of Greece; but this new expansion was far more powerful and, at least for Greek speakers, involved delicate balances of power between men and gods. Persaeus, the pupil of Zeno the Stoic, and others reminded their contemporaries that past benefactors and kings had been divinized (cf. Cicero, *On the Nature of the Gods* 1. 15. 38). Hecataeus of Abdera (c. 300 B.C.) distinguished two categories of gods: the celestial and the terrestrial. The second category was comprised of benefactors. (Diodorus Siculus in his *Bibliotheca historica* 1. 12 probably reflects his teaching.) In his *Sacred History*, Euhemerus (fl. 300 B.C.) claimed to have discovered on the island of Panchaia an inscription revealing that Zeus had been a mortal king who had received divine honors for his contribution to civilization; Zeus was born and died in Crete. Whether Euhemerus thought that all the gods had been men like Zeus is uncertain. Though Euhemerus shocked many with his ideas and his forgeries (the latter being the object of a virulent attack by Eratosthenes), his ideas had success: his book was translated into Latin by Ennius in the second century B.C., and was summarized by Diodorus in the first century B.C. Antoine Banier's *La mythologie et les fables expliquées par l'histoire* (3d ed., 1738–1740) shows that scholarship continued to be euhemeristic even in the eighteenth century.

In the second and first centuries B.C., many erudite Greek works tried to preserve the memory of ceremonies that were becoming obsolete. Most of these works were lost, except for what may have passed into later lexicons, such as the so-called *Suda*. A conspicuous model, known to the Latins, of this erudition was the work about Athens by Polemon of Ilium (fl. 200 B.C.). In Italy Alexander Polyhistor (d. 35? B.C.) gained a reputation for systematic compilations of this kind of information about foreign countries.

ROMAN THOUGHT

The Latins of the first century B.C. had a state with a vigorous religious tradition of its own; this tradition was considered to be the foundation of and the justification for Rome's enormous power. Roman religion had become a constitutive aspect of Roman prestige among her subjects. On the other hand, Greek philosophy had penetrated Roman thought: antiquarian devotion to the religious past was in conflict with rationalistic and irreverent tendencies. In this context a distinction among the theologies of poets, philosophers, and statesmen, probably borrowed from Greek philosophers, became popular in Rome. This distinction was formulated by the Roman lawyer and pontiff Q. Mucius Scaevola and was accepted by Marcus Terentius Varro and (by implication) by Cicero. Mucius Scaevola preferred the theology of statesmen, finding even the theology of the philosophers dangerous. The hesitation is conspicuous in Cicero who, however, is chiefly the protagonist of the introduction of systematic philosophical criticism into the interpretation of Roman religion. Others were oriented toward a guarded defense, or reconstruction, of Roman religion, though they were aware of philosophical argument. Even in Rome, Varro was something of an exception when he produced and dedicated to Julius Caesar his *Divine Antiquities*, a systematic description of Roman religion. He had reservations about the traditional religion of Rome, but he was mainly interested in saving what was in danger of being forgotten and in propounding it to the ruling class: unknowingly, he was preparing the ground for the restoration accomplished by Augustus. His work (which, much later, Augustine made the foundation of his criticism of Roman paganism) immediately became more authoritative than that of his contemporary Nigidius Figulus, who was strongly committed to religion. There was a great deal of antiquarian doctrine on Etruscan, Persian, and Egyptian religions—not to mention Greek cults—in Figulus's books (e.g., *On the Gods*). If Varro wanted a reasonable preservation of the Roman past, Nigidius Figulus seems to have been more aggressively in favor of a personal synthesis. He emphasized the power that religious practices give to the individual, not to the state. Varro and Nigidius could hardly ignore their Epicurean contemporaries, such as Lucretius, who preached an almost religious escape from religion.

Traditional Roman religion could never be simply taken for granted after the Caesarian age. Though Augustus put an accent on conservation of the past, the writers of the imperial age, even under Augustus, were explicitly or implicitly conditioned by new religious currents. Some writers remained within the frame of paganism ("Oriental cults"); others preached a god who was incompatible with other gods (Judaism and Christianity). The most difficult pagan writers to assess are those who composed their books when Judaism and Christianity were well known, and yet ignored or gave only perfunctory attention to these religions. There is perhaps no great antiquarian lore behind such writers, but they wrote primarily as historians, rather than as philosophers. It is not very clear why Plutarch (c. 46–after 119) writes what he writes about Isis and Osiris and other religious subjects. The same can be said about Pausanias's *Description of Greece* (second century A.D.) with its great attention to the history of cults in various parts of Greece. It is also difficult to separate autobiography from antiquarian lore in some of the religious speeches by Aelius Aristides in the same century. With Lucian (c. 120–after 180) we are indeed on the threshold of direct polemics with Christianity ("The Passing of Peregrinus"), though his main contributions to the history of religion are his study of his contemporary Alexander of Abonuteichos, the false prophet, and his description of the cult of Dea Syria in Hierapolis, which was composed in an archaizing style inspired by Herodotus.

CHRISTIAN-PAGAN POLEMICS

Though polemics between Christians and pagans became common in the second century, Judaic circles (as judged from preserved works) were no longer inclined to discuss religious differences either philosophically or historically. A possible exception is the recently published letter by "Anna" to Seneca, which may be a piece of Jewish propaganda on monotheism that was written not later than the fourth century (see Bernhard Bischoff, *Anecdota novissima*, Stuttgart, 1984). The Christians had to explain to the pagans why paganism, that is, polytheism, existed and was deplorable. This involved an element of historical explanation. The pagans, on the other hand, did not have to explain their own existence: it was sufficient for them to defend the rationality of their beliefs, as Celsus did, for instance, by explaining the function of polytheism in a plurinational world. Thus, in this exchange, there was more historical interest on the Christian side, a point worth remembering, as the Christian view prevailed. Whether the Christian view attributed polytheism to demonic influences or to the adulation by human beings of human beings, as the pagan Euhemerus had suggested, there was an element of historical conjecture in the Christian point of view. Indeed, Christian writers used pagan erudition to support their argument. It is enough to point to the use made of Varro by Augustine in the *City of God;* before Augustine, Varro's work was used by the Christian writers Arnobius and Lactantius. Furthermore, Augustine (and he was not alone in this) applied to the evolution of Jewish religion the biological scheme of the transition from infancy to maturity that he met in pagan historians (*City of God* 10).

SECOND TO FOURTH CENTURIES

It would be idle to pretend that the polemics between pagans and Christians in the second to fourth centuries represented more than a secondary contribution to the historical study of religion.

Actual historical work is rather to be found in two other types of writing. One is biography of holy men, both pagan and Christian, which was common in this period of conflict between paganism and Christianity. For example, the biography of Apollonius of Tyana by Philostratus (c. 170–c. 245) precedes the biography of Antony of Egypt by Athanasius (c. 293–373). Biographical exploration now becomes an essential way of describing and understanding religion. Next to it, and hardly less important, is the new form of ecclesiastical history with its peculiar techniques for following up the growth of the church or churches. There is a question about the relation between Eusebius's *Church History*, the prototype of the genre, and the Gospels and Acts of the Apostles. It is enough here to underline the fact that, within the tradition of Greco-Roman historiography, first the Gospels and then the *Church History* introduce new and revolutionary types of historiography of religion. Acts is, within this literary genre, less original. There is, furthermore, the wider question of whether what we now call pseudepigrapha intended to provide historical information about past situations. This question can be put to such different texts as 4 Maccabees, the *Martyrdom and Ascension of Isaiah*, and the *History of the Rechabites*: it can even be put to what to us is a novel, the story of *Joseph and Aseneth*. In any case, Eusebius appears to us to have been the first full-fledged historian of a specific religion.

THE MIDDLE AGES

Insofar as lives of saints and ecclesiastical histories remained extremely fertile genres of historiography in the Middle Ages, there was no shortage of recordings of religious events between the sixth and the fifteenth centuries. Furthermore, the ordinary chronicle was adapted to register events inside religious institutions (e.g., monasteries or cathedral churches), and it may be difficult to distinguish this chronicle from a local ecclesiastical history. Histories of wars had to take into account wars that had overwhelmingly religious meanings, such as the Crusades. Conversely, Ordericus Vitalis (1075–1142?) was not the only chronicler to worry about the encroachments of secular history on that ecclesiastical history that he had meant to write in the early twelfth century.

However mixed in character the single events reported, a definition of new religious experiences emerged everywhere. It is obvious in the "spirit of the Crusades," though one must remember that there were also crusades against heretics. These crusades had their historians (though not many, unfortunately, on the side of the heretics). Our notion of monastic life would be poorer without the autobiography by Abelard and the answer that Héloïse gave to it. The appearance of anchorites among the debris of rural Anglo-Saxon society after the Norman conquest is made vivid by the autobiography of Christina of Markyate, the recluse of the twelfth century. And, of course, there is the assiduous utilization of prophecies by historians of every kind, even by such a hard-boiled historian of the late twelfth century as Giraldus Cambrensis (Gerald de Barri).

These chronicles and biographies, however, seldom analyzed the religious phenomena they described. In the Middle Ages, understanding of religious diversity, if it was even attempted, is in sermons or philosophical treatises rather than in histories. This is true also of what Jews and Muslims wrote about religion: the former, in any case, had little historiography. Jews, Muslims, and Christians shared monotheistic presuppositions. The differences between the three faiths were debated theoretically rather than investigated historically. There was even less urgency among Jewish, Muslim, and Christian thinkers to understand polytheistic religions. Even Thomas Aquinas tended to follow the most unhistorical aspects of patristic thought in explaining the existence of polytheism. This tendency is also apparent in Jewish thought. Yehudah ha-Levi (c. 1075–1141) portrays the king of the Khazars discussing his own conversion with a rabbi without any serious reference to data derived from ordinary historical or ethnographical sources. Even Maimonides (Moses ben Maimon, 1135/8–1204), who claimed that he had read all he could in Arabic sources about the heathens and who had a keen sense of the social conditions of religious life, confined himself to philosophical or theological arguments. Some Muslim, Jewish, and Christian thinkers explained changes in religion by reference to astral influences (Abū Ma'shar, Avraham Ibn 'Ezra', William of Auvergne, etc.). The

Bible was of course the enormous exception; it was quoted by both Jews and Christians as a source of historical information. Though it would be wrong to underrate the medieval (especially Jewish) contribution to biblical criticism, the Bible as a sacred text was kept isolated from profane historiography.

The first beginnings of a different, more historical approach to religion, and especially to polytheism, is to be found in Islamic, Christian, and Jewish works of the eleventh to twelfth centuries that report on the religious situation in countries visited either by the authors or by their informants. Examples of this new approach are found in the writings of al-Bīrūnī on India, Adam of Bremen on northern Europe (as seen from the diocese of Bremen-Hamburg), and Benjamin of Tudela on the Jews of various parts of the world. This approach was developed further by Christian writers in the middle of the thirteenth century and coincides with the remarkable attempt of Christianity to come to terms with the Mongolian empire as a potential ally against Islam. Giovanni del Pian dei Carpini (John of Plano Carpini) and William of Rubrouck belong to this current, to which one can add Marco Polo. (An English translation of the reports by del Pian dei Carpini and W. Rubrouck is found in *Mission to Asia*, trans. Christopher Dawson, Toronto, 1980.) Knowledge gained through exploration and diplomacy restored paganism as a relevant part of the contemporary world and supplemented classical accounts of polytheism. At least one writer, the Icelandic historian Snorri Sturluson (1179–1241), in the thirteenth century collected the pagan myths of his own country. The accumulation of the new information on pagan countries must have modified Christians' awareness of their own pagan past in Christian countries. More research is needed if we are to fully understand the effect of this accumulation of new data on polytheism in the late Middle Ages. Needless to say, paganism was not something simple to medieval minds. Demons and satanic influences were often sufficient to explain the paganism of the uncultivated. But paganism had to be treated with some respect in reference to Greece and Rome. This may account for the tenacity with which the euhemerist interpretation of classical paganism survived in the Middle Ages (from Isidore of Seville to Vincent of Beauvais) and beyond.

THE RENAISSANCE

Fifteenth- and sixteenth-century humanism and the Renaissance would have been inconceivable without this double awareness of external and internal paganism. Ancient mythology, ancient religion, and ancient historiography acquired a new relevance in countries like Italy because the pagan past seemed to require reinterpretation. In Italian humanism (one may start with Giovanni Boccaccio's *Genealogia deorum gentilium*), the task of describing the pagans is inseparable from the task of explaining the existence of paganism. Even writers whose goal was the conversion of the infidel (and who used public theological controversy increasingly in efforts to convert Jews) sought more information about paganism. Arabic and Hebrew were studied by Christians in order to dispute with and convert Muslims and Jews. Foreign sacred texts, including the Talmud, were perused. An interest in Indian languages was born, though it did not fully emerge until the discovery and serious study of the sacred texts of India in the eighteenth century. The discovery of America opened up the exploration of a new pagan world in which Hebrew survivals were suspected.

The old interpretative models remained valid: euhemerism, demonic tricks, allegory, and the theory of successive revelations. But the new information acquired a value and created alternatives to the old models. First, the aim of informing readers about the religions of the world was in itself a novelty. One finds it in Johann Boem's *Omnium gentium mores, leges et ritus*, which appeared in 1520 and had successive editions, partly with additions by other authors, during the sixteenth century. Boem's work was followed, for instance, by Lilio Giraldi's *De deis gentium varia et multiplex historia* (1548) and by Alessandro Sardi's *De moribus ac ritibus gentium* (1557). Second, new speculations about languages and nations began to undermine the traditional picture of the early history of mankind. When, for instance, Jean Becan von Gorp made public his discovery that Dutch had been the primitive language of mankind and that Cimbri had taught wisdom to the

Greeks (*Origines antwerpianae*, 1569)—one of the many discoveries about the primitive language of mankind—the oddity of the claim was in itself an indication of change.

The new intellectual nationalists of the divided Europe of the sixteenth century could almost simultaneously sympathize with their pagan ancestors and accuse their enemies (most frequently Roman Catholics) of preserving pagan rituals. Such controversial literature is reported in J. A. Fabricius's *Bibliotheca antiquaria* (2d ed., 1716); a prototype, with a physiognomy of its own, is *Apologie pour Hérodote* (1566) by Henri Estienne. The relation between paganism and Christianity then became a question of historical continuity or discontinuity between specific aspects of paganism and Christianity. Conversely, elements in paganism that were judged to be true were ascribed to the survival within paganism of early revealed truths.

An important feature in all these works, notwithstanding the concern with immediate doctrinal issues, is an examination and analysis of the evidence with an attention to detail and with a philological skill that had been unknown to earlier authors. Though ecclesiastic history by Matthias Flacius Illyricus and his collaborators (the so-called *Centuriae Magdeburgenses*, 1559–1579) represents the Protestant point of view, and Cesare Baronio's refutation, the *Annales ecclesiastici* (1588–1607), represents a Catholic version, Flacius and Baronio have more or less the same critical method. The new style of collecting and sifting evidence became more conspicuous as religious polemics became less sharp in the seventeenth century and tended to peter out (or rather to be affected by Deism or by skepticism) in the eighteenth century. This is already manifest in the *Vitae sanctorum* (Lives of the Saints) of the Bollandists, and in the many works dedicated to the history of Christian institutions in given countries (for instance, Fernando Ughelli's *Italia sacra*, 1642, and William Dugdale's *Monasticon Anglicanum*, 1655). The Benedictine erudition in France and Italy of the late seventeenth and early eighteenth centuries is the crown of this method.

In the seventeenth and eighteenth centuries, pagan antiquities were studied in an effort to understand how the pagans preserved elements of the revelation to the Jews: the Phoenicians were assumed to be the transmitters. This is the subject of Samuel Bochart's *Geographia sacra seu Phales et Chanaan* (1646), G. J. Vos's *De theologia gentili* (1647), Theodore Gale's *The Court of the Gentiles* (1669–1677), and Pierre-Daniel Huet's *Demonstratio evangelica* (1690). At the end of the seventeenth century, the notions that Homer mirrored the age of the patriarchs (Gerard Croese, *Homeros Hebraios*, 1704) and that the religion of Delphi preserved traditions of the age of the Judges (Edmund Dickinson, *Delphi phoenicizantes*, 1655) were not unusual. This type of research went on for the whole of the eighteenth century. (See, for instance, Jacob Bryant, *A New System*, 1744–1746.) In fact one of the most telling titles appeared as late as 1786: Guérin du Rocher's *Hérodote historien du peuple hébreu sans le savoir* (1786) (the real author may be J. J. Bonnaud). At the same time, it was argued at great length and with great erudition that God had thought it wise to give the Hebrews pagan rites made venerable by antiquity (for example, in John Spencer's *De legibus Hebraeorum ritualibus eorumque rationibus*, 1685). Others, especially Spaniards such as Fray Bernardino de Sahagún in his *Historia general de las cosas de Nueva España*, wanted to insert the new American experience into the context of the old pagan world. But Sahagún's attempt, conducted between 1569 and 1582, was obviously premature: his book remained unpublished until 1829. Joseph-François Lafitau returned with greater maturity to the same subject in 1724. His *Mœurs des sauvages américains comparés aux mœurs des premiers temps* was not only published but found an immediate audience. Yet its importance as a pioneer work in anthropological research was not recognized until the twentieth century.

The gradual apprehension of the religions of India and China with their sacred texts remains one of the great achievements of

Western scholarship between the end of the sixteenth and the end
of the eighteenth century. For research on China, Juan González
de Mendoza's *Historia de las cosas mas notables . . . del gran
Reyno de la China* (1585) is considered epoch-making. For scholarship in the next century, I shall mention only Athanasius Kircher's *China illustrata* (1663) because the author, a Jesuit, was also
the author of *Oedipus Aegyptiacus* (1652–1654), a pioneering attempt to decipher the Egyptian hieroglyphs and to reconstruct
Egyptian religion. Kircher's work typifies the dual interest in ancient and modern pagan civilizations. Kircher was already in possession of a Sanskrit grammar, but it was not until the late
eighteenth century that the first successful interpretation of basic
Iranian and Indian texts was achieved. The translation of the Zand
Avesta by A.-H. Anquetil-Duperron appeared in 1771 (later Anquetil-Duperron turned to the Upaniṣads), while Charles Wil-
kins's translation of the *Bhagavadgītā* appeared in 1785. William
Jones gave the first clear formulation of the relations between Indian religion and Greek and Roman paganism (1784; see Jones's
Works, vol. 1, 1799, pp. 229–80). It is well to remember, however,
that the distribution in Europe in the 1760s of the translation of a
text called *Ezur Vedam* (True Veda) delayed the understanding of
early Indian religion and misled Voltaire; the text was a concoc-
tion by Christian missionaries with native help. Chinese wisdom
had the greater appeal for the rationalists and theists of the eighteenth century. It was left for the Romantic movement, especially
in Germany and France, to appreciate the religions of India. But
there are other works that confirm the eighteenth-century contribution to collecting the evidence about the religious history of
distant countries and sects, such as Thomas Hyde's *Historia reli-
gionis Veterum Persarum* (1700) and Isaac de Beausobre's *Histoire
critique de Manichée et du manichéisme* (1734).

THE RISE OF MODERN HISTORIOGRAPHY

The factual, empirical, almost antiquarian attitude of the historians of religion in the late Renaissance and in the Baroque age
was transmitted to the historians of the Enlightenment and of the
Romantic period. No doubt, as Hume and Voltaire show, erudition

was often conspicuously avoided for the sake of philosophic generalization. But erudition was always kept within reach even by the most dedicated philosopher. If there was a shift it occurred not in erudition itself, but rather in the purpose of erudition, which was increasingly used to support Deism (Edward Herbert of Cherbury), tolerance (Pierre Bayle), and religious emotions when contemplating nature, in preference to dogmas.

A new approach to religion emerged that can be described as typical of the Enlightenment: the attempt to determine and describe the various stages of the development of religion in mankind at large. In this approach new stages were identified, such as fetishism, that is, the adoration of objects, which was defined, after several predecessors, by Charles de Brosses in 1760, and animism, which was first tentatively postulated in various memoirs by Nicolas Fréret, while Banier resurrected the old euhemerism. It is here that Hume's insistence on the priority of polytheism over monotheism belongs. Hume's *Natural History of Religion* (1755) owed much even in its title to the *Natural History of Superstition* (1709) by John Trenchard. The intention behind these systems was not necessarily anti-Christian, though there were writers who were inclined to straight materialism, such as C. F. Dupuis during the French Revolution. One of the most radical and isolated thinkers, Giovanni Battista Vico, was a devout Catholic who tried to save the ancient Jews from the suspicion of myth-making that he saw as essential to ancient paganism. The overall result of this philosophical historical movement was to present schemes of human progress that theologians had to face. For the first time, philosophers and historians joined forces in presenting religion as something that had a history. It was an uneasy collaboration between philosophers and historians, but it was a new and significant one. It was even capable of transforming cultural events into religious experiences, as in Antoine Court de Gébelin's *Le monde primitif* (1773–1784).

NINETEENTH AND TWENTIETH CENTURIES

But what is this religious experience? What is religion? It is here that pre-Romantic and Romantic thought came out decisively, even against the Enlightenment, to restate the autonomy of religion as an emotion and as a need within the human experience. From G. E. Lessing and J. G. Herder to Friedrich Schleiermacher and F. L. J. von Schelling, the main effort was to rediscover religion as an emotional experience rather than as a culturally conditioned social manifestation. The philosophers parted company again with the historians, for whom the search for the social roots of religion remained a permanent bequest from the eighteenth century. Research in the field of religion during the nineteenth and twentieth centuries reveals an interaction between these two main approaches: the exploration of religious experience as such and the quest for a historical typology of religious attitudes and practices. The two currents seldom run parallel to each other; more often they cross each other, but never achieve confluence. This interaction can be seen in the continuity from Schleiermacher and Benjamin Constant de Rebecque to, say, Gerardus van der Leeuw and the Chicago school of Joachim Wach (with its German roots) in the effort to create a hermeneutic of religious experience. Though this effort must not be confused with that of the various psychological schools that have studied religious phenomena, such as William James's pragmatism and the psychoanalytic doctrines of Freud and Jung, it shares with the psychological schools a search for the roots of the religious experience as such. The relevance of such psychology or philosophy to theology is direct.

On the other side, the historical exploration of specific religions displayed unprecedented sophistication of methods and techniques. The deciphering of hieroglyphics and cuneiform conditioned the modern research on Egyptian and Mesopotamian religions, and even the partial interpretation of Etruscan texts added a new dimension to the knowledge of ancient Italian religions and helped to disentangle Roman from Greek religion. Knowledge of Buddhism, especially outside India, changed dramatically, and new information about so-called primitive tribes affected our knowledge of (and indeed the terminology we apply to) so-called advanced religions (consider, for example, the scholarly fortunes of the Melanesian term *mana*). The discovery of new texts such as the Dead Sea Scrolls modified the physiognomy of familiar religions.

To these changes, one has to add radical new methods and points of view regarding the examination of traditional texts. The succession (or rather superimposition) of source criticism, comparative studies (especially within Semitic studies), form criticism, redaction criticism, canon criticism, deconstruction, and so on, transformed our understanding of the Bible.

The problem that arose, and that dominated the study of religion since the early nineteenth century, was how to establish a real connection between theories on the nature of religion (with their hermeneutics of religious experience) and the new "factual" acquisitions about individual religions. Solutions have differed according to intellectual climate and individual preferences. At the beginning of the nineteenth century, for example, G. F. Creuzer tried to create a systematic, symbolic interpretation of ancient mythology (1810–1812). In 1825 K. O. Müller reacted to him when he declared Greek myths to be the expression of the emotions and vicissitudes of tribes in movement to occupy new lands. During the middle of the century, F. Max Müller began to develop what he called a "science of religion" on a model offered by the new Indo-European linguists such as Franz Bopp, and English anthropologists, such as E. B. Tylor, tried to improve on their eighteenth-century predecessors by using more modern concepts of evolution, such as Darwinism. The writings of Marx and Engels about the dependence of religion on the economic foundations of society should be mentioned here as well. At the turn of the twentieth century, Wilhelm Wundt developed his "psychology of the nations." Émile Durkheim, followed by his nephew Marcel Mauss, presented religion as the internal transfiguration of society that keeps society going, and Max Weber, followed by Ernst Troeltsch, proposed a sociology of religion with an inherent typology of religious experience as an answer to the never rigorously developed Marxist interpretation of religion.

Two aspects of this process of connecting history of religion with philosophy of religion deserve special notice. One aspect can be presented with the mere name of Ernest Renan. Though he was a radical critic of the Christian tradition, he communicated genuine religious sentiments in his books and exercised a decisive influence in the formation of modernist currents within Catholicism.

(He was, incidentally, also a pioneer in the study of Semitic epigraphy, which renewed our knowledge of Semitic religions.)

The other aspect is the increased scholarship of Jews in a field that had previously been dominated by scholars in the Christian tradition. In the late sixteenth century, the original scholar 'Azaria de' Rossi, the author of *Me'or einayim* (Light of the Eyes), remained almost unknown to non-Jews and little known to Jews themselves. He was recognized as a pioneer in the study of Judaism by Jews of the generation of Moses Mendelssohn in the late eighteenth century, and his work opened up the path to the so-called science of Judaism (*Wissenschaft des Judentums*) of the nineteenth and early twentieth centuries (Leopold Zunz, Solomon Munk, Heinrich Graetz, Ismar Elbogen, etc.). Other Jews contributed significantly to the understanding of other religions (James Darmesteter on Persian religion, Ignácz Goldziher on Islam) and to the comparative study of religion (Salomon Reinach). It should also be remembered that Durkheim brought a rabbinic education to his sociology.

At present there seems to be a definite preference for sociological interpretations of circumscribed aspects of religion: something less ambitious, say, than the phenomenology of van der Leeuw and Wach, and also less theoretically sophisticated than the sociology of Weber. This preference is due to the realization that many subjects (e.g., the position of women in religion, the function of holy men in different societies, the behavior of sectarians within the "greater societies," and even apocalyptic and messianic movements) have been studied without sufficient consideration of their social context. This preference for the social aspects of religion may well be a transitory fashion. The tension between the discovery of facts about individual religions and the need adequately to define religion itself is bound to continue. History and philosophy of religion are likely to go on disturbing each other, and theology will go on facing both. The triangle of history, philosophy, and theology is still with us.

Select Bibliography

Still fundamental to the study of the historiography of religion are the following works: Louis Henry Jordan's *Comparative Religion: Its*

Genesis and Growth (Edinburgh, 1905); Otto Gruppe's *Geschichte der klassischen Mythologie und Religionsgeschichte* (Leipzig, 1921); Henri Pinard de la Boullaye's *L'étude comparée des religions*, 2 vols. (Paris, 1922–1925); and Raffaele Pettazzoni's *Svolgimento e carattere della storia delle religioni* (Bari, 1924).

Among more modern books, special note should be made of Gustav Mensching's *Geschichte der Religionswissenschaft* (Bonn, 1948); Jan de Vries's *The Study of Religion: A Historical Approach* (New York, 1967), reprinted as *Perspectives in the History of Religions* (Berkeley, 1977); J. D. Bettis's *Phenomenology of Religion* (New York, 1969); Michel Meslin's *Pour une science des religions* (Paris, 1973); Eric J. Sharpe's *Comparative Religion: A History* (London, 1975); Giovanni Filoramo's *Religione e ragione tra Ottocento e Novecento* (Rome, 1985); and Joseph M. Kitagawa's *The History of Religions: Retrospect and Prospect* (Chicago, 1985).

Two very useful anthologies are Burton Feldman and Robert D. Richardson's *The Rise of Modern Mythology, 1680–1860* (Bloomington, Ind., 1972); and Jacques Waardenburg's *Classical Approaches to the Study of Religion*, 2 vols. (The Hague, 1973–1974).

For broad studies of the sixteenth through eighteenth centuries, see Giuliano Gliozzi's *Adamo e il nuovo mondo* (Florence, 1977), Sergio Landucci's *I filosofi e i selvaggi, 1580–1780* (Bari, 1972), and Dino Pastine's *La nascita dell'idolatria* (Florence, 1979). Studies focusing on the eighteenth century include Frank E. Manuel's *The Eighteenth Century Confronts the Gods* (Cambridge, Mass., 1959), Michèle Duchet's *Anthropologie et histoire au siècle des lumières* (Paris, 1971), P. Vidal-Naquet, "Hérodote et l'Atlantide entre les Grecs et les Juifs," *Quaderni di Storia* 8, 1982, 3–76, and Alfonso M. Iacono's *Teorie del feticismo* (Milan, 1985), which is also relevant to Marx. For studies of the nineteenth century, volume 3 of *Nineteenth-Century Religious Thought in the West* (Cambridge, 1985) is the most relevant to our topics. Also, see Kurt Rudolph's *Die Religionsgeschichte an der Leipziger Universität und die Entwicklung der Religionswissenschaft* (Berlin, 1962). For German antiquities, refer to Frank L. Borchardt's *German Antiquity in Renaissance Myth* (Baltimore, 1971). For American societies, see Antonello Gerbi's *La natura delle Indie Nove* (Milan, 1975). For Eastern religions, see also Raymond Schwab's *La renaissance orientale* (Paris, 1950) and Wilhelm Halbfass's *Indien und Europa* (Basel, 1981). Joachim Wach's *The Comparative Study of Religions* (New York, 1958), posthumously edited and with an introduction by Joseph M. Kitagawa, helps to bridge German and American studies. Three books may help to understand modern studies on Judaism: H. Liebeschütz, *Synagoge und Ecclesia* (Heidelberg, 1983, but written in 1938); *Wissenschaft des Judentums im deutschen Sprachbereich* (Tübingen, 1967), and A. H. and H. E. Cutler, *The Jew as Ally of the Muslim* (Notre Dame, 1986).

3

The Origins of Universal History

I

I WOULD BE MAKING the understatement of the century if I were
to say that universal history has never been a clear notion. Taken
literally, the idea of universal history verges on absurdity. Who can
tell everything that has happened? And who would like to listen if
he were told? But both in the Greek and in the Hebrew tradition of
history-writing the urge to tell the whole story from beginning to
end has been apparent, and universal history has become one
of the most problematic components of our twofold Jewish and
Greek heritage. Among the texts which have reached us directly
it is a Greek text—Hesiod's *Works and Days*—that gives us the
oldest scheme of the succession of ages; but the Jews of the
Hellenistic age outbid the Greeks by taking the story beyond
the present into the future and gliding from history into apocalypse. The mixture of the historic and the Messianic has seldom
been absent in the accounts of universal history which have been
produced by ecclesiastical and secular historians from the Revelation of St. John to Arnold Toynbee's *Study of History*; and there is
no sign that the universal-history industry is flagging.

Contrary to the prevailing opinion that most of the time universal history played only a small part in Greek culture, there was a
continuous and considerable production of patterns intended to
give, if not a meaning, at least some order to the story of mankind.

Presented at the University of Chicago and in the Christian Gauss Seminars in
Criticism at Princeton University in 1979. *Annali della Scuola Normale Superiore di Pisa*, Serie III, vol. XII, fasc. 2, 1982, pp. 533–60.

But the majority of these patterns had their origins in what we can loosely call the mythical or philosophical imagination of the Greeks rather than in the empirical collection and critical interpretation of past events called *historia*. Only the succession of world-empires can be said to have represented a guiding thought for real historians. I shall therefore devote the second part of this lecture to the development of the notion of the succession of world-empires within Greek historiography and I shall try to show that the Jews—and more precisely the authors of the Book of Daniel—derived this notion from the Greeks and turned it into an apocalyptic one. But before I do this I have to examine three other Greek schemes of universal history which are important in themselves, though they affected the historians only in a marginal way. These are the scheme of the succession of different races characterized by different metals; the biological scheme according to which not only individuals but nations and even mankind as a whole go through the stages of childhood, youth, maturity, and old age; and finally the scheme of the progress of mankind from barbarism to civilization through a series of technological discoveries. Each of these three schemes had high potential for proper historical research. In later ages each was adopted and developed by historians on a large scale. But the Greek historians, being mainly interested in politics and wars, took far less notice of these schemes than we should have liked. The first thing to learn from Greek historiography is that schemes of the evolution of mankind can be invented in a given culture before historical research makes its appearance and can be multiplied after historical research has established itself without necessarily taking into account what historians have to say. We historians are a rather marginal by-product of history.

The traditional father of Greek historiography, Hecataeus, lived at the end of the sixth century B.C.; the two men who shaped Greek historiography in the way we know it, Herodotus and Thucydides, operated in the second half of the fifth century B.C. But Hesiod presented a scheme of universal history which can hardly be later than the end of the eighth century B.C. It is also virtually certain that Hesiod had at his disposal a preexisting model for his cogitations on the development of mankind through a succession of various races, the golden race, the silver race, etc. Hesiod's

scheme is distinguished by two further complications. For mo-
tives which at least in the case of the golden race are entirely
mysterious and in the case of the successive races (silver, bronze,
heroic, iron) by no means self-evident, the gods, to say the least,
allow the elimination of the existing race and its replacement by
another which (with one exception) they like less than the one
just suppressed. The one exception—the race of heroes inserted
between the bronze and the iron age—is anomalous insofar as it
does not receive its name from a metal and interrupts for a while
the decline characterizing the process as a whole. Long ago it was
seen that the insertion of the race of heroes in the scheme of the
four races named according to metals was secondary and necessi-
tated by the importance attributed to heroes in the Greek tradition.
Whether it was in fact Hesiod who performed this adaptation of the
scheme of the four ages to specific Greek requirements we cannot
say. The races of gold and of bronze, and the heroic race, each seem
to be limited to one generation—which would mean that the gods
from the start did not endow them with the faculty of reproduction. Only the race of silver is explicitly given children, but it is
also the only race about which it is explicitly stated that it was
destroyed by the gods themselves. Hesiod has no remarks on this,
and nor have I.

All the later writers in Greek or Latin about the four races, outside Judaism or Christianity, depended directly or indirectly on
Hesiod. Plato used the myth freely, especially in the *Republic* (3.
415 a–c), to support the hierarchical structure of his State. Hellenistic poets like Aratus (third century B.C.) and Ovid refurbished
the Hesiodic myth to express a nostalgia for the golden race which
Hesiod, far more sensitive to the pains of the iron race than to the
attraction of previous times, had never really felt. The races could
be reduced in number—or increased. It will be remembered that
Juvenal in *Satura* XIII speaks of the ninth age without having a
metal for it; he defines the ninth as worse than the iron age (l. 28,
"nona aetas agitur peioraque saecula ferri temporibus"). He probably mixes up the scheme of the four ages with that of the ten
generations which is found in other contexts. It must here be observed that the transition from Greek to Latin in itself produced a
momentous difference. The *saeculum aureum* or *saeculum feli-
cissimum* of the Latins is not identical with the *genos chryseion*,

"the golden race" which it purports to translate. The Greeks underlined the type of man, the Romans put the character of the age to the fore. The difference made it easier for the Romans to exploit the myth for political propaganda. A good emperor could be expected to change the character of his age more easily than the race of his subjects. The return of the Golden Age was a more plausible theme for propaganda in poetry and inscriptions or coins than the return of the golden race. Altogether the Romans felt free to develop the implications of cyclical return to the Golden Age which the Greek versions had never stressed. In considering the evils of the iron race, Hesiod had been unable to repress the *cri de coeur:* "Would that I were not among the men of the fifth generation, but either had died before or been born afterwards." Yet it is very doubtful whether he implied circularity in the scheme of the ages and a possible return from iron to gold. Roman political propaganda on the contrary had to presuppose, or at least to imply, circularity in the scheme of the ages in order to make plausible the image of an emperor taking his empire back from the Iron Age to the Golden Age. In A.D. 400 the poet Claudian ominously depicted, not a Roman emperor, but the German general Stilicho as the man who brought the Golden Age back to Rome. This scene in the second book of the *Laudes Stilichonis* (vv. 422ff.), with the Sun going to the Cave of Eternity to retrieve the Golden Age for the consulate of Stilicho, is a memorable antithesis to the lines of Hesiod's *Works and Days* which more than a thousand years before had firmly placed Greek culture in the Iron Age.

Whether in the Greek or in the Roman form, there was very little historical observation behind this scheme of the ages. Whether we take Hesiod or Aratus or Ovid or Claudian—or the philosophers and moralists who played with this story—they did not really talk about any remembered or recorded past. The designation of the Bronze Age may have preserved some recollection of the time in which iron was not yet in use: it did not, however, define a technology. The collective image of the heroic age very probably preserved some obscure memory of the Mycenaean age—but no more than what one could find in the epic poems or some tragedy. The schematization did not add to knowledge, and in any case there was no folk memory behind the notions of gold and silver ages. For all practical purposes the Iron Age was the only age which belonged to the historical field: the four previous ages were ideal alternative forms of human life recaptured by myth and impervious to history. The scheme of the metal ages, as reported by non-Jewish and non-Christian writers, was part of classical mythology rather than of classical historiography. We shall see later that Persian and Jewish writers connected it with historical events.

II

Different considerations are suggested by the biological scheme, but again we shall find that in pre-Christian writers it was only marginal to history and hardly affected the writing of universal history. The biological scheme, in distinguishing between childhood, youth, maturity, and old age (with further optional refinements), proved to have relatively greater historiographical possibilities when applied to single nations than when applied to the whole of mankind. Confused ideas that certain nations are younger than others floated about in Greek ethnography. Since Herodotus it had been generally admitted that the Egyptians were a much older nation than the Greeks, and Herodotus also knew that as a nation the Scythians were about a thousand years old (4. 7). Here again the Romans seem to have derived more precise consequences from Greek premises. Lactantius in his *Institutiones* (7. 15. 14) states that Seneca—whether the rhetorician or the philosopher is debatable—constructed a scheme of Roman history from Romulus to Augustus based on this metaphor of stages of life. We do not know how Seneca elaborated this scheme, but under the Emperor Hadrian, Annaeus Florus composed his elegant summary of Roman history according to the same guiding principle. Since it is preserved (it proved to be immensely successful), it gives us the best idea we can form of this type of biological history. Florus attributes to Rome a childhood of 250 years under the kings, an adolescence of comparable length, and then a maturity of 200 years which ends with Augustus. The next hundred years under the emperors are old age, but Florus sees signs of rejuvenation under the Emperors Trajan and Hadrian in whose reigns he happens to live. Interestingly enough, he does not go beyond Augustus in his actual narration.

As the Roman Empire was often identified with the whole of the world, one might expect an easy transition from the notion of an aging Rome to the notion of an aging human race. But I have no evidence to show that any pagan historian took the step of presenting world history in terms of the aging of an individual. The notion of an aging Rome derived much of its historiographical strength from the realistic impression that beyond the borders of the Empire—or even inside them—there were nations ready to take advantage of the weakness of Rome. Tacitus would not have written the *Germania* without the uneasy feeling that the barbarians were ready to prey on aging Rome. Even more explicitly, in the late fourth century Ammianus Marcellinus connects the old age of Rome with the increasing frivolity and vulgarity of its ruling class which in turn provokes the enemies of the Empire to increasing audacity. It would not have made much sense for a historian rooted in the political tradition of Rome to identify the old age of Rome with the old age of the world: the danger, as he saw it, was in the contrast between the lethargy of Rome and the energy of her youthful enemies.

This may explain why, as far as I know, a clear formulation of the *senectus mundi*—of the old age of the world—is to be found only in Christian writers and does not become an operative historiographical notion until St. Augustine. A clear adaptation of the biological scheme to Christian notions of history is already to be found in Tertullian's *De Verginibus Velandis* (1. 7): the world reaches its infancy with the Mosaic Law, its youth with the Gospel, and its maturity with the Paraclete. But this is said in a perfunctory way. It takes a St. Augustine to face the *senectus mundi* in the precise clinical manifestation of the sack of Rome and to conclude that what appears to be old age in the City of Man may be youth in the Heavenly City: "Do not try to stick to this old World; do not refuse to find your youth in Christ who tells you the World is transient, the World is aging, the World declines, the World is breathless in its old age. Do not fear: your youth will be renewed as that of the eagle" (*Sermo* 81, *PL* 28. 505). It is by now evident that outside such audacious metahistorical applications there was little scope for the biological scheme in universal history. We must conclude that in classical pagan historiography the application of the biological scheme to the history of mankind was scarcely more successful than the application of the scheme of the metallic ages.

III

A further scheme remains to be considered which, though born outside historical research, like the previous two schemes, was soon felt to be open to empirical verifications and as such interested ancient philologists and antiquarians, if not historians. Gods or culture-heroes who reveal technological secrets to helpless mankind are of course to be found everywhere. The Yahwist account of Genesis 4 may be as old as the tenth century B.C. What seems to characterize the Greeks is that they did not remain content with their heroes, impressive as they may have been. Already in Aeschylus's *Prometheus* (the question whether Aeschylus is the real author of the *Prometheus* is here irrelevant) the culture-hero symbolizes mankind in its efforts to attain knowledge. Sophocles in the *Antigone* can dispense with the culture-hero and make man himself the source of all the ambiguous achievements which intelligence brings about. Even when mythical forms are retained (as in the new version of the Prometheus story told by Protagoras in Plato), the problem of how man acquired the arts becomes the focus for reflection. Individual men or individual cities were sometimes singled out for praise. The praise of Athens as a civilizing city goes back at least to Isocrates. The Epicureans would naturally emphasize the enlightened traditions of the city to which Epicurus, after all, belonged. We therefore find the praise of Athens in Lucretius, Book VI. But as a rule the effort to encompass the discovery of the arts went beyond individual names of gods, men, and cities and tried to envisage the conditions which favored discoveries in general. Climatic conditions, fear of animals, development of language, discovery of metals and forms of cultivation, organization of social life, the cumulative influence of observation in various fields, etc., are factors considered in the two most important discussions we have of the technical progress of mankind: Diodorus's *Bibliotheca* Book I and Lucretius's *De rerum natura* Book V, to which we may add Vitruvius's *De architectura* Book II and Manilius's *Astronomicon* Book I in the following century. Not much has come down to us—partly as a result of the classicistic selection operated by late Greeks and Romans—of the work of their predecessors, the Sophists of the fifth century B.C. and the specialized students of discoveries of the late fourth century B.C. and of the early Hellenistic period. We are informed about a refined study of sacrificial customs composed by Aristotle's pupil Theophrastus only because the philosopher Porphyry happened to be very interested in it in the third century A.D. Dicaearchus, who lent authority to the notion of a life of Greece and inspired Varro, apparently combined the cultural scheme with that of the decline from a golden to an iron age. He had some idea of technological stages, such as nomadism and agriculture. A couple of indications by Varro, one by Censorinus and one by Porphyry, give us a pale reflection of what must have been Dicaearchus's thinking on the evolution of Greece. We would expect Posidonius to have said something very influential on the subject of the discoveries of the arts in the generation before Lucretius and Diodorus. But sources being what they are, our main information about Posidonius's opinions on cultural history depends on Seneca's Letter 90. There Seneca agrees with Posidonius that the philosophers were the natural leaders of mankind during the golden age, but he does not accept Posidonius's further conjecture that the philosophers discovered the arts and techniques which myth had considered to be Prometheus's province. This is very little, and therefore scholars have been able to state or to deny with equal assurance that Posidonius is the source behind Diodorus's chapters in Book I about the evolution of mankind.

We must add that in Hellenistic and Roman times it was natural for Oriental writers in the Greek language to dispute the claim that the Greeks with their gods and heroes had been the civilizers. Moses was turned into a culture-hero by Jewish writers, like Artapanus in the second century B.C.; and in the late first century A.D. the Phoenician Philon of Byblos boasted of having found in Phoenician writers older than the Trojan war a clear description of how Phoenician gods and heroes had introduced the technology of civilization. In the wake of the discoveries at Ugarit, credulous Orientalists have been inclined to believe him. All these discussions hardly went beyond the zone of myth, and even within these limits they accepted the terms formulated by the Greeks.

The ravages of time, that is, the loss of so many original sources (like Posidonius himself), give perhaps an unjust impression of poverty of results in this field. We should be wiser if we had more of Posidonius or more of Theophrastus, or even more of Critias and Protagoras on this subject. The problems were recognized, and it is remarkable that such a variety of approaches—from fear of animals to climate and language—presented themselves to the Greeks (if not to their Oriental competitors) and remained present to the Romans. But even if we were much better informed, we would hardly find cultural developments as one of the central themes of Greek historical research. More specifically, we would not find universal histories built on schemes of cultural development. We are brought back to the hard fact that, before Christianity, Greek and Latin historians saw political and military events as the natural subject of their researches. If universal history was to have a central place in historical research, it had to have a place in political history. Whereas it was generally admitted that by studying political history one could avoid past mistakes and improve future performance, cultural history at best provided confirmation of some philosophic theory. It was not meant to help the future development of culture and remained at the level of curiosity and exemplification. To find universal history in full dress we must therefore go to Polybius, the political historian who claimed to be a universal historian or, to use his own expression *ta katholou graphein*, "to write general history" (5. 33). He is the first extant author to make this claim, though, as he himself knew, not the first to have made it.

IV

Polybius became a universal historian because he saw himself as seriously involved in a chain of political and military events which truly appeared to affect the whole world. According to Polybius, the Romans created universal history by conquering the world or at least by affecting directly or indirectly the future of the whole world. This meant that Polybius could not envisage universal history as the discovery of patterns of behavior common to all men qua men. To him universal history came into being at a certain date, say the second Punic War, about 220 B.C., because of a new historical development. The idea of a universal history from the origins of mankind was alien to Polybius. He was, however, prepared to admit that in the more remote past certain historical situations had already brought mankind near to political unity, and that some historians had understood this predicament and therefore examined the facts with something like the self-consciousness of the universal historian. In fact he indicated Ephorus, the historian of the middle of the fourth century B.C. who had examined Oriental events connected with Greek events, as his first and most serious predecessor as a universal historian.

The situations which Polybius believed to be comparable with Rome's conquests are the processes of formation of previous empires. Persia, Sparta, and Macedon are his explicit terms of reference. Characteristically he leaves out Athens, for he did not like Athenian democracy. He speaks of Rome and Carthage as the two powers which disputed the rule of the world before Rome won. Since the succession of empires is the central point of Polybius's historical vision, it is useful to remind ourselves of his precise words: "The paradoxicality and greatness of the spectacle with which I propose to deal will become most clear if we single out and compare with the Roman hegemony the most famous of the previous empires—the ones which have provided historians with their chief theme. Those worthy of being thus set aside and compared are the following: the Persians . . . the Spartans . . . the Macedonians . . . But the Romans have subjected to their rule not portions, but nearly the whole of the world" (1. 2) (trans. W. R. Paton, Loeb).

This was not only an intellectual perception, but an emotional finding. The fall of an empire is to Polybius an occasion on which a dignified man is entitled to let himself go, to be disturbed and even to cry. He knows he has a literary tradition behind him to justify his emotions and to give appropriate words to them. After having concluded his account of the fall of the Kingdom of Macedon under Perseus in 168 B.C., Polybius picked up a treatise on Fortune in which Demetrius of Phalerum had commented upon the fall of the Persian Empire and generally animadverted on the inconstancy of human fortunes. Polybius was impressed by the fact that in the generation after Alexander, Demetrius had foreseen that Macedon would one day fall in its turn. He quoted from Demetrius and concluded: "I, as I wrote and reflected on the time when the Macedonian monarchy perished, did not think it right to pass over the event without comment, as it was one I witnessed with my own eyes, but I considered it was for me also to say something befitting such an occasion, and recall the words of Demetrius" (29. 21) (trans. W. R. Paton).

It may seem superfluous to quote the other, more famous, passage (38. 21) in which Polybius tells of how he was near Scipio Aemilianus, the Roman commander, when Carthage was burning in 146 and had Scipio grasping his hand and repeating Homer's line "A day will come when sacred Troy shall perish" (*Iliad* 6. 448). But this passage raises a problem. We have not all of Polybius's original text, and we must reconstruct it as best we can from three quotations: one in the so-called excerpts *De sententiis*, another in Diodorus 32. 24, and a third in Appian, *Libyca* 132. Appian is the only one to tell us that Scipio Aemilianus was meditating on the fall of the empires of Assyria, Media, Persia, and Macedonia while weeping and reciting Homer to himself. This addition of the four world empires may be an improvement by Appian, who as an Egyptian writer of the second century A.D. was aware of them, but one would need very strong arguments to admit such interference by Appian with the account of the scene which he explicitly takes from Polybius. Prima facie, the reference to the four empires must be attributed to Polybius. If this is correct, it shows that although Polybius was interested as a historian in the succession Persia-Macedonia-Rome, he was acquainted with a longer list of world-empires in which Assyria and Media preceded Persia.

Indeed, we may immediately add that this list—the famous list of the four monarchies—must have been current in Polybius's time and therefore easily available both to him and to Scipio Aemilianus. We happen to know from a strange gloss inserted in Velleius Paterculus 1. 6 that Aemilius Sura, an otherwise unknown author of a book, *De annis populi romani*, placed the Romans at the end of a succession of empires starting with the Assyrians and continuing with the Medes, the Persians, and the Macedonians. More precisely Sura dated the beginnings of the Roman World Empire during the reigns of Philip V of Macedon and of

Antiochus III of Syria, that is, either before 179 B.C., the date of Philip's death, or before 187 B.C., the date of Antiochus III's death. There are too many difficulties in this text for us to be certain when it was written, but one is inclined to believe that Aemilius Sura gave such a precise and unconventional date because he wrote in the earlier part of the second century B.C. and was himself a witness of the Roman victories over Macedonia and Syria.

In fact the notion of the succession of the world-empires had been codified by Herodotus and Ctesias, the leading historians writing about Asia in the fifth and very early fourth century B.C. Herodotus had stated in so many words that the Persians had succeeded the Medes in the empire (I. 95; 130); he had furthermore promised to write a special account of Assyria, though for reasons unknown he did not do so (I. 184). Ctesias fulfilled this desideratum and introduced Median and Persian history by way of a long account of the previous Assyrian empire. Neither of them could of course foresee that the Persian world-monarchy would be replaced by the Macedonian monarchy. But the contemporaries of Alexander the Great must have been quick to add the Macedonian world-monarchy to the three empires codified by Herodotus and described by Ctesias. A man like Demetrius of Phalerum quoted by Polybius must be supposed to have been acquainted with Herodotus and Ctesias.

It is not surprising that Polybius should concentrate his real interests on Greece, Macedonia, Carthage, and Rome. Even Persia is to him a distant shadow. The succession of the four world-empires must have appeared far more significant in the late fourth century and in the early third century B.C. when the Hellenistic monarchies as a whole seemed to represent an obvious and lasting replacement of the Persian monarchy: Rome was still confined to Italy. Though the disappearance of most of the historical writing of early Hellenism makes it difficult to prove this statement, three considerations can be offered before I pass on to examine the only extant text of the third century B.C. about the four monarchies.

If one feature was evident in this scheme of the four monarchies—Assyria, Media, Persia, and Macedonia—it was that it kept Egypt out. This was of course noticed by Egyptians who came into contact with Hellenistic culture and by those Alexandrian intellectuals who persisted in the old Hellenic tradition of admiration for the Egyptians. Herodotus, without thinking of empires, had already presented the semimythical Egyptian King Sesostris as superior to Darius the Persian, who rather good-naturedly conceded the point (2. 110). But it was left to Hecataeus of Abdera—a Greek writing in Egypt about 300 B.C.—to elevate Sesostris to the dignity of a universal ruler. In Hecataeus's account, which we have in Diodorus's summary (1. 53), Sesostris's father gave his son the education befitting a future cosmocrator, and Sesostris proved to be the model emperor of the world. It does not matter very much whether the Egyptians put ideas into the head of Hecataeus of Abdera or vice versa. Three centuries later, when the geographer Strabo and the Emperor Tiberius's adoptive son Germanicus were separately traveling in Egypt, local priests told them stories similar to those of Hecataeus of Abdera (Strabo 17. 816; Tacitus *Annales* 2. 60). Native historians of Mesopotamia were of course in an easier position. In telling the history of Babylonia to the Greeks, Berossus was able to fit it into the scheme of four successive monarchies. On the other hand, it is impossible to understand all the anti-Roman propaganda of the last two centuries of the Republic without referring to these notions of successive world-empires. The Greeks and even more the Orientals who saw the Romans taking over everywhere found refuge in hopes, in prophecies, and even in actual revolutionary movements promising to put history in reverse and to give back to Greece or to the East the world-rule they had lost. Polybius says nothing of these outbursts. But some of them were registered by his contemporary Antisthenes of Rhodes, a historian and philosopher. In Antisthenes' account, both a dead Syrian officer and a dead Roman general announced Rome's fall and the return of Asia to power (*FGHist.* 257 F. 36). A forged letter from Hannibal to the Athenians circulated in which the Carthaginian promises to give the Romans a more severe lesson than that given by the Greeks to the ancestors of the Romans, namely the Trojans (R. Merkelbach, *Griechische Papyri der Hamburger Staats- und Universitätsbibliothek*, 1954, n. 129, ll. 106ff.).

The rebellions of the slaves in Italy, the struggle of Aristonicus in Asia Minor about 132 B.C., the wars of King Mithridates of Pontus against Rome for twenty-five years between 88 and 63 B.C., and finally Cleopatra's war against Octavian were accompanied and supported by prophecies of the return of the empire to the

Asiatic nations. As there were colonies of Persians with their magi in Asia Minor, somebody turned to them for help in this ideological warfare. The result was a document—the prophecy of Hystaspes, a king of Media supposed to have lived before the Trojan War. The prophecy was still circulating in the fourth century A.D., when it was amply summarized by Lactantius: it predicted the destruction of the Roman Empire and the return to power of the East.

Thirdly and finally, we have to turn to the universal histories which multiplied in the congenial atmosphere of Roman wars and conquests of the first century B.C., when Pompey and Caesar seemed to be challenging the reputation of Alexander the Great. Some of these universal historians accepted in full Polybius's premise that proper universal history could not be written until the rise of Rome as a world-empire. Therefore they continued Polybius down to their own day: Posidonius of Apamaea to about 60 B.C. at the latest and Strabo of Amaseia to the end of the civil wars, perhaps about 30 B.C. The novelty which Posidonius transmitted to Strabo, insofar as it was transmissible, was the use of Herodotean ethnography to describe cultures discovered—chiefly but not exclusively—by Roman conquest. Most of the world that Posidonius had managed to conjure up in his vivid, rich prose has, alas, disappeared with the loss of his work. Though Posidonius was probably superior to any of the other post-Polybian universal historians, those who did not accept the chronological limits imposed by Polybius and bravely imitated Ephorus in going back to remote antiquity are, as a group, more interesting for our inquiry.

I shall not take into account two Italians of the second half of the first century B.C. who, just because they were the first Italians to write universal history, naturally stimulate our curiosity: we know almost nothing of the contents of the three books of universal history by Cornelius Nepos which his friend Catullus commended; nor have we any precise idea of how Titus Pomponius Atticus selected his topics for the *liber annalis* which (Cicero claimed) "me inflammavit studio illustrium hominum aetates et tempora persequendi" (*Brutus* 18. 74). But we can read part of the universal history by the Sicilian Diodorus, and we have at least the summary made in the second or third century A.D. by Justin of the vast work strangely called *Historiae Philippicae* by Trogus

Pompeius, a Gaul from Gallia Narbonensis. We can also form some idea of what must have been the biggest universal history ever written in antiquity, a work in 144 books by Nicolas of Damascus, a Hellenized Syrian who managed to be tutor to the children of Cleopatra and Antony, secretary and envoy of King Herod of Judaea for many years, and finally a friend of Augustus, of whom he wrote a biography. We also have a faint notion of what must have been a universal history in Greek called "Kings" by Timagenes, who was forcibly removed from Alexandria to Rome about 56 B.C. and created for himself the reputation of being a bitter critic of anything Roman.

These four provincials—two from the West (Diodorus and Trogus) and two from the East (Nicolaus and Timagenes), one (Trogus) writing in Latin and the others writing in Greek—tried to offer some resistance to a view of world history which was an implicit, and even explicit, glorification of Rome. They gave pride of place to the old civilizations of the East and of Greece, and they emphasized either the relative barbarism of the Romans or their recent conversion to Greek customs (which amounted to the same thing). None of them could build up his history on a rigorous scheme of succession of world-monarchies. They all had to take account of the Celtic West which that scheme ignored. Trogus Pompeius, perhaps the most remarkable of the four, came from this Celtic West. Nor could Egypt be ignored after so many protests. Diodorus as a Greek could emphasize the superior merits of Greek education; and Nicolaus as a secretary of King Herod of Judaea had to accommodate the Jews and was altogether sympathetic to the minor nations of the Near East. But each of these four historians seems to have been very conscious of the scheme of the succession of Oriental monarchies. This is demonstrably the case with the two historians whom we can still read in a continuous way, not only relying on quotations, Diodorus and Trogus. Trogus's masterstroke—a piece of really good historical imagination—was to conclude his work by bringing together the free Parthians of the East and the no-longer-free Celts and Spaniards of the West. He simply declared that the Parthians were sharing the rule of the world with the Romans after having won three wars against them (41. 1). We know how these victories had hurt the Romans. Trogus had hit where it hurt most. He had furthermore made it plain that the conflict between East and West, of which so much had been said in the previous century, was by no means closed. The Parthian Empire was after all either the continuation or the revival of the Persian Empire, as everybody knew.

There is also a conspicuous reference to the four monarchies of Assyria, Media, Persia, and Macedon just at the beginning of the *Roman Antiquities* by Dionysius of Halicarnassus. This was written in 7 B.C. And we could follow up the allusions to this scheme until the early fifth century A.D. when Rutilius Namatianus was still comparing Rome, to her advantage, with the great empires of old. He called the Persian Empire of the Achaemenids "magni Parthorum reges" (*De reditu suo* 85). But we are ready to face the last text I propose to consider on this occasion—the Book of Daniel.

V

It was customary in the Hellenistic period both among Jews and among Gentiles to attribute sayings, visions, and books in general to wise men of the past. Daniel was not such a big name, but his reputation had been on the increase for some centuries. The prophet Ezekiel chose Noah, Daniel, and Job as the prototypes of righteousness (14 : 14, 20). Ezekiel 28 : 3 taunts the King of Tyre: "are you wiser than Daniel?" So Daniel was not only just, but wise. And he was probably not Jewish, as Noah and Job were not, strictly speaking, Jewish. In the Book of Jubilees (4 : 20), which is more or less contemporary with the final version of the Book of Daniel as we have it, we find a Daniel, or rather a Danel, whose daughter married Enoch, the other, more important biblical figure to whom apocalyptic books were attributed in the second century B.C. If Daniel and Danel are two variant spellings of the same name, which seems beyond doubt, the figure of the just man Danel may go back to an Ugaritic text of the fourteenth century B.C., "The Tale of Aqhat."

What is surprising is to find Daniel placed in the courts of Babylon and Persia by the book which bears his name. According to the book, he would have been taken prisoner at the fall of Jerusalem at the beginning of the sixth century B.C. We have no idea of when and how Daniel became a hero of the sixth century B.C. According to the Book of Daniel, he and three Jewish friends were successively at the court of Nebuchadnezzar, of Belshazzar, who is presented as the son of Nebuchadnezzar and the last King of Babylon (he was neither), and finally of that Darius the Mede, never heard of elsewhere, who is supposed to have conquered Belshazzar. In the first part of the book—which in our late-medieval division into chapters corresponds to chapters 1–6—Daniel interprets the visions and dreams of pagan kings. He and his companions exemplify steadfast Jews who prefer death to the cult of foreign gods or of living kings. But while (as we shall see) these chapters presuppose Alexander the Great and the formation of the Hellenistic monarchies, they do not allude specifically to Antiochus IV or his time. They envisage Jews living at the courts of kings and managing in spite of all to reconcile worldly success as courtiers with the duties of pious Jews. The situation resembles that of the Book of Esther rather more than that of the Books of Maccabees.

The second part of Daniel is differently oriented. It is clearly concerned with the situation of Jerusalem and the rest of Judaea under Antiochus IV, and his own visions are directly communicated by Daniel in the first person. The stories about Daniel and his companions are replaced by the words of Daniel himself. It seems obvious, however, that the author or authors who composed what now constitutes chapters 7–12 of the Book of Daniel knew the first part well. There are in fact signs that the Book of Daniel, though composed of heterogeneous elements, was put together with conspicuous care by an editor who was interested in producing an impression of coherence and even of stylistic harmony. The task was by no means easy because, as we all know, Daniel is one of the two books of the Bible which are written partly in Hebrew and partly in Aramaic. With the present division of chapters, the first chapter is in Hebrew, the next six chapters are in Aramaic; in the second section of the book the order and the proportions are inverted, one chapter in Aramaic being followed by six chapters in Hebrew. Even if we forget the existence of chapters, the proportions remain harmonic. This must be by design and indicates that the editor of the book did his best to give it an appearance of unity.

The link between the two sections is not only formal. The sec-

ond section of the book develops the philosophy of history which
we find in the second chapter of the first section. It is of course
inspired by the idea of the succession of empires.

In chapter 2 Nebuchadnezzar had a dream, as we all remember,
which none of the non-Jews could interpret, and he was determined to kill his professional advisers. Daniel was brought in,
gave the right interpretation, and thereby saved his Gentile colleagues or rivals. The dream is that of the great image with the
head of fine gold, breasts and arms of silver, belly and thighs of
bronze, legs of iron, feet part iron, part clay. A stone from heaven
(according to the dream) shattered the statue. In Daniel's interpretation the different metals in the different parts of the statue
each symbolize a kingdom, and the kingdoms are not concurrent
but successive. The stone is the true God, and what follows the
destruction of the statue is the establishment of the Kingdom of
God which will endure forever. However, there is an ambiguity in
the story. The stone smashes all the elements of the statue at the
same time, including the golden head. It puts an eternal Jewish
Kingdom of God in the place of all the empires of the past taken
together. Thus the statue is not meant to represent a succession of
empires: it rather symbolizes the coexistence of all the past, as it
had developed through a succession of kingdoms, at the moment
in which all the past is destroyed by the divine stone and replaced
by a new order.

The Book of Daniel does not say which are the four kingdoms
smashed by the stone. The writer of chapter 7, which took up the
same notion of four kingdoms but did not retain the symbolism of
the metals, undoubtedly identified the kingdoms with Babylonia,
Media, Persia, and Macedonia. In chapter 7 the fourth kingdom is
represented by a nameless monster with ten horns, and an eleventh little horn develops later. The ten horns of the fourth monster certainly symbolize three Macedonian and seven Seleucid
kings, and the eleventh little horn is Antiochus IV. One can date
chapter 7, from the details it provides, between 169 and 167 B.C.
Like the writer of chapter 2, the writer of chapter 7 expects a
Kingdom of God soon to replace the kingdom on earth.

Though there is a presumption that the author of chapter 7 was
capable of understanding what the author of chapter 2 meant by
four kingdoms, we need confirmation. The confirmation comes

from the fourth kingdom, which is partly iron, partly clay because, so *Daniel* explains, "it will be a divided kingdom with some elements of iron in it." This makes sense only for the Macedonian Kingdom or Empire which was divided by Alexander's successors. A further confirmation is in the apparently mysterious line 43: "Just as you saw the iron mixed with terra cotta of clay, they will be mingled by intermarriage, but they will not hold together, just as iron does not unite with terra cotta" (trans. L. F. Hartman, Anchor Bible, 1978). Here there is an allusion to an unlucky royal marriage. Now, there was one disastrous marriage among the successors of Alexander: that between the Seleucid Antioch II and Berenice, the daughter of Ptolemy II. This is indeed recorded more explictly in the second section of Daniel at 11:6. We must recognize the same allusion in chapter 2:43. As this marriage happened about 250 B.C. and is the most recent event alluded to in chapter 2, there is a fair chance that chapter 2 was written not much later. If so, we could tentatively date the first section of Daniel about 250–230 B.C., whereas the second section is made up of chapters written between 167 and 164 B.C.

If our reading of the text of Daniel is approximately correct, we have a Jew who in the second part of the third century B.C. expounded in symbolic form the doctrine of the four monarchies and reinterpreted it in an apocalyptic sense: the fifth kingdom, soon to come, would be the Kingdom of God. The idea was found acceptable, and was revived and given a new urgency in Jerusalem at the time of the resistance to Antiochus IV when the priest Mattathias and his son Judas Maccabeus took up arms to defend the Torah of the Fathers. The notion remained operative in Jewish thought, as a survey of Jewish Sibylline Books and other apocalyptic writings could easily show. But we must end with the obvious question. Where did the author of Daniel chapter 2 find this notion?

If we had only the second section of the Book of Daniel, which is directly inspired by the crisis in the reign of Antiochus IV and written while he was still alive, it would have been recognized long ago that the author or authors of these visions about kingdoms worked on the basis of the Greek concept of a succession of world-empires. The religious interpretation, the apocalyptic finale, is of course the specific Jewish contribution to the reading

of the situation. Furthermore, we must admit that Assyria is replaced by Babylonia in Daniel's vision: Babylonia was a natural
beginning for a Hellenistic Jew, who associated its empire with
the destruction of the First Temple. But the foundation of all this
Messianic structure is provided by the scheme of the succession
of empires which we found in Herodotus, Ctesias, and their successors. What is decisive is that no one has so far been able to
produce genuine evidence for the existence of the notion of four
world-empires outside Greek historical thought. There have been
many suggestions in the direction of India, Persia, and Babylonia,
but none has stood up to serious criticism. Four world ages of the
Hesiodic type are known in India; four kings in a descending order
of goodness within the Iranian state are described in Persian medieval commentaries on a lost book of the Avesta—the *Vohuman
Yasn.* Some serious scholars have suggested that such texts were
themselves written under Greek influence. If they were not, they
prove that the Hesiodic myth of decline had wide Indo-European
roots and ramifications. But the application of the quadripartite
scheme to the political notion of world-empires remains a Greek
peculiarity, if one excepts the Book of Daniel and its imitators. In
1975 Professor A. K. Grayson introduced a new pretender to the
title of Daniel's source by his meritorious discovery in the British
Museum of a late Babylonian text which he called "a dynastic
prophecy" (*Babylonian Historical-Literary Texts,* 24–37). This is
a chronicle in the form of a prophecy which lists a series of kings
who governed Babylon and indicates changes of dynasties and of
territorial boundaries. The text has some remarkable similarities
with Daniel, and I hope to show elsewhere that it was not com-
piled under the first Seleucid kings, as Grayson suggested, but
under Alexander the Great. It may in fact be the earliest document
we have of anti-Macedonian propaganda in Babylonia. But the
similarities between this dynastic prophecy and Daniel do not involve the scheme of the succession of empires, which is absent
from the Babylonian text.

There is, however, a very good reason why scholars should have
been slow to recognize that the Book of Daniel turns a Greek
summary of world-empires into a blueprint for the preparation of
the Messianic age. The reason is that no Greek source associates,

as Daniel chapter 2 does, the four empires with the four metals. A similar association of metals and kings is to be found in the medieval Persian texts *Denkard* and *Bahman Yasht* when they describe the four Iranian kings representing stages of declining respect toward Zoroaster and his doctrine. I believe, however, that this does not disprove our main point that no theory of the succession of world-empires circulated in the East before the Greeks imported it. It may well be that some such text which associated metals with kings, even if not universal kings, suggested to the author of Daniel chapter 2 the idea of characterizing each world-empire by one metal. But paradoxically this very association in Daniel between metals and world-empires is presented in such a way as to show that it is secondary. The metallic ingredients can hardly be said to make sense in Daniel's context. The four metals in order of decreasing value ought to represent successive stages in the decline of earthly kingdoms. Yet Daniel does not express any preference: all the empires will be destroyed together. Nor would we expect a Jewish writer to give the highest mark to Babylonia, which had destroyed the First Temple. It cannot be an accident that the scheme of the metals, where we find it outside Daniel chapter 2, has nothing to do with the scheme of the world-empires. Even Daniel chapter 7 drops the combination of world-empires and metals, thereby confirming that it was a peculiarity of Daniel chapter 2. The scheme of the world-empires in Daniel is in itself value-free, as the Greek scheme of world-empires was.

To judge from the fascination which the statue of the four metals has exercised throughout the centuries, we must admit that the author of Daniel chapter 2 had found a symbol which worked even if it was incongruous. While using the Greek notion of the succession of empires to illuminate the ways of God, he had also produced a quaint target for the destructive capacities of God. To repeat the words used in a similar context by Mandell Creighton: "No disappointment was rude enough to show men that this theory was but a dream" (*A History of the Papacy* I, 1882, p. 11).

We are no longer likely to be surprised that Jews talked to Greeks in the third century B.C. Even King Solomon, in his modern reincarnation as Ecclesiastes or Qohelet, was taking notice of the latest Epicurean treatises. In another context I hope to have shown that Herodotus was shown to the somewhat later author of the Book of Judith. What is remarkable is the energy and independence with which the Jews turned Greek ideas upside down.

Select Bibliography (mostly of recent works)

I

C. Trieber, "Die Idee der vier Weltreiche," *Hermes* 27, 1892, 321–44.
M. Büdinger, *Die Universalhistorie im Alterthume*, Wien, 1895.
M. Mühl, *Die antike Menschheitsidee in ihrer geschichtlichen Entwicklung*, Leipzig, 1928.
J. Kaerst, *Universalgeschichte*, Stuttgart, 1930.
W. Goetz, "Weltgeschichte," *Archiv für Kulturgeschichte* 24, 1934, 273–303.
R. Aron, *The Dawn of Universal History*, London, 1961.
J. Vogt, *Wege zum historischen Universum*, Stuttgart, 1961.
H. C. Baldry, *The Unity of Mankind in Greek Thought*, Cambridge, 1965.
R. Drews, "Assyria in Classical Universal History," *Historia* 14, 1965, 129–38.
A. B. Brebaart, "Weltgeschichte als Thema der antiken Geschichtschreibung," *Acta Historiae Neerlandica*, 1, 1966, 1–21.
A. Heuss, *Zur Theorie der Weltgeschichte*, Berlin, 1968.
A. Randa (ed.), *Mensch und Geschichte. Zur Geschichte der Universalgeschichtsschreibung*, Salzburg-München, 1969.
F. G. Maier, "Das Problem der Universalität," *Geschichte heute* (ed. G. Schulz), Göttingen, 1973, 84–108.
P. Burde, *Untersuchungen zur antiken Universalgeschichtsschreibung*, diss. München, 1974.
F. Hampl, *Geschichte als kritische Wissenschaft*, I, Darmstadt, 1975.
A. Heuss, "Über die Schwierigkeit, Weltgeschichte zu schreiben," *Saeculum* 27, 1976, 1–35.
G. Barraclough, *Main Trends in History*, New York–London 1978 (1979), 153–77.
H. Schwabl, "Weltalter" in *Pauly-Wissowa*, Suppl. 15, 1978, 783–850.
G. W. Trompf, *The Idea of Historical Recurrence in Western Thought from Antiquity to the Reformation*, Berkeley, 1979.

II

F. Kampers, *Alexander der Grosse und die Idee des Weltimperiums in Prophetie und Sage*, Freiburg, 1901.
A. Bauer, *Ursprung und Fortwirken der christlichen Weltchronik*, Graz, 1910.
A. O. Lovejoy and G. Boas, *Primitivism and Related Ideas in Antiquity*, Baltimore, 1935.
K. Löwith, *Weltgeschichte und Heilsgeschehen*, Stuttgart, 1953.

Anna-Dorothee v. den Brincken, *Studien zur lateinischen Weltchronistik bis in das Zeitalter Ottos von Freising*, Düsseldorf, 1957.

P. Meinhold, "Weltgeschichte-Kirchengeschichte-Heilsgeschichte," *Saeculum* 9, 1958, 261–81.

A. Klempt, *Die Säkularisierung der universalhistorischen Auffassung*, Göttingen, 1961.

K. Rahner, "Weltgeschichte und Heilsgeschichte," *Schriften zur Theologie*, V, Einsiedeln, 2 ed., 1964, 115–35.

G. Klingenstein, "Kultur- und universalgeschichtliche Aspekte in strukturaler Sicht," *Archiv für Kulturgeschichte* 52, 1970, 280–96.

J. Vogt, "Universalgeschichte und Kirchengeschichte unserer Zeit," *Theologische Quartalschrift* 155, 1975, 175–86.

III

E. Meyer, "Hesiods Erga und das Gedicht von den fünf Menschengeschlechtern" (1910) in *Kleine Schriften*, II, Halle 1924, 15–66.

F. Boll, "Die Lebensalter," *Neue Jahrbücher für das Klassische Altertum* 31, 1913, 89–145.

R. Schmidt, "Aetates mundi," *Zeitschrift für Kirchengeschichte* 67, 1955, 288–317.

U. Bianchi, "Razza aurea, unità delle cinque razze ed Elisio," *Studi Materiali Storia Religioni* 39, 1963, 143–210.

B. Gantz, *Weltalter, Goldene Zeit und sinnverwandte Vorstellungen*, Hildesheim, 1967.

J.-P. Vernant, *Mythe et pensée chez les Grecs*, 3 ed., Paris, 1971.

Jana Tumova, "Antike Bearbeitung des Mythos von den Vier Zeitaltern," *Graecolatina et Orientalia* 6, 1974, 3–46.

J. Fontenrose, "Work, Justice and Hesiod's Five Ages," *Classical Philology* 69, 1974, 1–16.

M. L. West, *Hesiod: Works and Days*, Oxford, 1978.

P. Vidal-Naquet, "Plato's Myth of the Statesman, the Ambiguities of the Golden Age and of History," *Journal of Hellenic Studies* 98, 1978, 132–41.

IV

K. Reinhardt, "Hekataios von Abdera und Demokrit," *Hermes* 47, 1912, 492–513 (*Vermächtnis der Antike*, Göttingen, 1960, 114–32).

W. Uxkull-Gyllenband, *Griechische Kulturentstehungslehren*, Berlin, 1924.

A. Kleingünther, "Πρῶτος Εὑρετής," *Philologus*, Suppl. 26, 1, 1933.

W. Spoerri, *Späthellenistische Berichte über Welt, Kultur und Götter*, Basel, 1959.

K. Thraede, "Erfinder" in *Reallexikon für Antike und Christentum*, V, 1962, 1190–1275.

A. Dihle and others, *Grecs et Barbares*, Entretiens Fondation Hardt, 8, Genève, 1962.

F. J. Worstbrock, "Translatio Artium. Über die Herkunft und Entwick-

54   On Pagans, Jews, and Christians

lung einer kulturhistorischen Theorie," *Archiv für Kulturgeschichte* 47, 1965, 1–22.
T. Cole, *Democritus and the Sources of Greek Anthropology*, American Philol. Assoc., 25, 1967.
E. R. Dodds, *The Ancient Concept of Progress*, Oxford, 1973..
B. Reischl, *Reflexe griechischer Kulturentstehungslehren bei augusteischen Dichtern*, diss. München, 1976.

V

S. Mazzarino, *Il pensiero storico classico*, I–III, Bari, 1966–67.
K. von Fritz, *Die griechische Geschichtsschreibung*, I, Berlin, 1967.
H.-A. Weber, *Herodots Verständnis von Historie*, Bern, 1976.
E. Cavaignac, "Réflexions sur Ephore," *Mélanges G. Glotz*, I, Paris, 1932, 143–61.
Th. J. G. Locher, "'Ephoros' jüngste Nachkommen," *Saeculum* 7, 1956, 127–35.
R. Drews, "Ephorus and History written 'χατὰ γένος'," *Amer. Journ. Philol.* 84, 1963, 244–55.
O. Murray, "Hecataeus of Abdera and Pharaonic Kingship," *Journ. Egypt. Archaeol.* 56, 1970, 141–71.
P. Pédech, *La méthode historique de Polybe*, Paris, 1964.
F. W. Walbank, *Polybius*, Berkeley, 1972.
E. Gabba (ed.), *Polybe*, Entretiens Fondation Hardt, 20, Genève, 1974.
S. Mohm, *Untersuchungen zu den historiographischen Anschauungen des Polybios*, diss. Saarbrücken, 1976.
K. E. Petzold, "Kyklos und Telos im Geschichtsdenken des Polybios," *Saeculum* 28, 1977, 253–90.
K. Bringmann, "Weltherrschaft und innere Krise Roms im Spiegel der Geschichtsschreibung des zweiten und ersten Jahrhunderts v. Chr.," *Antike und Abendland* 23, 1977, 28–49.
D. Musti, *Polibio e l'imperialismo romano*, Napoli, 1978.
F. W. Walbank, *A Historical Commentary on Polybius*, III, Oxford, 1979, 720–25.
Id., "The Idea of Decline in Polybios," in R. Koselleck and P. Widmer, *Niedergang*, Stuttgart 1980, 41–58.
K. Sachs, *Polybius on the Writing of History*, Berkeley, 1981, 96–121.
S. Blankert, *Seneca ep. 90 over natuur en cultuur en Posidonius als zijn bron*, Amsterdam, 1941.
K. Reinhardt, "Poseidonios" in *Pauly-Wissowa*, XXII, 1, 1954, 558–826.
J. Hermatta, "Poseidonios über die römische Urgeschichte," *Acta Class. Univ. Scient. Debreceniensis* 7, 1971, 21–25.
P. Desideri, "L'interpretazione dell'impero romano in Posidonio," *Rend. Istit. Lombardo* 106, 1972, 481–93.
K. von Fritz, "Posidonios als Historiker," *Historiographia antiqua*, Louvain 1977, 163–93.
K. Schmidt, *Kosmologische Aspekte im Geschichtswerk des Poseidonios*, Göttingen, 1980.
P. Merlan, "Lucretius, Primitivist or Progressivist?" *Journ. History of Ideas* 11, 1950, 364–68.

J.-P. Borle, "Progrès ou déclin de l'humanité. La conception de Lucrèce," *Mus. Helveticum* 19, 1962, 162–76.

B. Mannwald, "Der Aufbau der lukrezischen Kulturentstehungslehre," *Abh. Akad. Mainz*, Geistes- und Sozialwissensch. Klasse, 1980, Nr. 3.

E. Troilo, "Considerazioni su Diodoro Siculo e la sua storia universale," *Atti R. Istituto Veneto*, 1940–41, 17–42.

G. Vlastos, "On the Prehistory in Diodorus," *Amer. Journ. Philol.*, 67, 1946, 51–59.

B. Farrington, "Diodorus Siculus: Universal Historian" in *Head and Hand in Ancient Greece. Four Studies*, London 1947, 55–87.

R. Laqueur, "Diodorea," *Hermes*, 86, 1958, 257–90.

M. Pavan, "La teoresi storica di Diodoro Siculo," *Rend. Accad. Lincei*, N.S. 16, 1961, 19–52; 117–51.

M. Gigante, "Catullo, Cornelio e Cicerone," *Giornale Ital. Filologia* 20, 1967, 123–29.

F. Muenzer, "Atticus als Geschichtschreiber," *Hermes* 40, 1905, 50–100.

O. Seel, *Eine römische Weltgeschichte*, Nürnberg, 1972.

R. Urban, "Historiae Philippicae bei Pompeius Trogus," *Historia* 31, 1982, 82–96.

I. Lana, *Velleio Patercolo o della propaganda*, Torino, 1952.

R. J. Starr, "The Scope and Genre of Velleius' History," *Class. Quart.* 31, 1981, 162–74.

W. Den Boer, "Florus und die römische Geschichte," *Mnemosyne* 4, 18, 1965, 366–87.

Florus, ed. P. Jal, Paris, 1967.

H.-W. Goetz, *Die Geschichtstheologie des Orosius*, Darmstadt, 1980, 71–79.

VI

R. Reitzenstein and H. H. Schaeder, *Studien zum antiken Synkretismus aus Iran und Griechenland*, Leipzig, 1926.

H. Windisch, "Die Orakel des Hystaspes," *Verhandel. Kon. Akad. Wetensch.*, Afd. Letterkunde, N.R. XXVIII, 3, 1929.

F. Cumont, "La fin du monde selon les mages occidentaux," *Rev. Hist. Religons* 103, 1931, 29–96.

E. Kocken, *De Theorie van de vier wereldrijken en van de overdracht der wereldheerschappij tot op Innocentius III*, Nijmegen, 1935.

J. Bidez and F. Cumont, *Les mages hellénisés*, Paris, 1938.

H. Zimmern, "The Hindu View of World History according to the Purāṇas," *The Review of Religion* 6, 1942, 249–69.

R. Schmidt, "Aetates Mundi. Die Weltalter als Gliederungsprinzip der Geschichte," *Zeitschr. für Kirchengeschichte* 67, 1955, 288–317.

G. Widengren, "Quelques rapports entre juifs et iraniens à l'époque des Parthes," *Vetus Testamentum*, Suppl. 4, 1956, 197–241.

H. Wolfram, *Splendor Imperii. Die Epiphanie von Tugend und Heil in Herrschaft und Reich*, Graz-Köln, 1963.

F. König, *Zarathustras Jenseitsvorstellungen und das Alte Testament*, Freiburg, 1964.

M. Molé, *La légende de Zoroastre, selon les textes pehlevis*, Paris, 1967.

56   On Pagans, Jews, and Christians

M. Boyce, "Middle Persian Literature," *Handbuch der Orientalistik*, 4, 1, Sect. 2, Lit. 1, Leiden, 1968, 31–66.
C. Dimmitt Church, *The Yuga Story: a Myth of the Four Ages of the World as found in the Purānas*, diss. Syracuse, 1970.
G. Podskalsky, *Byzantinische Reichseschatologie*, München, 1972.
J. de Menasce, *Le troisième livre du Dēnkart*, Paris, 1974.
J. R. Hinnels, "The Zoroastrian Doctrine of Salvation in the Roman World: A Study of the Oracle of Hystaspes," *Man and His Salvation. Studies in Memory of S. G. F. Brandon*, Manchester, 1973, 125–48.
G. Widengren, "Iran and Israel in Parthian Times with special regard to the Ethiopic Book of Enoch," in *Religious Syncretism in Antiquity*, ed. B. A. Pearson, Missoula, 1975, 85–130.
D. König-Ockenfels, "Christliche Deutung der Weltgeschichte bei Euseb von Cäsarea," *Saeculum* 27, 1976, 348–65.
H. G. Kippenberg, "Die Geschichte der mittelpersischen apokalyptischen Traditionen," *Studia Iranica* 7, 1978, 49–60.
A. Alföldi, "Redeunt Saturnia Regna," *Chiron* 5, 1975, 165–92; 9, 1979, 553–606.

VII

H. Fuchs, *Der geistige Widerstand gegen Rom in der antiken Welt*, Berlin, 1938.
J. Swain, "The Theory of the Four Monarchies. Opposition History under the Roman Empire," *Class. Philology* 35, 1940, 1–21.
S. K. Eddy, *The King is Dead*, Lincoln, 1961.
J. Lebram, "Die Weltreiche in der jüdischen Apokalyptik. Bemerkungen zu Tobit, 14, 47," *Zeitschr. für Alttestam. Wissenschaft* 76, 1964, 328–31.
V. Nikiprowetzki, *La Troisième Sibylle*, Paris–La Haye 1970, 88–112.
D. Flusser, "The Four Empires in the Fourth Sibyl and in the Book of Daniel," *Israel Oriental Studies* 2, 1972, 148–75.
A. K. Grayson, *Babylonian Historical Literary Texts*, Toronto, 1975.
J. Schwartz, "L'Historiographie impériale des Oracula Sibyllina," *Cahiers Hist. Ancienne* 2, 1976, 413–21.
J. J. Collins (ed.), *Apocalypse. The Morphology of a Genre*, Semeia 14, 1979.
D. Mendels, "The Five Empires: A Note on a Propagandistic Topos," *Amer. Journ. Philol.* 102, 1981, 330–37.

VIII

H. H. Rowley, *Darius the Mede and the Four World Empires in the Book of Daniel*, Cardiff, 1935.
W. Baumgartner, "Ein Vierteljahrhundert Danielforschung," *Theolog. Rundschau* 11, 1939, 59–83; 125–44; 201–28.
H. L. Ginsberg, *Studies in Daniel*, New York, 1948.
H. H. Rowley, *The Servant of the Lord*, Oxford, 1952.
H. Gross, *Weltherrschaft als religiöse Idee im Alten Testament*, Bonn, 1953.
M. Noth, "Das Geschichtsverständnis der alttestamentlichen Apokalyp-

tik" (1954) in *Gesammelte Studien zum Alten Testament*, München, 1960, 248–73.

K. Koch, "Die Weltreiche im Danielbuch," *Theol. Liter.-Zeit.* 85, 1960, 829–32.

H. H. Rowley, *The Relevance of Apocalyptic*, 3 ed., London, 1963.

D. S. Russell, *The Method and Message of Jewish Apocalyptic*, London, 1964.

E. Bickerman, *Four Strange Books of the Bible*, New York, 1967.

O. Plöger, *Theokratie und Eschatalogie*, 3 ed., Neukirchen-Vluyn, 1968.

M. Delcor, "Les sources du chapitre VII de Daniel," *Vetus Testamentum* 18, 1968, 290–312.

F. Dexinger, *Das Buch Daniel und seine Probleme*, Stuttgart, 1969.

J. Schreiner, *Alttestamentlich-jüdische Apokalyptik*, München, 1969.

K. Koch, *Ratlos vor der Apokalyptik*, Gütersloh, 1970.

A. Mertens, *Das Buch Daniel im Lichte der Texte vom Toten Meer*, Stuttgart, 1971.

W. Schmithals, *Die Apokalyptik: Einführung und Deutung*, Göttingen, 1973.

J. J. Collins, "Jewish Apocalyptic against its Hellenistic Near Eastern Environment," *Bull. Amer. Soc. Oriental Research* 220, 1975, 27–36.

Id., "The Court Tales in Daniel and the Development of Jewish Apocalyptic," *Journ. Bibl. Literature* 94, 1975, 218–34.

P. R. Davies, "Daniel Chapter Two," *Journ. Theol. Studies* N.S. 27, 1976, 392–401.

J. G. Gamnie, "The Classification, Stages of Growth and Changing Intentions in the Book of Daniel," *Journ. Bibl. Literature* 95, 1976, 191–204.

J. M. Schmidt, *Die jüdische Apokalyptik. Die Geschichte ihrer Erforschung*, 2 ed., Neukirchen-Vluyn 1976.

J. J. Collins, *The Apocalyptic Vision of the Book of Daniel*, Missoula, 1977.

R. Raphael and others, *L'Apocalyptique*, Paris, 1977.

G. F. Hasel, "The Four World Empires of Daniel 2," *Journ. for the Study of the Old Testament* 12, 1979, 17–30.

P. R. Davies, "Eschatology in the Book of Daniel," *ibid.* 17, 1980, 33–53.

K. Koch and others, *Das Buch Daniel*, Darmstadt, 1980.

M. Stone, *Scriptures, Sects and Visions*, London and New York, 1980.

J. G. Gamnie, "On the Intention and Sources of Daniel I–VI," *Vetus Testamentum* 31, 1981, 282–92.

Among recent commentaries on Daniel I mention: J. A. Montgomery (1927), A. Bentzen (1952), E. Heaton (1956), J. Barr (1962), N. Porteous (1965), M. Delcor (1971), A. Lecoque (1976), L. F. Hartman and A. A. Di Lella (1978).

4

The Theological Efforts of the Roman
Upper Classes in the First Century B.C.

I

THERE IS NO DOUBT about what the Roman upper class had to face in the twenty years or so between 60 and 40 B.C.: a revolution which perhaps nobody wanted and to which everyone was contributing. An unparalleled series of conquests was at the same time the first stage and the ultimate condition of this revolution. Enormous armies had to be put together to regain—or perhaps gain for the first time—effective control of Spain in the Sertorian war (80–71 B.C.), and to extend Roman rule in Asia to the Euphrates over the ruins of the Seleucid kingdom and of the recent empire of Mithridates. Gaul was the prize for Caesar; and there was a moment in 54 B.C. in which even Britain was felt to be within reach. Egypt was forced for all practical purposes into the zone of Roman control. The great generals who engineered the conquests—Pompey and Caesar—also confronted each other in political and military battles. The elimination of Crassus in the only unmitigated disaster of the period—the failure to conquer Parthia—made the rivalry between the two surviving members of the triumvirate even more pressing. There had been other portents of the forthcoming replacement of senatorial government by military dictatorship: for instance, the rebellion of the slaves led by Spartacus; the wars against the pirates, one of the incidental consequences of which was the declaration of Crete as a Roman

Classical Philology, 79, 3, 1984, pp. 199–211.

province; and the mysterious Catilinarian conspiracy, which certainly appealed to discontented peasants.

It was in this revolutionary atmosphere that—perhaps not surprisingly—some of the Roman intellectuals began to think in earnest about religion.[1] These intellectuals were themselves members of the ruling class, although not of the *gentes* which could claim a natural right to rule the Roman state. The three best known of them—Nigidius Figulus, Terentius Varro, and Tullius Cicero—happened to be senators and followers of Pompey. But at least Varro and Cicero easily made their peace with Caesar, and, as we shall see, their most important work on religion was in fact written when they were at peace with Caesar, and with an eye toward Caesar. For Caesar turned out to be intensely concerned with questions of reorganizing religion.

This is not the place to discuss at length one of the most important books on Roman religion of the last decades—the *Divus Julius* by Stefan Weinstock, which appeared in 1971 not long after the author's death. Weinstock was convinced that Caesar was "an imaginative and daring religious reformer." He thought that by 44 B.C. Caesar had made himself a god—not just another god, but Iuppiter Iulius. As Iuppiter Iulius, Caesar would have become king of the gods just when he was preparing to become king of the Romans: godlike and kinglike honors would have coalesced, if he had lived long enough. It has already been objected by J. A. North that both parts of the construction are open to doubt.[2] The only evidence for Caesar's identification with Jupiter is in a passage of Dio Cassius (44. 6. 4) which is almost certainly the result of a misunderstanding. The parallel passage in Cicero's *Philippics* 2. 110—a contemporary and hostile witness—makes no mention of the identification with Jupiter: it shows that a cult of Iulius as Divus had been planned either in Caesar's last months or immediately after his death. Even less can we be certain that Caesar intended to be proclaimed king of Rome. All we know is that in the famous scene of the Lupercalia of 44 B.C., Antony called Caesar king and tried to put a diadem on his head, but Caesar refused the offer and sent the diadem to Jupiter—which he would not have done if he had himself become Jupiter. When, however, the obvious exaggerations of Weinstock's thesis are discounted, we are left with a considerable amount of evidence, for the first time properly examined by Weinstock himself, about Caesar's interest and that of his circle in changes and innovations in the rituals they had inherited. Caesar gave much thought to religious matters, and this explains why Varro after their reconciliation dedicated to him his *Antiquitates divinae*, his thorough study of Roman religion, in about 47 B.C. The following year it was the turn of Cicero to write *De natura deorum*.

Nigidius Figulus remains the most colorful of the three followers of Pompey we have mentioned, although his work is entirely lost: his misfortune in life was matched by the loss of his books in late antiquity.[3] A senator, he had advised Cicero during the Catilinarian crisis, had reached the position of praetor in 58 B.C., and had been a legate of Pompey. Unlike Varro and Cicero, he died in exile before he was able to obtain a pardon from Caesar: that he tried at least once to get the pardon through Cicero we know from a rather inept and embarrassed letter which Cicero wrote to him in 46 (*Epistulae ad Familiares* 4. 13). Nigidius did not study Roman religion, especially its augural rituals, simply to be informed and to inform. He developed divinatory gifts. He is supposed to have prophesied to the father of the future Augustus that his son would rule the world (Suetonius *Divus Augustus* 94). On a more modest level he helped a friend to discover where a small treasure had been buried (Varro ap. Apuleius *Apologia* 42). Obviously he did not aim at restoring traditional Roman practice either. Nigidius can have been nothing like a conventional Roman if St. Jerome chose to define him as "Pythagoricus et magus" (*Chron.* p. 156 Helm), that is, a Pythagorean of a modern cast, which would include occultism, astrology, and Persian doctrines about the ages of the world. He wrote on grammar, on gods, on the interpretation of dreams and *augurium privatum*, on animals, men, and land, and on stars and thunders. He seems to have reinterpreted traditional Etruscan doctrines in the light of Greek and Persian theories, if he is the source of Martianus Capella (who does not mention him by name) in the fifth century and of Johannes Lydus who mentions him, but in suspicious circumstances, in the sixth century. Like the hard-boiled Tories who established the "Catholic Apostolic Church" in the neighborhood of University College London in the early nineteenth century and combined the gift of tongues and prophetism with sound business ability, Nigidius Figulus and his friends were men of the world. They expected help from strange religious practices in trying to control what escaped them in the fast-moving world in which they lived. They had left behind the traditional ways of bargaining with the gods and were trying to discover safer rules for the interplay between men and gods. Divination seemed to them to offer the best chances, but it had to be based on a wide-ranging reassessment of the natural order: hence their interest in details from grammar to celestial spheres.

Varro would probably have agreed that ultimately a secret doctrine was needed if one wanted to feel safe in personal terms. We are unexpectedly told by Pliny the Elder that Varro arranged for himself by testament a burial in the Pythagorean style (*Naturalis Historia* 35. 160). He had been educated in Rome at the school of Aelius Stilo, who had commented on the language of the Twelve Tables and was of the Stoic persuasion. He had later been at the school of Antiochus of Ascalon, where the Platonic tradition had taken a definite turn toward skepticism and students were trained to produce arguments in favor of both sides. Yet if anything emerges from what Varro did and wrote, it is the need to separate one's religious and philosophic opinions from the role one is expected to play in one's own society. In Varro's time it was commonplace to distinguish three types of theology: the *genus mythicum*, which was appropriate to poets and was generally dismissed as unworthy of thoughtful people; the *genus physicum*, which represented the speculations of philosophers about gods; and finally the *genus civile*, or political type, which the citizens and especially the priests of a given state were required to know because it indicated the gods of the state itself, as well as the rites and sacrifices appropriate to them. The story of the research on the history of this "theologia tripartita" has been written by G. Lieberg.[4] What seems obvious from the evidence he brings together is that the distinction between the three kinds of theology acquired importance in Rome in the historical circumstances I am describing and in the authors I am dealing with—namely, Varro and Cicero. It was from Varro and Cicero that Tertullian and St. Augustine derived it and made it an important argument against paganism in general. The only other Christian theologian of antiquity who gave attention to this tripartition, Eusebius in the *Praeparatio evangelica* 4. 1, probably had no firsthand knowledge of the Western, Latin developments and merely reported what he had read in anti-Christian polemicists of the East. Although we must try to forget the importance which this tripartition assumed in the context of Christian-pagan polemics of later centuries, we cannot ignore the fact that this distinction first gained political relevance in Rome precisely among those who were concerned with the future of the Roman state in the first century B.C. In Rome the poets could be dismissed more easily than in Greece because after all it was known that the best stories about the gods were written in Greek and did not really belong to the original Roman tradition. But the conflict between philosophy and city-religion could not be equally briefly dismissed by turning against the Greek origins of philosophy. If there was something no one with any education would care to deny in Rome, it was the validity of philosophic argument. In the age of Caesar, philosophy had become part of Roman education in a more intimate way than Greek myths had become Roman through Greek poetry—or its Latin equivalent. It will be precisely my argument in the last pages of this paper that poetry replaces philosophy in the discussion about religion at the time of Augustus. In the period of Caesar, the men who discuss religion are concerned with the choice between the rational approach and the political approach to religion, not with any dubious relation between poetry and city-religion.

Seen against this dilemma, Varro's thought is straightforward. Whatever the merits of philosophical theology, cities live because citizens obey the regulations of civic religion. Insofar as civic religion is a series of rituals and obligations considered compulsory by the citizens themselves (and declared to be such in legal terms, whatever the details of the regulations), religion is part of the state. Thus, very self-consciously, Varro states that he has on purpose put the *Antiquitates divinae* after the *Antiquitates humanae.* The *civitas* must precede the institutions of the *civitas,* even the religious ones: even more daringly, the painter precedes the painting—"prior est pictor quam tabula picta." Here more than ever we must remind ourselves that most of what we know of Varro's *Antiquitates divinae* comes from St. Augustine's *Civitas Dei,* and St. Augustine may well have sharpened some of Varro's

formulations to fit his own style and suit his own argument. But I
do not know of any instance in which St. Augustine has betrayed
Varro's line of thinking. The difficulty which Varro had to face and
did face in his interpretation of civic religion was that such religion, being man-made, changed with the times. As Varro was specifically interested in Roman religion, the first change he thought
had happened was the introduction of images of gods in the shape
of men. I am not sure that for Varro this was equivalent to what we
would consider the anthropomorphization of the notion of God.
But it certainly occurred to Varro that a religion without human
images of gods existed in his own time among the Jews, and it was
not a bad thing either (Augustine *De civitate Dei* 4. 31). We even
know from Lydus *De mensibus* 4. 53—a text published in full for
the first time in 1898—that Varro knew the name of the Jewish
God: Iao.[5] Varro was therefore personally in sympathy with a religion which was non conic. Yet he did not feel he had to change his
attitude toward Roman religion. If the Romans had decided in
their wisdom to represent their gods in human form, there was
nothing left but to comply. The message which the *Antiquitates
divinae* intended to convey was that state religion had to be taken
as it was found. What mattered was to preserve it. Varro could
compare himself in his learned work to Aeneas, who had brought
away the Penates from burning Troy, or to the Roman L. Caecilius
Metellus, who in 241 B.C. had saved what could be saved of the
sacred objects from the burning temple of Vesta. The danger in
the face of which he was undertaking his rescue operation was not
that of enemy attack, but of *civium neglegentia,* the neglect by
his fellow-citizens of their ancestral cults. Varro was not the man
to conceal his preferences and convictions, but one of his convictions was precisely that there are truths which should remain unknown to the ordinary man and there are falsehoods which should
be spread among the mob as truths. Civic religion was ultimately
not a matter of truth but of civic cohesion: the Romans owed their
empire to their own piety. It was even useful that people should
consider themselves descended from gods, however false that
might be, if it added to their self-confidence in undertaking great
things. Varro was not going to take responsibility for the truth of
what he was trying to preserve. His report was subjective, in the

double sense that he gave his own impression and that he reported what was known to him: "hominis est enim haec opinari, dei scire" (August. *De civ. D.* 7. 17).

Even within the description of the religious system of Rome to which he devoted most of his *Divine Antiquities* Varro would not start from the gods and proceed to their cults. Very coherently he started from the pontiffs, the augurs, the *quindecimviri*, that is, from the men who were responsible for the cult. Next he turned to the buildings for the cult. The third section was on the festivals and rites, including games. This left only three books out of sixteen for the gods as such. St. Augustine inevitably found them the most interesting from his point of view, and therefore we know slightly more about them than about the other books. How far Varro's classification of the Roman gods reflected traditional Roman distinctions is not entirely clear to me. He certainly interspersed his own opinions and philosophical preoccupations with traditional terminology. The main result was a surprisingly long list of gods, in which functional gods for rare occasions loomed large. Cicero testifies in his eulogy of Varro (*Academica posteriora* 1. 9) to the surprise which Varro's *Antiquitates* produced among his contemporaries. They discovered a Rome they did not know in his pages. What impressed them was mainly this world of half-forgotten gods, ceremonies, and religious anecdotes. But of course we have to add to it that general reconstruction of the origins of Rome and of the changes in the Roman ways of life which Varro undertook in two other works, *De gente populi Romani* and *De vita populi Romani.* It was highly unusual to find a man who knew so much about the traditions of Rome and had such genuine respect for them, and yet was a recognizable freethinker with a taste for satire and wit. He may well have inspired some of the religious regulations of Caesar and later of Augustus. He remained up to the sixth century A.D. the source to which writers would turn for out-of-the-way details about the religious customs of earlier Rome.

Yet the most remarkable part of the story remains the elementary fact that Cicero, notwithstanding his admiration for Varro, never tried to assimilate all that evidence: indeed he bypassed Varro and may never have read the *Antiquitates,* whether human or divine, in their entirety. Which implies that even the man most suited by intellectual gifts and common experiences to appreciate Varro's efforts to save the old religious patrimony of Rome could not make sense of them. The crude question, once asked, remained: How could one believe in all these divine forces which were vaguely supposed to surround a Roman at each stage of his life and of his daily activities? What were all these goddesses— Adeona, Abeona, Interduca, Domiduca, Bubona, Mellona, Pomona, and so on—on whom St. Augustine was later to exercise his easy irony?

II

We are now left to decide what Cicero thought of this effort of his friend Varro apart from the compliments he formulated about his erudition. The thesis which I want to propose in this part of the paper is that Cicero basically agreed with Varro in his earlier philosophic works (*De republica* and *De legibus*), which were probably published before the *Antiquitates divinae* by Varro and may therefore even have influenced Varro. When, however, Cicero had before him Varro's works circa 46 B.C. he changed his mind and expressed profound skepticism both about the existence of the gods and about the validity of Roman divination. Whether Cicero in his later phase was shocked by Varro's sanctimonious attitudes is a secondary and not very interesting question. At this stage Cicero certainly worried about Caesar's religious policy, which Varro was supporting. What matters is that Cicero became more skeptical when his contemporaries became more credulous or at least more sanctimonious. And his skepticism is even more surprising and dramatic because in 45 Cicero's daughter Tullia died, and her father wanted to believe in her immortality.

I must add two points for preliminary clarification. In a remarkable article published in 1962,[6] the Polish scholar K. Kumaniecki observed from a different angle that Varro and Cicero had less in common than Cicero's public utterances would imply. Second, I cannot agree with the thesis, recently developed with interesting arguments by H. D. Jocelyn, that the *Antiquitates divinae* were written in the fifties rather than in the forties.[7] I still believe that when Cicero celebrated Varro's work about 46 B.C., he alluded to work which had recently appeared. The allusion to the third-century B.C. Metellus does not seem to me incompatible with this date; and the other passages quoted by Jocelyn admit of different interpretations. In other words, Cicero's most important philosophical work had already been done before Varro published his *Divine Antiquities*. In any case, the inspiration was different. The *De republica* was published in 51 B.C.: Cicero worked on it, at intervals, for about three years. The *De legibus* alludes to events of the same years and seems to have been composed concurrently with *De republica*.[8] *De legibus* was never formally published while Cicero was alive, and probably was never finished, although the text which circulated in antiquity was considerably longer and more complete than that which has reached us. In a letter to Varro of 46 B.C. (*Fam.* 9. 2. 5) Cicero indicates his intention of doing more work on the subject of laws, but we can only speculate on what he meant. What is obvious is that about 53 Cicero tried to give a Roman version of both the *Republic* and the *Laws* of Plato. He was not obliged to know what some modern scholars have discovered: that the *Republic* and the *Laws* represent two different stages of Plato's thought. In his version of Platonic thought, Cicero never tried to put philosophers in command or to expel poets. He rather accepted the notion of Polybius that the Roman state satisfied the conditions of a mixed constitution. Perhaps the most deeply felt conviction of his work on the *Republic* is that human virtue never comes so near to the *deorum numen*, to divine power, as in the founding or saving of a city (*Rep.* 1. 12). The religious interpretation of politics reaches its peak in that surprising and altogether mysterious *Somnium Scipionis* which concludes the *Republic*. Scipio Africanus appears to Scipio Aemilianus in a dream. The "grandfather" advises his "grandson" to exercise *iustitia* and *pietas* and promises him not only immortality of the soul but a better life in the celestial spheres. Cicero was never again to be so definite about the immortality of the soul or about the link between politics and salvation. But he was here indulging in a dream, and a careful reader cannot avoid noticing a certain contradiction between his deprecation of earthly life and his overpraise of political activity as conducive to salvation after death. There is the same ambiguity in the unfinished *Laws* which supplement the *Republic*. On the one hand, he argues that reason unites men and gods: "prima homini cum deo rationis societas" (1. 23); consequently, law can be founded on nature, which is reason. On the other hand, he is so far from envisaging a universal law that he makes a point of emphasizing in Book 2 of the *Laws* that he is even more a citizen of Arpinum than of Rome: "hinc enim orti stirpe antiquissima sumus, hic sacra, hic genus, hic maiorum multa vestigia" (2. 3). This is of course little more than a preparation for saying that the city, that is, Rome, which extended to the citizens of Arpinum the rights of her own citizenship, is now the real "patria," the city to which he, Cicero, owes allegiance. The conclusion of this sentimental outburst is a very practical one: as Rome has the most perfect form of constitution (2. 23), all a legislator has to do is to produce a slightly improved form of the *mos maiorum*, of the tradition of the ancestors (2. 23). Even the archaic language of the Twelve Tables must be preserved (2. 18). When, therefore, in a good Platonic spirit Cicero begins to formulate specific laws about religion, we know that nothing sensationally new will appear. The purpose is to reaffirm that Rome must worship the gods she has always worshiped in the forms she has received from immemorial tradition (2. 26). At the most, some rationalization may have to be introduced. One must divinize virtue, not vice (2. 28). Consequently, goddesses like Febris and Mala Fortuna who had their altars, if not their temples, inside Rome must be repudiated. The whole exposition of the sacred law in the second book of *De legibus* is characterized by three preoccupations: to preserve the main lines of Roman cult, to modify details which for personal or environmental reasons are no longer considered acceptable, and finally to avoid any systematic coverage of the subject which might turn out to be embarrassing. As is evident from the long excursus of 2. 47–69 on the interaction between civil and pontifical laws in the matter of family cults, Cicero was aware of contradictions between *ius civile* and *ius pontificium*. But he never puts the problem in sufficiently general terms to make it an important argument for reform. He was equally aware of the enormous importance which ordinary people still attributed to funeral rites. Although many of these customs have no appeal for him, he has no intention of interfering with them and speaks about them more to display his competence in comparative law than in the spirit of a reformer.

If one has to make a comparison between what Cicero wrote in
the *De republica* and in the *De legibus* and what was the general
trend of Varro's *Antiquities,* two differences seem to be evident,
but they are not profound. Cicero does not bother to collect the
whole of the evidence; at the same time he allows himself a
modicum of reform. While he is concerned with the preservation
of the tradition, of the *mos maiorum,* he is not obsessed by it, as
Varro was.

When about July 45 (*Epistulae ad Atticum* 13. 38. 1) he began
to write *De natura deorum,* he had the whole of Varro's *Antiquitates divinae* before him. He had also accumulated many more
sad experiences, not only political, but personal: a few months
before, in February 45, his daughter Tullia had died, and he had
tried to cope with this as well as he could by reading and writing
philosophy, by hopes of the immortality of the soul, and by plan-
ning a sort of *apotheosis* for his dead child. It was also the time of
the sudden end of his second marriage to Publilia. We therefore
expect to find in the *De natura deorum* an increased respect for
theism in general and for Roman traditional religion in particular.
The surprise is that there is no noticeable trace of all that in *De
natura deorum.* The *De natura deorum* is very different from
Varro in every respect.

De natura deorum is, as we all know, a discussion between an
Epicurean, a Stoic, and an Academic about the nature of the gods.
It does not matter who represents the three philosophies—except
for the representative of the Academy, C. Aurelius Cotta, the consul of 75 B.C. and *pontifex* who on his death in 73 B.C. had been
replaced by Caesar. Since Cotta as an Academic and as the final
speaker represented Cicero, the choice is pointed. Cicero himself
is supposed to have listened to the discussion, but not to have
taken part in it, as he was too young at the time when the imaginary encounter took place, during the *Feriae Latinae* of a year
between 75 and 73 B.C. It does not matter much either where
Cicero picked up his arguments for the three schools. He had
plenty of Epicurean and Stoic acquaintances. Lucretius had been
one of the Epicureans he knew well, and another, Philodemus,
was still alive. For the Stoics, Cicero certainly knew his Panaetius
and Posidonius, but may have used them indirectly through some
more scholastic summary of Stoic tenets. As we know much

less about contemporary Academics, it would be idle to mention names: in any case some of their arguments went back to Carneades, who had lived a hundred years earlier. The essential point is that Cotta, as an Academic, finds himself in greater sympathy with the Epicureans than with the Stoics when it comes to deciding whether gods intervene in human life. Cotta is really as uncertain about the existence of the gods as he is about the immortality of the soul. To be sure, before arguing against the proofs of the existence of the gods, Cotta takes the precaution of declaring that in ordinary life he, the ex-consul and pontiff, does not care about Zenon, Cleanthes, and Chrysippus, but about the welfare of Rome. There is one thing he knows about Rome: that Romulus and Numa founded her greatness on the observance of the rituals. *Sine summa placatione deorum* Rome could never have become as powerful as she is (3. 5). This is good enough, but very short and followed by a close argument for the impossibility of proving the existence of gods, to which there is no reply. The inescapable conclusion a reader was bound to draw from the end of the *De natura deorum* was that Cicero, with all due precautions (for which cf. 3. 95), intended to be negative. It was not the impression one would have derived a few years before from a reading of the *De republica* and *De legibus.*

The impression that from circa 51 to circa 45 Cicero has shifted his ground in the matter of religion cannot simply be contradicted by pointing to the mystical crisis he had experienced in 45 because of his daughter's death. As the *De consolatione,* the treatise he wrote to console himself after her death, is lost, we have no clear idea of what he was saying in it. Nor do we know how closely the idea of immortality was bound up with his belief in gods. The skepticism which unexpectedly emerges from the *De natura deorum* becomes even more conspicuous in the work which followed it, *De divinatione.* This work belongs to the end of 45 and early 44. It was probably drafted before the death of Caesar and revised immediately after the Ides of March. The proem to the second of the two books is certainly later than Caesar's murder and provides an invaluable summary of Cicero's intellectual activities in the previous year. In facing the question whether one had to believe in divination, Cicero was doing something more than supplementing his previous argument in the *De natura deorum.* Auspices were an essential part of Roman official religion. He was himself an augur, and in earlier days (so it appears) he had written a book *De auguriis*, of a technical character, which has not come down to us, but may be alluded to in one of his letters (*Fam.* 3. 9. 3) and in *De divinatione* 2. 75–76. He had of course taken a positive view of Roman divination in his book *De legibus.* At least in the past (he had argued in the *De legibus*) the Roman augurs had been authentic diviners (2. 32). The personal, almost intimate, character of the *De divinatione* is immediately made clear by the fact that it is a dialogue between Cicero and his brother Quintus in Cicero's villa at Tusculum, with nobody else present. The brother plays the part of the Stoic who defends the authenticity and legitimacy of divination: he seems to derive many of his arguments in favor of divination from Posidonius. Cicero plays his role of the skeptic from the point of view of the Academy. He has the final word. He ends by declaring that his denial of any value in divination is meant to save religion from a dubious and dangerous ally: religion must be separated from superstition. But the impossibility of defending religion from a serious philosophic point of view had already been demonstrated in the *De natura deorum*, to which Cicero pointedly refers in this final passage of *De divinatione* (2. 148). No attentive reader could take this escape clause too seriously. What on the contrary is striking is that Cicero so fiercely attacks all forms of divination— Roman or foreign—with the same two basic arguments, namely, the small proportion of verified prognostics in comparison with the multitude of prophecies, and the intrinsic improbability that the entrails of certain animals or the position of remote stars could tell us something specific about what was going to happen to single individuals at a given date. Cicero does not hesitate to use Roman examples and even his own personal experiences (such as one of his dreams, 2. 136) to show the inanity of divination. And it is, as I have said, a denunciation in very personal terms, with the clear intention of assuming full responsibility for what is being said. He repudiates explictly the arguments in favor of divination of his fellow augur Ap. Claudius Pulcher, who had dedicated a book on the subject to him (2. 75).

We are therefore brought back to my main point. In 51 B.C. or so we had found another Cicero—a man with ambitions to reform the Roman state on a religious basis. The *Somnium Scipionis* was a remarkable attempt to link the political program with religious aspirations: the good Roman leader was promised immortality in this precise sense. At the same time, the book on *Laws* modified, but substantially defended, the traditional Roman attitude to sacred laws, to *auspicia*, and to the ancestral cults. Six or seven years later very little of that was left. The *De natura deorum* had paid lip service to the traditional values of Roman religious tradition, including *auspicia*, but had been a rigorous denial of the possibility of demonstrating the existence of the gods. In the *De divinatione* the game was inverted: lip service was paid to religion, but any form of divination, including the traditional forms of Roman religion, was denied any merit and probability.[9]

The cleavage, as we have seen, was made more remarkable by two circumstances. Most probably between 51 B.C. and 45 B.C. Varro had published his *Divine Antiquities*, which Cicero himself greeted enthusiastically as a revelation. They provided a uniquely authoritative picture of Roman traditional religion. They invited a restoration of obsolete cults and in any case provided the evidence for a precise discussion of Roman cults. Cicero did not take any of this new material into account when he wrote *De natura deorum* and *De divinatione*. The other circumstance was that when he came to write these two works Cicero refused, only shortly after his daughter's death, to be carried away by his personal emotions and anxieties.

There is no safe interpretation of this change in Cicero's religious attitudes between 51 and 45–44 B.C. But it is impossible to avoid noticing that while Cicero was becoming more skeptical, Caesar and his direct entourage were becoming more religious or at least more concerned with religious questions. These are the years in which Victoria, Fortuna, and Felicitas were much broadcast in obvious connection with Caesar. In 45 a public sacrifice was decreed for Caesar's birthday, if we can trust Dio Cassius (44. 4. 4). On the other hand, as Cicero prominently records in *De divinatione*, Caesar had more than once refused to pay attention to prodigies and showed up their vanity: for instance, in 46 he had sailed to Africa in spite of the warning of the haruspices (Cic. *Div.* 2. 52; Suet. *Caes.* 59). Caesar had been *pontifex maximus* since 63. As such he was apparently entitled to a *domus publica* on the

Sacra Via (Suet. *Caes.* 46). In the last years of his life the senate decreed that a pediment should be placed on this house as if it were a temple (Cicero *Orationes Philippicae* 12. 110; Suet. *Caes.* 81. 3; Iul. Obseq. *Prod.* 67 and elsewhere). On the night of the Ides of March, Caesar's wife dreamed that the pediment had collapsed. The dream must soon have become known and opened up interesting questions about the relation between the validity of the dream and Caesar's ambitions in provoking the decree of the senate. Finally, there were the various, and by no means clear, steps toward the personal deification of Caesar. His statue was often exhibited among those of gods, and there may have been some decree to create a cult of Divus Iulius before Caesar's death. Let us add that Varro had not been the only one to dedicate a book on prayers and rituals to Caesar: a certain Granius Flaccus dedicated to him his *De indigitamentis* (Lactantius *Divinae institutiones* 1. 6. 7; Censor. 3. 2). Caesar, who had added to his dignity of *pontifex maximus* that of an *augur* in 47, clearly took pleasure in religious details. He passed a *lex Iulia de sacerdotiis* and (later?) increased the number of *pontifices, augures,* and *quinquennales.* May we suspect that Cicero was not amused? He had reconciled himself to Caesar's regime, as long as it lasted, and was bound to Caesar by intellectual ties which he was the last to underrate. But he was never with him at heart. The more Caesar was involved in religion, the more Cicero tried to escape it.

There was a sequel to the story in Augustus's time. Augustus was of course the great restorer of temples and rites. Like Caesar he became *pontifex maximus* and paraded his dignity as the son of Divus Iulus: *Divi filius.* He had learned people to advise him on religious matters, such as the great lawyer Ateius Capito, who was officially entrusted with the intrepretation of the Sibylline Books in 17 B.C. No doubt Varro's doctrine was gratefully used in Augustus's circles, although we know far less about this than we should like. But a difference between the Caesarean and the Augustan age is immediately apparent. The men who represented the new age were neither scholars like Varro nor philosophers like Cicero: they were poets—Horace, Virgil, Propertius, Ovid, Manilius. It was a poet, Ovid, who undertook and did not quite complete the task of collecting the stories attached to the various festivals of the Roman calendar.[10]

Next there were the historians, among whom Strabo should not be underrated. The lawyers (I shall add the name of Antistius Labeo) come third, the pure antiquarians (such as Verrius Flaccus) are fourth: philosophy in Latin, especially on religious matters, does not seem to have been conspicuous under Augustus. When a poet was encouraged to announce "Tuus iam regnat Apollo," there was less room for philosophers. There was perhaps less astrological speculation about Augustus than J. Gagé has repeatedly suggested,[11] but there was enough to offend the *dii manes* of Cicero (although, as we know, Octavian, as early as 30 B.C. when he was not yet Augustus, had made Cicero's son his ally as *consul suffectus* in order to demonstrate that he had had no share in Cicero's murder). But what would Cicero have said on hearing that a comet, the *sidus Iulium,* had become both the proof of Caesar's apotheosis and the confirmation of Augustus's power (Pliny *HN* 2. 94, from Augustus's autobiography)? Indeed the very title of Augustus alluded to *auguria* and more precisely to the *augusta auguria* which had accompanied the foundation of Rome. Even at their lowest number, there were too many horoscopes and other portents around Augustus. We can understand why Minucius Felix (by implication) and Arnobius (explicitly) thought the *De natura deorum* to be a refutation of paganism. Arnobius added that Cicero had taken the risk of appearing impious (3. 6). Lactantius, for all his admiration for Cicero (or because of it), declared: "totus liber tertius de natura deorum omnes funditus religiones evertit ac delet" (*Div. inst* 1. 17. 4). In a different context and in a different religious situation, St. Augustine was more severe (*De civ. D.* 5. 9: notice "philosophaster" in 2. 27).

What Petrarch thought of *De natura deorum* is no longer ancient history.[12]

5

Religion in Athens, Rome, and Jerusalem in the First Century B.C.[1]

I

I WOKE UP one winter morning to ask myself: "What do I know about what people believed in Athens, Rome, and Jerusalem in the first century B.C.?" I soon discovered that not only did I know very little, but also that it is not easy to get to know more. If you turn to Athens first, you soon realize that literary sources are rare, and epigraphic texts of the first century B.C. are inevitably more indicative of new institutional arrangements than of personal beliefs or traditional unmodified practices. On the other hand, if you start from Rome, the voice of the intellectuals—and especially the voice of that extraordinary survivor, Cicero—tends to prevail over that of any other group. Finally, it is surprising how little we know of what the Jewish sects really were when in the first century B.C. they competed for the loyalty of the Palestinian Jews: nor is it easy to define the boundary between Temple and Synagogue.

What I am trying to do in the present paper is not to offer any general picture, which I would be unable to draw, but to indicate some of the difficulties one meets when one makes the attempt to get at a picture. I shall begin where I feel the most serious difficulties lie.

Let us assume that for a brief moment we should like to be

Annali della Scuola Normale Superiore di Pisa, Serie III, vol. XIV, fasc. 3, 1984, pp. 873–92.

slightly ambitious and to ask a question like this: What was the place of Hope and Faith in Athens, Rome, and Jerusalem in the first century B.C.? These are notions which less than a hundred years later became central to Christianity.

We all remember that Hope, Elpis, was the last to remain inside Pandora's box in Hesiod's *Works and Days*. Elpis was not necessarily a good thing for the Greeks. Ambiguous in Hesiod and in Aeschylus's *Prometheus*, Hope becomes a plainly bad thing in Theognis 1. 637 and in Euripides, *Suppliants* 479 ("Hope delusive; it has embroiled many a State"), though not in other passages of Theognis or Euripides. I do not know of any official cult of Hope in Greek cities, though we find her as a goddess together with Nemesis and weeping Eros on the Chigi crater, and later by herself on coins of various cities (for instance of Alexandria). Neither Stoics nor Epicureans gave importance to Hope in their systems. "Prinzip Hoffnung" did not really find its Ernst Bloch in Greek thought. But could the Athenian man in the street live without Hope in the first century B.C.—or earlier? Or did he establish any relation between Hope and Fortune, between Elpis and Tyche, as after all some of the poets of the *Anthologia Palatina* occasionally did (for instance 9, 49, 1; 134, 1)? I wish I could give an answer.

In Rome we know at least that there was a cult of Spes. There was a temple to the "old Hope," "Spes vetus," not far from the Praenestine gate (Frontinus *De aquae* 1. 19). The name avoided confusion with another temple of Spes built by A. Atilius Calatinus during the first Punic war (Cicero, *De legibus*. 2, 28). Roman tradition associated the older temple with events of the fifth century B.C. (Liv. 2. 51. 2; Dion Hal. 9. 24. 4). Whatever the truth of the matter, there was in Rome, differently from Greece, an old tradition of official worship of Hope; we also hear of connections between Spes and Fortuna even in tombs. A temple of the triad Spes, Fides, Fortuna was built under Roman influence at Capua in 110 B.C. (Dessau *ILS*, 3770). But that does not give us enough to answer our question about what Hope meant to the Roman man in the street in the first century B.C.

Let us turn to Faith in Athens and Rome—and we may find ourselves in greater trouble. I shall here start from Rome, because *fides* was of course a current word in the political and religious terminology of the Romans in the first century B.C. Cicero, when it suited him as an advocate, denied that the Greeks respected or worshiped Faith (*Pro Flacco*, 9). As we might well expect, he extended the compliment to the Gauls (*Pro Fonteio*, 30). The Romans liked to consider themselves the people of *fides*. For Polybius this was a great characteristic of the Roman mind. According to tradition, Fides had been a Roman goddess since the time of Numa, who had given her a chapel (Livy 1. 21. 3). In Rome the handshake, the *dexterarum iunctio*, was an old symbol of faith. It probably went back to Indo-European origins, because it was known to Greeks, Persians (Xenophon *Anabasis* 2. 4. 1) and Celts. At the time of the Pyrrhic wars, Locri in Southern Italy had coined a piece of money representing Pistis, that is Fides, crowning Rome in order to pay homage to the Romans. This coin incidentally confirms that in the early third century B.C. the Greeks were already aware of the equivalence between Pistis and Fides. Fides traditionally protected oaths, but her range was wider. One famous story told by Livy 5. 21. 1 explained how Camillus refused to take advantage of the treachery of the schoolmaster of the Falerii and returned to their parents the aristocratic children the schoolmaster had offered as hostages to the Romans. In the first century B.C., Varro connected etymologically *fides* with *fetiales*, the magistrates Rome customarily sent to declare war and make peace. The cult which Numa was supposed to have started had been raised to the dignity of a proper temple by Atilius Calatinus, the same man who during the first Punic war built a temple to Spes. The new temple of Fides was placed near the temple of Jupiter on the Capitol to emphasize the close relation between Jupiter and Fides. It was large enough to allow assemblies of the Senate in it (e.g. Valerius Maximus 3. 2. 17) and became a sort of archive for documents on international relations. In the time of Cicero, Fides was also connected with commercial obligations. In the speech *Pro Marcello* which Cicero wrote in 46 to mark his reconciliation with Caesar—or rather Caesar's pardon—Fides also implies the restoration of commercial credit.

Let us now consult the Greek, or rather the Athenian, evidence. There is little trace of a cult of Pistis in Greece, though the poems attributed to Theognis speak of Pistis as a "great goddess" (l. 1137). In Athens in particular the traces of the cult of Pistis are late and doubtful. To my knowledge they are limited to one proverb in a collection of proverbs attributed to Diogenianus, a compiler of the second century A.D. (*Corpus Paraem. graec.* I, p. 80, Cent. II, 80). In Greece, too, faith, *pistis*, was traditionally connected with keeping oaths. An *apistos*, an unbeliever, may be a man who does not believe in anything connected with the gods. But there is no necessary connection between *pistis* and gods: *pistis* is not a specific term of classicial religious language. We must wait for Plutarch to give us plenty of references to Pistis as faith in gods or in traditional tenets, what he calls *patrios pistis* (*Pyth. Oracles,* 18). Even among the Stoics, the main note of *pistis* is still reliability; and it has been suggested that if Epictetus is the Stoic who attaches greater value to *pistis*, he may have had Roman *fides* in mind. And yet there is at least one detail which may point to an intimacy and intensity of Athenian customs concerning Pistis which we did not discover in the Roman *fides*. If we assume that hand-shaking was connected with Pistis in Athens as it was with Fides in Rome (and there are good reasons for that), the *Attic Grave Reliefs* so well collected by Fr. Johansen (1951) show hand-shaking as a symbol of Faith at the parting between the dead and the living. Thus hand-shaking was not only a sign of agreement among the living, but the gesture of trust and faith in the supreme departure. We are reminded of the several passages of Greek poetry—none more eloquent than Euripides' *Medea,* 21ff.—where the right hand is a symbol of Faith, of Pistis.

Thus, at first sight it would appear that the Romans worshiped Fides but had a rather cold and legal notion of it: nothing much of what we could call faith in God. The Athenians do not appear to have worshiped Pistis in any conspicuous way, but seem to have looked upon Faith as an emotional bond between the living and the dead: perhaps less so between man and gods. There are three famous studies of Roman *fides* in relation to Greek *pistis* which, taken together, seem to confirm this impression. In his pioneer study of *fides* of 1916, Eduard Fraenkel maintained that *fides* had originally less to do with persuasiveness than its Greek counterpart *pistis* (*Rh. Museum* 71 = *Kleine Beiträge* I, 1964). The Romans of the Republic seem to have emphasized in *fides* the "trustworthiness," "loyalty," "sincerity" of the person or institution to which they turned—or the objective value of the promise they had received. It was not until the age of Cicero, and probably under his influence, that rhetorical writers (Cicero *De inventione rhetorica* 1. 25; 1. 31) began to stress the subjective element of "inducing belief in something," of "convincing," "conviction" which would later characterize the Christian meaning of *fides*. In *De partitione oratoria* 9, Cicero defined *fides* as *firma opinio*. A closer approximation of *fides* to *pistis* may indeed have contributed to this evolution of *fides* from trustworthiness to belief. Richard Heinze, who controverted some of Fraenkel's conclusions in an article in *Hermes* in 1925 (now *Vom Geist des Römertums*, 3rd ed., 1960, 59–81), did not contest the general trend of the semantic evolution of *fides* as reconstructed by Fraenkel. Heinze, however, remarked, to my mind correctly, that Fraenkel had undervalued the element of moral commitment which existed even in the earlier examples of the word *fides*, just as much as in *pistis*. It was—one must add—a peculiar type of moral commitment. The conquered enemy who threw himself *in fidem populi Romani* committed both himself and the Romans to a definite type of behavior. The difference from the Greek *pistis* was that *pistis* often, not always, implied bilateral agreement: it often resulted in a treaty, rather than in surrender. As Polybius repeatedly observed (20. 9. 11 is the chief passage), the Greeks had great difficulty in reconciling themselves to the fact that for the Romans *in fidem p. R. venire* implied complete surrender to the conqueror which the corresponding word *pistis* could not possibly suggest. No doubt the words *in fidem p. R.* referred to a recognizable type of behavior: it presupposed an element of responsibility and moderation on the part of the Romans, but only insofar as they were the conquerors. In a similar mood the Roman woman about to give birth to a child invoked the *fides* of the goddess Iuno Lucina (*Iuno Lucina tuam fidem*, Plautus *Aulularia* 692): she implied an obligation, a bond, between herself and her goddess. To mention a third example, it was traditional for the Romans in an emergency—for instance a fire or a robbery—to *quiritare*, that is, as Varro explains (*De Lingua latina* 6. 68), to "claim the faith of the fellow-citizens," *Quiritium fidem clamans*. Here *fides* is the implicit moral obligation to help a fellow-citizen in danger. But even in this case the obligation presupposes the inferiority of one side. *Fides* is always a relation between nonequals, whereas *pistis*

seems to point to a relation between equals. Therefore I believe
that the third of the writers I was alluding to, Salvatore Calderone,
in his 1964 study on *pistis* and *fides*, was ultimately correct
in asserting that *fides*, being a word of basic inequality, defined
the program of Roman imperialism in international relations.[2]
Calderone was probably incorrect in trying to connect *fides* etymologically with the Greek φείδεσθαι, in the sense of "sparing
the enemy." But he went beyond the results of Fraenkel and
Heinze by underlining the fact that *fides* was more important to
the Romans in international relations than in religion. Paradoxically this is perhaps also true of *pistis*, at least as far as gods are
concerned, but for a different reason. *Pistis* was too much of an
egalitarian word, a word of reciprocity, to become important in the
relations between men and gods.

Elpis-Spes, Pistis-Fides, as we have seen, did exist in the everyday language and in the religious terminology of both Athens and
Rome in the first century B.C. Who can doubt that they needed
hope, as they needed trust, in their ordinary transactions? But I am
unable to say to what extent hope and faith were motive forces for
the many. The man who speaks most directly to us from that
period, Cicero, had his own terms of reference in honor or dis-
honor—and uncertainty. I do not know a better introduction to
his psychology than D. R. Shackleton Bailey's biography (1971).

We *must* be right in assuming that hope and faith were more
closely interrelated and made a stronger appeal in Jerusalem than
in Rome or Athens in the first century B.C.—if only we could find
the evidence! What Philo or any other Greek-speaking Jewish intellectual (say the author of the *Wisdom of Solomon*) thought in
Alexandria cannot of course be transferred to Jerusalem. The
same applies to the texts and ideas we know exclusively from the
Dead Sea Scrolls. It is a problem why some of the most conspicuous peculiarities of the Qumran Sect (the Teacher of Righteousness, the two or three Messiahs, the battle of the Sons of Light,
and even the precise terms of the quarrel with the authorities of
Jerusalem) did not leave any recognizable trace in Josephus, let
alone Philo. But for the moment we are no more entitled to assume that the man in the street in Jerusalem knew what was
going on in the minds of the men of Qumran than we are entitled
to assume that he paid attention to Philo. Our problem at present

is somewhat different. Hope and faith cried out from the pages of
the Bible. Scholars like K. H. Rengstorf, who in his notorious section on Elpis in Kittel's *Theologisches Wörterbuch* asserts that
post-biblical Jews had lost hope, by implication take it for granted
that the Jews had stopped taking the Bible seriously either in the
first century B.C. or later.[3] But the question of what they read into
it, and what they liked in it, remains. The question is closely
linked with the great enigma of what the synagogue was adding to
Jewish life by the first century B.C.

There is, however, a group of texts which can be safely located
in Jerusalem, and dated in the first century B.C., the Psalms of
Solomon. They can incidentally also reassure us that the Bible—
Torah, Prophets, and Psalms—was well present to their author or
authors. The allusions to Pompey's violation of the Temple and to
Pompey's death are certain. The allusion to Herod in 17 : 9 (Swete)
is far less certain because the "man foreign to our race" could still
be Pompey. Some of the Psalms are free from allusions to known
events and may well be earlier than 63 B.C. Altogether one feels
safe in dating the collection to about 70–40 B.C. and in assuming
that the original text was in Hebrew. The man who put together
these Psalms (if he did not actually write them himself) intentionally placed the experience of having the Temple entered by
Pompey at the beginning, in the middle, and at the end of the
collection. He made it the central experience. The foreigner is,
however, the instrument and the expression of God's dissatisfaction with his People. He had received help from Jews (8 : 18). The
diaspora, too, is seen as a punishment from God (9 : 2). Thus the
Psalms demand from God a native king of Davidic descent under
whom the diaspora Jews will return to their own Land. Trust in
God and obedience to God are of course the general presuppositions of the Psalms. God keeps faith with those who love him
truly (14 : 1, cf. 8 : 35, 17 : 12). Thus God is hope (17 : 3), and more
precisely is hope to the poor (5 : 13, 15 : 2).

Two points emerge from the collection as a whole. It is meant
as a reaction to defeat, humiliation, and submission to Roman
rule. If the Roman theology may be called a theology of victory,
here we have, once again, a theology of defeat. It is worth mentioning that we have no evidence that Sulla's entry into Athens produced a reaction comparable to Pompey's entry into Jerusalem. At

the same time, if the Temple is the center of the humiliation experience, it cannot be said to be the center of the moral preoccupations of the Psalmist. His devotion is not directed to the Temple or in general toward ritual purity. Justice, compassion, good faith are more prominent. Whatever he may mean by "Synagogues of Israel" (10:8) or "Synagogues of the saints" (19:18), he can hardly mean the temple service. The Psalms of Solomon indicate both an orientation and a mood which are different from anything we may surmise in Rome and Athens. Defeat is faced: it is directly related to God. No political interpretation is offered. What the writer hopes for, however, is a new *politeia* in the Davidic tradition: institutional concern is the consequence of religious scruples. We can relate all this to later texts, for instance to *Contra Apionem* 2, 169 where Josephus says that Moses planted the faith. We may even say that the Psalms of Solomon point toward the equivalence of perfect trust in God with salvation as formulated in the grand finale of the tract *Beshallah* of the *Mekhiltah de Rabbi Ishmael*, the date of which I do not know. But the fact remains that it would be foolish to generalize from a group of psalms of which we know how they originated but not how popular they were in Jerusalem in the first century B.C.[4] The religious orientation of the men of Jerusalem escapes us just as much as that of the men of Athens and Rome in the same period.

II

For the rest of this paper I shall abandon the deeper zone of Hope and Faith and concentrate instead on some of the most visible aspects of religious life—ceremonies, offerings, religious associations. But I shall do that only insofar as they can lead us to ask some questions (but not to give any answers) about the religious education of ordinary men and women of the three cities.

In Athens in the first century B.C., two different societies were meeting and interfering with each other, but never really coalesced: the international society of the students in philosophic schools and the old Athenian society now most prominently represented by a small aristocracy in political and religious control. The philosophic schools had their religious rituals: even the

Epicureans, if we listen to their first-century-B.C. philosopher Philodemus, did not abstain from religious acts. Foreigners, and more especially distinguished foreign students, were initiated into the mysteries of Eleusis, which maintained their prestige. Sulla, Cicero, and later Augustus were initiates. Cicero confirms this for himself in *De legibus* 2. 36. An Indian threw himself into the pyre "in accordance with ancestral customs" after having been initiated at Eleusis (Strabo 15. 1. 73; Dio Cassius 50. 9. 10). Local philosophers acted as Eleusinian priests: we find a Stoic as a priest at Eleusis. A curious mixture of philosophic influences, Roman patriotism, and new aspirations is to be found in a dedication by three brothers who were Roman citizens to Aion, the god of Eternity: the dedication prays for the greatness of Rome and was placed in Eleusis about Augustus's time (Ditt.³ 1125). The local religion was, however, mostly in the control of the local aristocrats. Wealthy men were needed because the state—or its subdivisions, the demes—had financial difficulties in restoring decaying buildings and satisfying ritual requirements. Thus in 52 B.C. the priest of Asclepios asked the Council of Athens for authorization to restore the Temple of Asclepios at his own expense. He was duly authorized, praised, quoted as an example, and given the text for two inscriptions to be set up in his own praise: a curious state of affairs, though no doubt technically correct. The decree of the senate which includes the text of the two future inscriptions is what we have in Ditt.³ 756.

The impression is that Athena, as the civic goddess, lost in popularity in Athens, while Apollon Patroos, as the god of the families, and in particular of the aristocratic families, held his own. Asclepios increased his popularity: he was a god in the ascendant. As a god of health he appealed to foreigners and was particularly good at communicating through dreams. So in the early first century A.D. we have an Athenian with Roman citizenship making a dedication to Asclepius after a dream (Ditt.³ 1150). Dedicators to the Mother of Gods, after having received a dream or an oracle, thought fit to declare that they worshiped all the gods (Ditt.³ 1153). This was indeed Plato's advice in the *Symposium* 180 E: "One must praise all the gods."

Groups or fraternities, however, specialized in some favorite god. The Soteriastae, about whom we hear from an inscription of about 37 B.C., were a fraternity in honor of Artemis Soteira. We happen to learn from the inscription (Ditt.³ 1104) that the sixty members present unanimously voted a crown in honor of their founder, a Diodorus son of a Socrates. A cult of Asclepios and Hygieia, about which we learn from a later inscription, was strictly private: it was founded by one man on his own ground and was open to his agricultural workers (= tenants?) and to the neighbors (Ditt.³ 1041). These were cults which appealed mainly to slaves. The best example is, however, an association introducing the cult of Men Tyrannos founded by Xanthos Lucius, a slave of Gaius Orbius (Ditt.³ 1042, of the second century). The text is remarkable for its details about purity regulations: such regulations help to explain or at least to place the contemporary Jewish obsession with purity. Sarapis and Isis of course appear among the well-established gods, and there are the first signs of imperial cult, to begin with a statue of Julius Caesar, but only as a "savior and benefactor of the demos of Athens" (Ditt.³ 759). A few years later the Athenians plumped for the more daring, and short-lived, cult of Antony as Neos Dionysos about 39 B.C.

How much survived of the old festivals? Probably more than we suspect, though there may have been drastic changes in the ritual. In the second century A.D. Pausanias described Attica as full of old-fashioned cults. He therefore considered the Athenians "far more devoted to religion than other men" (1, 24, 3), which was perhaps a pointed rebuff to those who had described the Romans as the most religious people. But even Pausanias was surprised to discover that aristocratic Athenian girls were still employed in his time to "carry unspoken things" by night through a subterranean passage of the Acropolis to an open-air sanctuary dedicated to Aphrodite (1. 27). It fell to the lot of the young archaeologist Oscar Broneer to confirm by local exploration that Pausanias's account is correct (cf. *Hesperia*, I, 1932, 51). Another Swedish archaeologist, Axel Boethius, put in order the epigraphic evidence (Ditt.³ 696–99) about the revival of the procession from Athens to Delphi, the *Pythais*. Restarted in 138 B.C., this irregular and costly ceremony does not seem in its new splendor to have survived the age of Sulla and the Mithridatic wars. The procession was of course another sign of the prestige of Apollo in late Hellenism: its main direction was toward the Apollo of Delphi, but the Apollo of Delos was not forgotten.

One is naturally curious to know what happened, apropos of Apollo, to the festival of the Thargelia which gave its name to the eleventh month of the Attic calendar. One day of the Thargelia was for purification, the second for offerings. In the old days, the purification had taken the form of selecting two individuals called *pharmakoi:* they were fed for some time at the expense of the city and then used as scapegoats. In the fourth century B.C., the two individuals (probably a man and a woman) were thrown out without being killed: whether they were killed in a more remote past is a notorious matter for controversy. Such human scapegoats had their parallels in other Greek cities. The account of the Athenian ceremony which is given by Helladius in the fourth century A.D. certainly presupposes that it was a custom of the past. I am not so certain that we can make the same inference from another account by the lexicographer Harpocration, who is usually placed in the second century A.D. without sufficient evidence. But in the same century Pausanias no longer talks about the *pharmakoi.* We may assume that the Athenian aristocracy in control of religion found it difficult to keep alive such discreditable features under Roman rule. Petronius, if it is correct that he lived in the first century A.D., speaks of analogous ceremonies in Massalia as things of the past.[5]

Everywhere in the Hellenistic world young people, especially of the upper class, were made to take part in religious ceremonies. The ephebes were often taught to sing hymns in religious festivals: they were also involved in the imperial cult. We are reminded that young Polybius, as an ephebe, was one of those who brought back the body of the divinized Philopoemen.

An inscription of the Athenian citizens resident in Delos to honor a poet who had composed a hymn to be sung by their children may give an idea of such performances (Ditt.[3] 662) and may also suggest that what Athenians did in Delos they would do in Athens. But the direct evidence for Athens is poor. No doubt the school calendar took notice of the religious calendar. Holidays were granted for religious festivals then as now. Furthermore, in their schools the boys were surrounded by images which reminded them of the faith of their fathers. The Muses, Hermes, Apollo, and Heracles were to be seen everywhere in schools and gymnasia. Sacrifices were performed also. And of course the literary texts which the schoolboys read were full of sacred stories. But we have still to answer the question whether, and how far, all this amounted to religious education. No doubt Homer and other poets taught children about the Greek gods and provided examples of divine intervention in the past which everybody respected. But Homer had not reached the first century B.C. as an undisputed authority. There were centuries of philosophic objections against him from Heraclitus to Epicurus. In the first century A.D. (or was it the first century B.C.?) the other Heraclitus had to start his defense of Homer with the admission that there was a whole tradition of sharp accusations against Homer because of his lack of reverence toward the gods. We do not know to what extent such criticisms affected the position of Homer in the schools, though we may suspect that sooner or later the young Athenian would come to know about them. What is more serious is that neither Homer nor any other poet read in the schools could act as a guide to an Athenian citizen of the first century B.C. in what he should do to please his own gods—or even help him to understand the ceremonies around him. Between the gods about whom one read in Homer and the gods of the polis there was quite a difference.[6]

This was even more marked in Rome. There was no equivalent to Homer in Roman literature before Virgil: and even Virgil was too much affected by Greek models to be able to provide a straight introduction to the peculiarities of the Capitoline triad. This is not to say that in Rome, as in Athens, the poets one read, at school or later, did not contribute to the religious imagination. But what one got out of them could not be simple and might be puzzling. In any case, we have to face in Rome, even more than in Athens, a strange absence of information about religious education. Romans who talk about themselves or their own education are not in short supply in the late first century B.C. Cicero tells us that he had to learn the Twelve Tables by heart (*Leg.* 2. 23. 59). Horace tells us how his father taught him morality; we are left in the dark about religion. Ovid in the *Tristia*, 4, 10, gives us that poignant picture of *fin de siècle* education in Rome, where he was sent with his brother from his native Sulmona. He does not utter one word about how he came to know religious practices when he was a boy.

Any father and mother (or grandfather and grandmother) would teach a minimum of prayers to be recited in given circumstances and to given gods. Lares, Penates, dii Manes had in any case to be taken care of. But it is arguable that in Rome, even more than in provincial Athens, the way to find out about religious practices was to be taken around or, if grown up, to go around the city. There was plenty to see in town or country almost every day. Even Ovid wants us to believe that the first step to become acquainted with Roman religion was to walk about town and to ask the expert: "on that day, as I was returning from Nomentum to Rome, a white-robed crowd blocked the middle of the road. A flamen was on his way to the grove of ancient Mildew [Robigo]. . . . I went up to him to inform myself of the rite." (Fasti 4. 905–9; trans. J. G. Frazer, Loeb.) If a flamen was not available, an old woman would do (6. 395–400; notice l. 417: "The rest of the tale I had learned long since in my boyish years"). Ovid of course notices in the Fasti the procession to the Capitol of the new consuls on the first of January: it used to attract a great crowd of spectators. Even more vivid is the description of the same ceremony which he sent from his exile at Tomi to the new consul Sextus Pompey (Ex Ponto 4. 4.): "Wretched am I that I shall not be seen in that throng, that my eyes will not be able to enjoy that sight."[7]

It may be a simple matter of chance that neither when he was in Rome nor later when everything Roman was made more intense for him by nostalgia did Ovid talk about another early January recurrence, the Compitalia. The feast was movable, and Ovid may have reserved it for the December section of his Fasti—which he did not write or at least preserve for posterity. It is Cicero who tells us that the Compitalia were a great occasion for strolls in town or country—a family affair, for which even the elder Cato had allowed an extra ration of wine for the slaves who took part in it as of right (De agricultura 57). The center of the festival was in the compita, that is, in the places where crossroads met and shrines abounded. We can imagine Cicero and Atticus, and Cicero's wife Terentia and Atticus's sister and mother turning up for that stroll in January 59, as Cicero suggests. On the other hand, it was polite not to trouble Pompey in his Alban villa on such an occasion (*Epistulae ad Atticum* 2. 3. 4, 7. 7. 3). With the help of Cicero, of Dionysius of Halicarnassus, of Ovid, and of other poets we could go on describing feasts and holidays. About 13 February the feast of the ovens (*Fornacalia*) started; it was a feast of the *curiae*, the obsolete divisions of the Roman people. Dionysius enjoyed seeing the simple offerings, "economical and lacking all vulgar display," as he says (2. 23). On 15 February the fertility rite of the Lupercalia, round the Palatine (or part of it) and up and down the Via Sacra, brought back to the spectators Romulus and Remus, the alleged founders of the two groups of performing Luperci. Centuries later, in A.D. 494, the festival still had enough attraction to compel Pope Gelasius I to superimpose on it a Feast of the Purification of the Virgin Mary.[8] On 17 February there were the *Quirinalia* which concluded the Feast of the Ovens and were reserved for the *stulti*, the fools who could not remember to which *curia* they belonged. On 23 February it was the turn of the god of the boundaries, Terminus. Ovid is again our witness to the vitality of the ceremony. The boundary stones of each estate were crowned by the owners of the two sides, and an altar was built. On each side the fire was brought out by the rustic wife, the little daughter presented honeycombs, the boy stood by with a large basket in his hands from which the landowner thrice threw corn into the fire. Finally the opposite sides joined in a simple meal and sang the praises of Terminus. And so the year went on—with more festivals and meals, public and private, politically colored or entirely domestic. The living and the dead were involved.

Cicero's political career shows how religious weapons were used at every step for political purposes. The tragicomic story which is behind his orations *Pro domo sua* and *De haruspicum responsis* shows the impossibility of getting away from accusations of sacrilege even when no senator could possibly take them seriously. When Clodius accused Cicero of having aroused the anger of the gods by reoccupying his own house which had been pulled down during his exile and consecrated to Liberty, Cicero had no choice but to retort the charge upon Clodius and to accuse him of having perverted the games of the Great Mother and of having taken possession of the house of Seius after having murdered its owner. Sacrilege had to be admitted, because indicated by the haruspices. The question one could discuss was: Who is guilty of sacrilege? In a public debate it was obviously impossible to say what every educated person knew—that the soothsayers were not to be taken seriously. Traditional practices implied collective responsibility for the prosperity of the country. They were the tissue of daily life, the occasions for social reconciliation or conflict. New gods and ceremonies came in. Rome had long developed mechanisms for absorbing foreign gods. But these produced their problems. The path of Isis, for instance, was not simple in Rome in the first century B.C. A tradition still alive in the time of Apuleius (*Metamorphoses* 11. 30) dated back the introduction of Isis into Rome to about the time of Sulla. This must be roughly right. There was enough opposition to it in 59 B.C. to persuade the Senate to order the destruction of an altar to Isis on the Capitol. We know indeed of a *Sacerdos Isidis Capitolinae*, perhaps in the middle of the first century B.C. (Degrassi, *ILLRP* I. 159). Varro, we hear, was indignant that Alexandrian gods were worshiped in Rome (Tertullian, *Ad nationes* 1. 10. 17 and parallel texts). The worshipers were faithful, and in 43 the Senate had to reverse the decision and promise to erect a temple to Isis at public expense. However, the war against Antony and Cleopatra delayed the return of Isis, for Isis became a sort of enemy goddess. In 28, Augustus prohibited the erection of chapels to Isis within the pomoerium. In 21, Agrippa intensified the prohibition. Isis had to wait until the Emperor Caligula to get her temple in Rome. But Ovid had already remarked that nobody would refuse to make an offering to the priests of Isis, if asked (*Epistulae ex Ponto* 1. 1. 37).

Most of the people had their favorite gods and their favorite superstitions. They put pressures on each other, though few would go so far as the elder Cato, who did not allow his slave steward to consult Chaldean soothsayers (*De agr.* 5. 4). Some gods were more politically relevant than others, but not even Jupiter was identified with Rome. There was the further complication that some of the political leaders were turned into divine beings by the internal logic of this interplay between religion and politics. If the god was king, would not a king become god? Very few people were, however, prepared to be absolutely exclusive in their devotion. The great exception were the Jews, who were beginning to be noticeably numerous and, according to Cicero (*Pro Flacco* 66), dangerously noisy in Rome.

III

The Jews had only one God—and a very jealous one at that. This was enough to give a distinctive character to Jerusalem, or to any Jewish group of the diaspora. But Jerusalem was also different from any other place because its Temple had long been the symbol of the unity of Judaism. I do not know of any other ancient god who had a sanctuary as exclusive as the Temple of Jerusalem. This exclusivity conditioned of course the influence of the Temple authorities on the calendar. The official cult of the Temple was the obvious emotional center of Jewish life. The half-shekel for its upkeep became a bond of loyalty for the diaspora. The ancient figures about pilgrims in Jerusalem are wildly inflated, as ancient figures tend to be. Alexandria was not so far from Jerusalem, but the wealthy and pious Philo seems to have gone to Jerusalem only once in his life. Yet Jerusalem was a place for pilgrims unmatched by Athens or Rome, with all their attractions.

The real surprise is that the third and perhaps most essential difference between Jerusalem and the other two cities did not spring from this second difference and might perhaps even seem to contradict it. If the Temple of Jerusalem was almost (not quite) unique, the Jews had been supplementing it by houses of prayer and of meetings which, in the first century B.C., probably still defeated any attempt at normalization.[9] The *proseuche* prevailing in Egypt—mainly a house of prayer, to judge from the name—was different from at least that synagogue of Jerusalem which its founder Theodotus, a priest and an archisynagogos, described as being "for the reading of the Law and for the teaching of the commandments," with no mention of prayers (*Corpus Inscriptionum Judaeorum*, II, 1404). This inscription is certainly earlier than the destruction of the Temple. As Theodotus introduces himself as son and grandson of archisynagogoi, the probability is that synagogues existed in Jerusalem in the first century B.C. But there is at least one passage in Philo which makes it certain that texts from the Bible were read and commented upon in the Egyptian *proseuchai* on the Sabbath. This is the alleged speech by a Roman governor of Egypt in *De somniis* 2. 127: "and will you sit in your conventicles and assemble your regular company and read in security your holy books, expounding any obscure point and in leisurely comfort discussing at length your ancestral philosophy?" (trans. F. H. Colson and G. H. Whitaker, Loeb). So we can perhaps assume that a common feature of the various gatherings of the Jews was the study of the Bible on the Sabbath, either in the original text or in translation or both. The reading of prophetic texts in addition to the Torah and the practice of sermons are confirmed for Palestine by the New Testament (Acts 13:15; 15:21. Luke 4:16–17). It is important that according to Flavius Josephus (*Antiquitates Judaicae* 16. 43), Nicolas of Damascus in his address to Agrippa on behalf of the Jews should have stated: "We give every seventh day over to the study of our customs and law." The reading of the Law on Mondays and Thursdays can only be inferred from later evidence, though it seems likely enough for the first century B.C. The mere existence of a minimum of weekly reading and interpretation of the Bible in public seems to me a new departure in the religious life of the classical world. It was considered such at the end of the first century A.D. by Flavius Josephus, admittedly a biased witness: "every week men should desert their other occupations and assemble to listen to the Law and to obtain thorough and accurate knowledge of it, a practice which all other legislators seem to have neglected" (*Contra Apionem* 2. 175; trans. H. St. J. Thackeray, Loeb). No doubt some mystery cults included the reading of sacred texts.[10] One can also argue that the reading of Homer in the schools might be considered a quasi-religious performance, though I have indicated the difficulties of this interpretation. But what an adult Jew was now asked to do was to come back at least once a week to learn about his past history and his present obligations: by implication he was also asked to accept the expounders of the Law in his own synagogue or *proseuche* as his own teachers. There is no point in speculating here on the relation between the rise of the scribes and the development and intellectualization of the synagogue. There is also no point in trying to be more precise about the relation between synagogues and schools for children which undoubtedly existed, though the very tradition that schooling became compulsory in Judaea under Alexander Jannaeus in the early first century B.C. is full of difficulties (cf. *y. Ket.* 32c. with *b. B. B.*, 21a). Above all, we must not confuse this elementary synagogue instruction with the higher learning which Jewish masters communicated to their disciples on a level comparable with that of pagan philosophers and jurisprudents. The mere fact that one had to study in order to be pious is a strange notion which made Judaism increasingly intellectual—not what cults were known for in the Greco-Roman world. It favored separation of the learned from the ignorant and it caused (and allowed) basic doctrinal disagreements; in the end it introduced schism and excommunication. But, to confine ourselves to the first century B.C., we should recognize that while in Athens and Rome thinking about religion usually made people less religious, among Jews the more you thought about religion the more religious you became. As it happened, one of the sects which developed in the atmosphere of Jerusalem was to replace the old religions of Rome and Athens.

6

How Roman Emperors Became Gods

I

GERTRUD BING, the director of the Warburg Institute, used to tell with great gusto a story that apparently has not found its way into the biography of Aby Warburg by Ernst Gombrich. Bing happened to be in Rome with Warburg, the founder and patron saint of the Warburg Institute, on that day, February 11, 1929, on which Mussolini and the Pope proclaimed the reconciliation between Italy and the Catholic Church and signed a concordat, the first bilateral agreement to be reached between post-Risorgimento Italy and the Church of Rome. There were in Rome tremendous popular demonstrations, whether orchestrated from above or from below. Mussolini became overnight the "man of providence," and in such an inconvenient position he remained for many years. Circulation in the streets of Rome was not very easy on that day, and it so happened that Warburg disappeared from the sight of his companions. They anxiously waited for him back in the Hotel Eden, but there was no sign of him for dinner. Bing and the others even telephoned the police. But Warburg reappeared in the hotel before midnight, and when he was reproached he soberly replied something like this in his picturesque German: "You know that throughout my life I have been interested in the revival of paganism and pagan festivals. Today I had the chance of my life to be present at the re-paganization of Rome, and you complain that I remained to watch it."

American Scholar, Spring 1986, pp. 181–93.

Warburg's remarks may help to explain to people younger than myself why some of the most original work on the Roman imperial cult should have been done around the years 1929–1934 in that ambiguous atmosphere of the revival of emperor-worship in which it was difficult to separate adulation from political emotion, and political emotion from religious or superstitious excitement. E. J. Bickerman's seminal essay on apotheosis appeared in 1929; L. R. Taylor's great book *Divinity of the Roman Emperor* in 1931; A. Alföldi's on the monarchic ceremonial in 1934; several of A. D. Nock's capital studies on the imperial cult and related notions between 1930 and 1934, including his chapter in *Cambridge Ancient History* X of 1934.

If one looks at these studies now, it is easy to notice two not necessarily contradictory features. On the one hand, the authors are keen to show how the imperial cult was grafted into the traditional patterns of Greco-Roman religion. On the other hand, they are trying to keep the imperial cult below and perhaps outside the zone of true religion. We owe to A. D. Nock the much-repeated formulation that the emperor's cult was homage, not worship. As James Frazer's *Golden Bough* had made everyone familiar with primitive divine kings, the distinction between homage and worship was therefore meant to define the difference between the alleged primitive confusion of god with king and this later, more sophisticated Greco-Roman phenomenon of ruler-cult. For good or ill the imperial cult was seen as a symptom of absolutism and treated more as an expression of political allegiance than of religious emotion. This, incidentally, allowed scholars divided between their Fascist sympathies and their religious convictions, such as A. Alföldi and J. Carcopino, to avoid religious problems.

A marked reaction against the political interpretation of the imperial cult was to be expected in the post-Fascist era, and at last we have it. If anything is surprising, it is that it has taken so long to come, but we classical scholars are notoriously slow-witted. A number of anthropologically minded scholars, taking their cue from the anthropological work of Clifford Geertz—for instance in his essay "Centers, Kings and Charisma: Reflections on the Symbols of Power"—have been arguing that to deny the religious value of the imperial cult is equivalent to taking a Christianizing view of religion.

I find the first clear expression of this view in the well-argued chapter on the divine emperors in the 1978 volume *Conquerors and Slaves* by Keith Hopkins. The most recent and complete expression is the book by Simon Price, *Rituals and Power: The Roman Imperial Cult in Asia Minor* (1984), which has deservedly received much favorable attention. But beyond this theoretical display, which has become characteristic of classical scholars in fear of not being sufficiently up-to-date, there is the serious purpose of discovering the meaning of the imperial cult by analyzing the acts and the words that were the substance of the cult.

Much of Price's work is concerned with making sense of the combination of public space and private time that characterizes the performance of the imperial cult. While the various monuments in honor of the emperor placed him "within the physical framework of the city," according to Price, individual or group initiative conditioned the forms, frequency, and emotional intensity of the cult in each place. This is particularly evident in small communities, even villages, where the imperial cult is often found associated with ancestral gods. But perhaps the need for personal initiative is most clearly demonstrated by those places in which the imperial cult is absent, simply because the local people were not Hellenized enough to want it. The concluding chapter of Price's book is a very valuable attempt to explain the imperial cult as an effort by the Greeks to make sense of "an otherwise incomprehensible intrusion of authority into their world."

The imperial cult, in Price's terms, stabilized the religious order of the Greek world. As the imperial cult enhanced the dominance of local elites over the lower classes, it was also a reaffirmation of the structure of local power that was then coordinated at city level with the symbolism of the imperial cult. This is what Clifford Geertz would call the inherent sacredness of sovereign power. In Geertz's words: "The gravity of high politics and the solemnity of high worship spring from liker impulses than might first appear." Clifford Geertz himself had an easy time finding confirmation not only in Java, which he likes and knows so well, but in Elizabethan England, in nineteenth-century Morocco, and in American presidential elections.

In fact, however, the real difficulty we feel in interpreting the

Greco-Roman monarchic or ruler-cult is not now about questions of relations between religion and politics. I think we can cope with these without much trouble. In our contemporary world there is no lack of politically religious emotions or of religiously political emotions; and it is our personal responsibility as rational beings to decide whether we want these emotions to prevail. What the Greco-Roman world contributes to our education, or at least to our experience, is that such tangled emotions had been kept remarkably under control for some centuries by both Greeks and Romans. For a long time the Greeks and Romans did without monarchy or at least divine monarchy. Even in Sparta the kings were not gods. In the Greece we know from the seventh to the fourth century B.C., political power was in the hands of magistrates who were elected in assemblies by their peers. Even tyrants had to receive legitimization from assemblies. In Rome, monarchy disappeared toward the end of the sixth century. Whatever this monarchy might have been, it was not remembered as a monarchy by divine right. Why, then, was divine monarchy resurrected in Greece and Rome in an age of philosophic discussion about the nature of the gods and about the place of men in the world? The imperial cult prospered at a time in which a philosophically minded doctor like Galen argued that true piety is not to be found in bloody sacrifices to gods but in the study of nature. And how could a monarch be at the same time a man and a god, and more precisely, in Rome, a magistrate and a god?

I am not sure that I know the answer to these questions. But in the following pages I shall try to argue a partial answer on the presupposition that people were finding it easy to call exceptionally powerful men gods because they were losing faith in the existence, or at least in the effectiveness, of their traditional gods. One has to add, about the Roman Empire, that these powerful men were aliens importing powerful alien ideas and institutions, such as Roman citizenship and Roman peace. Not by chance was the worship of Roman emperors associated with that of Roman abstract ideas like Fides or Pax or Roma herself turned into a goddess. In the provinces, the Roman rulers were the importers of an alien system of values and habits that did not contradict, and might even support, the extant polytheistic establishment. The association of an obviously powerful emperor with gods whose power was not so obvious might well reassure the believers in those gods.

II

There was a notion of the hero among the Greeks that connected (in an obscure way for us but, no doubt, more clearly for the Greeks) the zone of the gods with the zone of men. The heroes were dead men of special value whose tombs received the tribute of some sort of cult. The Spartans chose Orestes as a hero, and the Thebans imported the bones of Hector for that purpose—and of course the Athenians had Theseus and Oedipus. The presence of the bodies of such men was considered a blessing for the place. Real or imaginary founders of a city were naturally entitled to such tomb-worship by the city concerned. That the range was vast is indicated by the example of the Spartan Brasidas who, in 422 B.C., was rewarded with a cult of this kind at Amphipolis, where he had died defending the interests of Sparta. We may also remind ourselves that at the beginning of the fifth century the mad boxer Cleomedes, according to Pausanias, received such a cult at Astypalaia after having mysteriously disappeared in a homicidal bout. The Delphic priestess proclaimed him "the last of the heroes. . . . Honor him with sacrifices as being no longer a mortal." As Thucydides confirms, games and yearly sacrifices were the most obvious forms of cult for heroes.

But though Cleomedes was by no means to remain the last of the heroes, the Delphic priestess intimated more than she could know with that adjective *last*. In the fourth century the notion of hero lost in importance compared with that of divine man or indeed of man recognized to be god. It is an essential aspect of the ruler-cult in Hellenistic and Roman times that it develops this notion of divine man and is not founded upon the notion of hero. One excellent reason, among others, is that the ruler-cult, though interested in past rulers, was basically oriented toward living sovereigns: it was meant to explain, justify, and recognize present, not past, power. If the oracle of Delphi, according to Herodotus, had difficulty in deciding whether Lycurgus, a legislator in Sparta, was a man or a god, fourth-century people seem to have had less difficulty in deciding that the Spartan Lysander, having destroyed the Athenian empire, deserved in his lifetime altars like a god, a hymn (paean) sung to him, and the transformation of a festival for the goddess Hera into a festival for Lysander (the Lysandreia). Attempts were made to adapt the notion of a dead hero to a living man; for instance, Dio of Syracuse was considered to be a hero while alive.

But the trend was toward blurring the distinction between man and god. Thus King Philip, the father of Alexander, got a sanctuary at Olympia while alive and a statue to keep company with the statues of the Twelve Olympian Gods. We have here the transition to the frank demand in 324 by Alexander the Great that the Greek cities should recognize him as a god. We do not know exactly what his envoys said, and even less what the poor Greek cities actually answered. We do not even know whether Demosthenes was talking tongue in cheek when he suggested leaving to Alexander the choice between being the son of Zeus or the son of Poseidon. We happen to know that the sons of Poseidon did not enjoy a very good reputation, but the text that reports Demosthenes' words—Hyperides' speech against Demosthenes—is badly fragmented at this point.[1] Perhaps what matters most for our purpose is that in ordinary parlance, both in Greece and in Rome, the word *god* or *godlike* could be attached to a "man" without thinking twice—in affection, in admiration, or in adulation. If Speusippus and Cicero called Plato a god, Cicero could also call the father of P. Lentulus "deum ac parentem fortunae et nominis mei," and of course Virgil says in a private context "namque erit ille mihi semper deus." After all, even Epicurus could be a god to Lucretius.

Hellenistic kings had their dynastic cults in various forms, while individual cities were able to introduce the cult of individual kings, not necessarily their own rulers. Individuals were free to display loyalty or gratitude by acts of cults to sovereigns. Acts of cult varied from building temples and setting up statues to performing sacrifices and organizing festivals; but perhaps sacrifices were the most obvious sign of cult. There were territorial and local differences. In Pergamum they seem to have built temples only to dead kings and to have treated living kings as *Synnaoi*, as associates in a temple, of traditional gods. *Synnaoi* to gods have been made famous by a classic piece of research by A. D. Nock in *Harvard Studies* of 1930. Roman magistrates and governors soon joined or replaced Hellenistic kings in the divine honors among Greek and Hellenized people. A list of Roman magistrates in Greek cities is given by G. W. Bowersock in *Augustus and the Greek World*. It begins with M. Claudius Marcellus in Syracuse at the end of the third century B.C. and ends in the early first century A.D., oddly enough at Miletus, in a cult for the governor of Egypt, Cn. Vergilius Capito. A cult of a Roman magistrate could last three centuries, like that of Titus Flamininus, who had the reputation of having proclaimed the freedom of the Greeks, or could last only a few years, such as that of Sulla in Athens. It is worth remembering that Cicero, though vain, firmly declined worship when he was a provincial governor. During the time of Augustus, the cult of Roman provincial governors disappeared to the exclusive benefit of the cult of the emperor.

But the cult bestowed on the Roman governors in the Greek provinces that they ruled or visited was not always a simple application of Hellenistic ruler-cult. The Greeks, or rather some Greek city, put Dea Roma among their gods; so did Smyrna, according to Tacitus, as early as 195 B.C. Fides was also acceptable to Greeks as a goddess personifying Roman rule. Plutarch tells us in his account of Titus Flamininus that he was invoked in a hymn at Chalcis together with Zeus or Jupiter, Roma and Fides, and that, though he had his own priest, he shared a temple with Heracles and Apollo. About the end of the second century B.C. three cities of Asia Minor agreed not to harm the Romans and put this agreement under the protection of Zeus, Concord, and Dea Roma.

III

If the intervention of Dea Roma and Fides shows that it was not simply a question of Hellenistic ruler-cult transferred to Roman rulers, we have also to take into account the existence in Rome itself in the last centuries of the Republic of a need for legitimization of exceptional power. The problem was bound to present itself as soon as the military leaders and conquerors began to claim privileges that were incompatible with the traditional aristocratic structure of the Roman Republic. Scipio Africanus, like Alexander, was supposed to have been born from the intercourse of his mother with a nonhuman being, a divine snake.

Another member of the gens Cornelia, Sulla, was Felix and a protégé of Venus, while his rival Marius received homage of food and drink in Rome like a god. Caesar went beyond all of them, first because the Julii claimed descent from Venus, and second because he received religious honors before his death, the limits of which are in dispute, and full deification after his death. In 45 B.C., while he was alive, his cult-statue was placed in the temple of Quirinus with the inscription "To the Invincible God." His *clementia* had a cult. That he was alive when he was given a priest, a *flamen*, in the person of Antony seems to be put beyond doubt by Cicero in *Philippics*. Octavian, being Caesar's adopted son, became *divi filius* in 42 B.C. For a while he had to compete with Antony, who paraded as a new Dionysus in Athens and elsewhere. In the East he was soon associated with the cult of Rome.

But Octavian was presenting himself as a restorer of the Roman republican traditions. There was a limit to the divinity of an alleged republican leader. In Rome itself, therefore, he was satisfied with being the son of a god and being called Augustus, which was a borderline qualification between heaven and earth. Besides, he was a protégé of Apollo. Yet forms of his cult crept in even in Rome through individuals and groups: they were even more obvious in the rest of Italy and in the Western provinces, not to speak of the East. On the Western side the cult of the ruler's *genius* became especially acceptable. I wish we really knew what a *genius* was, a sort of guardian angel, perhaps even mortal like his possessor, if we have to follow Horace (*Epistles* 2. 2. 188).

Generally speaking, the emperor had to approve to limit, and occasionally to refuse, ruler-cult. He had to be worshiped, and yet he had to remain a man in order to live on social terms with the Roman aristocracy of which he was supposed to be the *Princeps*. It suffices to remember that, on the formal side, the emperor was also the *Pontifex Maximus* of the Roman state: being both the first of the priests and a god was not so obvious. Emperors who acquired a bad reputation, such as Caligula, Nero, Domitian, and Commodus, are also those who, in our tradition,

appeared to have requested or received more than their decent
share of worship. Emperors had to decide at every step how far
they could go. They knew instinctively that what suited Egypt
would not suit Rome, but the intermediate stages were not self-
evident. Cult after death was perhaps easier: it had a recognized
model in the apotheosis of Romulus; it had something to do with
ancestor cult; it had a Roman ritual; it was easily acceptable
everywhere as a sign of the stability and continuity of the Empire.
Yet even apotheosis, harmless as it was, could provoke irony and
criticism, as Seneca's *Apocolocyntosis* against the divinization of
Claudius shows.

It is probably fair to say that the emperor during his lifetime
was more of a god in his absence than in his presence, and that the
success (for success it was) of the imperial cult in the provinces
was owing to the presence with which it invested an absentee
sovereign. His statues, his temples, his priests, the games, sacrifices, and other ceremonial acts that were performed in his honor
helped to make him present: they also helped people to express
their own interest in the preservation of the world in which they
lived. We have an obvious difficulty in assessing how distant the
power of Rome appeared to the provincials. After all, Rome was
not a police state: internal security of towns was only moderately
ensured by the central government. The army was of course very
strong, but it was usually stationed at the boundaries of the Empire and interfered little with city life. Solidarity was hardly created by war efforts, except in emergencies. Tax collecting was a
tangible, and inevitably unpopular, reality: few can have been
aware of what they got in return for taxation. If the tribute was
supposed to be for the emperor, it would not improve the image of
the emperor. Again, the emperor was known to make laws and
regulations and to answer petitions of various kinds. The great
amount of paperwork passing from center to periphery and vice
versa (about which we have now the learned work by Fergus
Millar) was not the kind that would strike the imagination and
create widespread loyalty. It was not in the language of the Roman
administrative machine that people could express ambitions, pray
for peace and prosperity, or dream of victory and greatness, even if
vicariously.

Occasionally no doubt, though very seldom, the emperor appeared. His *adventus*, his arrival, would give scope for emotional outbursts and even for miracles, as the case of Vespasian in Egypt shows. But the *adventus* itself, to which I shall return, was already conditioned by the recognized method of facing the Roman emperor while not seeing him, which was the imperial cult. The *adventus* presupposed the imperial cult, not vice versa. I leave out here certain technical difficulties that one has to deal with in grasping the imperial cult—for instance, the types of sacrifice that were available to the worshiper—though not indiscriminately. The imperial cult is fraught with terminological little traps. For instance, though Greek makes a distinction between a real cult-statue, an *agalma*, and an image with only complimentary implications, an *eikon*, it is by no means evident that the distinction is invariably observed and that, consequently, we know that a text alludes to a cult-statue. But there is one aspect of the imperial cult that must be stressed because it is essential. An element of its strength was paradoxically the fact that it was *not* universally accepted. Indeed it was often imposed on indifferent or reluctant subjects by zealous governors. *The Acts of the Christian Martyrs* will soon remind us that there was an element of brutal imposition in the imperial cult. Not everybody liked it. After all, even Vespasian joked about becoming a god after death, and it was not a cheerful joke.

Other intellectuals, among them Tacitus, spoke of the ruler-cult as *Graeca adulatio*, and we may assume that the idea was shared by many cultivated Greeks. In the third century a Greek historian such as Dio Cassius could attribute to Maecenas a total condemnation of the imperial cult. Apart from these intellectuals who were annoyed or who smiled at the notion that a mortal became a god because of his office, there were of course those who hated the Roman Empire or an individual emperor. Most naturally, if something went wrong, portraits of the emperor, whether *agalmata* or *eikones*, would be the first target, as the story of the Four Emperors in A.D. 69 shows and the famous Antiochian riots of the fourth century confirm. Second, there was an increasing number of subjects of the Empire who had religious objections to the imperial cult. They were the Jews and, soon, the growing number of Christians. The Jews, especially after the attempt of Gaius to place his own statue in the Temple of Jerusalem, were more or less exempt from direct cult: they only prayed for the emperor. But, as the complicated story of the great Jewish rebellions shows, this was not enough to keep the Roman government pleased or the Jewish subjects quiet. The feeling that the Jews did not deserve their privileges must have been widespread. As a well-known passage in *Mishnah, Abodah Zarah,* 3, shows, statues were felt by the Jews to be potential troubles. The problem was basically the one we have mentioned: how would you recognize a cult-image if you saw one? As for the Christians, there was no privilege for them. The accusation that they did not worship the emperors—"deos non colitis et pro imperatoribus sacrificia non penditis"—is for Tertullian (*Apologeticum* 10) the standard accusation. The rest of the tradition largely confirms his contention. It is unnecessary here to quote the well-known texts, such as the letter of Pliny the Younger to Trajan (10. 96), or the most reliable *Acts of the Martyrs,* such as those of the Scyllitan martyrs or of Pionius or of Polycarpus, where the test of loyalty to the emperor is precisely the recognition of his cult.

After all, ordinary men took an oath to the emperor and his *genius* even in private transactions. We all remember the poor Alexandrian sailors who emotionally saluted the emperor, as Suetonius tells us: "per illum se vivere, per illum navigare." The poor sailors knew about Roman peace, if not about ruler-cult. But nothing is emotionally acceptable if it does not provoke contrasts, and it can hardly be doubted that the imperial cult gained from the existence of dubious characters, such as the Jews and the Christians, outsiders whether by birth or by choice, who did not worship the emperors. What happened to the imperial cult when the Christians conquered the Empire under Constantine and turned the tables on the pagans and the Jews is a story to which I shall soon return.

For now let me add that other sectional differences contributed to the imperial cult. The slaves who were entitled by law to take refuge near the statue of an emperor to protest against ill-treatment by their master or his injunction to prostitute themselves had their own emotional interest in the sacredness of these imperial statues. On the other hand, even a governor could seek refuge near the statue of his emperor when he was persecuted by rioters who wanted to burn him alive. (The story is told by Philostratus in his *Life of Apollonius of Tyana* I, 15.) Rich people, as we know from so many inscriptions, found satisfaction in erecting their monuments in honor of the emperor. As there was scope for individual fancies and combinations, each donor had reasonable freedom in expressing his preference. He could worship the emperor alone or associate him with his favorite god. What can we say about those two Spaniards who chose or invented Aesculapius Augustus and Iuppiter Pantheus Augustus that crop up in *Corpus Inscriptionum Latinarum* 2. 2004 and 2008?

Even better: there were theological questions about these new-fangled gods, the emperors. How much were they affected by astrology? Correspondingly, could anyone endanger an emperor by getting hold of his horoscope? The story of how emperors were afraid of astrologers and of those who used the astrologers to learn about the destiny of emperors is a well-known one. Horoscopes of emperors were certainly made and preserved, whether retrospectively or not. The opinion we find in Firmicus Maternus in the fourth century that the emperor is not subject to the stars because his destiny is determined by higher authority (*Mathesis* 2. 30) is somewhat isolated, though not unique. Firmicus Maternus wrote that opinion when he was on the way to becoming a Christian. More frequently there was tension between astrology and worship of emperors as gods, and that again did no harm to the imperial cult. Theological difficulties have always contributed to making beliefs more interesting.

What we know about least is the pleasure that the various groups derived from setting up statues, building temples, performing sacrifices, composing speeches, arranging banquets to honor the sovereign or the *genius* of the sovereign or the gods connected with the sovereign. Athletes would be given prizes, musicians and poets would be employed, children and adolescents would be involved in performances. Each community and group had its own calendar; different military units would differ in their worship, as would different cities; but probably no one would have felt a complete stranger if he traveled from one military unit to the next or from one city to another. In the Hellenized provinces of the Empire, where the cult of local rulers had preceded the emperor's cult, ordinary people were confirmed in their habit of adding new gods to the old gods. In the provinces of Western Europe and Northern Africa people were offered the new pleasure of getting nearer to the gods through earthly divine rulers. Most remarkably, we even have some evidence, albeit vague, which H. W. Pleket collected years ago (in *Harvard Theological Review*, 58, 1965, 331ff.) that some groups were treating the imperial cult as a mystery religion. In some inscriptions, priests called *sebastophantai* appear: they seem to have the task of revealing some secrets about emperors. I wish we knew more about this.

IV

Rule by the grace of God was the only form of rule compatible with the Christian faith: indeed, there had been pagan emperors like Aurelian who had thought on those lines. But it is not difficult to see that the Christian emperors were in no hurry to eliminate the imperial cult. It had taken root, it had become an organic part of the relation between sovereign and subject: indeed, it indicated the exact point at which the subject felt himself to be a subject. Sacrifices, perhaps, had to be eliminated by Christian emperors. The ecclesiastical historian Philostorgius is explicitly critical of Christians who offered sacrifices to the statue of Constantine in Constantinople. When Constantine wrote his letter to the citizens of Hispellum in Umbria to authorize the building of a temple to himself and to his family, he had to stipulate that the cult should not be polluted by the deception of any contagious superstition. He must have meant sacrifices, though he did not say so. Another text, this time by Constantius in 341, makes it evident that Constantine had in fact tried to prevent "the madness of sacrifices," but the precise occasion is not indicated. The imperial cult, however reformed, went on.

We know that in the early sixth century there was still in the small African town Ammaedara a good man who was proud of calling himself *flamen perpetuus Christianus*, without realizing that there was some contradiction between *flamen* and *Christianus*. As G. W. Bowersock was quick to point out, what really minimized the importance of being *divus* for a Christian emperor was the chance of becoming *sanctus*. Constantine himself was treated in the East like a saint, indeed like one of the apostles, soon after his death. When prayers for the performance of miracles began to be addressed to saints, paradoxically the last barrier which separated a deified emperor from an old Olympian god fell down, or at least was occasionally broken down. As has been well known since at least A. D. Nock's chapter on religion in *Cambridge Ancient History* X (1934), there is a characteristic absence of evidence that prayers were offered to emperors to perform a miracle (or even to induce a dream). Ex-voto inscriptions registering acts of grace by emperors after prayers to them are few and unclear for the three pagan centuries of the Empire.

To make things worse, there is some evidence that the boyfriend of Hadrian, Antinous, who was deified to please Hadrian, did accomplish miracles after his death. We have an explicit ex-voto in that sense from Bithynia. So a mere Antinous was better than the Emperor Hadrian in performing miracles after death. But it must be a consequence of the new atmosphere of the fourth century—when an emperor could perform miracles qua a saint—that even a pagan emperor became capable of authentic miracles after death. We learn from Libanius that worshipers were given miracles by Julian after his death. As A. D. Nock immediately perceived when M. P. Charlesworth directed his attention to that passage by Libanius, it must have been competition with Christian saints that endowed the dead Julian with such power.

Even Theodosius II, who took his Christianity seriously, still had to recognize in 425 the reality of the statues, images, and games for an emperor, though he wanted these honors "without the vainglorious heights of adoration." The limits between worship and homage remained unclear.

But we must consider the *adventus*, the moment when the emperor, usually remote and unseen, would become present to his subjects. The moment was solemn and therefore a frequent subject on monuments. Since 1938 we have had marble reliefs found beneath the Palazzo della Cancelleria in Rome that have been dated to the reign of Domitian. One panel presents Rome presiding over the *adventus* of the emperor Vespasian. Several other scenes of *adventus*—for Trajan, Hadrian, Marcus Aurelius, etc.—had been known before. The *adventus* of an emperor might happen in a moment of need, when his position was not yet safe. Such was the case of the *adventus* of Vespasian at Alexandria in 69. Tacitus notices that Vespasian was still lacking "auctoritas et maiestas." He acquired it there by performing miracles in collaboration with Serapis. He did not have the king's touch by right, as legitimate monarchs of later ages had: he was just lucky at that moment.

Normally, *adventus* was not an occasion for miracles, but for eloquence, rejoicing, and religious ceremonies. Eloquence for *adventus* was theorized, and we hear plenty about it in the third-century treatise by the rhetorician Menander—a book that has come back into fashion among classicists in recent years. It is, perhaps, more important to refer to the long tradition of religious acts that would greet the visitor. It had of course precedents in the reception of Roman leaders in the provinces. Metellus Pius, we are told by Valerius Maximus, had his *adventus* in Spain greeted with altars and incense. Augustus tried to arrive incognito to avoid giving trouble. Sacrifices are noted by Suetonius for the *adventus* of the Emperor Gaius. They must have happened for almost every emperor who traveled about. If we know more about *adventus* in the third or fourth century, it is partly a question of sources: most of the imperial panegyrics belong to that period, and they are, as we have said, particularly sensitive to *adventus*. But it may well be that the new religious atmosphere, combined with the new military situation, gave *adventus* a greater, though perhaps different, share in the imperial ceremonial. We know from Ammianus that Julian was received in Antioch "like some divinity with public prayers." In any case, as the emperor was seldom in Rome in the fourth century, his appearance in Rome became a ceremony of special significance. Constantius's entry into Rome in 357 was memorably described by Ammianus; and we have one of the speeches written for the occasion by Themistius. According to Ammianus's description, Constantius "kept the gaze of his eyes straight ahead and turned his face neither to right nor left." He was seeing things rather than seeing people. Sabine MacCormack in *Art and Ceremony in Late Antiquity* has already observed that there was in fact an increasing tendency, especially in figurative art, to emphasize the presence rather than the arrival of the emperor. How can we explain this?

One element is perhaps to be found in the new climate of modified emperor-worship by Christians. There was less one could do in terms of cultic ceremonies as such. The crowd could no longer take part in sacrifices or direct prayer. The crowd, therefore, tended to recede in the descriptions of the *adventus*—whether in literature or in monuments. There remained the emperor in a new solitude—present rather than arriving. His presence was still, or perhaps more so, a divine presence: the presence of a lonely superior being. Thus the *adventus* was involved in the difficulties that surrounded the imperial cult in a Christian empire. For a while, *adventus* and the modified imperial cult supported each other, in the sense that the *adventus* supplied the imperial cult with an immediate presence of the divine being, and the modified imperial cult supplied the *adventus* with something of the sanctity of the Christian sovereign. In the long run, both *adventus* and the imperial cult were doomed. The introduction of the patriarch into the ceremony of coronation (first perhaps with Leo I, in 457) made it definitely clear that the emperor could be a saint, but not a god.

People were again seriously believing in a god or gods. On the one hand, the emperors were no longer the victorious and efficient rulers they used to be; and, on the other, they were no longer felt to be an alien power where they were still ruling. The imperial cult was primarily a sign of indifference or doubt or anxiety about the gods; it was, furthermore, an expression of admiration for efficient, but alien, rule.

7

What Josephus Did Not See

I

PIERRE VIDAL-NAQUET's book *Flavius Josèphe ou du bon usage de la trahison* evolved from an introduction to Savinel's French translation of Josephus's *Jewish War*. Vidal-Naquet holds a well-established position among scholars in the circle of J.-P. Vernant who work on the reinterpretation of Greek thought. This distinguished group of scholars, who have also been influential in Italy, base themselves on nondogmatic premises in which historical psychology, Marxism, and structuralism (both the Dumézil and the Lévi-Strauss variety) are brought together. They have aroused and revitalized interest in mythology, poetry, and various strands of philosophy which are viewed as expressions of the Greeks' apprehension of reality. Of this group, Pierre Vidal-Naquet, who was born in 1930, is the most involved in direct research into political and social history. Such interests are demonstrated by the volume he wrote in 1964 in collaboration with Pierre Levêque on *Clisthène l'Athénien* and by his penetrating work *Le bordereau d'ensemencement dans l'Égypte ptolémaïque* (1967). Besides these works, and perhaps even more indicative, is the essential part he played in presenting and advancing the economico-

This article originally appeared as "Ciò che Flavio Giuseppe non vide" in *Settimo contributo alla storia degli studi classici e del mondo antico*, Rome, 1984, pp. 305–17. Translated here by Joanna Weinberg. Introduction to the Italian translation, *Il buon uso del tradimento* (Editori Riuniti, Rome 1980), of Pierre Vidal-Naquet's *Flavius Josèphe ou du bon usage de la trahison*.

sociological researches of his friend M. I. Finley for the French public.[1] To a certain extent, one may simply account for these scholarly interests of Vidal-Naquet as being the result of his orthodox training as classicist and ancient historian—he was the pupil of H.-I. Marrou, Victor Goldschmidt, L. Robert, A. Aymard, and of that curious "Socratic" Henri Margueritte. However (and this is also well known), one cannot dissociate Vidal-Naquet's historical interests from his conspicuous involvement in two decisive moments in recent French history. Unaffiliated to any particular political party, Vidal-Naquet took a stand during the Algerian crisis against the repressive methods of the French government (cf. his work *Torture: Cancer of Democracy*, Harmondsworth, 1963). He also participated in the student revolt of 1968 which he later recorded in *Journal de la Commune étudiante*, 1969, a documentary volume written in collaboration with Alain Schnapp. The volume was translated into English.

In 1960–1961 Vidal-Naquet was suspended from his teaching post as assistant professor at the University of Caen because he had signed the declaration of the 121 on the right "à l'insoumission" in the Algerian war. More recently, he has been the object of attack both in France and Italy, not only by scholars of the right, but also by those of the left (B. Hemmerdinger and V. Di Benedetto).[2] After spending several years at the CNRS and at the University of Lyons, Vidal-Naquet was appointed subdirector of studies in 1966 and in 1969 became A. Aymard's successor as director of studies at the École Pratique des Hautes Études. He is also a fully engaged editor of the *Annales* and works in particularly close collaboration with the medievalist J. Le Goff.

There was every good reason to expect that one day Vidal-Naquet's historiographical interests would have to include Judaism. Yet somehow, the book on Josephus came as a greater surprise to the author than to the usual readers of his writings on Greek subjects. Vidal-Naquet has never forgotten nor can he ever forget that he is a Jew, hailing from the Arba' Kehillot (the "Four Communities") of the Comtat-Venaissin centered at Carpentras. From the Middle Ages on, these communities produced dynasties of great rabbis and doctors, and more recently, musicians, politicians, writers, and scientists quite disproportionate to their smallness in numbers. Both Vidal-Naquet's father, who was in the Resistance from 1940, and his mother were deported and murdered in Auschwitz by the Nazis.

It is here that Vidal-Naquet's intervention on behalf of the Arabs (and Berbers) of Algeria has its roots. From here too stems his constant preoccupation with the problem of Israel. This preoccupation cannot be explained in a few words. Essentially, however, it consists of Vidal-Naquet's claim that a dialogue between Israelis and Palestinians is possible.

Similarly, there can be no definite explanation to account for the link between the French Jew's preoccupation with the future of Judaism and his interpretation of Josephus's position during and after the Jewish war of A.D. 66–70. Here it may be sufficient to underline the profound emotional roots from which there emerged a new (and perhaps more personal) Vidal-Naquet the historian. This can now be traced in his chapter on Hellenistic-Roman Judaism which was published in the second volume of *Rome et la conquête du monde méditerranéen* (1978) produced by Claude Nicolet and others in the series "La nouvelle Clio." It is not difficult to predict that these are just the beginnings of his endeavors in these areas.

II

The connection between Vidal-Naquet's contemporary concerns as a Jew of the modern diaspora and his narration of the Jewish war of A.D. 70 takes on a more clearly defined shape in one respect. It is made manifest by the attention he devotes to the ancient diaspora before, during, and after the war of A.D. 70, while stressing (which becomes a variant of the same phenomenon) Josephus's twofold training in rabbinics (Hebrew) and rhetoric (Greek). That these two facts are connected is beyond any dispute. The Jews of the diaspora (at least for the most part) took no part in that war. Later, during the rule of Trajan, they were to throw themselves into a heroic and violent revolt which ended in their total destruction. The Jews of Palestine, on the other hand, seem to have remained uninvolved in that revolt. But the latter, in their turn, found themselves on their own to challenge Hadrian's troops in the Bar Kokhba revolt, the final disaster. As for the historian of the war of A.D. 70, he was a Jew who spoke and initially wrote in Aramaic. It was only after he had received Roman citizenship and settled in Rome that he became with effort a writer in the Greek language. His absorption of Greek modes of thinking indicates his break from Palestinian Jewry. And yet he concurrently evolved an apologia of Judaism which in many ways reflected the situation in the diaspora. It is telling that the *Contra Apionem* is a response to a detractor who was a Greek-speaking Egyptian.

There was no novelty in being a fugitive. Polybius had found himself in the same situation. But, as Vidal-Naquet correctly states, as a fugitive Polybius had to settle accounts with his Achaean compatriots, not with God. Josephus had to justify himself to the God of his fathers. Like Polybius, he wrote contemporary history; but in addition, he wrote about his people's past in defense of his religious tradition. After becoming an exile, Flavius Josephus remained loyal to his God and to his people. His situation, as regards the objective elements in it, was not so unlike that of the Jews of the diaspora who did not fight in the war of A.D. 70 Living dispersed in different linguistic areas, they still remained Jews. Traitor with respect to his comrades-in-arms in Palestine, Josephus went to take refuge among those who had not fought and did not yet know that they were destined to fight.

III

The reason for our speaking of Josephus's isolation should not be attributed to moralistic prejudice. He does not give us any indication of having understood the institution which held the Jews together even before the destruction of the Temple—the synagogue. He demonstrates even less understanding of the apocalyptic fervors of the time to which he was antagonistic. He does not seem to have realized that this apocalyptic fervor involved not only Palestinian revolutionaries, but also extended to the Jews of the diaspora and included groups of Christians. In the end, it subsided in the territory inflamed by hostility to Rome in the provinces. It is at this point in my interpretation that I begin to part company from my friend Vidal-Naquet.

1. The history of the survival of national cultures in the Roman Empire is a history which does not permit generalizations. It includes opposite cases: Greeks who became Romans when Christianized (the designation "Hellene" was reserved for the pagans); Egyptians (or Syrians) who regained the best of their national awareness when their language (Coptic and Syriac respectively) became the language of their religion after their conversion to Christianity. In the Latin West, the old regional cultures seemed to lead a subterranean life until they reemerged (at least, to a certain extent) in Latin or neo-Latin garb after the fall of the Empire in the West.

Even prior to 70, the national life of the Jews was mainly identified with the institutions which were predominantly designated by the Greek word *synagoge*.[3] There were synagogues both in Palestine and the diaspora. As present knowledge stands, we do not know the place and date when synagogues originated (certainly at least from the first century B.C.) and then proliferated wherever Jews lived. In Palestine, as long as the Temple stood, and indeed, as long as the majority of the population remained Jewish, the purpose of the synagogue was not to distinguish Jew from Gentile and thus to preserve the identity of the Jews. But in Palestine, and likewise in the diaspora, the synagogue came to represent the establishment of a cult which was based on the reading and interpretation of the Bible (particularly the Pentateuch). Directly or indirectly, its function was to educate children and adults. It was also an administrative and charitable organization. Each synagogue was set up by private enterprise, which meant that there could be many synagogues in one city. Such a situation did not prevent open collaboration and communication between synagogues. The religious service of the synagogue was such that the biblical text was also made accessible to those who did not know Hebrew. As a consequence there were oral and written translations of the Bible into Greek, Aramaic, and later into Latin—a unique phenomenon in the ancient world. It was in the synagogues that the Jews first became the people of the book. But still a long time was to elapse before they were to accept as their ideal Maimonides' rule that every Jew, rich or poor, young or old, healthy or sick, was duty-bound to assign part of every day until death to the study of the Torah. The synagogue offered the possibility of expression—and to a certain extent also resolution—of the increasing number of economic, social, and specifically religious disputes. As linguistic unity was lost, the synagogue maintained and developed cultic unity. Chaotic conditions would have prevailed in the many synagogues without the presence of authoritative interpreters of the Law: they depended on the rabbinic academies.

To gain awareness of all this, one need go no further than the Gospels, the Acts of the Apostles, and St. Paul. But we learn practically nothing about the synagogue from Josephus. He barely informs us about the custom, introduced by Moses, of studying the Law on the Sabbath (*Antiquitates Judaicae* 16. 43; *Contra Apionem* 2. 175). He never refers to the synagogue as a working institution.

2. Nowadays, it may not be necessary to emphasize the point that the internal social conflicts of the Jewish people in A.D. 70 and thereabouts—so acutely analyzed by Vidal-Naquet—were partly generated and partly confined by the presence of Rome. In this respect, they cannot be dissociated from the situation created by Rome and from the hostility which was consequently aroused throughout the Empire. While exploiting the common provincials and holding them in the greatest contempt, the ruling class singled out a limited number of the rich ones, Romanizing them and gradually allowing them to hold public office. The presence of the Roman authorities sharpened the disputes between rich and poor in the provinces. Nevertheless, they did not totally succeed in winning over the privileged provincials. Plutarch makes a fleeting but revealing allusion to the boots of the Roman soldiers on the heads of the Greeks (*Praecepta gerendae reipublicae* 813 E). It is obviously impossible to isolate the Jewish revolt from those of other provincials. The years 66–70 were a time of general upheaval in the Empire. Yet Josephus does not connect but rather disconnects the events in Palestine from what was happening in the rest of the Empire. More generally, he does not appear to realize that the apocalyptic expectations of certain revolutionary parties in Judaea, which were familiar to him, were also shared by Jews in the diaspora and appropriated by Christian groups. In fact,

their expectations were not so different from those of the provincials who hoped for the return of Nero to combat the tyranny of Rome as avenger of the Eastern and Greek provinces.[4]

More precise information about this state of mind is provided not by Josephus, but from John's Apocalypse. The return of Nero widely awaited in pagan circles is transformed in the Apocalypse into the advent of the anti-Christ. The destruction of Rome, the new Babylon, signifies the advent of the millennium.[5] The Apocalypse gives extreme messianic expression to the feelings of resentment against Rome. It is telling that it was written by a Christian, since Eusebius's tradition tends to dissociate Christians completely from Jews by their refusal to rebel against Rome. The precise dating of the Apocalypse, which Irenaeus had located in the period of Domitian (*Adversus Haereses* 5. 30. 3), is relatively unimportant when compared to its anti-Roman and more specifically anti-Neronian content. However, it should not be forgotten that there are two internal and precise clues which enable us to date the work to A.D. 68–69, i.e., the time of the Jewish rebellion. The book presupposes the existence of the Temple of Jerusalem (11. 1) and predicts (ch. 17) the rule of seven Roman emperors, the last of whom was to rule briefly. Beginning with Caesar, as does Suetonius, the seventh emperor is Galba, who did indeed rule briefly. This cannot be purely coincidental.[6]

Partly political, partly messianic, these expectations were not limited to Judaea or to the year of the four emperors (and that is why the question of the date and place of origin of each apocalyptic document is of limited importance). The extant collection of the Sibylline Books which contains texts purporting to be the prophecies of pagan Sibyls was written outside Palestine by Jews and Christians between the second and the third century A.D. (if not later). The fourth and fifth books are a less obvious but still clear expression of the same state of mind which produced John's Apocalypse. Both books are of Jewish origin. The fifth book contains some Christian interpolations (ll. 68; 256–59), thus proving that a group of Christians had accepted and appropriated the book. The fourth book alludes to the eruption of Vesuvius in A.D. 79, the approximate date of the work. The idea of the succession of the Kingdoms, which first appears in Jewish thought in the Book of Daniel (3–2 c. B.C.),[7] is accepted with modifications in the fourth book. It describes the expectations for the forthcoming end of the fifth Empire (Rome), which is heralded by the rebellion in the East with the return of Nero as the central episode in the event. Although the fifth book appears to have undergone reworking up to the time of Marcus Aurelius, it contains a nucleus which may be dated to A.D. 76.[8] The expectation for the end of the world is explicitly connected with the end of Rome. It is not accidental that the eighth book of the Sibylline Oracles was redacted in the age of Marcus Aurelius—it is a totally Christian text in its present form. The fall of Rome is also anticipated and predicted in this book.

By the time of Marcus Aurelius, the Jews had become enervated by three messianic uprisings, and abandoned, or at least suppressed, their messianic and eschatological hopes which had sustained them in their armed struggle against Rome. On the whole, the rabbis discouraged messianic speculation, especially if it meant revolutionary activity. Their thought is expressed in the *Mishnah* and *Tosefta*, the great legal compilations of the third century A.D. After A.D. 130 there was a diminution in Jewish production of purely apocalyptic works. (There are, however, later texts: chapters 15–16 of II Esdras, for example, which is also called V Esdras, are often dated to about A.D. 270 by modern scholars.) What was already written gradually passed into Christian hands. Groups of medieval Christians ensured the survival of these works of Jewish origin. Josephus had not anticipated that the rabbis, who were not historians by profession, would condemn this literature. He disregarded it because he did not appreciate its importance.

IV

It is now our task to elucidate more precisely the meaning of Josephus's twofold blindness about the synagogue and the widespread Jewish and Christian apocalyptic trends of his time.

Of course, Josephus had to justify himself: he was a fugitive. However, he applied himself not without serious commitment to the writing of historical works which were constructed with due attention to detail. The maturing process took place slowly as he wrote on the borders of two cultures. He wrote his works in Greek with particular consideration for his upper-class Greco-Roman readers; but he could not avoid bearing in mind (more than he would like to claim) his Jewish readers who could understand Greek. The fact that he wrote in Greek—as Vidal-Naquet does not fail to point out—implies that he accepted the criteria of exposition and explication inherent in Greek historiography. He characterizes the Jewish sects in Greek fashion: the main features are described with an abundant use of rhetorical modes which could not be paralleled in the terse style of contemporary Hebrew or Aramaic. Linguistic reasons alone militated against the use of Greek historical prose to express either apocalyptic emotions or, on the other hand, the customary activities of synagogue-goers. Outside historiography it was only an original artist who succeeded in rendering apocalyptic emotions in Greek, precisely because he was involved in them—John, the author of the Apocalypse; and this was at the expense of tortuous grammar and syntax.[9] Writing in historical prose is "Luke" of the Acts of the Apostles, who tells us something about the synagogues and the churches which derived from them; but this was only achieved through the creation of a new type of narrative which could adequately describe the revolutionary situation he wished to portray. In Josephus's case, the adoption of Greek meant the reverse. It implied that Judaism, just as he conceived it, should ideally exist within the bounds of the Greco-Roman civilization. But the apocalypse and the synagogue are alien to the model of Judaism which rightly or wrongly he derived from the Bible, from a few other documents, and from his own experience and which he then presented to his Gentile or, if Jews, Hellenized Jewish readers.

Holding the upper classes of his people responsible for the disaster (e.g., *Ant.* 1. 23), Flavius Josephus has little intention of secularizing his own judgmental categories. True, he refuses to share the messianic hopes which sustained the fighters. Yet Josephus does not express just a vague loyalty for his ancestral religion (which he states in *Ant.* 3. 317–22 and elsewhere), but goes further in that he is convinced that the prophets of the past had already predicted the Roman dominion and the limits of its duration. Theoretically, there is a large area of agreement between him and his coreligionists. Josephus acknowledges that the prophecy concerning Israel included the fate of the Roman Empire. Predicted were both its present successes and its downfall in the future. The downfall was inevitable because it was the condition or one of the conditions required for the establishment of the reign of the Messiah. For the Jew, and likewise for the Christian, there could be no "Roma aeterna." Yet he, Flavius Josephus, preferred to emphasize what had already come true, i.e., the dominion of Rome, and to play down that which was still undivulged because it belonged to the future. His distrust of the apocalyptic fervors of the Zealots combined to an unquantifiable extent with the prudence of one who was under surveillance. On the one hand, he explicitly tells us that Roman rule had been predicted by Jeremiah, Ezekiel, and Daniel (*Ant.* 10. 79; 10. 276) as well as, apparently, by the much earlier Azariah (*Ant.* 8. 294–96; cf. II Chron. 15 : 1). On the other hand, he suppresses certain points in Daniel's prophecy. He omits the vision of the beasts, i.e., the vision of the empires, which is described in chapter 7 of Daniel. Its reference to Rome is actually attributed to God in a remarkable passage in II Esdras 12. 1off. (an apocalyptic work from the end of the first century A.D.). For the same reason and betraying obvious embarrassment, Josephus refuses to explain the prophecy of the divine stone which shatters the statue of the empires (Daniel 2 : 34). He knew that it had been reinterpreted as a prediction of the fall of Rome (*Ant.* 10. 210).[10]

He follows the same procedure when speaking of Alexander the Great. In his visit to Jerusalem, Alexander enters the Temple and consults the Book of Daniel. The information he gathers is sufficient to apprise him of his impending victory over the Persians (*Ant.* 11. 337), but does not go as far as telling him of the destruction in the more remote future of the Empire which he had founded.[11] In fact, Josephus's Hebrew prophets predominantly seem to promise the Empire to non-Jewish rulers. Josephus manages to make some of his own additions to the account of Cyrus, who is explicitly mentioned in the prophecy of Isaiah. He says that Cyrus himself had read the prophecy two hundred and ten years after it had been pronounced (*Ant.* 11. 5) and was inspired to act in accordance with its provisions.

Josephus preserves the prophetic component of the biblical

books. At the same time, he divests them of any subversive tendency by showing that the foreign monarchs appeared to be satisfied with them. Daniel was one of his favorite seers of the past (*Ant.* 10. 267); he was a prophet of good tidings and accurate in his chronology. It is impossible to suppress the feeling that somewhere in his conscience Josephus was equating himself with Daniel. He is convinced of his own prophetic qualities and of his ability to interpret dreams. He had demonstrated it not only in his prediction of Vespasian's enthronement (*Bellum Judaicum* 3. 400–8), but also at the very moment of betraying his own compatriots (3. 351–54). He ascribes the gift of prophecy to the Pharisee sect to which he had belonged (*Ant.* 17. 43) and to certain individual Pharisees (*Ant.* 15. 3). Furthermore, he claims to be a descendant on his mother's side of John Hyrcanus the Hasmonean who had possessed the gift of the prophetic spirit (*Ant.* 13. 299; *Bellum* 1. 68).

Confident in his own prophetic gifts, he predicted the victory of the Romans, and on these grounds he justifies his own decision not to commit suicide and to give himself up. As Vidal-Naquet observes, Josephus's approach was the antithesis of that which he ascribes to the leader of the defenders of Masada, who in his discourse advises resistance and suicide (*Bellum* 7. 320–88). However, it is perhaps only an arbitrary use of language, if, as does Vidal-Naquet, one explains Eleazar's discourse as an apocalypse which has no outlet, an apocalypse of death. Eleazar's discourse has nothing in common, neither in its form nor in its content, with an apocalypse. It is an invitation to suicide based on arguments which are more understandable to a Greco-Roman than to a Jew. In fact, in his presentation of the discourse, Josephus implies that Eleazar had chosen suicide because he recognized that the immediate apocalyptic expectations had failed.

Fortified by his prophetic legacy, Josephus could predict the future and survive. In so doing he was somehow pronouncing his loyalty to the God of his fathers and to the law of the Bible. But he was divorced from the two vital currents in the Judaism of his time, the apocalypse and the synagogue. To us, these appear to be two counterflowing currents, and so they were from the second century onward. In the first century, however, they often converged and enriched each other. The same thing happened in primitive Christianity, which derived both its eschatology and its ecclesiastical organization from Judaism. As a result, Josephus's Judaism was colorless, not false and not trivial, but rhetorical, generic, and rather unreal.[12] There are many superficial similarities with the religious and practical attitudes of the group of rabbis who under the guidance of Johanan ben Zakkai tried to rehabilitate the structures of the Jewish people after the disaster of 70. The rabbis, too, repressed their apocalyptic hopes, emphasized the exemplary nature of the biblical narrative, and sought to come to an agreement with the Romans and win their support. In his own way, Johanan ben Zakkai was a fugitive. It may be telling that rabbinic tradition attributes to him the prophecy of Vespasian's enthronement which Flavius Josephus (corroborated by Suetonius, *Vesp.* 5) had attributed to himself.[13] But the similarities remain on the surface. Josephus knows nothing of the joy in the Law, the sense of the disciplined life of the community, the concern and love for the younger generations, and trust in God. These, combined with a considerable degree of intellectual freedom, juridical competence, and obsession with the laws of purity, were the characteristic features of the rabbis who emerged as leaders of a nation without a state, without land, and without linguistic unity.

Even before Greek, the language in which Josephus wrote, had become obsolete as a Jewish cultural language, his works had already ceased to interest his coreligionists.[14] In the Middle Ages, the resumption of contact between the Jews and their historian was through the medium of reworkings which left little of the original spirit of the works. The authentic text was to be preserved by Christians and used by them as an independent witness of the downfall of the old Israel in defense of the new. It was a "testimonium flavianum" rather more ample and certainly more authentic than the short passage mentioning Jesus (*Ant.* 18. 63–64) for which the designation is usually reserved.[15]

8

Some Preliminary Remarks
on the "Religious Opposition"
to the Roman Empire

I

FOR MY GENERATION two books, both in German, and both re-
acting to the Fascist-Nazi worldview, determined the interest in
the religious situation of the Roman Empire: H. Fuchs, *Der
geistige Widerstand gegen Rom in der antiken Welt*, 1938, and
E. Peterson, *Der Monotheismus als politisches Problem*, 1935.
After the Second World War, with other preoccupations, different
approaches prevailed. An attempt to revive Mommsen's legal approach to the problem of persecutions was made by Hugh Last,
but, profound as it was, it had little appeal in the circumstances.
Typically, race was discussed by A. N. Sherwin-White, Last's pupil, in his *Racial Prejudice in Imperial Rome*, 1967. W. Den Boer
could easily object in his review of Sherwin-White (*Classical
Journal*, January 1970) that there was no conscious racism in the
Roman Empire. More in keeping with the new mood has been the
evaluation of the Roman State from the point of view of Christian
theology, as for instance in the book by Oscar Cullmann, *Der
Staat im Neuen Testament*, 1955; of the resistance of the natives
in the provinces (for instance *La résistance africaine à la ro-
manisation* by M. Benabou, 1976); and of the relation between

An address delivered at the Fondation Hardt, Geneva, in October 1986 [and published in *Entretiens* Tome XXXIII (1986), Fondation Hardt, Vandoeuvres-Genève,
1987, pp. 103–133].

imperial cult and the loyalty of Roman subjects, an item which received much attention in the 1972 Entretiens of the Fondation Hardt on *Le Culte des Souverains*. In 1966 Ramsay MacMullen produced what was perhaps the first attempt to put together these postwar tendencies in his book *Enemies of the Roman Order*. It remains a remarkable book. But other lines of research, at first sight unconcerned with the opposition to the Roman Empire as such, were destined to be of great influence on this very question of the opposition to the Roman Empire. I allude to the studies on the relations between Jews and Christians in the Empire. One can see how the two lines of research—the relations between Jews and Christians and the relations between them and the Roman state—increasingly tended to converge if one compares Marcel Simon's *Verus Israel* of 1948 with W. H. C. Frend's *Martyrdom and Persecution in the Early Church*, 1965. More recent products of the same trend are, for instance, Johann Maier, *Jüdische Auseinandersetzung mit dem Christentum in der Antike* and David Rokeah, *Jews, Pagans and Christians in Conflict*, both 1982; Günter Stemberger, *Die römische Herrschaft im Urteil der Juden*, 1983; R. L. Wilken, *The Christians as the Romans Saw Them*, 1984—to make an arbitrary selection among a vast literature.

I have no intention to climb this mountain of paper on the present occasion. There are some preliminary difficulties to sort out about the evidence we have received from antiquity. Striking as the Roman toleration of foreign cults was, it never amounted, of course, to an ancient equivalent of the modern idea of separation between state and church. On the other hand, our knowledge of what Celts, Pannonians, Punics, Egyptians, etc., thought of the Roman treatment of their native cults is very vague and not comparable with what we know about the Jewish and Christian reactions to the Roman policies. I should like to illustrate three elementary points: first, the ambiguities inherent in the Roman attitude to tolerance; second, our profound ignorance of what the Druids, the worshipers of Iuno Caelestis, and the Egyptian priests and seers—to take three examples—thought about the behavior of the Roman authorities; and third, the complexities of the Jewish and Christian attitudes to the Roman State, which are the only ones we can really analyze.

II

We of course have to make some distinction between opposition to Rome by independent states and opposition to the Roman government by the subjects of the Roman State—provincials or otherwise. Those who fought against Rome to preserve their independence at best knew the Roman government from afar: they were not, or not yet, enmeshed in the peculiarities of Roman State religion. Though it may be somewhat crude to draw a line between the Druids before Caesar's conquest of Gaul and the Druids after it, we have to take into consideration the bilateral relation between subjects and sovereigns which exists after any conquest. But another distinction has to be considered. Almost invariably the Greeks of Greece felt that their disputes with Macedonian, and later with Roman, power were to be conducted as well as they could in terms of prudence, shrewdness, and patience: these were disputes between men, not between gods. The Greeks after all had Demosthenes behind them and Polybius with them. Nobody, to my knowledge, has so far commented on the paradox that Demosthenes should have become a model to Roman politicians precisely in the century in which he was being read by the Greeks who wanted to learn from him how to resist the Romans. In the East it was different. We all know the "strange stories" told by Phlegon of Tralles, a freedman of the Emperor Hadrian, about the oracles uttered by the Roman general Publius during the war between Antiochus III and the Romans. Though I was not persuaded by Jörg-Dieter Gauger in his very acute article in *Chiron*, 10, 1980, 225–63 that these oracles belong to the time of Mithridates Eupator, I have no difficulty in believing that such oracles were reused when Mithridates marched from Asia to Greece, and Athens opened her gates to him. We are not surprised either that Eunus, the organizer of the first slave war in 135–131 B.C., relied on the help of the Syrian goddess and displayed the arts of prophecy and wonder—working, we expect, from a desperate charismatic leader. The source of Diodorus, probably Posidonius, considered him a charlatan.

But we have also to admit that between 70 and 20 B.C. the prophets of doom seem to have prospered everywhere within the Roman Empire. Etruscan prophets at the end of the saeculum encouraged the Catilinarians (Cicero *In Catilinam* 3. 9, 19). Sallust, or rather the author of the second letter to Caesar, envisaged the possibility of the end of Rome, and of course Horace foresaw the bones of Romulus being scattered about the Forum and a journey for the reprieved toward the Island of the Blessed. Caesar was suspected of having entertained the notion of abandoning Rome, and Livy must have remembered something like that when he showed Camillus refusing to move away from Rome after the Gallic disaster (5. 49). No doubt people felt that there were enemies of the Empire other than the visible ones beyond the borders. No wonder. Pompey introduced Judaea into the Empire; Caesar annexed Gaul; Octavian made Egypt a province. These were regions where prophets and visionaries prospered.

III

Such as they were in the first century B.C. and would go on being for some centuries afterward, the members of the ruling class of Rome were ready to transact business with people who worshiped different gods and were used to different political traditions. Roman polytheism could adapt itself to, and indeed merge with, what we may call the provincial traditions. Greek and Roman gods became practically identical. Celtic, Semitic, Pannonian, and African gods were either assimilated to Greco-Roman gods or accepted as respectable gods in their own right to an extent which is no less stupendous for being obvious. The lack of a priestly class in what Dumézil would like us to consider a trifunctional society gave a secular tone to the whole of private life; religious instruction was not a major item of Roman education to anyone. But there was another side to Roman tolerance. The ordinary activities of the Roman authorities both in Italy and in the provinces implied continuous attention to the approval of the gods and continuous participation of the gods in the public life of the Romans. The question of believing was seldom made explicit, but the question of performing correctly was ever present and committed the ruling class to the preservation of the religious tradition. Nor was that all. The Roman magistrates, the Roman Senate, and, above all, the emperors were qualified to decide who was an enemy of the Roman State and to take consequent action. The tolerant could turn intolerant with little warning. In the second century A.D., we are told by Ulpian, there were laws condemning to death those who consulted astrologers about the health, that is, the expectation of life, of the emperors (*Collatio Legum Mosaicarum et Romanarum* 15. 2. 2). As Juvenal observed (6. 560), no mathematicus can claim true inspiration without being condemned. The Roman authorities either centrally or peripherally could take steps which, to say the least, were unexpected. If we today are puzzled by the contrast between the easygoing tolerance of Roman society at large and the harshness of some Roman governmental actions, one wonders what the persons involved and affected thought.

Our difficulty in assessing the position of the Druids in the first century A.D. is partly due to this conflict in Roman attitudes and partly to the absence of texts explaining the Druidic point of view. It is perhaps worth adding that even the Roman point of view is not so easy to gather from the extant sources.

Caesar, who knew something about religion, is remarkably silent about the part of religion in the resistance of the Celts against himself. That Augustus prohibited the participation of Roman citizens in the Druidic "religion" (Suetonius *Divus Claudius* 25. 5), that Tiberius did away with the Druids (Pliny *Naturalis Historia* 30. 4. 13), and that Claudius confirmed the abolition of Druidic rituals are stated in our sources. It is also implied in these sources that the Roman government strongly objected to the human sacrifices which were part of the Druidic religion. Success in the abolition of human sacrifices is claimed by Strabo under Tiberius (Strabo IV. 4. 5, p. 198) and by Pomponius Mela (III. 18) under Claudius. What our sources forget to tell us is whether the problem of human sacrifices was exclusively Druidic or Celtic. Prohibition of human sacrifices had apparently become law in Rome by a *senatus consultum* of 97 B.C. (Pliny *N.H.* 30. 3. 12). Even after that date we hear of several episodes of human sacrifices in Italy during the civil wars. We remember that in 46 B.C., according to Dio Cassius (43. 24. 4), two enemies of Caesar were sacrificed by the pontiffs and the Flamen Martialis in Campus Martius, and their heads were hung from the Regia. There may also be some reality in other stories of which S. Weinstock provides a list in his *Divus Julius*, p. 399. The minimum we can ask is whether the human sacrifices were an exclusive feature of the Druidic rituals. The role of the Druids as opponents of Rome is unclear. Mariccus, the "adsertor Galliarum et deus" of A.D. 69, is implicitly excluded from the Druidic aristocracy by Tacitus when he calls him "e plebe Boiorum" (*Historiae* 2. 61). In the story of the conquest of Britain, Tacitus confines the Druids to the episode of the conquest of Mona (*Annales* 14. 30). Only about the fire of the Capitolium in 69 does he explicitly state that it was interpreted by the Druids as a sign of the transition of power to the transalpine nations: "possessionem rerum humanarum Transalpinis gentibus portendi superstitione vana Druidae canebant" (Tac. *Hist.* 4. 54). It is not surprising that three recent essays on the Druids—by Cesare Letta in *Rivista Storica Italiana*, 1984; Giuseppe Zecchini, *I Druidi*, 1984; and M. Clavel-Lévêque, *Dialogues d'histoire ancienne*, 1985—reach different conclusions from the same evidence; more particularly, while Letta minimizes the political repression of the Druids by the Romans, Zecchini ascribes a part to the Druids in the Imperium Galliarum. The role of prophetess is better established for A.D. 70 by the story of Veleda. That she sooner or later became a prisoner of the Romans is said by Statius, *Silvae* I. 4. 90: "captivaeque preces Veledae"; but I still do not know what to do with the inscription of Veleda published by M. Guarducci in *Rend. Pont.* 21, 1945–46, 163–76 (cf. *ib.* 25–26, 1949–1951, 75–87, and G. Walser, *P.-W.* s.v. Veleda).

When we hear again of Druids, and indeed for the first time of female Druids, "dryades," in the fourth century in the *Historia Augusta* (with references to previous centuries) and in Ausonius, they operate inside Roman society and are no longer guilty of human sacrifices. But less than linear development is again suggested by Nennius's *Historia Brittonum* with its reference to "magi" and to at least one human sacrifice under Vortigern in the middle of the fifth century. If Nennius's magi are Druids, some tradition of human sacrifice had survived with them to grace the regime of Vortigern whom J. N. L. Myres in an impressive article in *Journal of Roman Studies* 50, 1960, called a "Pelagian tyrannus" (p. 35). What a fascinating end for the supporters of independent Britain—the alliance between the followers of the Briton Pelagius and of the Druids.

IV

The changing position of the Druids in relation to Rome in Celtic territory could no doubt be matched by similar oscillations in other provinces—if we only knew. Let us consider briefly Dea Caelestis, who used to be Tanit in the good old days in which Carthage was powerful and, maybe, friendly to the Romans. There are hints in our tradition that the Romans, in conformity with their customs, evoked Tanit before destroying Carthage (Macrobius, *Saturnalia* 3. 9. 7). But Tanit as Dea Caelestis had been back in her old city since at least 122 B.C. when the Colonia Iunonia was planted in the place of Carthage. Locally the goddess was protected and even privileged by the Romans. According to a well-known Regula by Ulpian "deos heredes instituere non possumus praeter. . . . Caelestem Salinensem Carthagini" (22. 6). In the third century the empress Julia Domna was identified with Caelestis in an inscription of Magontiacum (*CIL*, 13. 6171); in 221 Dea Caelestis was given a place in Rome together with Sol Invictus by Elagabalus (Herodianus 5. 6. 4), which was apparently also a good occasion for transferring to Rome the Carthaginian treasure of the goddess. She survived Elagabalus, for she had a temple on the Capitol in Rome from at least A.D. 259 (Dessau, *ILS* 4438; M. Guarducci, *Bull. Com. Arch.* 72, 1946–1948, 11–25). We are assured by the *Historia Augusta* that Roman governors of Africa consulted the goddess regularly (Macrob. 3. 1). But here trouble begins. First, because in general we do not know what value to attribute to such statements of the *Historia Augusta* (cf. T. D. Barnes, *Journal of Theological Studies* 21, 1970, 96–104). Secondly, and more specifically, because a statement in the life of Pertinax has been interpreted to imply that Pertinax suppressed rebellions in Africa which had been provoked by prophecies issued by the temple of Caelestis (4. 1). In the late second century A.D., the cult of Caelestis would have been hostile to the Roman government. I do not intend here to go into the text, which is probably corrupt: "multas seditiones perpessus dicitur vaticinationibus earum quae de templo Caelestis emergunt." I shall only add that I do not feel entitled to follow G. C. Picard in his acute but daring emendation *canum* instead of *earum*, founded on the comparison with other texts (cf. *Revue de l'histoire des religions* 155, 1959, 41–62). What matters to me is that we can never be certain that these provincial cults could not, on certain occasions, and almost unexpectedly, turn into centers of dissatisfaction and protest against Rome.

My third case concerns Egypt. The Potter's Oracle is much better known since the publication of *Pap. Oxyrhynchus* 2332 and its republication by L. Koonen in *Zeitschr. f. Papyrologie und Epigraphik* 2, 1968, 178–209 (an appendix *ib.* 13, 1974, 313–14). The potter's prophecy is addressed to King Amenophis and presents itself as a Greek translation from an Egyptian original; but it seems doubtful whether there ever was an Egyptian original. The potter himself was probably an incarnation of the potter-god Chnum. The oracle, as we have it, presupposes the existence of the city of Alexandria and the cult of Serapis. It is anti-Greek and seems to foresee, and to hope for, the dissolution of Greek rule through internal struggles. Certain indications in the text seem to allude more precisely to events of the second century B.C., such as Antiochus IV's invasion of Egypt about 170–168 and the troubles with the natives of about 131–127 under Ptolemy Euergetes II. In any case, the return of a previous king, presumably a native, is promised as a gift by the sun-god Re. The Potter's Oracle has reached us in different versions and was still read in Roman imperial times. If so, it must have acquired an anti-Roman connotation. There can be no doubt about the anti-imperial bias of another text which is closely connected with, and possibly inspired by, the Potter's Oracle, namely the apocalyptic section of the so-called *Asclepius* in the *Corpus Hermeticum*. As is well known, the *Asclepius* in its original Greek form was read by Lactantius: it must be earlier than the fourth century A.D. The Latin and Coptic translations of the apocalyptic section, which alone preserve for us the text in full, have some allusions to religious persecutions of pagans which may have been interpolated after Lactantius and before St. Augustine. If we accept chapter 27 of the

Asclepius as the conclusive part of this Apocalypse, the demi-urgos is expected to restore to power the ancient Egyptian gods who had retired to a Libyan mountain while the foreigners ruled Egypt. Jewish apocalyptic influences, perhaps transmitted by Sibylline texts, combine with the tradition of Egyptian prophecy to convey an image of present desecration by barbarians which the "god first in power and demiurgos of one god" (deus pri-mipotens et unius gubernator dei) will paradoxically heal by re-storing the ancient gods and collecting all the right people of the world in a sort of Egyptian counterpart to Messianic Jerusalem.

The traffic between Jewish apocalyptic and Egyptian prophecy was perhaps not one way only. It has been suggested that the Lamb of St. John's Revelation has a predecessor in the Lamb which gives its name to another Egyptian oracle. The surviving text of the Lamb's Oracle is dated under Augustus (A.D. 4/5) but refers to the reign of King Bocchoris of the XXIV dynasty (about 715 B.C.). The Lamb announces that a disaster will break over Egypt after nine hundred years, and it also pronounces that ultimately God will care again for the Egyptians and will give them back the sa-cred objects which the Assyrians had taken away. The historical allusions may not be too clear, and the nine hundred years may just be a round figure. I am also doubtful about the connection between the Egyptian Lamb and St. John's Lamb. But it seems be-yond doubt that in the Lamb's prophecy the Assyrians symbolize all the foreign invaders—and therefore also the Romans. We are reminded of the symbolic value of the Assyrians in the Books of Judith and Tobit.

We have therefore at least three texts of religious inspiration which circulated in Egypt during the Empire and expressed op-position to foreigners. Do they, however, really imply definite hos-tility to the Roman Empire as such? Two texts, the Potter's Oracle and the Lamb's Oracle, may simply transmit the echo of previous conflicts. The text which is in fact rooted in the conditions of the imperial age is the *Asclepius*. Before the publication of the Coptic version, which happened only in 1971 (M. Krause and P. Labib, *Gnostische und hermetische Schriften aus Codex II und Codex VI*, 1971, 187–206; cf. *The Nag Hammadi Library in English*, 1977, 300–307), scholars tended to take the Latin version as an interpolated text suggested by the Christian persecutions of pagans in Egypt in the fourth century. An acute judge like Professor A. S. Ferguson had, however, argued in 1936 for a date of this Apocalypse under Trajan or Hadrian and had connected it with the great uprising of the Jews: the text would originally have been not against the Christian emperors, but against the Jewish rebels. There is indeed a fragment of an anti-Jewish prophecy preserved by *Pap. Soc. It.* 982 (*Corp. Pap. Jud.* 520; third cent.). But the text of the *Asclepius*, which in the Coptic version definitely says that the "Egyptians will be prohibited from worshiping God," does not seem to me to fit into the context of the Jewish rebellion under Trajan. I cannot visualize the situation which the author of the original Greek text, which is lost, must have had in mind. If the Coptic and the Latin versions of the apocalyptic section of the *Asclepius* allude to a pre-Christian situation, I am also unable to guess what it was. I can only say that I do not see in the extant texts an unambiguous protest against Roman rule in Egypt. I still suspect with all reservations that the Coptic and Latin versions of the *Asclepius* are anti-Christian.

V

When we pass from such fragmentary information to the massive evidence about Jews and Christians, we may well hope to be on more solid ground. Perhaps we are, but qualifications are required. If we look at the legal aspects of the position of the Jews within the Roman Empire before its Christianization, we are struck by the large number of texts which allow the Jews to keep up their cult and to regulate their lives in the places of their residence. Some of the *Acts of the Alexandrian Martyrs* accuse Roman emperors like Hadrian and Commodus of favoring the Jews. For most of the time and the places, the pagan Roman State recognized the right of the Jews to live as Jews and did not curtail their movements. Imperial cult (except under Gaius) was no serious problem. Except in times of rebellion (that is, of war), the expulsions of Jews from Rome and other cities had to be justified in ordinary terms of public order: they were not frequent, though, like many other administrative measures of the Roman government in religious matters, both provocative and inane. The real moments of persecution and intolerance toward the Jews were subsequent to or connected with the great rebellions from Nero to Hadrian. This of course must not be confused with the widespread dislike of Jews among the educated and the uneducated, though the memory of the Jewish rebellions was used by hostile circles for anti-Jewish demonstrations, such as the annual festival still celebrated at Oxyrhynchus in the year 199 to commemorate the Roman repression of the Jewish rebellion of 116 (*Corp. Pap. Jud.* 450) or the ban of the Jews from Cyprus on the same pretext (Dio Cassius 68. 32). We are therefore brought back to the three Jewish rebellions as the main events in the relation between Jews and pagans. How can we explain them?

We have no ancient extended account of the two rebellions under Trajan and Hadrian. The two versions we have of the rebellion of A.D. 66–70 which led to the destruction of the Temple do not make it easy for us to assess the part played by religious convictions and expectations in this rebellion. Neither Tacitus, who speaks, so to say, for the Roman Empire, nor Josephus, who has a Jewish point of view, presents a coherent account of what happened.

It is characteristic of Tacitus, as has long been recognized, that notwithstanding his total dislike of the Jews, he is basically inclined to think that they were provoked to rebellion by the errors and misbehavior of the Roman governors: "duravit tamen patientia Iudaeis usque ad Gessium Florum" (*Hist.* 5. 10. 1). Nor is Tacitus the man to speak without some element of sympathy about people who refuse to put up statues in their towns either to their own kings or to Roman Caesars: "non regibus haec adulatio, non Caesaribus honor." Tacitus is well aware of the part played by prophecy in the rebellion of a "gens superstitioni obnoxia religionibus adversa," and though he does not make it explicit may well consider an aspect of this "superstitio" the "maior vitae metus quam mortis" of such men and women. But it is not an obvious conclusion that Tacitus makes the rebellion of 66–70 a simple consequence of the Jewish "superstitio." Tacitus is far more aware than Josephus of the general unrest in the Empire in the last years of Nero (*Hist.* 4. 3. 3). He sees the crisis of the Roman Empire more clearly than the Jewish episode of it.

For different reasons, the religious component of the Jewish rebellion is left undefined in our most important source, Flavius Josephus. Josephus speaks for himself alone. This is true in the deeper sense, to which I shall return, that the Jews who survived the destruction of the Temple without passing over to the Roman side apparently ceased to write history. But even on a superficial level we have the paradox of a Josephus in conflict with Justus of Tiberias, though they shared full acceptance of the Roman victory. We should like to know why Justus apparently kept the text of his history of the Jewish war in his drawer for twenty years before publishing it. It is no use speculating on the precise relation between a work which is lost and a work which is extant, but we are confirmed by Justus in our impression that Josephus spoke only for himself. Josephus was obviously determined to show that there was no basic incompatibility between the Jewish religion and the Roman Empire. He plays down the apocalyptic expectations among the Jews. He even avoids talking, apropos of Daniel, of the fourth and last kingdom. He must have been aware of its identification with Rome, which we find for instance in the almost contemporary IV Ezra (12:11). The speech which Josephus attributes to Agrippa II (*Bellum* 2. 345–401) explains why the Jews should accept Roman rule. As Emilio Gabba rightly observed (*Riv. Stor. dell'Ant.* 6–7, 1976–1977, 189–94), Josephus claims that King Agrippa read and approved his account of the war (*Vita* 364–67). He must have identified himself with Agrippa's speeches. It is therefore important that Josephus should feel obliged to recognize at least one religious element in the Jewish rebellion against the Romans. He states that the followers of Judah the Galilean, the future "sicarii," were committed to the principle that God, and nobody else, was their ruler (*Bellum* 2. 118). We need go no further, and we can leave aside all the questions concerning the relations between "sicarii" and Zealots. What the interpreters of Josephus must not forget is that Josephus was never of one mind. He wrote his *Bellum* in order to explain that the catastrophic conclusion of the rebellion brought about the elimination of the bad Jews. But as his ambiguous attitude to the *sicarii*, confirmed by the speeches he attributes to their leader in Masada, shows, there was another Josephus in Josephus. The other Josephus in Josephus would perhaps have liked to have died in Masada.

The evidence about the rebellions under Trajan and Hadrian is not such as to shed much light on this religious side. The new letters of Bar Kokhba or Bar Chosiba show the ritual concerns of the rebels, but do not say much about their religious motivations. At most the usage of the word "brothers" in the letters may indicate that the fighters considered themselves members of a religious community. Later texts may perhaps suggest something more specific. The notion that Edom is Rome and therefore that Edom and Israel are brothers-enemies seems to have developed in the generation of the Bar Kokhba rebellion and more precisely in Rabbi Akiba's circle. It was obviously not meant to express sympathy for Rome. A good analysis of this identification was given recently by Mireille Hadas-Lebel in *Rev. Hist. Rel.* 201, 1984. Most of the Talmudic texts about Edom are anti-Roman.

On the other hand, the failure of the rebellions undoubtedly brought about some changes in attitude on the Jewish side. In one passage of uncertain date in *Midrash Rabbah* of Genesis 9:15 (9:13 in the English Soncino translation), the earthly kingdom is said to be very good because it exacts justice for men: the passage seems to include a pun between Adam (man) and Edom; in any case it alludes to Rome. More significant are the dialogues between Jewish sages and Roman dignitaries studied in a well-known paper by Moshe David Herr (*Scripta Hierosolymitana* 22, 1971). These dialogues present Jewish sages, especially of the second and third centuries, engaged in discussions with Roman aristocrats, both men and women, and even with emperors. The question whether any of these conversations ever happened cannot be answered with certainty. What matters is that they were considered possible and that women are made to take part in them: the interest of women in philosophic and religious controversies is especially well documented for the second and third centuries. The tone is often friendly, and one Roman senator is presented as a proselyte who gave his life to save the Jewish people from a hostile decree of the Senate (*Deuter. Rabbah* 2. 24). The decline of militancy and a certain effort to adapt oneself to a situation in which the Jewish diaspora counted at least as much as the survivors in Palestine are altogether clear. Most of the rabbis became suspicious of apocalyptic speculations and even said that although the Messiah was sure to come in the future, they would not like to be present at his arrival (T. Bab. *Sanhedrin* 98a). There is also less in the Talmudic sources against the imperial cult than we would expect. The issue does not seem to be vital for the present. In the *Mekhilta de-Rabbi Ishmael*, tractate *Shirata*, chapter 8 (II, 61, ed. J. Lauterbach), Pharaoh, Sennacherib, Nebuchadnezzar, and the prince of Tyre call themselves gods. There may be prudence in avoiding any mention of the Roman emperor, but the tone is academic. We must rather remember that most of the rabbinic sayings were put together in the fourth century or later, when the imperial cult was less and less a burning issue. We would like to have the Sayings of the Sages in the form in which they were uttered, instead of the form in which they were later edited. Yet the general impression is one of reduced tension between Jews and Empire in the third century.

VI

One suspects that these attempts at a rapprochement are not unconnected with the alliance which the Christians assumed to exist between Jews and pagans in denouncing the Christians. We shall never know how much of these accusations by Christian writers against the Jews is true; but the mere fact that these accusations were uttered contributed to the atmosphere (see for instance Hippolytus *In Daniel* 1. 15. 2). In any case, the Christianization of the Empire by Constantine and his successors forced a rapprochement between Jews and pagans and even between Jews and Christian heretics. I think that Lellia Ruggini was right in recognizing a sign of this rapprochement in the fourth-century compilation of the *Collatio Legum Mosaicarum et Romanarum*. Edoardo Volterra had already made it obvious that this text was of Jewish, not Christian, origin. Lellia Ruggini has now pointed out (*Italia Judaica*, 1983, 38–65) that in creating a sort of concordance between Biblical Law and Roman Law the *Collatio* was in fact trying to refute the Christian accusation that the Jews were hostile to Roman Law. We must remember that this opinion, expressed by St. Ambrose and St. John Chrysostom, has literally been codified by Theodosius II when he calls the Jews "Romanis legibus inimici" (*Nov. Theodos.* 3. 2 of A.D. 438). The decision of the Emperor Julian to rebuild the Temple of Jerusalem was the main consequence of this convergence of Jewish and pagan interests. The failure of Julian made the position of the Jews even more uncomfortable. The Jews had at least one advantage over the Christians in dealing with the pagans. They were not so certain of having an exclusive right to salvation. In rabbinic circles there was much weight of opinion in favor of Joshua ben Hananiah's dictum: "there are righteous men among the nations who have a share in the World to come" (*Tosefta, Sanhedrin* 13. 2; cf. *Sifra, Ahare Mot* 13. 13 [12] and E. E. Urbach, *Sages*, 1975, 932; *T. B. Baba Kamma* 38a).

I shall conclude this section on the Jews with a text which has been attributed to a Jew and would express anti-Roman feelings. M. Guarducci has the great merit of having published twice a curious "tabula defixionis," first in *Bull. Com. Arch.* 74, 1951–1952, 57–70, then in *Rend. Linc.* 8, 24, 1969, 275–83. The text is exceptional insofar as the writer curses not only the doctor who killed his brother, but also the Italian land and Rome which he intends to leave soon in order to return to his own country. Guarducci thought that the writer was a Jew full of hatred for Rome. J. and L. Robert were quick to notice in "Bull. Épigr.," *Rev. Ét. Gr.* 84, 1971, 535–36 that there was nothing Jewish in the text. People cursing their doctors, Rome, and Italy before returning to their native land must have been many and varied.

VII

What exactly caused the first persecutions of the Christians, how they were legally justified, and how the Christians came to be distinguished from Jews "impulsore Chresto assidue tumultuantis" (Suetonius *Divus Claudius* 25,4) are questions into which I do not intend to go. According to Luke 22 : 36, Jesus himself in the decisive moment advised his disciples to buy swords, and we are still discussing the precise meaning of this advice. The Revelation of St. John reflects some of the immediate apocalyptic expectations. The text presupposes the existence (albeit a precarious existence) of the Temple in Jerusalem and therefore is likely to have been written about A.D. 69–70, whatever may have been the reasons of Irenaeus for thinking otherwise. The relation of the preliminary letters to the Churches of Asia to the main text of Revelation may be doubtful, but the fact that the text was at a certain point so precisely addressed indicates the extent and publicity of such apocalyptic emotions.

We shall only remind ourselves of the opinion voiced by Celsus (ap. Origen Contra Celsum 8. 17) that the circumstance that the Christians had no image of God was a sign that they belonged to a secret society. The same accusation was still repeated by Porphyry (if Arnobius Adversus nationes 6. 1 quarrels with him). Abstinence from communal festivals and doubts (confirmed by Tertullian, De Corona) about their serving in the Roman army contributed to the unpopularity of the Christians. In moments of crisis, such as the persecution of Septimius Severus and during the Montanist predication in the early third century, many Christians expected the end of the World to come soon. Daniel became fashionable again. The chronographer Judas, interpreting Daniel, found that the anti-Christ would appear in or not much after the tenth year of Septimius Severus (Eusebius Historia ecclesiastica 6. 7). About the same year, 202, Hippolytus had no hesitation in saying explicitly that the fourth beast of Daniel is Rome, which tries to imitate the Christian unification of the World in a satanic style (In Daniel 4. 9). What Hippolytus discourages is the calculation of the time for the end of the fourth beast because it coincides with the arrival of the anti-Christ (4. 21).

These and similar facts only make the early acceptance by the apostles and their followers of the providential character of the Roman Empire more conspicuous. Paul's letter to the Romans (13 : 1–7) reiterates and develops Jesus' acceptance of the imperial authority (Mark 12 : 17), and he is supported by I Peter 2 : 13–17. Augustus had been a contemporary of Jesus; the "pax romana" was readily recognized as the main condition for the spreading of Christianity. By destroying the Jewish Temple of Jerusalem, the Romans had not only punished the Jews for their lack of faith, but had demonstrated the correctness of the claim of the Christian Church to be the legitimate successor to the Hebrew Temple. The theme of the contemporary rise of the Augustan Empire and of the

Christian Church is clear in Melito of Sardis (*ap.* Euseb. *Hist. Eccl.* 4. 26. 7–8). The argument from the destruction of the Jewish Temple is implicit in Justin, *I Apology* 47. 53, in Minucius Felix, *Octavius* 33, and takes shape in Origen, *c. Celsum* 2. 30 and 7. 26. It is developed by Eusebius *Demonstratio evangelica* 3. 7. 140; 6. 18. 286. Tertullian *Apologeticus* 21. 24 had added to it the touch of Pilate, "iam pro sua conscientia Christianus." I have discussed contiguous points in an article soon to appear in *Classic Philology* 1986 and shall only emphasize the very remarkable attitude of those Christians who, though persecuted by the Roman Empire, defended the notion that the Roman Empire had been providentially created to foster and support the Christian message.

One among the many factors of this attitude was (as in the case of the Jews) the genuine fear of the end of the World, which it was felt was approaching and inevitable. As long as the Roman Empire lasted, the end of the World was deferred. Even Tertullian was ready to admit that the end of time is a threat of terrible sufferings and that the Roman Empire affords us a respite from it (*Apol.* 32; *De resurrectione carnis* 24). Apart from these considerations, the coherence of which is not for us to judge, it is worth underlining that the Christian writers in the period of persecution are firm in stating that the Christians accept their obligations as citizens. The condition of a Christian as a stranger in this World does not abolish his duties as a citizen. To put it in the subtle language of the letter to Diognetus (second century A.D.): "they share all things as citizens and suffer all things as strangers."

There were evidently pagans who were ready to settle their differences with the Christians on the basis of recognition by the Christians of their obligations toward the Roman State. Even such an elaborate attack on Christianity as that by Celsus includes an invitation to the Christians not to create difficulties for the Empire by refusing to serve in the army and in the imperial administration (*c. Celsum* 8. 75). Furthermore, the correspondence between Pliny and Trajan and the very texts of the Acts of the Christian Martyrs show that the Roman authorities did not find it easy to explain why they were persecuting the Christians. No doubt the mere fact of being a Christian had created a presumption of disloyalty toward the emperor. It was easy to apply tests of loyalty: "deos appellare et imagini tuae. . . . ture ac vino supplicare" (Pliny *Epistulae* 10. 96). But men like Pliny were clearly embarrassed to have to do that. The Acts of the Christian Martyrs show Roman officials, most usually governors of provinces, very determined to apply the law against the Christians, but very vague or uncertain in explaining or supporting the law they were allegedly applying. As, after all, the persecution of the Christians is the main example of the systematic condemnation of a religious group for its hostility to the Roman Empire, we must register the paradox inherent in the attitude of both sides.

On the Christian side there was what we can call a predominant attitude of acceptance of, and respect for, the Roman Empire: there was even the attribution of providentiality to the Roman Empire. Perhaps it could hardly be otherwise, because the Church was then and remained long afterward interested above all in the conversion of the pagans of the Roman Empire. On the side of the Roman authorities there were preoccupations with public order, fears for the loyalty of the army, and possibly the knowledge that not all Christians shared the respect for the Empire shown by their apologists. But there was no elementary incompatibility with the Christian way of life. The army and the local administration had de facto become careers for volunteers. The ordinary Christian did nothing which menaced his pagan neighbors. At a higher level, men like Galen and perhaps Marcus Aurelius (if we accept the traditional text of *Meditations* 11. 3. 1–2) had some respect for Christian attitudes. With Celsus we have some hints of the theory that would please the Emperor Julian—how plurality of gods corresponded to the plurality of the nations of the Roman Empire (5. 32, 7. 70, 8. 35). But it was a double-edged theory which was never pursued systematically by the pagans. The Christians had the possibility of answering either that they were, after all, a new nation or alternatively that one god was better for one kingdom. These two arguments are already unified at the end of the *Contra Celsum* by Origen. What is perhaps most remarkable in Roman paganism is that there was no basic objection to conversion: all that was required was acceptance of the consequences of one's own conversion. This is really what Constantine, not a very sophisticated mind, understood better than anybody else. He converted. The problem of the Christian opposition to the Empire was solved by one stroke. Or almost.

VIII

There remains a puzzle with which I should like to end. As we all know, the Jews began to write Sibylline oracles in the style of the authentic Sibylline oracles in the second century B.C. or perhaps earlier. The precise purpose of these compositions is not necessarily always the same. The oracles were meant to express reaction (not inevitably hostile) to pagan powers, whether Hellenistic or Roman; they were also meant to express apocalyptic expectations. But perhaps, more than anything, the oracles were meant to convey to Jews and proselytes—and pagans who cared to read—a reflection on, or a reaction to, historical events. They were cheap philosophy of history supported by apocalyptic expectations. It is worth reminding ourselves that the Jews stopped writing history after A.D. 100 and the Christians did not write political history before the fifth century. The Sibylline oracles filled a historiographic gap. The oracles were, it seems, regularly attributed to a daughter or daughter-in-law of Noah: a detail which gave them a very respectable authority, a quasi-Jewish (but not a totally Jewish) character, and an endless possibility to refer to the past as if it were the future. Pagan oracles were incorporated in the Jewish texts.

In Rome, consultation of the Sibylline Books was controlled by the Senate and reserved to Roman officers. A law prohibiting the consultation of Sibylline Books is obscurely mentioned by Justin in his *I Apology* (44. 12) about the middle of the second century. But there seems to have been no serious attempt to prevent consultation and consequently fabrication of Sibylline Books outside Rome. What nobody ever claimed to have seen (except, I must hasten to report, Trimalchio according to Petronius) was a Sibyl in the flesh. Therefore the Sibylline Books, whether pagan or Jewish, were in a strict sense all forged. The Jews went on forging Sibylline oracles in Greek until the seventh century, if it is true that some of the oracles of our main collection of Sibylline texts (in Book XIV) refer to the Arab conquest of Alexandria.

Now what does interest me in this familiar picture is that the

Collection of Sibylline Oracles which has reached us contains both Jewish and Christian Sibylline oracles. The Collection as it is now was put together and transmitted by Christians. Here we find Christian forgers using Jewish forgeries and adding their own more or less for the same purposes: anti-Roman feeling, apocalyptic expectations, and generic reflection on past history presented as future. Fathers of the Church (notably Lactantius) hurried to quote these texts; and of course the Christians went on composing their Sibylline texts (now also in Latin) throughout the Middle Ages.

There is a text outside our main Collection which precisely shows that the Christians were conscious of the Jewish interest in Sibyls. It deserves more attention than has been given to it. Paul Alexander in his volume *The Oracle of Baalbek* (1967) admirably edited a text which Silvio Giuseppe Mercati had discovered on Mount Athos, but which was not published. Alexander showed this text to be an expanded version put together between A.D. 502 and 506 of an earlier Greek oracle composed about A.D. 378–390. The earlier Greek text is still recognizable under the Latin guise of medieval Tiburtine oracles. Unlike the ordinary Jewish-Christian Sibylline oracles, the Mount Athos text explains the occasion and gives the locality of the prophecy. The Sibyl is made to speak on the Roman Capitol and to answer questions put by a hundred Roman judges. The text is definitely Christian. Yet Jewish priests intervene in the dialogue and respectfully question the Sibyl about rumors in the pagan world regarding the birth of Christ. The Sibyl, of course, gives a precise confirmation, and the Jewish priests are not heard again. What concerns us is that Jews are here shown to question a pagan Sibyl as a matter of course.

The Christians inherited and preserved many Greek texts of Jewish origin in which the Jews had lost interest, partly for linguistic reasons. Philo and Flavius Josephus are among them. But the preservation of the Jewish Sibylline Books is something different because the Christian composers of Sibylline texts continued the work of their Jewish predecessors or contemporaries in the same spirit of critical evaluation of the past and visionary conjecture of the future. The very existence of the Jewish-Christian Sibylline Books is evidence for an underground reaction to the political and social events of the Roman Empire, an underground reaction which probably implies some exchange between Jews

and Christians and certainly presupposes a Christian interest in
what the Jews thought about the Roman Empire. Even taking into
account the Acts of the Martyrs, whether Alexandrian or Christian, I do not know of any other set of texts which brings us nearer
to an anonymous, religiously inspired, public opinion in the Roman Empire. We need further research on this conglomerate of
Jewish and Christian documents—and on the way in which it was
gradually put together.

This strange fact of finding Christians picking up and reutiliz-
ing Jewish Sibylline texts must, however, also be compared with
the other strange episode of Christianization of a text—namely
the Christianization of the oracles of Hystaspes. These oracles
predicted the destruction of the Roman Empire and the return to
power of the East. The collapse of Rome, apparently at the end of
six thousand years, would be followed by wars and natural disasters. After that, the world would enjoy peace and prosperity for
one thousand years, presumably under Eastern kings. The prophecy of the fall of Rome took the form of a dream by a king of
Media, Hystaspes, who lived before the Trojan War: the dream
itself is interpreted by a child, "Romanum nomen quo nunc re-
gitur orbis tolletur e terra et imperium in Asiam revertetur" (Lactantius *Divinae Institutiones* 7. 15. 11). Justin in his Apology
knew that the circulation of the oracle of Hystaspes had been prohibited on penalty of death (1. 44. 12). One version of the oracle
had been Christianized before Clement of Alexandria. Clement in
fact attributes a quotation of Hystaspes to St. Paul (*Stromata* 6. 5.
43. 1). He must have found a reference to it in some apocryphal
text attributed to Paul. In this Christianized version, Hystaspes
alludes to Christ. Lactantius, who directly or indirectly summa-
rizes most of the oracle, had a text before him which was not
interpolated by Christians, though it provided confirmation to his
own Christian eschatology. In this non-Christian version, the text
of Hystaspes may be dated at any time between the victory of
Rome over Antiochus III and the publication of Justin's Apology.
It may be due to friends of Mithridates or to friends of the Parthians either outside or inside the Roman Empire. We know from
Pausanias (5. 27. 5) and later from a letter of St. Basil (258) that
there were Persian colonies in Asia Minor with their magi (cf. A.
Peretti, *Wiener Studien* 69, 1956, 350–62). The original anti-

Roman bias of the oracle of Hystaspes is evident. But was this oracle still used by the Christians, either in its original form or in Christianized versions, for rejoicing at the impending doom of Rome?

For the last time this morning I confess my inability to separate in each case what was precise hostility to the Roman State from what was apocalyptic expectation by people used to thinking in apocalyptic terms about nothing definite.

9

The Disadvantages of Monotheism for a Universal State

For Edward Shils

I

IF WE WANT TO KNOW what the Roman Empire was and why in the East it survived until 1453, we must of course turn to military history, not to religious history. In the past, states and especially empires have survived because they were capable of defending themselves and offending their enemies. Whether it will be different in the future is the task of the future historian to establish. What is self-evident to the historians of ancient Rome is the superiority of the Roman war machine if judged with the criteria of the *longue durée*, sheer survival. There is, however, one facet of this long-term military history which has a direct bearing on the cultural physiognomy of the Roman Empire and consequently on religious history. The army was mainly stationed at the borders of the empire and tended to have a life of its own. The ordinary life of the provincials was shaped by their local institutions and by the intervention of the Roman authorities in matters of law, taxation, and public works. Within this frame a largely spontaneous process of assimilation took place which had some paradoxical aspects. Linguistically, it produced the absolute domination of the Latin language in the West and confirmed (and extended) the previously existing superiority of the Greek language in the East. Culturally,

Classical Philology, 81, 1–4, 1986, pp. 285–297.

however, it meant a type of education and intellectual interests which, whether expressed in Greek or in Latin, was basically uniform. The rhetorical and philosophical schools might speak Latin or Greek but thought basically about the same things. Only the language of law remained prevalently Latin, and even in the Eastern part of the Empire the law schools trained pupils to understand legal Latin and eventually to express themselves in Latin. Culturally, the Greeks remained convinced that they were intellectually superior to everybody else, including the Latins; and curiously enough the Latin-speakers seldom contested this assumption. But the realities were, as always, less simple than the assumptions. There was no work in the Greek world from 100 B.C. to A.D. 300 that could compare with the literature in Latin of the Caesarean and Augustan period: the imperial Greeks never had their Cicero nor their Virgil, not even their Horace and their Propertius. On the other hand, there was nothing in Latin comparable in revolutionary importance with the New Testament—a product of Greek culture. Of course that meant that Christian literature in Greek was of decisive importance in shaping the intellectual physiognomy of Christianity. But again simplification is discouraged as soon as we recall the name of St. Augustine, whose Greek was bad.

In religious terms one can easily see that Christianity was bound to insist on the parallelism between the unity of the Empire and the unity of the Christian Church. Even a priori one can easily guess that the old parallelism perhaps introduced by Aristotle between one god and one king would come back in Christianity with a vengeance, and indeed it did come back. We shall return to this point. But what we have first to ask ourselves is whether and how the pagans saw the relation between polytheism and the Roman Empire. The cultural standardization of the Roman Empire had produced a vast syncretism. Local cults and local gods from the provinces of Western Europe and Africa had been identified with Latin and Greek gods and cults, while it was traditional for Roman gods to be taken as identical with Greek gods at least in terms of myths. Furthermore, the imperial cult—partly a spontaneous practice, partly a practice enforced from above—was an expression of allegiance to the Roman State, whatever degree of emotional sincerity and depth we are prepared to attribute to it.

The two questions I want to ask are: first, whether and how plurality of gods was related to the plurinational character of the Empire; and secondly, how was plurality of gods thought to help the emperors? If the Empire justified itself by victory, how was victory related to polytheism? Some answer to these questions is possible, but let me say immediately that I have found it easier to produce evidence for the Christian criticisms of the polytheistic structure of the Roman Empire than for the pagan interpretation of the Roman Empire. While it is not difficult to explain what Jupiter, or indeed Janus, Ceres, Bacchus, Fides, and Terra Mater meant to the pagans of the Roman Empire, it is much more difficult to find the evidence for the pagan interpretation of the Roman Empire. The famous or notorious *Aufstieg und Niedergang der römischen Welt* (1981) contains three thick volumes on paganism which are very valuable but do not contain one chapter, as far as I can see, relevant to my two questions.

II

I shall try to put together some of the texts which seem to me relevant to my question about the pagan interpretation of the Roman Empire. I am taking it for granted that an ordinary Roman pagan was certain of helping his country by performing specific rituals and by showing respect for the traditional gods of Rome. What we are asking is whether somebody found the Roman Empire more intelligible or more easily amenable to improvement if examined in terms of a society willed and controlled by a plurality of gods, each of whom had a specific physiognomy and definite powers. Virgil undoubtedly has a theology of history: the Roman Empire gains recognition from Jupiter because of Aeneas's *pietas*. There are few Roman poets who have not something to say on the providential nature of the Roman State or even, more generally, of human society. It was Tibullus (2. 1) who claimed "rura cano, rurisque deos," "I sing the country and the country's gods. They were the guides when man first ceased to chase his hunger with the acorns from the oak." Propertius saw the conflict between Octavian and Antony as a match between "our Roman Jove" and "barking Anubis" (III, 11) and proclaimed "the gods founded the walls" of Rome "and the gods protect them." We could go on reminding ourselves of similar thoughts in Horace and Ovid. But on the whole it is surprising that this patriotic literature has so little to say about the divine custodians of the Roman State. And I have found even less in post-Augustan poets such as Statius who a hundred years later was so indiscreet in his descriptions of people and so inclined to make provincials and freedmen uncomfortable by his faint praise. We remember how he complimented a young man of equestrian family from Africa (*Silvae* 2. 14): "Neither your speech nor your dress is Punic, yours is no stranger's mind: Italian are you, Italian." Statius talks of gods continually, but not of imperial gods.

What is perhaps more remarkable is that similar poverty of religious thought about the Empire is to be found in writers who discuss the nature of Roman monarchy and the structure of the Empire. Take for instance the four speeches on Kingship which Dio Chrysostomus of Prusa wrote in the first years of the second century under Trajan. Of course the Roman emperor must be "like Zeus in counsel" and must imitate Zeus and Heracles. A third model is the god Helios, the Sun, not yet an important god for old-fashioned Romans: "You see how greatly the sun, being a god, surpasses man in felicity and yet throughout the ages does not grow weary in ministering to us and doing everything to promote our welfare" (*Orat.* 3. 73, trans. J. W. Cohoon, Loeb). The gods provide models to the emperors; they do not explain the Empire. Fifty years later, probably in A.D. 155, it was the turn of Aelius Aristides to produce a very sophisticated analysis of the Roman Empire on one of his journeys to Rome. We all know with what skill Aelius Aristides compared the Roman Empire with previous empires and characterized the Roman administration. As one would expect, Aelius Aristides ends his speech by declaring that the gods are delighted with Rome and feel more comfortable in Roman cities than in other places and in previous times. More specifically, he remarks that some of his favorite gods, Asclepius and Isis and Serapis, have extended their authority because of the favor bestowed upon them by the Romans: which is only too true. But there is no attempt to relate the structure of the Roman Empire to the structure of the divine world. What is stated is that the "Sun watches over your empire with the greatest pleasure" and

that the gods in general "join with you in making your empire
successful and they confirm your possession of it." If one considers that in his private life Aelius Aristides was directly experienc-
ing mystical and magic contacts with the gods and had plenty of
conversations (or, if you like, dreams) with them, the lack of
imagination in his political thinking about the gods can be better
appreciated.

Another basic text for political thinking in Rome about the Empire is provided by two speeches which in the early third century
Dio Cassius put into the mouths of Agrippa and Maecenas. They
are to be found in Book LII of the *Histories* by Dio Cassius and,
needless to say, are a rhetorical invention by the historian himself. The text is therefore a document for the early third-century
attitudes by a man of the provincial aristocracy of the East toward
the Empire. Dio Cassius goes into details about several aspects of
the Roman government. By encouraging Augustus to develop his
monarchic powers against the previous advice formulated by Agrippa, Maecenas is supposed to give a picture of the ideal monarchy. Well, there is advice about imperial cult and about the
necessary repression of any attempt at destroying the traditional
cults. Dio Cassius obviously dislikes Christianity, but is not
pleased to see the emperor dressed as a god. Apart from these two
points he has nothing to offer. It is worth repeating his main advice to the emperor: "You should not permit gold or silver images
of yourself to be made . . . Neither should you ever permit the
raising of a temple to you . . . For it is virtue that raises men to the
level of gods. And no man ever became a god by popular vote . . .
Worship the divine power everywhere and in every way in accordance with the traditions of our fathers and compel all others to
honor it. Those who attempt to distort our religion with strange
rites, you should abhor and punish not merely for the sake of the
gods . . . but because such men, by bringing new divinities in
place of the old, persuade many to adopt foreign practices from
which spring up conspiracies, factions and cabals which are far
from profitable to monarchy. Do not, therefore, permit anybody to
be an atheist or sorcerer. For such men, by speaking the truth
sometimes, but generally falsehood, often encourage a great many
to attempt revolutions. The same thing is done also by many who

pretend to be philosophers, hence I advise you to be on your guard against them too" (trans. E. Cary, Loeb).

The importance of this statement is obvious. A responsible writer of the early third century like Dio Cassius can combine a frank disapproval of the imperial cult as generally practiced with an invitation to persecute all new forms of religious practice. What he does not think of giving—and would probably have been surprised at being asked to give—is a reasoned explanation of the interrelation between gods and Roman Empire.

I have looked for other texts. I have looked for instance into the so-called *Acts of the Pagan Martyrs*, which one can find conveniently collected in the excellent edition by Herbert Musurillo published at Oxford in 1956. These texts are expressions of upper-class Alexandrian culture and patriotism of the first and second centuries A.D.—with its consistent anti-Semitism and its widespread (but not equally consistent) anti-Roman feelings. They celebrate men who spoke up for Alexandria and Greek culture and present them in scenes of formal and informal contacts with Roman authorities. There are scenes of trial before Roman authorities. The most extraordinary scene is a sort of trial of Alexandrian ambassadors which is conducted by the Emperor Trajan. The Alexandrian ambassadors stand up to him and reproach him with being pro-Jewish. The bust of the god Serapis which stood where the trial took place "suddenly broke into a sweat, and Trajan was astounded when he saw it." Serapis was showing his approval of the courage of his Alexandrians. One would expect texts of this kind, with their religious and nationalistic commitments, to give some views on what the gods thought of the Roman Empire. But the gods apparently did not go beyond silent sweating. As these Alexandrian texts have indisputable connections with Cynic literature, it is not irrelevant to add that the specific Cynic texts written in the Roman Empire—such as most of the letters attributed to Diogenes—show the same indifference to the actual religious structure of the Roman Empire. These are texts of moral protest, occasionally raising some social problems and mostly displaying contempt for luxury and social destruction. A letter attributed to Diogenes (Letter 19) may reflect the years of transition from Caesar to Augustus. But on the whole, pure Cynic texts confirm what we could have deduced from the texts which I have already mentioned by a man profoundly influenced by Cynicism, such as Dio of Prusa, and that is that the problem of the structure of Olympus in relation to the structure of the Roman Empire did not preoccupy the minds of educated pagan members of the Roman Empire in its first centuries.

It is therefore significant that the first time we come across some serious concern with the relation between Roman polytheism and Roman Empire is in that man Celsus who in about A.D. 180 polemized against the Christians and whom eighty years later Origen chose as his adversary in his devastating *Contra Celsum*. Celsus was mainly aiming at a double target: he wanted to prove that the Christians were rebels, first rebels against the Jews, and secondly and worse, rebels against the emperor. The Christians, according to Celsus, abandoned the laws of the Jews in order to disobey the emperor and refuse military service. In pursuing this double argument, Celsus came to maintain (as far as we can see from the quotations in Origen, Book VII) that the gods ruled the world under a supreme god more or less as the satraps governed the Persian Empire under a king of kings. Origen could make short shrift of all this by answering that Christians had been told to worship the creator and not his creatures (8. 65). Moreover, he could turn to the prophet Zephaniah 3. 7–13, a *locus classicus* for the unity of mankind (at least in the Christian interpretation). Celsus's argument was obviously becoming more dangerous when he invited the Christians to serve the country in which they lived. The reply, to which we shall soon have to return from another point of view, was that the Christians served the Church as the alternative to serving the State. Celsus's objections to Christianity being known to us only from Origen's replies to them, it is impossible to isolate Celsus's arguments from Origen's replies: it is indeed impossible to be certain that Celsus is fairly represented by the texts Origen quotes to refute him. But the impression remains that, though he had gone farther than his pagan predecessors in presenting a theological parallelism between Olympus and Roman Empire, Celsus had not relied on this argument and had not developed it. It is interesting that Celsus left Origen doubtful about his philosophic presuppositions: Origen took him to be an Epicurean, but recognized Platonic elements in his book. This ambiguity must have its roots in a certain opacity of Celsus's convictions about the intervention of the gods in the world.

Vastly superior to Celsus in learning and acumen, Porphyry's attack on the Christians (which he must have written after A.D. 270) does not seem to me to add much to what Celsus said about monarchy in heaven and empire on earth—except that he is more definite about the impossibility of distinguishing Christian angels from pagan subordinate gods (fr. 76, Harnack). Porphyry was no doubt ready to praise Egyptians and other barbarians, in comparison with the Greeks, for their religious beliefs, but that hardly had political implications. Even when faced by Christianity, the pagans had difficulty in finding arguments for a rational connection between their religion and their politics. Celsus perhaps went as far as anybody could go in presenting the Roman Empire as a safeguard of polytheism; the Roman Empire allows each nation and city to worship its own gods and to observe its own laws. After seeing Celsus in action, we are not surprised that the Roman magistrates in charge of enforcing laws against the Christians did not show any particular inclination to go beyond the letter of the law in a search for some higher justification of what they were doing. *The Acts of the Christian Martyrs* are a mirror not only of Christian attitudes during persecution, but also of pagan attitudes in persecuting. The most reliable of the Acts are also reliable witnesses to the way in which Roman magistrates (most usually governors of provinces) questioned the Christians and attributed a meaning to the persecutions. What strikes me is the legalistic attitude, the more conspicuous because it is often accompanied by an obvious reluctance to put people to death simply because they refuse to sacrifice to the gods and to swear by the genius of the emperor. None of these judges seems really to know why he is doing what he is doing—except for his determination to apply the law. I shall confine myself to the twenty-eight Acts of Martyrs collected by Musurillo in his other volume, *The Acts of the Christian Martyrs*, published at Oxford in 1972. The few statements by Roman governors which I have been able to extract from these twenty-eight documents show how embarrassed the persecutors were to justify their persecutions. In questioning the Scyllitan martyrs, the proconsul of Africa Saturninus (we are in the year

180) tells the accused people: "We too are a religious people, and our religion is a simple one: we swear by the genius of our lord the Emperor and we offer prayers for his health—as you also ought to do." In the Acts of Apollonius (end of the second century), the judge Perennis is rather in sympathy with the Christians and goes so far as to say: "We too are aware that the word of God is that which begets the soul and the body of the just in expressing and teaching what is dear to God." A fine statement, but not much of a comprehensive view of imperial power. In the Acts of Pionius, the proconsul declares that "Zeus is the ruler of all the gods." In the Acts of Conon, the prefect tells the martyr: "If you have recognized Christ, then recognize our gods too." Some of the most famous texts, such as the Acts of Perpetua and Felicitas, yield nothing for our inquiry. The Acts of the military martyrs are particularly poor in general statements by the judges: after all, in trying to get out of the military service because it was contrary to their Christian conscience, the martyrs had infringed military rules. Part of this reticence is just a question of judicial style. But in the Acts of Phileas as preserved in the Bodmer Papyrus, the questioner (in this case Culcianus, prefect of Egypt, 303–306) was ready to discuss with the accused. Culcianus even volunteered the opinion that St. Paul did not belong to the same class as Plato. We are really faced by a tradition of thought which takes for granted, but has difficulty in making explicit, the connection between the structure of the body politic and the structure of religion.

III

The Christians seem to have found it much easier to evaluate themselves in political terms. Of course they were helped by the Book of Daniel or, if you like, by the identification of the fourth kingdom with Rome. The theory of the four empires, having pagan roots and Oriental colors, also had the great advantage of being intelligible to the people who came to Christianity from a pagan background. But what interests us here is not the theory of the succession of empires, which I have tried to study elsewhere, at least in its origins. What interests us here is that the existence of a universal monarchy was explicitly recognized by this theory of the four monarchies. The foundations were laid for the parallelism "one god—one empire." No doubt, as the Apocalypse of John is enough to show, there were formidable difficulties in turning the Roman Empire into a good thing, from the Christian point of view. But two supplementary arguments soon emerged: one was that by destroying the Temple of Jerusalem the Roman Empire had punished the Jews for their refusal to recognize the Christ in Jesus; the other was that the birth of Jesus in the time of Augustus was a providential preparation for the spreading of the Gospel in a unified and peaceful world.

We do not have to follow in detail how these three arguments were developed and ultimately fused—the monarchy of God, the destruction of the Jewish State, and the providential unification and pacification of the world under Augustus. It will be enough to mention that the notion of the monarchy of God and the notion of the providential character of Augustus's peace were already in Philo, though not developed in depth. The real Christian novelty was the argument that the providentiality of the Roman Empire was confirmed by the destruction of the Jewish Temple. The notion of the monarchy of God was apparently analyzed in detail by Justin about the middle of the second century in a work which has not reached us (Eusebius *Historia ecclesiastica* 4. 18. 4). But the three notions together are found perfectly fused in Origen, *Contra Celsum*: "God was preparing the nations for his teaching by submitting them all to one single Roman Emperor" (2. 30). The same Providence saw to it that the Romans should destroy the Jewish State in order to facilitate the gathering of the Gentiles (7. 26). In its turn, the synthesis by Origen was accepted by his pupil Eusebius and made the cornerstone of his *Demonstratio Evangelica*: "It was not by mere human accident that the greater part of the nations of the world were never before under the one empire of Rome, but only from the times of Jesus . . . And no one could deny that the synchronizing of this with the beginning of the teaching about our Saviour is of God's arrangement, if he considered the difficulty of the disciples taking their journey, had the nations been at variance one with another, and not uniting together because of varieties of government" (3. 7. 140; trans. W. J. Ferrar). "For as soon as Jesus our Lord and Saviour had come and the Jews had outraged Him everything that had been predicted was fulfilled against them without exception 500 years after the prediction: from the time of Pontius Pilate to the ages under Nero, Titus and Vespasian they were never free from all kinds of successive calamities, as you may gather from the history of Flavius Josephus" (6. 18. 286). If for men like Celsus paganism protected the variety of customs of the nations within the Roman Empire, for men like Eusebius the new dispensation meant the reduction of the plurality of innumerable nations to unity: "And thus it is reckoned the deepest peace, there being no diversity of government or national rule, that nation should not take sword against nation . . . As this state of things was never achieved at any other time but during the Roman Empire, from our Saviour's birth till now, I consider the proof irrefutable that the prophet refers to the time of our Saviour's coming among men" (8. 3. 407).

As we might expect, such philosophy of history remained dominant in Christian circles during the fourth century, which was the century of victory for the Church under the protection and with the help of the Roman Empire. It would be easy to quote passages from John Chrysostom, Ambrose, and even Jerome in this sense. It will be enough to remind ourselves of the words of a poet, Prudentius, in *Contra Symmachum* (2. 620–22): "Christo iam tunc venienti crede parata via est, quam dudum publica nostrae pacis amicitia struxit moderamine Romae." ("For the time of Christ's coming, be assured, was the way prepared which the general good will of peace among us had just built under the rule of Rome"; trans. H. J. Thomson, Loeb). What is more remarkable is that Christian thinkers of the first three centuries should have built up a theology of history of this kind during persecutions, however intermittent, and while claiming religious obligations incompatible with the ordinary loyalties of the Roman State. The Christians built their interpretation of the Roman Empire as a providential instrument for the Church while they were declared enemies of Rome. Their opponents, the defenders of polytheism, never reached comparable clarity in their arguments for the plurality of gods in a pluralist empire. Toward the end of the fourth century it was no longer so evident that the survival of Christianity would depend on the survival of Roman Empire. The notion which had seemed self-evident to Eusebius—of a Constantine who integrates the work of Augustus—lost glamour. Basic disagreements developed on this issue, as we can see in the different orientation of St. Augustine and his pupil Orosius. Augustine was less certain than Orosius that one god in heaven should be mirrored by one king on earth. In the most remarkable book ever produced on *Der Monotheismus als politisches Problem*, Erik Peterson reached the conclusion that the Christological controversies of the fourth century effectively destroyed the doctrine of a correspondence between God's Kingdom and the Roman Empire as it had been presented by Origen and Eusebius. As he put it, "The orthodox doctrine about the Trinity made questionable the political theology of the Roman Empire" (p. 96). Even more explictly, he stated that the doctrine of the divine monarchy had been made impossible by the trinitarian dogma. With the new Christology, monotheism as a political problem had been put aside, and the Christian faith had been freed from its ties with the Roman Empire (p. 99). Peterson's little book was published in 1935 and made its target explicit in its last note: Carl Schmitt's *Politische Theologie* of 1922. Schmitt had meanwhile become the chief speaker for a sort of theological Nazism, and Peterson had to leave Germany for Italy and Rome, where he was never quite at home either. This of course is not the place to examine the extraordinary complexities of this battle about political theology which has not yet come to an end (there is a strong revival of the ideas of Carl Schmitt both in Germany and in Italy and perhaps elsewhere). I want simply to say that Peterson's interpretation of the decline of political theology after the fourth century was perhaps too unilateral. One of the factors, as I have already mentioned, was the obvious weakening of the Empire at the beginning of the fifth century. Another factor was the surprise of the pagan revival by Julian.

Julian may have passed away as a cloud, as Athanasius foresaw (Rufinus X, 35), but he had shown the possibility of a pagan emperor emerging from a Christian family. The danger was not easily forgotten. The case of Julian, with which I shall end this paper, showed that the religious pluralism of Celsus could be revived by an emperor and given new depth and meaning. Julian may have been a failure, but was once a real menace. And he presented the case for polytheism far more consistently. One of the most insistent arguments one finds in Julian's apology for paganism is precisely that polytheism accounts for the diversities between nations. Julian is one of the pagans of late antiquity who regard the Sun or Helios as the Supreme God and subordinate to him the hierarchy of the other gods. In the books against the Galileans which have come down to us only in the fragments quoted by his opponents, Julian invites the Christians to compare their doctrines with those of the Greeks: "Our writers say that the creator is the common father and king of all things, but that the other functions have been assigned by him to national gods of the peoples and to gods that protect the cities, everyone of whom administers his own department in accordance with his own nature. For since in the father all things are complete and all things are one, while in the separate deities one quality or another predominates, therefore Ares rules over the warlike nations, Athena over those that are wise as well as warlike, Hermes over those that are more shrewd than adventurous, and in short the nations over which the gods preside follow each the essential character of their proper god" (115 E, p. 345, trans. W. C. Wright, Loeb). Julian challenges the Christian opponents to deny the truth of such an elementary fact of nature: "Come, tell me why it is that the Celts and the Germans are fierce, while the Hellenes and the Romans are generally speaking inclined to political life and humane though at the same time unyielding and warlike? Why the Egyptians are more intelligent and more given to crafts and the Syrians more unwarlike and effeminate, but at the same time intelligent, hot-tempered, vain and quick to learn? . . . Whence then come these differences of characters and laws among the nations?" (131 D, p. 347). Julian had been educated as a Christian, had served as lector in the church and therefore knew the story of the Tower of Babel which at least explained the dissimilarity of language among the nations. But he does not consider it a good explanation. Julian gives a long refutation of the story of the Tower of Babel and we shall only retain two points of it. First, the story of the Tower of Babel, while explaining the differences between languages, did not explain the differences in customs and political institutions. Secondly, if you are not prepared to admit that the differences in customs and institutions were willed by Divine Providence, in what sort of Providence do you believe? If you do not believe that the Supreme God gave divine rulers to each nation, you imply that the Supreme God does not care for his creatures. It is good to know from the Bible that there was a God taking special care of the Jews, but can we believe that the other nations had been left without their own gods and legislators? In fact, we may infer from the existence among the pagans of legislators not inferior to Moses that the pagan nations also had their national gods (176 A B C). As one would expect, the Bible provides Julian with some good arguments for the existence of pagan gods: "Did not Solomon serve our Gods, if only because he had been deluded by his wife, as they assert?" (224 D, p. 383). The existence of Asclepius is one of the great arguments of Julian for the existence of local or sectional gods. For he, Julian, knew Asclepius by direct experience. Asclepius used to present himself in dreams to Julian: "When I have been sick, Asclepius has often cured me by prescribing remedies" (235 D, p. 389). If we take into account other writings by Julian, his conception of the divine world becomes even more complex. Julian, as we all know, elaborated his religious convictions in a prose hymn to Helios, to the Sun, whch is to a great extent a reinstatement of Iamblichus's philosophy. Here Julian treats Helios as an intermediary god between the absolute God—who is also absolute Goodness, but is now nameless—and the minor gods who supervise departments of nature and sections of mankind. As the hymn is to Helios, the functions of the individual subordinate gods are not here described in detail, but they are presupposed. In a letter to a pagan priest Julian developed both his notion of piety and his notion of priesthood. What we must retain from this letter is that Julian, with due respect for the national differences in habits and laws, tends to privilege what he calls "the sacred tradition of the Gods which has been handed down to us by the theurgists of earlier days (tōn archaiōn hēmin theourgōn)" (292 B, p. 306). This sacred tradition is fundamentally Greek and not very distinguishable from the mystery cults and Neoplatonic speculations for which Julian had abandoned Christianity. An interesting, but not surprising, element of this faith is the insistence on prayer: "We ought also to pray often to the gods, both in private and in public, if possible three times a day, but if not so often, certainly at dawn and in the evening" (302 A, p. 329).

From Julian's faith one could certainly not deduce his decision to rebuild the Temple of Jerusalem. This anti-Christian move shows Julian well acquainted with the Christian argument that the destruction of the Temple had been divine punishment for the part the Jews had played in the death of Jesus. Julian was obviously aware that for Origen and Eusebius (both of whom he had read) the destruction of the Temple was an essential part of the Christian interpretation of the Roman Empire. The destruction of the Temple was considered final by the Christians: indeed only permament obliteration made sense as a theological argument. But there was no need for Julian to reread Eusebius in order to formulate the purpose of rebuilding the Temple of Jerusalem for the Jews. He had been brought up among people who had considered the destruction of the Temple a primary argument on behalf of the Christian truth. It is more difficult to say whether Julian also had other aims in promising the Jews that he would rebuild their Temple. In the letter to a pagan priest he declares his intention of restoring the Temple "in honor of the god whose name has been associated with it" (2. 295 C, p. 313). In a letter to the community of the Jews (25 Hertlein = 51 Loeb) he speaks of a series of measures for restoring equality of rights to the Jews and giving them back Jerusalem. The authenticity of the letter has been contested, but it is difficult to imagine either a Jewish or a Christian or a pagan forger for such an idiosyncratic document; it has all the signs of having been written by Julian himself. If so, it may indicate another purpose beyond the obvious challenge to the Christians. At a certain point of the letter, Julian expresses the hope that the Jews "may have security of mind during my reign everywhere and in the enjoyment of peace may offer more fervid prayers for my reign to the most High God, the creator, who had deigned to crown me with his immaculate right hand." This passage incidentally is referred to by Sozomenus in his *Historia ecclesiastica* 5. 22, which at least shows that Sozomenus believed in its authenticity. Julian, therefore, asks the Jews, in exchange for reconstruction of the Temple, to pray for him to the most High God. I cannot go quite so far as Hans Lewy did in an article which he published in Hebrew in *Zion* 1941 and others translated into English in the periodical *Jerusalem Cathedra* for 1983 about forty years after that great scholar's death. Hans Lewy basically made his own the interpretation of John Chrysostom, *Against the Jews* V 1 (*P.G.* 48. 900), according to which Julian had been trying to persuade the Jews to sacrifice to a pagan god and therefore to commit impiety.

Put into Hans Lewy's language, Julian's purpose was to include the Jewish God in the hierarchy of pagan gods. I wonder whether Julian was so subtle—or perhaps so crude. He wanted the restoration of the Temple to be a proof that Jesus was no god. But he probably also liked the idea of the Jews honoring the Roman emperor in their own way side by side with the pagans. After all, he was committed to pluralism both in heaven and on earth. He respected national gods and like Celsus was divided in his mind about the Jews. As a pluralist he was bound to accept their national god, but as a polytheist he disliked the exclusiveness of the Jewish God.

Ultimately we must recognize that there was an internal weakness even in the pluralistic conception of Julian. It showed itself in this business of the Temple of Jerusalem. Essentially Julian was not much interested in the individual nations of the Roman Empire, if we except the Greeks and, at times, the Romans. He felt himself to be a Greek, he looked to the Athenians as his real fellow-citizens. Perhaps his most sincere words are in his address to his friend Sallust, the Neoplatonic author of the treatise on the gods and the world: "Among the Greeks I was born and brought up and hence I have a deeply rooted affection for them and for those parts and the cities there." The Greeks (adds Julian) "sought after truth, as its nature requires, by the aid of reason and did not suffer us to pay heed to incredible fables or impossible miracles like most of the barbarians" (251 D, 252 B). In Julian we can see the effort to break the alliance between monotheism and monarchy which the Christians had built up in three centuries of apologetic efforts. Though one cannot say that in practical terms his brief reign, which ended in military disaster, accomplished much in any field, least of all in the field of religion, the shadow of Julian was slow to disappear from the minds of Christian theologians. Gregory of Nazianzus (Orations 3) and John Chrysostom preached against this shadow: as John Chrysostom said, it had given a new hope to the Jews (Adversus Judaeos VII, 1; P.G. 48, 916). Almost eighty years after Julian's death, Cyril of Alexandria wrote in Against Julian his refutation of Julian's Against the Galileans. It may well be that Julian's pluralism helped to persuade the Christian theologians to think again about the providentiality of the Roman Empire.

Yet my last words must be to admit that the pagans never managed, even with Julian, to produce a consistent case for the
interdependence between polytheism and political pluralism in
the Roman Empire. If one considers texts carefully, one can see
that both sides of the pagan argument were weak. As polytheists,
men like Celsus and Julian were making too many concessions
to monotheism. Julian at least never really ceased to be a mono-
theist—which does not mean a Christian. On the other hand, the
superiority of Greco-Roman pagan culture was still overwhelming
and never allowed other cultures to assert their autonomy within
the Empire. Celts, Iberians, Pannonians, Punics, and Berbers were
Latinized, and the Orientals were expected to remain or to become Greeks. As we all know, it was mostly through Christianity
that Syrians, Egyptians, and Armenians saved their languages and
their souls. We are, however, free to wonder whether at least in the
West the Roman Empire would not have been better able to stand
up to the barbaric invasions if its plural structure had been taken
more seriously both in heaven and on earth. Paradoxically, the
plural structure of the pagan state favored an intellectual and linguistic unification which Christianity was unable to preserve.
The pagans and the heretics, not to speak of the Jews, lost interest
in the Roman State. Furthermore, the new loyalties toward the
Church or rather the churches diminished the loyalty toward the
State; and the churches attracted the best men, the best leaders.
The gain of the Church became the loss of the State. We shall hear
again the case for the superiority of enlightened polytheism in a
pluralist Roman Empire from an eighteenth-century historian
educated, or rather not educated, at Oxford. But it was perhaps
Moses Mendelssohn who came nearest to Julian the Apostate at
the end of his *Jerusalem* of 1783, though I doubt whether Mendelssohn had ever read Julian: "Brothers, if you care for true piety,
let us not feign agreement, where diversity is evidently the plan
and purpose of Providence. None of us thinks and feels exactly
like his fellow man: why then do we wish to deceive each other
with delusive words?" (trans. A. Arkush, 1983).

10

Ancient Biography and the Study of Religion in the Roman Empire

I

WHILE I WAS involved in research on the development of religion in the Roman Empire, I was also trying to clarify my ideas about the development of biography and autobiography in the Empire. What would have been obvious in any case became even more obvious in the circumstances. How could I use biographical and autobiographical materials for reconstructing the religious history of the Roman Empire? The question, which is in itself trivial, becomes slightly less trivial if seen against the present situation of the study of Roman religion.

The classic approach to Roman religion by Mommsen, Wissowa, and ultimately even Kurt Latte in his *Römische Religions Geschichte* of 1960 was to emphasize the centrality of Roman State religion, with its official calendar, its colleges of priests, its state rituals. Against Mommsen's approach there had been several objections for a long time: the actual religious experience of the Romans had not been sufficiently considered; the comparative method was still unknown to Mommsen (this, however, was not true); and finally Mommsen, in accordance with his habits of mind, had exaggerated the isolation of the Romans even in relation to Greek religion, though any Roman came to identify Jupiter

Annali della Scuola Normale Superiore di Pisa, Serie III, vol. XVI, fasc. 1, 1986, pp. 25–44.

with Zeus, Minerva with Athena, and so on. These objections were expressed in various types of books. The very sensitive W. Warde Fowler, Virgil in his hand, insisted on the religious experience of the Romans and added some anthropological material for comparison. H. J. Rose followed him with more systematic comparisons. The title of the most significant of his books is *Primitive Culture in Italy* (1926). Behind both Warde Fowler and Rose there was James Frazer, but in fact Frazer's major contribution to Roman religion, his commentary on Ovid's *Fasti*, appeared only in 1929. In the 1930s Franz Altheim published books which assumed the existence of very early relations between Greek and Roman religion. After the war it was the turn of Georges Dumézil to stress what he called the Indo-European heritage in Rome; he was looking rather at the Celtic, Germanic, and Indian religions for comparison with Rome. Whatever the merits or demerits of the various theories, they were no help in understanding Roman religion beyond the period of its origins. Mommsen had at least presented a scheme which applied to the whole of Roman religion, as long as there was a Roman State to support it. F. Cumont's study on Mithraism remained for decades the most substantial contribution to the study of Roman paganism. Then in 1933 A. D. Nock seemed to open up a new epoch with his *Conversion*, but, curiously, it was a book which remained alone, even in its author's production. Only in the late 1970s did a new generation begin to notice the poverty of the work done on the religion of the Roman imperial period in comparison with the attention given to earlier ages.

Four recent books can give an idea of recent orientations of research. J. H. W. G. Liebeschuetz's *Continuity and Change in Roman Religion* appeared in 1979; R. MacMullen's *Paganism in the Roman Empire* was published at Yale in 1981; A. Wardman's *Religion and Statecraft Among the Romans* is dated 1982; and in 1983 John Scheid, who was born in Luxembourg and teaches in Paris, published in Italy *La religione a Roma*.

Scheid and Wardman agree on the point that Roman religion was a religion of victory. They therefore attribute basic importance to the Roman imperial cult as a cult of victory. Their emphasis is obviously on the imperial period. Consequently both Scheid and Wardman see in the political and military crisis of the third century A.D. the turning point in Roman paganism which will not survive the military defeats. Constantine persuaded himself that Christian monotheism was more likely to save the empire than traditional polytheism. Yet there are differences between Wardman and Scheid. For instance, the latter considers the cults of Isis and Mithras to be extraneous to the state religion of the Romans, and nearer to personal faith. For Wardman the so-called Oriental cults of Isis and Mithras are complementary to the cults of the cities. But for the victory of Christianity they would have been absorbed completely into the Roman official religion.

Liebeschuetz too is convinced that Roman religion was meant to ensure victory for the state rather than safety or certainty for the individual. But he limits his attention to more literary, especially poetical, texts which seem to express the faith of the upper class, of the educated few. This attention to the literature of the upper class is of course well justified. It allows Liebeschuetz to make observations which his predecessors too often missed. Liebeschuetz observes that the scrupulous care of the Roman magistrate for the acts of cult was a way of gaining freedom of action against superstition. The Roman politician or general, after having obtained the formal approval of the gods through specific ritual acts, considered himself free to do whatever he wanted. It is also Liebeschuetz who observed that the Romans were capable of laughing at their own gods. But Liebeschuetz's approach being systematically limited to the upper class makes one suspect that he takes less than seriously his own point of departure, which is that Roman religion was intended to give victory to the Roman State.

The last of the four authors to be here considered, R. Mac-Mullen, is just the opposite of Liebeschuetz. He treats Roman religion of the imperial period essentially as a popular religion, a way for people to get together, to find, in sanctuaries and festivals, places and times of encounter or reunion, as the case may be. It is, however, implicit in this populist approach that MacMullen, like Liebeschuetz, should pay less attention to the state religion. State religion is for MacMullen just one of the aspects of the universal search for the social organization of pleasure. Miracles, oracles, and sacrifices are not different in quality if prearranged by political institutions. Perhaps the point on which MacMullen insists most is that it is wrong to present Oriental cults as competing against state cults. MacMullen consciously plays the role of the anti-Cumont. Whereas Franz Cumont saw the cult of Mithras as a typical nonstatal cult which offered hope of salvation and ultimately competed with Christianity, MacMullen denies that Mithras provided more salvation than other cults. Nor would people have cared much if Mithras did. What people cared for was to be free from bad dreams, obsessions, and anxieties: they looked for exorcists, miracle-makers, or, more normally, for a pleasant day out, when the weather was fine. If paganism yielded to Christianity in the third or fourth centuries, it is because the plurality of gods was too expensive in a period of economic and political contraction. The urban upper class simply was unable to pay for the festivals. Christianity, according to MacMullen, offered not only cheaper and better-organized social life, but also more efficient exorcists and miracle-makers.

I am not here to sit in judgment and to decide whether Mac-Mullen is more correct than Scheid or Wardman or Liebeschuetz. The reason I have introduced them is that for the first time we have a climate of opinion in the study of Roman religion in which problems of origins count for less than the social realities of the age in which people lived. The paganism—or indeed the Christianity—in which these historians are interested is the urban society of the first centuries of the Empire and has dimensions corresponding to the territory of the Roman State. It is characterized, in the matter of documentation, by a high degree of literacy which takes the form of private inscriptions and private letters and contracts just as much as of literary texts and legal texts. The countryside, being much less vocal, is by definition left out; it can be heard only indirectly. There is indeed no way of eliminating the disparity of documentation between country and town, though the ingenuity of researchers and greater attention to documents in languages other than Latin and Greek have done wonders in the direction of recovering the state of affairs outside the more cultivated urban centers.

There are, however, some disquieting features in this new enthusiasm for such an easy sociology of religion in its application to the situation of the Roman Empire. Most of the pagan religious texts can be classified either as records of specific acts (such as a dedication or a funeral formula) or as theological texts declaring a belief. Philosophic texts are usually reflections on religion in order to establish the relation of popular cults to specific philosophic tenets: Stoics interpret religion from the Stoic point of view; Epicureans from an Epicurean point of view, etc.

What is more difficult to know is how people lived a faith or, to put it in a less Christian way, how they behaved according to a religious tradition. For the non-Jews and non-Christians of the Roman Empire, there is the additional difficulty of knowing how they were educated to be pagans. It is hard to visualize how a good Roman or Athenian boy learned about the religion which he was supposed to consider his own. Not that the problem is entirely absent when Jews or Christians are investigated. If we have an approximate idea of what a sabbath in a synagogue was like for any adult Jew, we are left in the dark about what a Jewish boy was supposed to learn at school about the written and unwritten Torah. Nor is our information about Christian schools of the first centuries satisfactory. But where there is a sacred text, an Old or New Testament, as a foundation of a religion, we know at least that it was read, though the modalities may be obscure. In the case of so-called paganism there was no comparable text. Homer or Virgil did not represent religious texts comparable with the Bible for the pagan boy or adult of Athens and Rome. No doubt, religious groups such as the Orphics or the initiates of certain mysteries had their sacred texts, but these texts had none of the complexities of the Old or New Testament (to begin with, as far as we know, they were much shorter). Above all, they were considered to be supplementary to what an ordinary pagan was supposed to know. The question of the ordinary education of an ordinary pagan is left paradoxically untouched by the existence of mystery texts for the adepts in specific sects.

Apart from the question of education, which is a particularly difficult one for the pagans, there is the general difficulty, in which Jews and Christians are also involved, that we know little of how an individual behaved during his life in relation to the religious community to which he belonged. We know even less of how he behaved in relation to the religious communities to which he did not belong. The Roman Empire was religiously an agglomeration of competitive groups, some mutually exclusive, some mutually compatible or even mutually integrative, but still competitive. A Christian normally ceased to be a Jew or a pagan, and Jews seldom paganized, but do we really know what we mean when we say that? Problems about saints and demons are a warning. We think we know that most of the pagans did not feel that the special devotion they might profess for Asclepius or Mithras or even Minerva excluded devotion to other gods—among whom the god of the Jews or of the Christians might be one. But do we really know? The priorities and conflicting claims existing for pagans, Jews, and Christians are not easy to define.

The lack of attention to, or the lack of information about, the way of life of an individual as such does of course produce problems for the evaluation of the group to which the individual belonged. By general admission we know more about the faith of individual Christians than about the faith of individual pagans in the first century A.D. Yet recent books on the social structure of early Christianity have only confirmed that to know to what religious group you belong is not identical with knowing what you believe. One of the most important books on the sociology of early Christianity is Wayne Meeks's *The First Urban Christians, The Social World of the Apostle Paul*, 1983. Not by chance, Meeks is a colleague of MacMullen at Yale: one recognizes the same preoccupations. Meeks has certainly done much to define the social structure of the group of Christians guided by St. Paul: he has shown that it was a middle-class group characterized by much social mobility and de facto elimination of the traditional cultic separation between men and women. But at the end of the book I have been left wondering how such a well-integrated sect, so neatly defined in its internal rules, could through the centuries (and not even many centuries) emerge as the paradigmatic Christian society. Fourth-century Roman society was very different from the little groups for which St. Paul wrote. If we want to understand what St. Paul taught to the fourth century, I suspect we must stick to the old-fashioned notion that the message of St. Paul was not founded on social premises, but on universal expectations of immortality, resurrection, and salvation. If we had the biography or autobiography of one disciple of St. Paul—a real biography or autobiography, not just one letter which may have slipped into the Pauline collection—the book by Meeks would have been written differently—valuable as it is in its present form. With pagan religious groups the situation is more or less the same. If we had a biography of a real devotee of Isis or Mithras, we should be capable of better judgment about the religious groups specifically interested in Isis or Mithras. In the case of Isis we can at least ask the question, though it is an absurd question: Does Apuleius's *Metamorphosis* qualify as a biography of a follower of Isis? For Mithras we cannot even ask the absurd question. The life of the Emperor Julian by Eunapius is not preserved, and it is no use trying to reconstruct it for our purpose from what Zosimus borrowed from it for his own story of Julian.

II

These are banalities but perhaps necessary banalities. At the present stage of the studies of religion in the Roman Empire what we need is something allowing us to break the stereotypes of sociological generalization either about paganism or about Judaism or about Christianity. We need personal stories—whether biographical or autobiographical. Personal education, personal religious commitments, punctual relations between social life and personal experience (dreams included) are what we want to know. But biography can do more for us than give us personal stories in which religion may be conspicuous either by its presence or by its absence. Biography can by itself express the religious or irreligious attitudes of the biographer. We have to distinguish between what a biographer tells about his hero and what he wants to say for himself. This applies (though not so rigorously) to autobiography, where what a man tells about his own past does not necessarily coincide with what he currently believes and wants us to believe. The available materials are unevenly distributed and of different intrinsic value: after Flavius Josephus there is little Jewish biography or autobiography, and one cannot help asking why biographies of poets are altogether less searching and perhaps less informative than biographies of philosophers, rhetoricians, and even grammarians. But there is enough evidence to make the study rewarding for the history of religion in the Roman Empire. I can only give some examples, first about personal stories and then about what the biographer has to say for himself.

Presence or absence of formal religious education interests me for the reasons I have already explained. It is still surprising to me that if one considers the relative abundance of the autobiographical and biographical material at our disposal for the period of Caesar and Augustus, there is so little about the initiation of people into their own national religion. In his exile Ovid remembered his education in Rome where he was sent with his brother from his native Sulmona, but there is no sign that education included religion. The same of course applies to what Horace says he learned from his father.

More than one century later, Tacitus wrote a life of his father-in-law. Agricola's education is duly registered, and we learn that there was a moment in which young Agricola ran the risk of being more involved in philosophy than a Roman should: it was a passing phase. Religion is not mentioned at all among the troubles of the education of Agricola. We are naturally brought to the comparison with what his contemporary Flavius Josephus has to tell about himself and about his own education in Judaea. As we all remember, young Josephus claims that he acquainted himself thoroughly with all the three sects of Judaism in order to choose ultimately Pharisaism. But it is obvious if one looks a bit more closely at the text of Flavius Josephus's autobiography that Josephus had no time in the three crucial years he mentions to be initiated into the three sects. He was passing those three years—between the ages of sixteen and nineteen—in the desert with a master, Bannus, who apparently was neither a Sadducee nor a Pharisee nor an Essene. Josephus wrote his *Vita* either for hellenizing Jews or for educated pagans or rather for both. He thought he had to introduce himself as a Jew who had made his choice between alternative conceptions of Jewish life, just as a young Greek would make a choice between alternative philosophic schools. In full coherence with this attitude, Josephus stops talking about religion after the pages devoted to his own education. The rest of his life, like Tacitus's Agricola, is mainly a record of political and military activities. There is no intention to impose religious details on the reader. Josephus instinctively knew that in the pagan world in which by now he lived he was expected to say as little as possible about religion either in biography or in autobiography.

We feel we are entering into a different world when in the second century A.D. we read Marcus Aurelius's word of thanks to his dead mother for having given him τὸ θεοσεβές καὶ μετα-δοτικόν, the veneration of gods and generosity. Commentators from Gataker to Farquharson do not seem to know anything comparable with this little sentence. Another text brings us a step further and gives us what to my knowledge is the oldest autobiographical account of involvement on the grand scale by a Roman citizen in religion and magic. Apuleius's *De magia* or *Apologia* is a speech in self-defense pronounced by him about A.D. 155 in the African city of Oea where he was accused of magical practices before the Roman proconsul of Africa, Claudius Maximus. Autobiography, as we know, often took the form of a speech of defense before an imaginary tribunal. One of the prototypes of Greek biography, the speech on the *Antidosis* by Isocrates, is an imaginary speech. It is, however, improbable that Apuleius would present himself, even for autobiographical purposes, as accused of magical practices, if the trial had not been real. Some details he gives about his family and its linguistic situation seem to confirm the authenticity of the circumstances. The woman he had married at Oea was older than himself, had been married before, and had grown-up children: she had offended the family of her first husband and her own sons by the new marriage. She used to write her letters in Greek, not in Latin, and one of her sons from the first marriage is described as knowing Punic better than Latin and having as much Greek as his mother had given him. Apuleius does not feel it necessary to explain why his wife wrote to him in Greek. But he has to explain at length why his propensity for mystery cults and his scientific curiosity must not be confused with the habits of a magician.

We have every reason to believe that Apuleius came out well from his trial. But that did not save him from being considered a magician in later centuries. Lactantius put him together with Apollonius of Tyana among the pagan thaumaturges (*Div. Inst.* 5. 3. 21). Augustine knew that it was usual to associate Apuleius with Apollonius of Tyana (ep. 138), but, admiring him as a writer and being more perceptive than Lactantius, he saw that the *Apo-*

logia could not have been written by a real magician. Apuleius's autobiographical text can therefore be studied from three angles: as a document of what Apuleius thought about himself when he was confronted by an accusation of magical practices; as evidence for the mentality of a small African community of the Roman Empire when an outsider with an unusual education came to settle down and marry in their midst; and finally as a text which in the third and fourth centuries was interpreted in a way which seems absurd to us, but placed Apuleius in the company of that rival of Jesus, Apollonius of Tyana.

Lucian offers another side, or rather two other sides, of the religious situation of the second century by his portraits of the philosopher Demonax and of the false prophet Alexander of Abonuteichos. Lucian says that he had been a pupil of Demonax. He also claims direct acquaintance with the false prophet Alexander. Even if not true, this is in the best style of biography.

Demonax made a point of not being initiated into the mysteries of Eleusis, even though he lived in Athens. He also did not sacrifice to Athena, because she had no need of his offerings. When a friend told him, "Let's go to the temple of Aesculapius and pray for my son," he replied, "You must think Aesculapius very deaf, that he can't hear our prayers from where we are." Such answers would not have been reported if they were considered to be normal. As for Alexander, the representative of the opposite trend, it is enough to remember that when people accused him of trickery he used to retort by accusing them of being Christians or atheists. He claimed, and apparently found, allies among the Platonists and the Stoics. He even burned texts by Epicurus in public. Less than a century later it was the turn of the Christian Origen, according to his pupil Gregory Thaumaturgus, to welcome all the pagan philosophers, except Epicurus. Another quasi-Christian trait of Alexander of Abonuteichos was that he gave oracles to barbarian followers in barbarian languages—such as Syriac and Celtic. Lucian dedicated his piece on Alexander to a man called Celsus who had sympathy for Epicurus. Origen attacked an anti-Christian writer of the same name whom he thought to be an Epicurean, but modern scholars take to be Platonic. The identification of the two Celsi, if it were possible, would make sense. We shall soon see that in the Roman Empire a sympathy for Epicurus was not always incompatible with an addiction to Plato. In any case, Demonax was for Lucian the philosopher capable of gaining respect in a city even if he did not adhere to her traditions. Alexander was the new type of adventurer in religion, the Cagliostro of the second century; he brought confusion into cities.

Among the other writings by Lucian I shall only mention his allegedly autobiographical account of how he chose his own career. His family expected him to become a sculptor; he chose to become a rhetorician, following a dream which he reported at length. This is a conspicuous example of how dreams came to count in the biographical or autobiographical tradition. Dreams were registered either to indicate peculiarities of the mind of the dreamer or more often to mark the point at which a superhuman power interfered with the human mind. One wonders how the biographers knew of the dreams of their heroes. Plutarch and Suetonius diligently reported dreams, though in Suetonius the Emperor Claudius does not dream. Septimius Severus registered dreams and portents in his autobiography and was echoed by Dio Cassius. Diogenes Laertius tends to ignore the dreams of the philosophers, and Philostratus, as far as I remember, does not report dreams of Sophists. But in the life of Apollonius of Tyana by the same Philostratus there is a theoretical chapter about dreams (2. 37), and Apollonius, inter alia, is prevented by a dream from going to Crete (4. 34). However, even in the miraculous life of Apollonius dreams do not amount to much. Did dreams mean less in the third century than in the age of Aelius Aristides and Lucian?

III

With Diogenes Laertius and Philostratus we have arrived at the point at which we must ask whether the mere construction of a collection of biographies—whether of philosophers or Sophists—acquires a religious significance. At least for Diogenes Laertius, my answer is positive.

Even the name of Diogenes Laertius is mysterious, not to speak of the date at which he lived. He was no doubt called Diogenes, but Laertius may be a learned joke, an allusion to the Homeric expression to designate Ulysses. The form Laertius points to a

date not earlier than the late second century A.D. when nick-
names or signa of that type became common. Diogenes Laertius's
work, which seems to have been called "Lives and Opinions of
Famous Philosophers and According to Their Sects," is not quoted
before Stephanus Byzantinus, who in his turn appears to have lived
in the sixth century. Thus Diogenes Laertius may in theory have
lived at any time between the late second century and the early
sixth century A.D., but I still find probable, though not absolutely
cogent, the arguments which have suggested a date in the early
third century. The most recent philosopher Diogenes Laertius
mentions is a pupil of the skeptic Sextus Empiricus called Saturninus (9. 116). As the date of Sextus Empiricus cannot be fixed
within narrow limits, all we can say is that Saturninus, as a direct
pupil of Sextus Empiricus, can hardly have lived before A.D. 150 or
later than A.D. 250. The other indications go in the same direction.
Diogenes Laertius gives us no sign of knowing about thinkers like
Plotinus and Porphyry who lived after A.D. 250. He dedicates his
work to a woman whose name is not given, but who is described
as an enthusiastic Platonist (3. 47). It would have been difficult to
speak to a Platonist in late antiquity without mentioning names
like Plotinus or Porphyry. The phenomenon of women intensely
interested in pagan philosophy seems to be widespread precisely
between A.D. 150 and A.D. 250. Galen, writing in the middle of
the second century, mentions a woman, Arria, who was enthusiastic about Plato. Later of course we meet Julia Domna, the wife
of the Emperor Septimius Severus, who allegedly asked Philostratus to write the life of Apollonius of Tyana. Some decades later,
Julia Mamaea, the mother of Alexander Severus, "a woman religious if ever there was one," as Eusebius put it in his Ecclesiastical History (6. 21), summoned the Christian Origen into her
upper-class presence at Antioch and gave him a military escort.
Hippolytus of Rome dedicated a book on resurrection to Mamaea
and a *Protrepticus* to another woman. The aristocratic women
who lived between the second and the third century A.D. were
faced with a Christianity which was emerging as a sophisticated
system of thought and was increasingly absorbing elements of the
Greek philosophic tradition. It is no wonder that they turned to
reputable thinkers among their contemporaries for illumination
and guidance. The question thus arises whether Diogenes Laer-

tius was writing for a woman, or, if you like, for a reader in general, who wanted orientation in the spiritual conflicts of her or his time.

For the purpose of interpretation, we have to devote more attention than is customary to the *Prooemium*. It opens with the statement, "There are some who say that the study of philosophy had its beginning among the barbarians." This statement about the non-Greek origin of philosophy is rapidly disposed of: "The authors forget [Diogenes says] that the achievements which they attribute to the barbarians belong to the Greeks, with whom not merely philosophy, but the human race itself began" (trans. R. D. Hicks, Loeb Library). The whole work by Diogenes Laertius is a demonstration that philosophy is a Greek phenomenon. Diogenes divides Greek philosophy into two big currents: the Ionian school which started with Thales and Anaximander and the Italian school which started with Pythagoras and went on with Democritus and Epicurus. Each of those two great currents is of course divided into several schools. Here Diogenes follows conventional divisions of Greek philosophy, though he seems to pride himself on calling the skeptics a sect or school, contrary to the opinions of those who denied the skeptics the status of a sect because they had no positive doctrines (1. 20). Now, Diogenes Laertius is quite aware that some of these schools were still alive in his time. But for the purpose of telling the lives of the philosophers, he does not follow the schools down to his own time—whatever that time may be. In the case of the Stoics he does not go beyond the first half of the first century A.D.—and this is true only if we admit that Book VII has reached us in an incomplete form. Generally speaking, Diogenes stops with the third century B.C. In this way he can easily avoid including any Roman philosopher (he does not mention either Cicero or Seneca). He sticks literally to his assertion that philosophy is a purely Greek phenomenon. Even in Italy the real philosophers are for him exclusively Greek. And he calls "Italian philosophers" thinkers like Epicurus who had never seen Italy. Thus we have a total exclusion of the barbarians from the realm of philosophy. The exclusion affects the Romans just as much as the Egyptians, the Chaldaeans, the Persians, and the Jews. As for the Jews, he tells us that some of his predecessors thought they had their philosophers who could be compared to the Iranian magi. The exclusion of the Jews therefore stands and falls with that of the magi. The silence on the Christians is total. We need hardly add that no educated man of the second or third century could be unacquainted with the elementary fact of life that the Christians existed and were persecuted. Diogenes wrote as if they did not exist and there were no Christian philosophy. The silence on Christian philosophy, like the silence on Roman philosophy, was intentional. What Diogenes tries to present is a world of philosophy which is exclusively Greek, pre-Roman and pre-Christian.

At this point the dedication of the book to a woman Platonist becomes central. The letter of dedication which must have opened the book is lost; alternatively it may never have been written if the book was published posthumously before it was finished, as some people suspect. But that a dedication was intended is beyond question. In two passages Diogenes Laertius speaks directly to the woman. One of the two passages is in the life of Plato (3. 47) and emphasizes her competence and her interest in Plato. But Diogenes did not write in order to subscribe to the philosophic preferences of his patroness, though quite obviously he wanted to give her pleasure by providing a summary of Platonic tenets she would be able to accept. The other passage in which she is addressed is in the life of Epicurus (10. 29). The tone is suitably different. Diogenes implies that the woman has neither a profound knowledge of nor much sympathy with Epicurus. He wants to give her an opportunity to form a better opinion of this philosopher. It is indeed unusual for Diogenes to quote so many texts by a philosopher; three entire letters apart from the Sovran Maxims which were the standard introduction to Epicurean philosophy. Epicurus is shown as a good son, a good brother, even a pious and patriotic man. "His piety towards the gods and his affection for his country no words can describe" (10. 10).

These words are incredible enough, yet they are not necessarily words by an Epicurean. There is no reason to think that Epicurus was nearer to Diogenes Laertius than Plato, or Diogenes the Cynic, Aristotle, or Zeno the Stoic, all of whom are presented most sympathetically. Diogenes Laertius is not holding up one philosopher or one school as a model; what he is doing is producing a gallery of memorable philosophers. His vision of Greek phi-

losophers is a symposium of various sages, each with his brand of
wit and wisdom. Personally, after all, he may have been a skeptic.
That would explain the troubles he took to give hospitality to the
skeptics in his sanctuary. He was certainly very sympathetic to
Pyrrho. He attributes to one Ascanius of Abdera the opinion that
skepticism was a most noble philosophy (9. 61) in a context in
which he seems to share this opinion. What is more, in talking
about another skeptic, Timon, not to be confused with Timon the
Misanthrope, he quotes one of his sources in a most unusual way:
he calls him "our Apollonides of Nicaea," ὁ παε ἡμῶν (9. 109).
The expression has intrigued all the commentators and transla-
tors of Diogenes Laertius. It can of course mean either "my fellow-citizen" or "my fellow-philosopher" Apollonides of Nicaea,
but the second meaning is more natural in philosophic literature.
Cicero calls "nostri" his friends of the Academic sect, and Strabo
calls the Stoics "our." A skeptic attitude of mind would not contradict, and may even confirm, the posture of general sympathy
for Greek philosophy. Greek philosophy was to Diogenes Laertius
a form of notable rationality with many possible variants. A
Greek was entitled to be a skeptic, a Christian was not. Diogenes
was not out to sell a special brand of philosophy, he was out to
recommend Greek philosophy to those who were in danger of pro-
fessing barbarous doctrines, Christian or otherwise. Such an attitude, at the same time committed and detached, is inseparable
from the learned and almost pedantic turn of mind which Diogenes displays. His image of the world implied awareness of recondite information, of contradictory opinions, and of the difficulty
of ascertaining basic facts.

IV

There is indeed one author who can be usefully compared with
Diogenes Laertius. He is Flavius Philostratus, a near-contempo-
rary to all appearances. The comparison is useful, because it
shows that the world of Greek philosophy which Diogenes was
still offering as a defense against Christianity was in fact falling
apart. Philostratus, the author of the life of Apollonius of Tyana,
wrote his *Lives of the Sophists* at a later stage of his activity and

dedicated them to Antonius Gordianus a few years before Gordianus became an emperor in 238; the exact date of the *Lives* is a notorious difficulty. Philostratus was himself a Sophist and was basically interested in the readers and colleagues who had transformed the intellectual scene of the Roman Empire in the preceding hundred years or so. He is the man who gave the name of Second Sophistic (p. 481) to this intellectual movement. He was anxious to find ancestors among the old Sophists and orators of the fifth and fourth centuries B.C. To help himself he also created the category of the philosophers who were thought to be Sophists, such as Eudoxus and Carneades; this category would have had its last representatives in Dio of Prusa and Favorinus of Arelate in the early second century A.D. But Philostratus does not feel that he can make a serious case for continuity; his world is a contemporary world, of men who by the mastery of subtle techniques of eloquence have acquired power, influence, and wealth in the Roman Empire. Their prototype is Herodes Atticus, the extremely wealthy, prestigious, and quarrelsome declaimer who reached consulship in A.D. 143 and managed to survive quarrels and emperors. While Diogenes Laertius is careful not to touch the contemporary scene, Philostratus in the *Lives of the Sophists* is unable to give real predecessors to his contemporary heroes. The world Diogenes paints is a world of the past which can still appear meaningful and coherent. The world Philostratus paints is a world of the present which is all show and no substance. However, let us not forget that Philostratus had previously found a hero in a man of the past of a quite different kind: Apollonius of Tyana. True enough, the past of Apollonius was not so remote, since he had lived in the first century A.D. But his prototype was Pythagoras, and his style of life was that of a dedicated ascetic in contact with the gods.

In the *Lives of the Sophists* there are occasional contacts with religion. We learn, for instance, that Antiochus the Sophist used to spend many nights in the temple of Asclepius both on account of the dreams he had there and for the social contacts he had with other fellows; besides, the god used to speak to him even while he was awake (568), but this is incidental. We would never deduce from the long account Philostratus gives of Aelius Aristides that his life was dominated by religious obsessions. There is therefore a precise conflict between the religious outlook of the life of Apollonius by Philostratus and the nonreligious, mundane outlook of his *Lives of the Sophists*. It would be impertinent to decide which of the two books, the life of Apollonius or the *Lives of the Sophists*, was nearer to Philostratus's heart. What we do know is that the Life of Apollonius, that man of the past, had the future to itself.

When we find a conscious continuation of Philostratus in the *Lives of the Philosophers and the Sophists* by Eunapius, written about 396, it was no longer possible to evaluate a Sophist simply in terms of his technical abilities. The very category of Sophist had lost precise significance: Eunapius combined philosophers and Sophists; in fact, the majority of the people about whom he was speaking were Neoplatonists. Eunapius recognized as his predecessors Porphyry who had written on Plato, Sotion who had written on later philosophers, and Philostratus who had dealt with the Sophists of the imperial age. But he also made the point that the aim of his narrative was not to write of the casual doings of distinguished men, but of their main achievements. By implication he broke with Philostratus. While the world of Philostratus in the *Lives of the Sophists* had been that of dazzling orators whose lives and beliefs were basically irrelevant to their performances, Eunapius tried to rebuild the unity between life and thought. It is, however, a unity in which character as such is no longer the center of personality. What counts for Eunapius is the experience of a supernatural reality induced by education, initiation into mysteries, and frequentation of men who directly speak to the gods. The atmosphere is obviously pagan. Eunapius makes no secret of his dislike of Christianity. He was by then a very old man with little to lose. He explains the Gothic invasion of Greece in A.D. 395 as the result of treason by men "clad in black raiment" (476), that is, Christian monks. He has bitter words about the destruction of the temple of Serapis in Alexandria (472). All this is not surprising; what is surprising is to be told that among the teachers of Eunapius at Athens there was Proairesius, a Christian rhetorician who had the distinction of becoming the teacher of St. Basil and of Gregory of Nazianzus. Eunapius devotes to him one of the detailed accounts in his biographies and has to admit in a rather embarrassed tone that the man who "loved him like his

own son" was one of those who had to retire when the Emperor
Julian decreed that Christian Sophists should be barred from
teaching Hellenic literature (493).

The difference between pagan and Christian intellectuals was
in fact much smaller than they themselves would have owned. On
both sides of the iron curtain the notion of character, the experience of the interchange between individual ambitions and political circumstances was being replaced by mystical experiences and
contacts with divine beings. As political life ceased to be the primary term of reference for the individual, women reasserted themselves far more easily. The primary text for a woman's life is of
course the life of Macrina by her brother Gregory of Nyssa.

Generally speaking, one can say that Gregory of Nyssa in the
variety of his biographical experiments is at the center of the
transformation of biography in the fourth century. No other author gives us a sequence comparable with that provided by Gregory of Nyssa in the lives of Moses, of Gregory Thaumaturgus, of
his brother Basilius, and of his sister Macrina, not to speak of
minor but by no means insignificant pieces such as the sermon on
Bishop Meletius of Antioch. We need not discuss the authenticity
of the biography of St. Ephraim the Syrian which is attributed to
Gregory of Nyssa. Yet, if the Christian biographers are the most
determined creators of new biographical models, the pagans are
not far behind. Eunapius of all people provides a parallel to Gregory's life of Macrina in his relatively long and detailed account of
Sosipatra, the wife of the Sophist Eustathius.

As a child, Sosipatra, like Macrina, grew up on her father's
country estate—this time near Ephesus. She was in the care of the
mysterious individuals who administered the estate in the absence of her father. They ultimately proved to be "gods in the
likeness of strangers" (468) and disappeared without notice after
having initiated the girl into unusual mysteries. Sosipatra grew up
to predict the future in all details.

Lives of holy men, whether pagan or Christian, have some positive and some negative qualities in common. First, they present
the holy man as a philosopher, not as a poet, though poets traditionally had the reputation of a special relationship with gods. It
would take us too far here to explain why poets were unsuitable
predecessors for the holy men, though my passing mention of bi-

ography of poets provides a hint. Second, biographies of holy men avoided allegorization. Allegorization of gods and heroic figures had of course a long tradition in pagan thought before it was transferred by men like Philo of Alexandria to biblical figures. Gregory of Nyssa went beyond Philo in allegorizing the life of Moses. But neither Gregory of Nyssa nor any other Christian biographer I know of allegorized the life of a saint, and I do not know either of any allegorization of pagan holy men, such as Plotinus or Proclus. Third, to be a creditable biographer of a holy man one had to claim close personal knowledge. There was need of intimacy with a holy man. The biographer mediated the intimacy between saint and reader by asserting the intimacy between saint and biographer. Positively, a holy man, whether Christian or pagan, was described as a man who "had made rapid progress towards affinity with the divine, despised his body, freed himself from its pleasures, and embraced a wisdom that was hidden from the crowd." These are words of Eunapius, about Sosipatra's son, Antoninus, who had studied with Hypatia at Alexandria. They might apply to a Christian monk.

The real difference between a pagan and a Christian holy man, as far as I know, was never written down in antiquity. The difference, to use Peter Brown's language in inverted commas, was the invisible presence of the bishop in the life of a Christian holy man. The pagan holy man was a law unto himself: as such he was often a crank, and Garth Fowden was right in describing his drift toward social marginality. The Christian saint had to reckon with the bishop, if he was not himself a bishop. It is no accident that the prototype of the saint's life was written by a bishop. There was no Athanasius to mark the boundary for the pagan equivalent of St. Anthony.

Roman Religion: The Imperial Period

THE ROMAN STATE'S extraordinary and unexpected transformation from one that had hegemony over the greater part of Italy into a world state in the second and first centuries B.C. had implications for Roman religion which are not easy to come to terms with. After all, Christianity, a religion wholly "foreign" in its origins, arose during this period of Roman ascendancy. We shall confine ourselves to three elementary and obviously related facts.

The first is that the old Roman practice of inviting the chief gods of their enemies to become gods of Rome (*evocatio*) played little or no part in the new stage of imperialism. *Evocatio* does not seem to have had any role in the wars in Spain, Gaul, and the East; it is mentioned only, and on dubious evidence (Servius, *Ad Aeneidem* 12. 841), in relation to Rome's conquest of Carthage.

The second fact is that while it was conquering the Hellenistic world Rome was involved in a massive absorption of Greek language, literature, and religion, with the consequence that the Roman gods became victorious over Greece at precisely the time that they came to be identified with Greek gods. As the gods were expected to take sides and to favor their own worshipers, this must have created some problems.

The third fact is that the conquest of Africa, Spain, and, ulti-

"Roman Religion: The Imperial Period" by Arnaldo Momigliano. Reprinted by permission of the publisher from *The Encyclopedia of Religion*, Mircea Eliade, Editor in Chief. Copyright © 1986 by Macmillan Publishing Company, a Division of Macmillan, Inc.

mately, Gaul produced the opposite phenomenon of a large, though by no means systematic, identification of Punic, Iberian, and Celtic gods with Roman gods. This, in turn, is connected with two opposite aspects of the Roman conquest of the West. On the one hand, the Romans had little sympathy and understanding for the religion of their Western subjects. Although occasionally guilty of human sacrifice, they found the various forms of human sacrifices which were practiced more frequently in Africa, Spain, and Gaul repugnant (hence their later efforts to eliminate the Druids in Gaul and in Britain). On the other hand, northern Africa, outside Egypt, and western Europe were deeply latinized in language and romanized in institutions, thereby creating the conditions for the assimilation of native gods to Roman gods.

Yet the Mars, the Mercurius, and even the Jupiter and the Diana we meet so frequently in Gaul under the Romans are not exactly the same as in Rome. The individuality of the Celtic equivalent of Mercurius has already been neatly noted by Caesar. Some Roman gods, such as Janus and Quirinus, do not seem to have penetrated Gaul. Similarly, in Africa, Saturnus preserved much of the Baal Hammon with whom he was identified. There, Juno Caelestis (or simply Caelestis, destined to considerable veneration outside Africa) is Tanit (Tinnit), the female companion of Baal Hammon. The assimilation of the native god is often revealed by an accompanying adjective (Mars Lenus, Mercurius Dumiatis, etc., in Gaul). An analogous phenomenon had occurred in the East under the Hellenistic monarchies: native, especially Semitic, gods were assimilated to Greek gods, especially to Zeus and Apollo. The Eastern assimilation went on under Roman rule (as seen, for example, with Zeus Panamaros in Caria).

Roman soldiers, becoming increasingly professional and living among natives for long periods of time, played a part in these syncretistic tendencies. A further consequence of imperialism was the emphasis on victory and on certain gods of Greek origin (such as Heracles and Apollo) as gods of victory. Victoria was already recognized as a goddess during the Samnite Wars; she was later associated with various leaders, from Scipio Africanus to Sulla and Pompey. Roman emperors used an elaborate religious language in their discussions of victory. Augustine of Hippo depicted Victory as God's angel (*City of God* 4. 17).

The Romans also turned certain gods of Greek origin into gods of victory. As early as 145 B.C., L. Mummius dedicated a temple to Hercules Victor after his triumph over Greece. After a victory, generals often offered 10 percent of their booty to Hercules, and Hercules Invictus was a favorite god of Pompey. Apollo was connected with Victory as early as 212 B.C. Caesar boosted her ancestress Venus in the form of Venus Victrix. But it was Apollo who helped Octavian, the future Augustus, to win the battle of Actium in September of 31 B.C.

IMPERIAL ATTITUDES TOWARD AND USES OF RELIGION

Augustus and his contemporaries thought, or perhaps in some cases wanted other people to think, that the preceding age (roughly the period from the Gracchi to Caesar) had seen a decline in the ancient Roman care for gods. Augustus himself stated in the autobiographical record known as the *Res gestae* that he and his friends had restored eighty-two temples. He revived cults and religious associations, such as the Arval Brothers and the fraternity of the Titii, and appointed a *flamen dialis*, a priestly office that had been left vacant since 87 B.C. This revivalist feeling was not entirely new: it was behind the enormous collection of evidence concerning ancient Roman cults, the "divine antiquities," which Varro had dedicated to Caesar about 47 B.C., in his *Antiquitatum rerum humanarum et divinarum libri*; the rest of the work, the "human antiquities," was devoted to Roman political institutions and customs. Varro's work became as much a codification of Roman religion for succeeding generations as existed, and as such it was used for polemical purposes by Christian apologists; it was, however, never a guide for ordinary worshipers.

For us, inevitably, it is difficult to do justice at the same time to the mood of the Augustan restoration and to the unquestionable seriousness with which the political and military leaders of the previous century tried to support their unusual adventures by unusual religious attitudes. Marius, a devotee of the Magna Mater, was accompanied in his campaigns by a Syrian prophetess. Sulla apparently brought from Cappadocia the goddess Ma, soon identified with Bellona, whose orgiastic and prophetic cult had wide appeal. Furthermore, he developed a personal devotion to Venus and Fortuna and set an example for Caesar, who claimed Venus as the ancestress of the *gens Julia*. As *pontifex maximus* for twenty years, Caesar reformed not only individual cults but also the calendar, which had great religious significance. He tried to support his claim to dictatorial powers by collecting religious honors which, though obscure in detail and debated by modern scholars, anticipate later imperial cult.

Unusual religious attitudes were not confined to leaders. A Roman senator, Nigidius Figulus, made religious combinations of his own both in his writings and in his practice: magic, astrology, and Pythagoreanism were some of the ingredients. Cicero, above all, epitomized the search of educated men of the first century B.C. for the right balance between respect for the ancestral cults and the requirements of philosophy. Cicero could no longer believe in traditional divination. When his daughter died in 45 B.C., he embarked briefly on a project for making her divine. This was no less typical of the age than the attempt by Clodius in 62 B.C. to desecrate the festival of Bona Dea, reserved to women, in order to contact Caesar's wife; he escaped punishment.

The imperial age was inclined to distinctions and to compromises. The Roman *pontifex maximus* Q. Mucius Scaevola is credited with the popularization of the distinction, originally Greek, between the gods of the poets as represented in myths, the gods of ordinary people to be found in cults and sacred laws, and finally the gods of the philosophers, confined to books and private discussion. It was the distinction underlying the thought of Varro and Cicero. No wonder, therefore, that in that atmosphere of civil wars and personal hatreds, cultic rules and practices were exploited ruthlessly to embarrass enemies while no one could publicly challenge the ultimate validity of traditional practices.

The Augustan restoration discouraged philosophical speculation about the nature of the gods: Lucretius's *De Rerum Natura* remains characteristic of the age of Caesar. Augustan poets (Horace, Tibullus, Propertius, and Ovid) evoked obsolescent rites and emphasized piety. Virgil interpreted the Roman past in religious terms. Nevertheless, the combined effect of the initiatives of Caesar and Augustus amounted to a new religious situation.

For centuries the aristocracy in Rome had controlled what was called *ius sacrum* (sacred law), the religious aspect of Roman life, but the association of priesthood with political magistracy, though frequent and obviously convenient, had never been institutionalized. In 27 B.C. the assumption by Octavian of the permanent title *Augustus* implied, though not very clearly, permanent approval of the gods (*augustus* may connote a holder of permanent favorable auspices). In 12 B.C. Augustus assumed the position of *pontifex maximus*, which became permanently associated with the figure of the emperor (*imperator*), the new head for life of the Roman State. Augustus's new role resulted in an identification of religious with political power, which had not existed in Rome since at least the end of the monarchy. Furthermore, the divinization of Caesar after his death had made Augustus, as his adoptive son, the son of a *divus*. In turn Augustus was officially divinized (*apotheosis*) after his death by the Roman Senate. Divinization after death did not become automatic for his successors (Tiberius, Gaius, and Nero was not divinized); nevertheless, Augustus's divinization created a presumption that there was a divine component in an ordinary emperor who had not misbehaved in his lifetime. It also reinforced the trend toward the cult of the living emperor, which had been most obvious during Augustus's life. With the Flavian dynasty and later with the Antonines, it was normal for the head of the Roman State to be both the head of the state religion and a potential, or even actual, god.

As the head of Roman religion, the Roman emperor was therefore in the paradoxical situation of being responsible not only for relations between the Roman State and the gods but also for a fair assessment of his own qualifications to be considered a god, if not after his life, at least while he was alive. This situation, however, must not be assumed to have applied universally. Much of the religious life in individual towns was in the hands of local authorities or simply left to private initiative. The financial support for public cults was in any case very complex, too complex to be discussed here. It will be enough to mention that the Roman State granted or confirmed to certain gods in certain sanctuaries the right to receive legacies (Ulpian, *Regulae* 22. 6). In providing money for a local shrine an emperor implied no more than benevolence toward the city or group involved.

Within the city of Rome, however, the emperor was in virtual control of the public cults. As a Greek god, Apollo had been kept outside of the *pomerium* since his introduction into Rome: his temple was in the Campus Martius. Under Augustus, however, Apollo received a temple inside the *pomerium* on the Palatine in recognition of the special protection he had offered to Octavian. The Sibylline oracles, an ancient collection of prophecies that had been previously preserved on the Capitol, were now transferred to the new temple. Later, Augustus demonstrated his preference for Mars as a family god, and a temple to Mars Ultor (the avenger of Caesar's murder) was built. It was no doubt on the direct initiative of Hadrian that the cult of Rome as a goddess (in association with Venus) was finally introduced into the city centuries after the cult had spread outside of Italy. A temple to the Sun (Sol), a cult popular in the Empire at large, and not without some roots in the archaic religion of Rome, had to wait until the Emperor Aurelian in A.D. 274, if one discounts the cult of the Ba'al of Emesa, a sun god, which came and went with the Emperor Elagabalus in 220–221. Another example of these changes inside Rome is the full romanization of the Etruscan haruspices performed by the Emperor Claudius in A.D. 47 (Tacitus, *Annales* 11. 15).

A further step in the admission of Oriental gods to the official religion of Rome was the building of a temple to Isis under Gaius. The cult of Isis had been contested and ultimately confined outside the *pomerium,* associated as it was with memories of Cleopatra, the Egyptian enemy of Augustus. Jupiter Dolichenus, an Oriental god popular among soldiers, was probably given a temple on the Aventine in the second century A.D.

We have some evidence that the Roman priestly colleges intervened in the cults of *municipia* and *coloniae,* but on the whole we cannot expect the cults of Rome herself to remain exemplary for Roman citizens living elsewhere. For example, Vitruvius, who dedicated his work on architecture of Octavian before the latter became Augustus in 27, assumes that in an Italian city there should be a temple to Isis and Sarapis (*De architectura* I. 7. I); Isis, we know, was kept out of Rome in those years. Caracalla, however, presented his grant of Roman citizenship to the provincials in A.D. 212 in hope of contributing to religious unification (*Papyrus Giessen* 40). Although the cult of the Capitoline triad appears in Egypt, the results of this grant were modest in religious terms.

Coins and medals, insofar as they were issued under the control of the central government, provide some indication of imperial preferences in the matter of gods and cults. They allow us to say when and how certain Oriental cults (such as that of Isis, as reflected on coins of Vespasian) or certain attributes of a specific god were considered helpful to the Empire and altogether suitable for the man in the street who used coins. But since as a rule it avoided references to cults of rulers, coinage can be misleading if taken alone. Imperial cult and Oriental cults are, in fact, two of the most important features of Roman religion in the imperial period. But we also have to take into consideration popular, not easily definable, trends; the religious beliefs or disbeliefs of the intellectuals; the greater participation of women in religious and in intellectual life generally; and, finally, the peculiar problems presented by the persecution of Christianity.

THE IMPERIAL CULTS

Imperial cult was many things to many people. The emperor never became a complete god, even if he was considered a god, because he was not requested to produce miracles, even for supposed deliverance from peril. Vespasian performed miracles in Alexandria soon after his proclamation as emperor, but these had no precise connection to his potential divine status; he remained an exception in any case. Hadrian never performed miracles, but his boyfriend Antinous, who was divinized after death, is known to have performed some (F. K. Dörner, *Denkschriften Wiener Akademie* 75, 1952, p. 40, no. 78).

Apotheosis, decided by the Senate, was the only official form of deification valid for everyone in the Empire and was occasionally extended to members of the imperial family (Drusilla, the sister of Gaius, received apotheosis in A.D. 38). It had its precedent, of course, in the apotheosis of Romulus. Ultimately, the cult of the living emperor mattered more. It was the result of a mixture of spontaneous initiative by provincial and local councils (and even by private individuals) and promptings from provincial governors

and the emperor himself. It had precedents not only in the Hellenistic ruler cult but also in the more or less spontaneous worship of
Roman generals and governors, especially in the hellenized East.
Cicero, for example, had to decline such worship when he was a
provincial governor (*Ad Atticum* 5. 21. 7).

The cult of Roman provincial governors disappeared with Augustus, to the exclusive benefit of the emperor and his family.
When he did not directly encourage the ruler cult, the emperor
still had to approve, limit, and occasionally to refuse it. Although
he had to be worshiped, he also had to remain a man in order to
live on social terms with the Roman aristocracy, of which he was
supposed to be the *princeps*. It was a delicate balancing act. It is
probably fair to say that during his lifetime the emperor was a god
more in proportion to his remoteness, rather than his proximity,
and that the success (for success it was) of the imperial cult in the
provinces was due to the presence it endowed to an absent and
alien sovereign. His statues, his temples, and his priests, as well as
the games, sacrifices, and other ceremonial acts, helped make the
emperor present; they also helped people to express their interest
in the preservation of the world in which they lived.

The imperial cult was not universally accepted and liked. Seneca ridiculed the cult of Claudius, and Tacitus spoke of the cult in
general as Greek adulation. In the third century the historian Dio
Cassius attributed to Augustus's friend Maecenas a total condemnation of the imperial cult. Jews and Christians objected to it on
principle, and the Acts of the Christian Martyrs remind us that
there was an element of brutal imposition in the imperial cult.
But its controversial nature in certain circles may well have been
another factor of the cult's success: conflicts help any cause.
There is even some vague evidence (Pleket, 1965, p. 331) that
some groups treated the imperial cult as a mystery religion in
which priests revealed some secrets about the emperors.

Schematically it can be said that in Rome and Italy Augustus
favored the association of the cult of his life spirit (*genius*) with
the old cult of the public *lares* of the crossroads (*lares com-
pitales*): such a combined cult was in the hands of humble people.
Similar associations (Augustales) developed along various lines in
Italy and gave respectability to the freedmen who ran them. Augustus's birthday was considered a public holiday. His *genius* was

included in public oaths between Jupiter Optimus Maximus and the *penates*. In Augustus's last years Tiberius dedicated an altar to the *numen Augusti* in Rome; the four great priestly colleges had to make yearly sacrifices at it. *Numen*, in an obscure way, implied divine will.

In the West, central initiative created the altar of Roma and Augustus in Lyons, to be administered by the Council of the Gauls (12 B.C.). A similar altar was built at Oppidum Ubiorum (Cologne). Later temples to Augustus (by then officially divinized) were erected in western provinces. In the East, temples to Roma and Divus Julius and to Roma and Augustus were erected as early as 29 B.C. There, as in the West, provincial assemblies took a leading part in the establishment of the cult. Individual cities were also active: priests of Augustus are found in thirty-four different cities of Asia Minor. The organization of the cult varied locally. There was no collective provincial cult of the emperor in Egypt, though there was a cult in Alexandria. And any poet, indeed any man, could have his own idea about the divine nature of the emperor. Horace, for example, suggested that Augustus might be Mercurius.

Augustus's successors tended to be worshiped either individually, without the addition of Roma, or collectively with past emperors. In Asia Minor the last individual emperor known to have received a personal priesthood or temple is Caracalla. In this province—though not necessarily elsewhere—the imperial cult petered out at the end of the third century. Nevertheless, Constantine, in the fourth century, authorized the building of a temple for the *gens Flavia* (his own family) in Italy at Hispellum but without "contagion of superstition"—whatever he may have meant by this (*Corpus Inscriptionum Latinarum*, Berlin, 1863, vol. 11, no. 5265).

It is difficult to say how much the ceremonial of the imperial court reflected divinization of the emperors. We hear, however, that Domitian wanted to be called "dominus et deus" (Suetonius, *Domitian* 13.2). In the third century a specific identification of the living emperor with a known god seems to be more frequent (for instance, Septimius Severus and his wife, Julia Domna, with Jupiter and Juno). When the imperial cult died out, the emperor had to be justified as the choice of god; he became emperor by the grace of god. Thus Diocletian and Maximian, the persecutors of

Christianity, present themselves not as Jupiter and Hercules but as Jovius and Herculius, that is, the protégés of Jupiter and Hercules. It must be added that during the first centuries of the Empire the divinization of the emperor was accompanied by a multiplication of divinizations of private individuals, in the West often of humble origin. Such divinization took the form of identifying the dead, and occasionally the living, with a known hero or god. Sometimes the divinization was nothing more than an expression of affection by relatives or friends. But it indicated a tendency to reduce the distance between men and gods, which helped the fortunes of the imperial cult. We need to know more about private divinizations (but see H. Wrede, *Consecratio in formam deorum*, Mainz, 1981).

ORIENTAL INFLUENCES

Oriental cults penetrated the Roman Empire at various dates, in different circumstances, and with varying appeal, although on the whole they seem to have supplemented religious needs in the Latin West more than in the hellenized East. They tended, though not in equal measure, to present themselves as mystery cults: they often required initiation and, perhaps more often, some religious instruction.

The Magna Mater, the first Oriental divinity to be found acceptable in Rome since the end of the third century B.C. was long an oddity in the city. She had been imported by governmental decision, she had a temple within the *pomerium*, and she was under the protection of members of the highest Roman aristocracy. Yet her professional priests, singing in Greek and living by their temple, were considered alien fanatics even in imperial times. What is worse, the goddess also had servants, the *Galli*, who had castrated themselves to express their devotion to her.

Under the Emperor Claudius, Roman citizens were probably allowed some priestly functions, though the matter is very obscure. Even more obscure is the way in which Attis, who is practically absent from the republican written evidence concerning Cybele, became Cybele's major partner. A new festival, from 15 to 27 March, apparently put special emphasis on the resurrection of

Attis. Concurrently, the cult of Cybele became associated with the ritual of the slaying of the sacred bull (*taurobolium*), which Prudentius (*Peristephanon* 10. 1006–1050) interpreted as a baptism of blood. The ritual was performed for the prosperity of the emperor or of the Empire and, more frequently, for the benefit of private individuals. Normally it was considered valid for twenty years, which makes it questionable whether it was meant to confer immortality on the baptized.

Although Isis appealed to men as well as to women—and indeed her priests were male—it seems clear that her prestige as a goddess was due to the unusual powers she was supposed to have as a woman. The so-called aretalogies (description of the powers) of Isis insist on this. Thus the earliest aretalogy, found at Maroneia in Macedonia, tells of Isis as legislator and as protector of the respect of children for their parents (Merkelbach, 1976, p. 234). The Kyme text declares that she compelled husbands to love their wives (H. Engelmann, ed., *Kyme* 1.97), and the Oxyrhynchus hymn in her honor explicitly states that she made the power of women equal to that of men (*Oxyrhynchus Papyri* 11. 1380). No god or goddess of Greece and Rome had achievements comparable with those of Isis. The girlfriends of the Augustan poets Tibullus and Propertius were captivated by her. In association with Osiris or Sarapis, Isis seems to have become the object of a mystery cult in the first century A.D.; as such she appears in Apuleius's *Golden Ass*.

Late in the first century A.D., Mithraism began to spread throughout the Roman Empire, especially in the Danubian countries and in Italy (in particular, as far as we know, in Ostia and Rome). A developed mystery cult, it had ranks of initiation and leadership and was, to the best of our present knowledge, reserved to men—a clear difference from the cult of Isis. It was practiced in subterranean chapels rather than in temples, although his identification with the sun god gave Mithra some temples. The environment of the Mithraic cult, as revealed in numerous extant chapels, was one of darkness, secrecy, dramatic lighting effects, and magic.

What promise Mithra held for his devotees we do not know for certain. The cult seems to have encouraged soldierly qualities, including sexual abstinence. It certainly presented some correspondence between the degrees of initiation and the levels of the celestial spheres, which may or may not imply an ascent of the soul to these spheres. The killing of the bull (in itself different from the *taurobolium* and perhaps without any implication of baptism) was apparently felt to be a sacrifice performed not for the god but by the god. The initiates reenacted this sacrifice and shared sacred meals in a sort of communal life. Tertullian considered Mithraism a devilish imitation of Christianity, but the Neoplatonist Porphyry found in it allegorical depths.

The cult of Sabazios may have been originally Phrygian. Sabazios appears in Athens in the fifth century B.C. as an orgiastic god. He was known to Aristophanes, and later the orator Aeschines became his priest. There is evidence of mysteries of Sabazios in Lydia dating from the fourth century B.C. In Rome the cult was already known in 139 B.C. It may at that time have been confused with Judaism, but Sabazios was often identified with Jupiter or Zeus, and there seems to be no clear evidence of syncretism between Sabazios and Yahweh. Sabazios was most popular in the second century A.D., especially in the Danubian region. In Rome his cult left a particularly curious document in the tomb of Vincentius, located in the catacomb of Praetextatus; it includes scenes of banquets and of judgment after death. Whether this is evidence of mystery ceremonies or of Christian influence remains uncertain. (See Erwin R. Goodenough, *Jewish Symbols in the Greco-Roman Period*, vol. 2, 1953, p. 45, for a description.) The tomb of Vincentius appears to belong to the third century, when, judging by the epigraphic evidence, there seems to have been a decline of the cult of Sabazios and, indeed, of all mystery cults. Although a shortage of inscriptions does not necessarily imply a shortage of adepts, one has the impression that by then Christianity was seriously interfering with the popularity of Oriental cults.

Another popular Oriental god occupies a place by himself. This is Jupiter Dolichenus, who emerged from Doliche in Commagene in the first century A.D. and for whom we have about six hundred monuments. Of the Oriental gods, he seems to have been the least sophisticated and to have disappeared earliest (in the third century). He was ignored by Christian polemicists. While he circulated in the Empire, he preserved his native attributes: he is depicted as a warrior with Phrygian cap, double ax, and lightning bolt, standing erect over a bull. He was often accompanied by a goddess, called Juno Regina in the Roman interpretation. Twins, identified with the Castores, followed him; their lower parts were unshaped, and they were probably demons. Soldiers seem to have loved the cult of Jupiter Dolichenus. Its priests were not professional, and the adepts called each other brother. Admission to the cult presupposed instruction, if not initiation.

EXTENT OF SYNCRETISM

We are in constant danger of either overrating or underrating the influence of these Oriental cults on the fabric of the Roman Empire. If, for instance, Mithraists knew of Zoroastrian Angra Mainyu, what did he mean to them and how did this knowledge affect the larger society? At a superficial level we can take these cults as a sort of antidote to the imperial cult, an attempt to retreat from the public sphere of political allegiance to the private sphere of small, free associations. The need for small loyalties was widely felt during the imperial peace. Distinctions between social, charitable, and religious purposes in these multiform associations are impossible. Tavern-keepers devoted to their wine god and poor people meeting regularly in burial clubs are examples of such associations (*collegia*). Ritualization of ordinary life emerged from their activities. Nor is it surprising that what to one was religion was superstition to another (to use two Latin terms which ordinary Latin speakers would have been hard-pressed to define). Although allegiance to the local gods (and respect for them, if one happened to be a visitor) was deeply rooted, people were experimenting with new private gods and finding satisfaction in them. Concern with magic and astrology, with dreams and demons, seems ubiquitous. Conviviality was part of religion. Aelius Aristides has good things to say about Sarapis as patron of the *symposium*. Pilgrimages to sanctuaries were made easier by relative social stability. Several gods, not only Asclepius (Gr. Asklepios), offered healing to the sick. (Here again we have Aelius Aristides as chief witness for the second century.) Hence miracles, duly registered in inscriptions; hence also single individuals, perhaps cranks, attaching themselves to temples and living in their precincts.

The real difficulties in understanding the atmosphere of paganism in the Roman Empire perhaps lie elsewhere. It remains a puzzle how, and how much, ordinary people were supposed to know about official Roman religion. The same problem exists concerning the Greeks in relation to the religions of individual Greek cities. But in Greek cities the collective education of adolescents, as *epheboi*, implied participation in religious activities (for instance, singing hymns in festivals) which were a form of religious education. In the Latin-speaking world, however, there is no indication of generalized practices of this kind. People who tell us something about their own education, for example, Cicero, Horace, and Ovid, do not imply that it included a religious side. The situation does not seem to have changed in later times, as illustrated, for instance, in Tacitus's life of Agricola. Children at school no doubt absorbed a great deal from classical authors, but whether they read Homer or Virgil, they did not absorb the religion of their own city. Temples carried inscriptions explaining what was expected from worshipers as well as the qualities of the relevant god. Cultic performances, often in a theater adjoining the temple, helped to explain what the god was capable of. We cannot, however, draw a distinguishing line between cultic performances, perhaps with an element of initiation, and simple entertainment.

Another element difficult to evaluate is the continuous, and perhaps increased, appeal of impersonal gods within Roman religion. There is no indication that Faith (Fides) and Hope (Spes) increased their appeal. (They came to play a different part in Christianity by combining with Jewish and Greek ideas.) At best, Fides gained prestige as a symbol of return to loyalty and good faith during the reign of Augustus. But Fortuna, Tutela, and Virtus were popular; the typology of Virtus on coins seems to be identical with that of Roma. Genius was generalized to indicate the spirit of a place or of a corporation. Strangely, an old Latin god of the woods, Silvanus, whose name does not appear in the Roman calendar, became important, partly because of his identification with the Greek Pan and with a Pannonian god but above all because of his equation with Genius: we find the god protector of Roman barracks called Genius Castrorum or Silvanus Castrorum or Fortuna Castrorum. We have already mentioned Victoria, often connected with individual emperors and individual victories (Victoria Augusti, Ludi Victoriae Claudi, etc.).

A third element of complication is what is called syncretism, by which we really mean two different things. One is the positive identification of two or more gods; the other is the tendency to mix different cults by using symbols of other gods in the sanctuary of one god, with the result that the presence of Sarapis, Juno, and even Isis was implied in the shrine of Jupiter Dolichenus on the Aventine in Rome. In either form, syncretism may have encouraged the idea that all gods are aspects, or manifestations, of one god.

Vaguely monotheistic attitudes were in any case encouraged by philosophical reflection, quite apart from suggestions coming from Judaism, Christianity, and Zoroastrianism. It is therefore legitimate to consider the cult of Sol Invictus, patronized by Aurelian, as a monotheistic or henotheistic predecessor of Christianity. But believers had to visualize the relation between the one and the many. This relation was complicated by the admission of intermediate demons, either occupying zones between god or gods and men or going about the earth and perhaps more capable of evil than of good. Even those who could think through, in some depth, the idea of one god (such as Plutarch) were still interested in Zeus or Isis or Dionysos, whatever their relation to the god beyond the gods. Those educated people who in late antiquity liked to collect priesthoods and initiations to several gods, in pointed contrast with Christianity, evidently did so because they did not look upon the gods concerned as one god only. The classic example of such a person is given by the inscription concerning Vettius Agorius Praetextatus dated A.D. 385 (*Corpus Inscriptionum Latinarum*, Berlin, 1863, vol. 6, no. 1779).

This is not to deny the convergence of certain beliefs and experiences. To quote only an extreme case, a mystical experience like ascension to heaven was shared by Paul, Jewish rabbis, gnostics such as the author of the *Gospel of Truth*, and Plotinus.

ROLE OF WOMEN

Women seem to have taken a more active, and perhaps a more creative, part in the religious life of the imperial period. This was connected with the considerable freedom of movement and of administration of one's own estate which women, and especially wealthy women, had in the Roman Empire. Roman empresses of Oriental origin (Julia Domna, wife of Septimius Severus, and Julia Mamaea, mother of Severus Alexander) contributed to the diffusion outside Africa of the cult of Caelestis, who received a temple on the Capitol in Rome. The wife of a Roman consul, Pompeia Agrippinilla, managed to put together a private association of about four hundred devotees of Liber-Dionysus in the Roman Campagna in the middle of the second century A.D. (See the inscription published by Achille Vogliano in the *American Journal of Archaeology* 37, 1933, p. 215.) Women could be asked to act as *theologoi*, that is, to preach about gods in ceremonies even of a mystery nature. We have seen that Isis appealed to, and was supported by, women. It is revealing that Marcus Aurelius declared himself grateful to his mother for teaching him veneration of the gods.

The intellectual and religious achievements of women become more conspicuous in the fourth century. Women such as Sosipatra, described in Eunapius's account of the lives of the Sophists, and Hypatia of Alexandria are the counterparts (though apparently more broadly educated and more independent in their social actions) of Christian women such as Macrina, sister of Gregory of Nyssa (who wrote her biography), and the followers of Jerome. We are not surprised to find in the city of Thasos during the late Roman Empire a woman with a resounding Latin name, Flavia Vibia Sabina, honored by the local senate "as a most noteworthy high priestess . . . the only woman, first in all times to have honours equal to those of the senators" (H. W. Pleket, *Texts on the Social History of the Greek World*, 1969).

Dedications of religious and philosophical books by men to women appear in the imperial period. Plutarch dedicated his

treatise on Isis and Osiris to Clea, a priestess of Delphi; Diogenes
Laertius dedicated his book on Greek philosophers (which has
anti-Christian implications) to a female Platonist. Philostratus
claims that Julia Domna encouraged him to write the life of Apollonius of Tyana. What is more, Bishop Hippolytus apparently
wrote a book on resurrection dedicated to the pagan Julia Mamaea.
We know from Eusebius that this same woman invited Origen to
visit her in Antioch, obviously to discuss Christianity.

LITERARY EVIDENCE

Epigraphy and archaeology have taught us much, but the religion of the Roman Empire survives mainly through writings in
Latin, Greek, Syriac, and Coptic (not to speak of other languages):
biographies, philosophical disputations, epic poems, antiquarian books, exchanges of letters, novels, and specific religious
books. Most of the authors speak only for themselves. But taken
together, they convey an atmosphere of sophisticated cross-
questioning which would have prevented minds from shutting
out alternatives or concentrating solely on ritual. We can only give
examples. The Stoic Lucan in his *Pharsalia*, a poem on the civil
wars, excludes the gods but admits fate and fortune, magic and
divination. Two generations later, Silius Italicus wrote an optimistic poem, turning on Scipio as a Roman Heracles supported
by his father, Jupiter. More or less at the same time, Plutarch was
reflecting on new and old cults, on the delays in divine justice,
and (if the work in question is indeed his) on superstition.

In the second part of the second century Lucian passed from the
caricature of an assembly of gods and from attacks against oracles
to a sympathetic description of the cult of Dea Syria; he abused
such religious fanatics as Peregrinus, as well as Alexander of
Abonuteichos, the author of a cult, whom he considered to be an
impostor. Perhaps what Lucian wanted to give is, in fact, what we
get from him—the impression of a mind that refuses to be imposed upon. Fronto's correspondence with Marcus Aurelius confirms what we deduce from other texts (such as Aelius Aristides'
speeches): preoccupation with one's own health was a source of
intense religious experience in the second century A.D. Apuleius,

in *De Magia*, gives a glimpse of a small African community in which suspicion of magic practices can upset the town (as well as the author). In *The Golden Ass* Apuleius offers an account of the mysteries of Isis which may be based on personal experiences. But Apuleius's *Golden Ass* is only one of the many novels which were fashionable in the Roman empire. The appeal of such novels probably resided in their ability to offer readers vicarious experiences of love, magic, and mystery ritual.

The variety of moods and experiences conveyed by these texts, from the skeptical to the mystical, from the egotistic to the political in the old Greek sense, gives us an approximate notion of the thoughts of educated people on religious subjects. These books provide the background for an understanding of the Christian apologists who wrote for the pagan upper class. Conversely, we are compelled to ask how much of pagan religious thinking was conditioned by the presence of Jews and even more of Christians in the neighborhood. The anti-Jewish attitudes of a Tacitus or of a Juvenal offer no special problem: they are explicit. The same can be said about the anti-Christian polemics of Celsus; here the problem, if any, is that the text is lost and we are compelled to make inferences from the reply given in changed circumstances by the Christian Origen. But there are far more writers who seldom or never refer to Christianity yet can hardly have formulated their thoughts without implicit reference to it.

How much Lucian or Philostratus (in his life of Apollonius of Tyana) was trying to put across pagan points of view in answer to the Christian message is an old question. The biography by Philostratus was translated into Latin by a pagan leader, Nicomachus Flavianus, in the late fourth century. Another author who may be suspected of knowing more about Christianity than his silence about it would indicate is Diogenes Laertius. In his lives of philosophers, he pointedly refuses to admit non-Greek wisdom and enumerates all the Greek schools, from Plato to Epicurus, as worthy of study and admiration. With the renascence of Neoplatonic thought in the third and fourth centuries and the combination of Platonism with mystical and magical practices (the so-called theurgy) in the circles to which Julian the Apostate belonged, the attempt to erect a barrier to Christianity is patent but, even then, not necessarily explicit.

The most problematic texts are perhaps those which try to formulate explicit religious beliefs. Even a simple military religious
calendar (such as the third-century Feriale Duranum, copied for
the benefit of the garrison of Dura-Europos) raises the question of
its purpose and validity: how many of these old-fashioned Roman
festivals were still respected? When we come to such books as the
Chaldean Oracles (late second century?) or the Hermetica texts,
composed in Greek at various dates in Egypt (and clearly showing
the influence of Jewish ideas), it is difficult to decide who believed
in them and to what extent. Such texts present themselves as revealed: they speak of man's soul imprisoned in the body, of fate,
and of demonic power with only a minimum of coherence. They
are distantly related to what modern scholars call gnosticism, a
creed with many variants which was supposed to be a deviation
from Christianity and, as such, was fought by early Christian
apologists. We now know much more about gnostics, thanks to
the discovery of the Nag Hammadi library, which supplemented,
indeed dwarfed, previous discoveries of Coptic gnostic texts. As-
sembled in the fourth century from books mainly translated from
Greek, the Nag Hammadi library represents an isolated survival.
It points to a previous, more central movement thriving in the
exchange of ideas. Can we assess the impact of the gnostic sects
when they placed themselves between pagans and Christians (and
Jews) in the first centuries of the Empire?

STATE REPRESSION AND PERSECUTION

The Roman State had always interfered with the freedom to
teach and worship. In republican times astrologers, magicians,
philosophers, and even rhetoricians, not to speak of adepts of certain religious groups, had been victims of such intrusion. Under
which precise legal category this interference was exercised
remains a question, except perhaps in cases of sacrilege. From
Tacitus we know that Augustus considered adultery in his own
family a crime of *laesa religio* (*Annales* 3. 24). Whatever the legal
details, there was persecution of Druidic cults and circles in Gaul
and Britain in the first century. Augustus prohibited Roman citizens from participating in Druidic cults, and Claudius prohibited

the cult of the Druids altogether. Details are not clear, and consequences not obvious, though one hears little of the Druids from
this time on. Abhorrence of Druidic human sacrifices no doubt
counted for much. But Augustus also did not like the practice of
foretelling the future, for which the Druids were conspicuous, and
he is credited with the destruction of two thousand *fatidici libri*
(Suetonius, *Augustus*, 31). The Druids were also known to be magicians, and Claudius condemned to death a Roman knight who
had brought to court a Druidic magic egg (Pliny, *Naturalis Historia* 29. 54).

This being said, we must emphasize how unusual it was for the
Roman government to come to such decisions. Existing cults
might or might not be encouraged, but they were seldom persecuted. Even Jews and Egyptians were ordinarily protected in
their cults, although there were exceptions. The long-standing
conflict between the Christians and the Roman State—even taking into account that persecution was desultory—remains unique
for several reasons which depended more on Christian than on
imperial behavior. First, the Christians obviously did not yield or
retreat, as did the Druids. Second, the Christians hardly ever became outright enemies of, or rebels against, the Roman State. The
providential character of the Roman State was a basic assumption
of Christianity. The workings of providence were shown, for
Christians, by the fact that Jesus was born under Roman rule,
while the Roman State had destroyed the Temple of Jerusalem and
dispersed the Jews, thus making the Church the heiress to the
Temple. Third, the Christians were interested in what we may call
classical culture. Their debate with the pagans became, increasingly, a debate within the terms of reference of classical culture;
the Jews, however, soon lost their contact with classical thought
and even with such men as Philo, who had represented them in
the dialogue with classical culture. Fourth, Christianity and its
ecclesiastical organization provided what could alternatively be
either a rival or a subsidiary structure to the imperial government; the choice was left to the Roman government, which under
Constantine chose the church as a subsidiary institution (without quite knowing on what conditions).

The novelty of the conflict explains the novelty of the solution—not tolerance but conversion. The emperor had to become

Christian and to accept the implications of his conversion. It took about eighty years to turn the pagan state into a Christian state. The process took the form of a series of decisions about public non-Christian acts of worship. The first prohibition of pagan sacrifices seems to have been enacted in 341 (*Codex Theodosianus* 16. 10. 2). Closing of the pagan temples and prohibition of sacrifices in public places under penalty of death was stated or restated at an uncertain date between 346 and 354 (ibid., 16. 10. 4).

Even leaving aside the reaction of Julian, these measures cannot have been effective. The emperor remained *pontifex maximus* until Gratian gave up the position in 379 (Zosimus, 4. 36. 5). Gratian was the emperor who removed the altar of Victoria from the Roman Senate and provoked the controversy between Symmachus and Bishop Ambrose, the most important controversy about the relative merits of tolerance and conversion in late antiquity. Then, in 391, Theodosius forbade even the private pagan cult (*Codex Theodosianus* 16. 10. 12). In the same year, following riots provoked by a special law against pagan cults in Egypt, the Serapeum of Alexandria was destroyed, an act whose significance was felt worldwide. The brief pagan revival of 393, initiated by the usurper Eugenius, a nominal Christian who sympathized with the pagans, was soon followed by other antipagan laws. Pagan priests were deprived of their privileges in 396 (ibid., 16. 10. 4). Pagan temples in the country (not in towns) were ordered to be destroyed in 399 (ibid., 16. 10. 16). But in the same year festivals which appear pagan to us were allowed (ibid., 16. 10. 17).

No doubt the Christians knew how and where they could proceed to direct action. The economic independence and traditional prestige of local pagan aristocrats, especially in Rome, allowed them to survive for a time and to go on elaborating pagan thought, as we can see from Macrobius's *Saturnalia* and even from Boethius's *De Consolatione Philosophiae*, although Boethius was technically a Christian who knew his Christian texts. The Neoplatonists of Athens had to be expelled by Justinian in 529. But in Africa Synesius became the first Neoplatonist to be baptized in the early fifth century (about 403–410).

Hopes that the pagan gods would come back excited the Eastern provinces during the rebellion against the Emperor Zeno in about 483, in which the pagan rhetorician and poet Pampremius had a prominent part (Zacharias of Mitylene, *Vita Severi*, in *Patrologia Orient*. 2. 1. 40; M. A. Kugener, ed., Paris, 1903). The peasants (*rustici*), about whom Bishop Martin of Bracara in Spain had so many complaints, gave more trouble to the ecclesiastical authorities than did the philosophers and the aristocrats of the cities. Sacrifices, just because they were generally recognized as efficient ways of persuading the gods to act, were at the center of Christian suspicion. According to a widespread opinion shared by Paul the Apostle (but not by all the Fathers) pagan gods existed—as demons.

Select Bibliography

Georg Wissowa's *Religion und Kultus der Römer*, 2d ed. (Munich, 1912), and Kurt Latte's *Römische Religionsgeschichte* (Munich, 1960) are basic reading on the topic. They are supplemented by Martin P. Nilsson's *Geschichte der griechischen Religion*, vol. 2, 3d ed. (Munich, 1974), for the eastern side of the Roman Empire. Jean Bayet's *Histoire politique et psychologique de la religion romaine* (Paris, 1957) proposes an alternative approach and is improved in the Italian translation, *La religione romana: Storia politica e psicologica* (Turin, 1959). All the publications by Franz Cumont and Arthur Darby Nock remain enormously valuable and influential. See, for instance, Cumont's *Astrology and Religion among the Greeks and Romans* (New York, 1912), *After Life in Roman Paganism* (New Haven, 1922), *Les religions orientales dans le paganisme romain*, 4th ed. (Paris, 1929), *Recherches sur le symbolisme funéraire des Romains* (Paris, 1942), and *Lux Perpetua* (Paris, 1949); see also Nock's *Conversion: The Old and the New in Religion from Alexander the Great to Augustine of Hippo* (Oxford, 1933) and his essays in *The Cambridge Ancient History*, vol. 10 (Cambridge, 1934) and vol. 12 (Cambridge, 1939), and in *Essays on Religion and the Ancient World*, 2 vols., edited by Zeph Stewart (Cambridge, Mass., 1972). The scattered contributions by Louis Robert on epigraphic evidence are also indispensable; see, for instance, his *Hellenica*, 13 vols. (Limoges and Paris, 1940–1965).

Among more recent general books are J. H. W. G. Liebeschuetz's *Continuity and Change in Roman Religion* (Oxford, 1979), Ramsay MacMullen's *Paganism in the Roman Empire* (New Haven, 1981), Alan Wardman's *Religion and Statecraft among the Romans* (London, 1982), and John Scheid's *Religion et piété à Rome* (Paris, 1985). Volumes 2.16, 2.17, and 2.23 of *Aufstieg und Niedergang der römischen Welt* (Berlin and New York, 1978–1984) are mostly devoted to Roman imperial paganism and are of great importance. Ramsay MacMullen's *Christianizing the Roman Empire, A.D. 100–400* (New Haven, 1984) supplements his previous book from the Christian side.

Numerous monographs have been published on various topics. Here I can indicate only a few.

On the basic changes in Roman religion: Arthur Bernard Cook, *Zeus: A Study in Ancient Religion*, 3 vols. (Cambridge, 1914–1940); Johannes

Geffcken, *Der Ausgang des griechisch-römischen Heidentums* (Heidelberg, 1920); Bernhard Kötting, *Peregrinatio religiosa: Wallfahrten in der Antike und das Pilgerwesen in der alten Kirche* (Münster, 1950); Frederick H. Cramer, *Astrology in Roman Law and Politics* (Philadelphia, 1954); Arnaldo Momigliano, ed., *The Conflict between Paganism and Christianity in the Fourth Century* (Oxford, 1963); E. R. Dodds, *Pagan and Christian in an Age of Anxiety* (Cambridge, 1965); Clara Gallini, *Protesta e integrazione nella Roma antica* (Bari, 1970); Peter Brown, *Religion and Society in the Age of Saint Augustine* (London, 1972); Javier Teixidor, *The Pagan God: Popular Religion in the Greco-Roman Near East* (Princeton, 1977); Sabine G. MacCormack, *Art and Ceremony in Late Antiquity* (Berkeley, 1981); Peter Brown, *Society and the Holy in Late Antiquity* (Berkeley, 1982). See also Morton Smith's article "Prolegomena to a Discussion of Aretalogies, Divine Men, the Gospels and Jesus," *Journal of Biblical Literature* 90 (June 1971), 174–99.

On the imperial cult: Christian Habicht, *Gottmenschentum und griechische Städte*, 2d ed. (Munich, 1970); Stefan Weinstock, *Divus Julius* (Oxford, 1971); Elias J. Bickerman et al., eds., *Le culte des souverains dans l'empire romain* (Geneva, 1973); J. Rufus Fears, *Princeps a diis electus: The Divine Election of the Emperor as a Political Concept at Rome* (Rome, 1977); S. R. F. Price, *Rituals and Power: The Roman Imperial Cult in Asia Minor* (Cambridge, 1984). Price's book should be supplemented by his article "Gods and Emperors: The Greek Language of the Roman Imperial Cult," *Journal of Hellenic Studies* 94 (1984), 79–95. See also H. W. Pleket's "An Aspect of the Emperor Cult: Imperial Mysteries," *Harvard Theological Review* 58 (October 1965), 331–47; Lellia Cracco Ruggini's "Apoteosi e politica senatoria nel IV sec. C.," *Rivista storica italiana* (1977), 425–89; and Keith Hopkins's *Conquerors and Slaves* (Cambridge, 1978), 197–242.

On specific periods or individual gods: Jean Beaujeu, *La religion romaine à l'apogée de l'empire*, vol. 1, *La politique religieuse des Antonins* (Paris, 1955), 96–192; Marcel Leglay, *Saturne africaine* (Paris, 1966); R. E. Witt, *Isis in the Graeco-Roman World* (London, 1971); Robert Turcan, *Mithras Platonicus: Recherches sur l'hellénisation philosophique de Mithra* (Leiden, 1975); Maarten J. Vermaseren, *Cybele and Attis* (London, 1977); Friedrich Solmsen, *Isis among the Greeks and Romans* (Cambridge, Mass., 1979); Reinhold Merkelbach, *Mithras* (Königstein, West Germany, 1984). See also Merkelbach's article "Zum neuen Isistext aus Maroneia," *Zeitschrift für Papyrologie und Epigraphik* 23 (1976), 234–35.

On Roman sacrifice (not yet studied so thoroughly as Greek practices), see *Le sacrifice dans l'antiquité*, Entretiens Fondation Hardt, no. 27 (Geneva, 1981), and for a theory of the mystery cult in the novels, see Reinhold Merkelbach's *Roman und Mysterium in der Antike* (Munich, 1962). Kurt Rudolph's *Gnosis: The Nature and History of Gnosticism* (San Francisco, 1983) and Giovanni Filoramo's *L'attesa della fine: Storia della gnosi* (Bari, 1983) are the best introductions to the subject, while *Gnosis und Gnostizismus*, edited by Rudolph (Darmstadt, 1975), provides a retrospective anthology of opinions. The collective volumes *Die orientalischen Religionen im Römerreich*, edited by Maarten J. Vermaseren (Leiden, 1981), and *La soteriologia dei culti orientali*, edited by Ugo Bianchi and Vermaseren (Leiden, 1982), provide further guidance in current research on various topics. Noteworthy also are the seminal essays in *Jewish and Christian Self-definition*, vol. 3, *Self-definition in the Graeco-Roman World*, edited by B. F. Meyer and E. P. Sanders (London, 1982).

For the transition from paganism to Christianity, the work of Lellia Cracco Ruggini is essential. See, for example, her "Simboli di battaglia ideologica nel tardo ellenismo" in *Studi storici in onore di Ottorino Bertolini* (Pisa, 1972), 117–300; *Il paganesimo romano tra religione e politica, 384–394 d.C.*, "Memorie della classe di scienze morali, Accademia Nazionale dei Lincei," 8.23.1 (Rome, 1979); and "Pagani, ebrei e cristiani: Odio sociologico e odio teologico nel mondo antico," *Gli ebrei nell'Alto Medioevo* (Spoleto) 26 (1980), 13–101.

12

The New Letter by "Anna" to "Seneca" [1]

BERNHARD BISCHOFF, the great Munich master of medieval Latin philology, has just published one of those books which were customary in the eighteenth and nineteenth centuries, but are now very unusual: a collection of 42 medieval Latin literary texts discovered in various European libraries. The title of the book indicates its contents: *Anecdota novissima. Texte des vierten bis sechzehnten Jahrhunderts* (Hiersemann, Stuttgart, 1984). Several of these new texts touch upon Jewish subjects: a Hebrew-Latin glossary of the tenth century, an anti-Jewish Easter sermon by Liutprandus of Cremona, a parody of a biblical text, etc. But the most important of these texts presents itself as a letter written by an individual called Anna to Seneca: "Incipit Epistola Anne ad Senecam de Superbia et Idolis." This text is preserved in the Library of the Archbishops of Cologne in a manuscript of the early ninth century. The text is not complete, though it is fairly long for a letter, about four pages of a modern book. Professor Bischoff calls his *editio princeps* "Der Brief des Hohenpriesters Annas an den Philosophen Seneca—eine jüdischapologetische Missionsschrift (Viertes Jahrhundert?)."

What this man Anna tells Seneca is that pagan polytheism is indefensible—even in its philosophic forms. The truth is to be found in strict monotheism: "iactant sese creaturae signa cognoscere, cum ignorent ipsum Dominum creatorem mundi." The

Athenaem, N.S. 63, fasc. 1–2, 1985, pp. 217–19.

author does not explicitly mention Jews or Judaism, but he repeatedly alludes to passages to the Old Testament from Genesis to Job. Furthermore, he uses the apocryphal *Sapientia Salomonis* (which he may have read in Greek rather than in Latin). He speaks on behalf of a faith which he calls "veritas nostra." The abundant allusions to the Old Testament are in marked contrast with the absence of references to Christian texts or events. The text shows no sign of Christianity (or of polemical concern with Christianity). The author is evidently neither Christian nor disturbed by Christianity. He criticizes ordinary paganism (with special reference to the cult of Liber Pater). He speaks to educated pagans from the point of view of the Old Testament, but with emphasis on the immortality of the soul: "quod de terra natum est, in terra revertetur; anima autem caeleste munus expectabit."

As we all know from Flavius Josephus, there was a contemporary of Seneca called Anna (Ananos, Hanan) who was eminent enough to be (or to be considered to be) suitable to correspond with Seneca: this Anna was a high priest for a brief period in 62 and was deposed as being responsible for condemning James the brother of Jesus (*Antiquitates Judaicae* 20. 199). After his deposition he remained very authoritative until he was killed in 68: a pro-Roman Sadducee who accepted, however, to play a part in the struggle against Rome.

Josephus admired him, at least when he wrote the *Bellum* (4. 319–25). What he wrote in his autobiography is another story. Professor Bischoff suggests that we should identify this Sadducee leader Anna with the alleged author of the letter to Seneca, and he must be right as far as the incipit of the text goes. Who wrote that incipit probably thought that Anna was the high priest of 62.

But a glance at the text of the letter by Anna is enough to show that there are further complications, some of which have already been noticed by Bischoff himself. True enough, the incipit says that this is a letter from Anna to Seneca. But the text is not addressed to Seneca. The writer clearly speaks to several people whom he addresses as *fratres:* "vehementer admiror, fratres. . . Videtis ergo, fratres. . . ." These *fratres,* to whom the letter is addressed, must be potential proselytes. In other words, the name of Seneca is a secondary interpolation. Somebody turned a letter or a sermon directed to a group of potential proselytes into a letter to Seneca. If this is true, we have to ask ourselves whether the interpolator who introduced Seneca also introduced Anna. This of course is entirely possible. But I do not see how we can exclude the other possibility that an otherwise unknown Jewish propagandist called Anna actually wrote a letter or sermon in Latin for the benefit of *fratres*, potential converts, if not to Judaism, at least to monotheism. An Anna dissociated from Seneca need not be identical with the famous high priest contemporary with Seneca who, being a Sadducee, did not believe in the immortality of the soul.

We have to reckon with the possibility, or rather probability, that our text had originally nothing to do with Seneca and with the high priest of 62. Only at a later stage was the text provided with the present incipit which turned it into a letter to Seneca from (presumably) the high priest Anna. Future research into the Latinity of the text and into the biblical references should help us to give an approximate date to the text apart from the incipit. It will not be an easy task, because we know little about the Latin of the Jews of the West and about their Bible. Our text—apart from scribal interference—shows signs of having been written by someone whose Latin was strongly influenced by Greek. On the other hand, it is a text of some sophistication. One is reminded of the famous epitaph of Rome for Regina (*Corpus Inscr. Iud.* 476 of the second century). In any case, a text in Latin written to attract proselytes to Judaism is not, as far as I know, something we encounter at every corner. Proselytes in Rome certainly existed. Another Roman inscription (*CII* 523) celebrates a woman who became a proselyte at the age of seventy and died at the age of eighty six after having been "mother" of two synagogues.

We may now face the obvious. At the end of the fourth century St. Jerome knew of a correspondence between Seneca and St. Paul. Alcuin offered it to Charlemagne and it has duly come down to us. As these fourteen letters were still unknown to Lactantius in the early fourth century, it is generally agreed that they were forged later in the same century. A voice of disagreement was heard a few years ago from a noble and scrupulous scholar who was entitled to his opinion. Not long before his regretted death, Ezio Franceschini attempted to defend the authenticity of this correspondence (*Studi E. Paratore*, Bologna, 1981, 827–41). One wonders what Franceschini would have said about this new letter by Anna to Seneca which is a Jewish counterpart to the (Christian) correspondence between Seneca and St. Paul.

What *we* can say, who take the fourth-century origin of the correspondence between Seneca and St. Paul for granted, is not very much. As we have seen, the letter published by Bischoff was not originally addressed to Seneca; it may, however, have been written by *an* Anna. We may therefore conjecture that somebody interpolated the name of Seneca into the incipit because he knew of the existence of the correspondence between Seneca and St. Paul. On this hypothesis, someone, obviously a Jew, wanted to compete with the implicit Christian propaganda of these letters. This hypothesis has the advantage of simplicity, but is not very illuminating. If the interpolator meant to compete with the Christians, he ought to have inserted some suitable sentence into the text itself. At least in the present stage of the discussion I would not like to exclude a priori the other possibility that a Jew, by interpolating the name of Seneca (and perhaps of Anna) into a preexisting letter, created the precedent for the idea of the correspondence between Seneca and St. Paul. A third possibility (though not a very likely one) is that the introduction of the name of Seneca into Anna's letter and the forgery of the correspondence between Seneca and St. Paul are two unrelated events. What I do not want to ask is whether Anna reminded someone of Annaeus: hence the introduction of (Annaeus) Seneca. I do not like puns.[2]

13

The Life of St. Macrina by Gregory of Nyssa

I

IT HAS BEEN REMARKED that there is a change in the Greek and Roman upper-class attitude to marriage about the end of the first century A.D. It can at least be said that the letters from Pliny the Younger to his wife, when they happened to be separated even for a short period, are unusual. There is also something unusual in the advice about marriage given by Plutarch. His insistence on husband and wife sharing religious practices and beliefs betrays the fear of a religious split in the family and recognizes the importance of an understanding between the two partners in religious matters (*Moralia* 140 D). What Plutarch actually says in his *Advice to Bride and Groom* 19 is: "A wife ought not to make friends of her own, but to enjoy her husband's friends in common with him. The gods are the first and most important friends. Wherefore it is becoming for a wife to worship and to know only the gods that her husband believes in and to shut the door tight upon the queer rituals and outlandish superstitions. For with no god do stealthy and secret rules performed by a woman find any favour" (trans. Loeb). Plutarch is obviously aware of a danger point. He must have known that Christianity was one of those cults which both attracted and accepted unaccompanied women.

The Craft of the Ancient Historian: Essays in Honor of Chester G. Starr, New York, 1985, pp. 443–58.

Indeed, it is difficult to separate what we sense to be a heightened interest by women in philosophy from their increasing independence in religious orientation. Galen knows a woman, Arria, who is interested in Platonic philosophy (XIV 218 Kuhn: *De Theriaca* 14). She was perhaps the wife of N. Nonius Macrinus and is said by Galen to be a friend of emperors (Septimius Severus and Caracalla). We all remember that Philostratus claimed to have been encouraged by Julia Domna, wife of Septimius Severus, to write the life of Apollonius of Tyana. A few decades later the mother of Alexander Severus, Julia Mamaea, invited the Christian philosopher Origen to visit her in Antioch and gave him a military escort. This unlikely piece of news, provided by Eusebius in his *Historia ecclesiastica* 6. 21, is confirmed by the list of the works attributed to Hippolytus, Bishop of Rome, which includes a treatise on resurrection probably dedicated to the same imperial lady (cf. Theodoretus, *Eranistes Dialogues* 2 and 3, "letter to a certain queen," with *Dict. Spiritualité* VII. 543–44). Later in the same century, if this is the correct date, Diogenes Laertius dedicated his lives of Greek philosophers to a woman who was a follower of Plato, but whom he wanted to interest in other philosophic tenets, and especially in Epicureanism. These aristocratic women playing a part in intellectual discussions paved the way for their descendants of the fourth century who played a leading role either in defending paganism or in building up the new monastic style of Christianity.

On the pagan side Hypatia is the best known; but the most intriguing is Sosipatra, who is described by Eunapius as an aristocratic girl educated on her father's estate by mysterious individuals, gods or demons. As a widow she later presided over a philosophic discussion group in her palace at Pergamum (467ff.). Greater and more respectful attention is reserved in our tradition to the Christian aristocratic women: they belonged to the winning side. Most of them were allies of some of the great leaders who both exploited the victory of Christianity and gave it stable intellectual foundations. Olympias is permanently associated with John Chrysostom, though her biography, a contemporary document, is anonymous: the relevant texts are collected in the *Sources Chrétiennes* by A.-M. Malingrey, 1968. Paula—allegedly a descendant of the Scipiones and of the Gracchi and even of

Agamemnon—got her memorial in the long epistle 108 by St. Jerome to her daughter Eustochium: it is known as Epitaphium Sanctae Paulae and has recently (1975) received critical treatment by Jan W. Smit in the Lorenzo Valla series of texts. Macrina is the subject of a biography by her brother, none other than Gregory of Nyssa. Before we concentrate our attention on Macrina, let us mention in passing two other biographical documents of Christian aristocratic women who lived in about the end of the fourth century. Both are anonymous and both were rediscovered in the late nineteenth century: the so-called *Peregrinatio Aetheriae* and the life of Sancta Melania, the former edited by P. Maraval and M. C. Diaz y Diaz, 1982, and the latter by D. Gorce in 1962, both in the *Sources Chrétiennes*. The *Peregrinatio* was identified as a work by the nun Aetheria or Egeria in 1903. The life of Melania seems to have been written by the priest Gerontius whom Cyrillus of Scythopolis in the life of Saint Euthymius calls the successor of the blessed Melania (27 Schwartz).

The victory of Christianity was helped by the decisive intervention of women: it was therefore consecrated by memorable biographies of Christian women. What gives the *Vita* of Macrina its special value is that it comes from her brother. It was not usual for a brother to write the life of his sister. In our case the exceptionality of the performance was increased by the exceptionality of the man who wrote it—not simply a great thinker, but specifically the most versatile and creative Christian biographer of the fourth century. Furthermore, the life of Macrina is the most accomplished and the least conventional biography he ever wrote, the most closely related to his philosophic meditations. This biography was written together with a dialogue "on the soul and resurrection," which is a conscious Christian version of the Platonic *Phaedo*: Macrina is here Socrates to her brother Gregory.

The family background was aristocratic in the ordinary sense: great landowners of Cappadocia and Pontus, Christians for some generations. The father was a reputable rhetorician; at least two of the sons, Basil and Gregory, had rhetorical training before devoting themselves to ecclesiastical affairs. The paternal grandmother, Macrina, from whom our Macrina derived her name, had been under the influence of Gregory Thaumaturgus, himself a pupil of

Origen. The family of the elder Macrina had suffered persecution under Diocletian.

As in the case of the aristocratic pagan Sosipatra, the family of Macrina developed its own physiognomy in the relative isolation and self-sufficiency of the family estate in Pontus with its cohort of slaves and *coloni*. But there are several differences between Sosipatra and Macrina. The former was guarded and educated in her childhood by superhuman beings, so her biographer Eunapius tells us. Macrina had a normal childhood. On the other hand, Sosipatra was a wife and mother before turning to spiritual life as a widow. But even as a widow her spiritual life was disturbed, and therefore her leadership imperiled, by a profane love which seemed induced by magic practices and had to be chased away by appropriate countermeasures. For Macrina there was an engagement with an aristocratic boy at the proper age of twelve, but when the boy died prematurely she refused any other offer of marriage. Her reply to such offers was that the boy she had loved had gone on a long journey: it would have been wrong to betray a husband who was traveling far. She would rejoin her husband in heaven. Here the identification of engagement with marriage is patent: and the mystical interpretation of the Roman quality of *univira* is equally precise. With this decision, which was the beginning of the religious life of Macrina, one detail of her birth acquired its full meaning. Gregory tells us that before giving birth to Macrina her mother dreamt that a figure more majestic than that of an ordinary man named the girl to be born Thecla, "from that Thecla who is famous among the virgins." Therefore, although the girl was called Macrina after her grandmother, her secret name remained Thecla.

It will be remembered that at least since the end of the second century A.D. the Acts of Paul and Thecla had been circulating with increasing authority. They are first mentioned by Tertullian in *De baptismo* about A.D. 205. These Acts, of which Tertullian thought he knew the forger, put forward the memorable figure of Thecla who refused marriage, baptized herself, and with the approval of St. Paul devoted herself to the diffusion of the Gospel. Methodius included Thecla among the exemplary virgins of his *Symposium* at the end of the third century. In the fourth century

Thecla is to be found everywhere: in Ambrosius, *De virginibus* 2. 3. 19–21; in St. Jerome, *Ep.* 22 to Eustochium; in the life of Olympias; and so on.

For the male members of this Christian family, as we have seen, rhetorical education was still paradigmatic. Basil, Gregory, and perhaps the other boys received this worldly training. We know this not only from Basil's and Gregory's own works, but from the other Gregory's, Gregory of Nazianzus's, autobiography: he had shared Basil's life as a student in Athens. For Macrina the Bible seems to have been the main education under her mother's supervision. Education of women had never progressed very far even in pagan aristocratic circles. The decisive moment for this family came when the children had grown up—and the father was already dead. It was decided to turn an estate at Annesoi in Pontus into a double monastery, for women under Macrina and her mother, for men under Macrina's brother Peter. This must have happened about A.D. 350. Another brother, Naucratius, apparently preferred a hermit's life with a friend, in a corner of the same family estate: he was killed in an accident. Also Basil seems to have lived in the neighborhood on family land during his years of retreat between c. 358 and c. 365. We know that his mother was able to bring food to him and to his companion Gregory of Nazianzus (Greg. Naz. *Ep.* 5. 4). Whether Basil's retreat, which provided the first model for Basilian monasticism, was identical with the hermitage of Naucratius, as suggested by J. Gribomont (*Rev. d'Ascétique et de Mystique* 43 [1967], 249–66) is not certain. But Basil's letter 14 to Gregory of Nazianzus in which he playfully extols his own estate over his friend's estate, and his letter 3 to the governor of Cappadocia, Candidianus, asking for protection of his own property, imply that Basil turned land which he owned into a monastic retreat. Even Gregory of Nyssa may have spent some time on this estate, but all we actually know is that Gregory of Nyssa in his letter 9 invites someone to visit him in a hermitage; where and what kind of hermitage it was we do not know (cf. G. Pasquali, *Stud. Ital.* n.s. 3 [1923], 103).

Altogether, Gregory of Nyssa seems to have been least connected with these monastic experiments of the members of his family: he was mainly involved in teaching rhetoric until about 372 when he became rather reluctantly the Bishop of Nyssa. It was only during his own unsatisfactory episcopal life that he came to appreciate fully the value of a monastic existence. After the death of Basil in 379 and of Macrina about 380, Gregory found himself heir to a unique family tradition in pioneering monasticism: then, indeed, he theorized monasticism, if *De instituto christiano* in the form rediscovered and published by W. Jaeger (1952) belongs to the last years of his life. The foundation of monastic institutions on family estates was by no means exceptional. In the same years about 350, under the influence of St. Jerome, Marcella turned her Roman palace into a monastery (Jerome, *Ep.* 127. 5). The later establishment by Paula in Palestine seems to have been started by a personal purchase of land followed by the construction of appropriate buildings (*Epitaphium Paulae* 14. 4). We shall soon see the lasting consequences for the character of these foundations from such aristocratic origins. What is immediately evident is that the founders of these monastic establishments organized their new life in a style likely to safeguard their own aristocratic leadership. Macrina, Melania, Paula, and Olympias were firmly in control of their own institutions.

The aristocratic spirit is especially evident in Macrina's monastic houses because her biographer was her brother—an aristocrat himself in no doubt about the distinction of his own family and of its right to rule. It was generally recognized that a biography written by an eyewitness was a better biography. For a saint, either male or female, to have a biographer among personal acquaintances was even more necessary than for any other mortal being. Sanctity was a private, almost a recondite, condition which required direct experience to be fully appreciated. Furthermore, as miracles were the most authoritative signs of sanctity, having watched miracles became the best qualification for writing the life of a saint. The claim of being an eyewitness is therefore more insistent in the case of biographers of saints than in the case of other biographers. The anonymous biographer of Sancta Melania claims personal acquaintance for part of the facts. St. Jerome was of course the guide and teacher of Paula, who even learned the rudiments of Hebrew from him. Paulinus, who wrote the life of St. Ambrose for the benefit of St. Augustine, was Ambrose's secretary and witnessed a miracle while he was taking down dictation from him. In the case of Macrina, as I have said, it is exceptional that the eyewitness biographer should be her brother. *Laudationes funebres*, a Roman custom (the evidence for which was admirably collected by F. Vollmer, *Jahrb. für class. Philologie* Suppl. 18 [1892]) were a different matter. Relatives eulogized their dead relatives in formal public speeches according to set rules. Gregory of Nazianzus eulogized both his brother Caesarius and his sister Gorgonia. The difference of the genre prevents us from comparing the funeral speech by Gregory of Nazianzus about Gorgonia with Gregory of Nyssa's biography of Macrina. But any study of the female image in fourth-century Christianity will certainly have to take more notice of how Gregory of Nazianzus describes and sanctifies the basically normal married life of his sister Gorgonia, the mother of several not even very saintly children. What was for a woman even rarer than having a brother as a biographer was to have a woman—let alone a sister—as a biographer. I shall not expand on this because I am not widely read in hagiography and much may have escaped me. But it struck me as something of an exception that the abbess Sergia should tell the posthumous adventures of Olympias's body in the "Narratio Sergiae de translatione sanctae Olympiadis" which was edited by Père Delehaye in *Analecta Bollandiana* 16 (1897), 44–51.

II

It follows that if Gregory of Nyssa was probably exceptional in being the biographer of a saintly sister and was certainly even more exceptional in having a brother of overwhelming sanctity like Basil, he was not exceptional in writing a panegyric—that is ultimately a funeral speech—on the same Basil. What is interesting is that he chose two different literary genres to speak about his sister and his brother. While Macrina is brought near by a biography, Basil is made distant by a panegyric. No doubt, being the self-conscious aristocrat he was, Gregory of Nyssa puts both his brother and his sister into the category of greatness: the "great" Basil is a counterpart to the "great" Macrina. But the similarity stops there. Gregory speaks of his sister as his sister, but does not speak of his brother as his brother. Brother Basil is turned into a distant biblical figure, to be compared with Moses, Elijah, St. John the Baptist, and St. Paul. Everybody in the audience undoubtedly knew that Gregory was talking about his brother. But this only increases the sense of timelessness, the biblical proportions, which Gregory attributes to Basil. Macrina brings to Gregory her message of faith and immortality by being active in a small society and caring for a small group—in fact for Gregory himself. The most serious question about Basil is whether he can be considered inferior to St. Paul because he never experienced a bodily ascent to heaven.

To understand the mood and consequently the style with which Gregory of Nyssa confronts his brother Basil, one has to compare his speech on Basil with the speech on Basil written by his friend Gregory of Nazianzus. The Nazianzen is obviously aware of having been preceded by Gregory of Nyssa, and he says all the things Gregory of Nyssa avoided saying. He speaks about Basil's aristocratic background, about his education in Athens—which, as we know, Gregory of Nazianzus had shared—and, at some length, about his struggles with civil and ecclesiastical authorities. The biblical comparisons which represent the substructures of Gregory of Nyssa's eulogy of his brother are not absent from the Nazianzen's speech, but are not a central element of it.

There is more in common between what Gregory of Nyssa had to say about Basil and what he said about Gregory Thaumaturgus, the other figure to which he turned his attention as a panegyrist. Gregory of Nyssa probably owed his name to the connection of his family with Gregory Thaumaturgus, the spiritual guide of the elder Macrina. But this family connection is known to us from Basil (*Ep.* 204), not from Gregory of Nyssa. He keeps his namesake distant, as he keeps his brother distant. He turns the Thaumaturgus, as he turns his brother, into a biblical figure, but this time the emphasis is on miracles rather than on pastoral care and on theology. It will negatively be noticed that Gregory of Nyssa does not say much about the relation between Gregory Thaumaturgus and Origen, though, as we know, Origen was never absent from his mind. There is no mention of the speech of thanks the Thaumaturgus had written on leaving Origen's school, though, as H. Crouzel proved in *Gregorianum* 60 (1979), 312–19, Gregory of Nyssa remembered some expressions in it. The recent valuable analysis of this life or rather panegyric by Raymond Van Dam

(*Classical Antiquity* 1 [1982], 272–308) overlooks the negative approach by Gregory of Nyssa. As in the case of Basil, Gregory of Nyssa tends to focus his attention on those aspects of the Thaumaturgus which are most distant from himself.

At the same time, Gregory of Nyssa expresses in his account of Gregory Thaumaturgus some of the most realistic and even brutal aspects of the policy of Christianization pursued by the clergy in the eastern provinces of the Empire. Gregory Thaumaturgus is the man who found only seventeen Christians in his city, Neocaesarea of Pontus, when he started his mission and left only seventeen pagans when he died. How he managed to achieve this triumph is explained by Gregory of Nyssa under two interconnected headings. First, Gregory Thaumaturgus avoided martyrdom for himself and his flock during the persecution of about A.D. 250 by leaving the city and fleeing to the mountains. Second, the Thaumaturgus persuaded the people that an epidemic was the punishment for pagans who had enjoyed their festivals: the decimation of the population did wonders for Christianity. With this charitable note the panegyric of the Thaumaturgus ends. Not long before, he had turned into real death the simulated death of a Jewish swindler who was giving to a compère the opportunity of collecting some alms. It is to be noticed that according to the Syriac Life of the Thaumaturgus (translated by V. Ryssel, *Theologische Zeitschrift aus der Schweiz* 11 [1894], 241–54) the Thaumaturgus was subsequently persuaded to revive the deceased: hence the conversion of the Jews who became monks. Gregory of Nyssa does not know or ignores this happier end (cf. P. Devos, "Le manteau partagé," *Analecta Bollandiana* 93 [1975], 160–64).

Yet another style was adopted by Gregory of Nyssa in writing the panegyric to Bishop Meletius of Antioch who had died far from his see. This is a lament for the death of an orthodox bishop and friend. And there is a still different approach in the eulogies of the two imperial women who had died within a short time of each other, Pulcheria and her mother, Aelia Flacilla. The characterization of idealized Christian princesses had to express the satisfaction with what was still a newly Christianized Roman Empire. These are slight sketches, obviously at the margins of Gregory's biographical works, but their political importance must not be

underrated. Bishops are now asked to console, celebrate, and flat-
ter emperors.

The connection between the new Christian order and the old
imperial Rome is shown in much stronger colors in the remarkable panegyric to the prototype of military martyrs, Theodorus of
Amasea (the man who was credited with having burned down the
temple of the Magna Mater in Amasea about 305). This panegyric
was written in 381, less than one year after the Emperor Theodosius's baptism. Gregory turns the soldier Theodorus, who in his
day had been a rebel and an incendiary, into the holy or magic
protector of the province Pontus against barbaric invasions.

We should have to attribute very considerable importance to the
life of Ephrem the Syrian which has come to us under the name of
Gregory of Nyssa, if we could be certain that it was written by
him. Ephrem, a contemporary of Gregory, was of course famous
both for the power of his utterances in Syriac and for his ignorance
or near-ignorance of Greek. This life tells of Ephrem going to visit
Basil at Caesarea. The authenticity of the life partly depends on
the authenticity of this encounter between Ephrem and Basil, as
Gregory could hardly have reported an encounter between his
brother and the other great man if they had never met. O. Rous-
seau (*L'Orient Syrien* 2 [1957], 261–84; 3 [1958], 73–90) has given
serious reasons for denying the reality of this visit and consequently the authenticity of the speech. But I must add that I
would remain skeptical about the authenticity of the speech even
if the authenticity of the visit had been proved. I would expect
Gregory of Nyssa to tell of the visit in a different way: either more
biblically or more intimately. There is a strange indifference to
this event in our text.

These and other sketches of saints and martyrs (apparently
there is one still unpublished) cannot be separated from Gregory's
meditation upon biblical figures. The two panegyrics to Stephen
Protomartyr still need elementary study. We have a critical edition
only of the first by O. Lendle (1968), and the second is of doubtful
authenticity. What is obvious even in a superficial analysis of the
first panegyric is that Gregory of Nyssa tries to make the protomartyr relevant to the Christological controversies of the fourth
century.

Paradoxically, the life of Moses by Gregory of Nyssa has suffered perhaps from too much attention, for it has been studied in isolation from the rest of Gregory of Nyssa's biographical work. Thanks to the beautiful French commentary by J. Daniélou (1955), to the commentary accompanying the English translation by Abraham Malherbe and Everett Ferguson, and finally to the critical edition with an Italian translation and commentary by Manlio Simonetti (Fondazione Valla, 1984), this life of Moses has become the best known of Gregory of Nyssa's biographical works. It certainly shows his determination—probably in the last years of his life—to submit the figure of Moses to that allegorical interpretation which the Jewish master of allegorical interpretation, Philo, had pointedly refused to undertake. Philo had allegorized the three patriarchs—the allegorization of Abraham is the only one extant. He had also, though to a far lesser degree, allegorized Joseph in whom he saw a better governor of Egypt than the contemporary Roman governors. But he had almost entirely eliminated allegory from his life of Moses. From the first paragraphs of this life of Moses it is apparent that Philo had envisaged not only Jewish, but Gentile readers of it. This, however, cannot be a meaningful explanation for the avoidance of allegory in the interpretation of the life of Moses. The real explanation is the simpler one that Moses had to remain the legislator of the Jews—nothing more but also nothing less than that. Any allegory would have made him less specifically Jewish. By contrast, Gregory of Nyssa, for whom Jewish Law had been abolished by the new dispensation, had every reason for extending the Philonic method of allegory to the life of Moses which Philo had refrained from allegorizing. So Moses was turned by Gregory into an allegory of spiritual life, or rather of the sinless life of the saved. A brief factual "historia" is followed by a long "theoria," the allegory.

One has to take due account of the capacity for allegorization which is characteristic of Gregory of Nyssa in order to appreciate the absence of allegory in the life of Macrina. First, Gregory respects the convention which Athanasius had established in which saints could be compared with biblical figures, but could not be allegorized as could biblical figures. Saints, even for Gregory of Nyssa, must remain firmly in everyday life. Second, Macrina can teach immortality and resurrection to her far more educated brother because she remains the sister who talks to him about her own life and asks about his own life. In simple words, Gregory and Macrina did speak to each other; but if Basil spoke to Gregory, I am not sure that Gregory ever answered Basil.

III

In this complex experimentation with religious figures, the life of Macrina is therefore eccentric. It is the life of a sister surrounded by mother, brothers, and sisters; it is at the same time the story of an aristocratic clan fully conscious of its own distinction. But the author is also aware that he is himself slightly outside the mainstream of what he tells. He says that he had not seen Macrina for nine years when he went back to Annesoi about 380 to find her dying. There is thus an obvious explanation for the fact that the biography is full and explicit only for Macrina's younger years, when the family was still united and she was the religious conscience of the family. The rest is really not told except from retrospective allusions suggested by the last days of her life, when she was about fifty. But Gregory knows how to give a mysterious meaning to this chronological perspective. The arch of time is built in such a way that adolescence is in direct contact with death. As I have already mentioned, Macrina had decided to remain faithful to her dead fiancé and never to marry. On her deathbed the love for the young boy is transfigured into love for the celestial bridegroom—for Jesus himself. Gregory is a sufficiently refined writer not to be too explicit: he implies all this in chapters 22–23, and we must respect this reserve which, however, constitutes no real ambiguity. The transformation of the love for the earthly fiancé into love for the celestial bridegroom is inseparable from Macrina's Socratic role in leading Gregory toward the contemplation of the world of immortality and resurrection. Between these two moments there is the stark and uncompromising *contemplatio mortis* with its explicit details.

Aristocrats take their aristocracy for granted, and we shall not expect much reflection by Gregory of Nyssa on the social phenomenon of this new aristocratic activity by women: the foundation of monasteries not only for women, but also for men. St.

Jerome is more likely to give us details about that. Yet what Gregory tells us on this subject is not to be overlooked and can be combined with what we know from Jerome and other sources.

The characteristic features of these female foundations were of course equality of duties toward God, common renunciation of luxury and of worldly pleasures, and an agreed code of behavior. In fact, many of the members of a foundation were direct dependents of the founder—members of her household, servants of some sort. It is clear that these people accepted the leadership of their former employers, but each establishment must have solved in its own way the problem of reconciling the new equality in God with the old social hierarchy. In this pioneering stage of monastic life we cannot assume uniformity. I would not even make inferences from the Basilian rule (a complicated affair in itself) to the rule of Basilius's sister Macrina. Nor do I know whether it made a difference if the former household was prevalently one of free people (perhaps *coloni*) rather than of slaves.

In the case of Macrina, we learn from her brother that she had persuaded their mother to accept a monastic life in which differences of rank would be eliminated (ch. 11). At the same time, we are told that Macrina remained rich, and was even richer than her parents, even though the family fortune had been divided between nine brothers and sisters (ch. 20). One is reminded of the pride with which Gregory of Nyssa speaks of the increasing wealth of his family in his letter 1, 33, the attribution of which to the Nyssenus, rather than to the Nazianzenus, has been made certain by Pierre Maraval in *Anal. Bollandiana* 102, 1984, 61–70. The girls whom Macrina had collected in a period of famine and whom she had fed and educated were particularly devoted to her (ch. 26). Macrina was evidently the leader of the establishment, though a priest acted as administrator of the patrimony (ch. 20). According to Gregory, Macrina emphasized in her conversation with him before she died that she was aware of her high birth. The whole of chapter 21 is a highly sophisticated account of how she would reconcile Christian humility with the awareness of the distinction of her parents and of the authority of her brothers, and more particularly of Gregory himself.

Our difficulties in visualizing how this peculiar compromise between Christian equality and humility on the one hand and Roman aristocratic wealth and leadership on the other actually worked can be exemplified by the more detailed statements of Jerome in a similar case. Jerome tells us that Paula divided the many virgins she had collected from different provinces into three companies or monasteries. He adds that these women belonged to three different classes, some being aristocratic, some middle-class, and some of low birth. He does not say whether the three monasteries corresponded to the three classes or whether each monastery had members from all three classes. Common sense would prefer the second solution, of course. And St. Jerome adds that if there was any aristocratic woman, she was not allowed to have a member of her former household as her companion—which would seem to confirm the common-sense interpretation that the three orders were mixed, but that an aristocratic woman was not allowed to have old servants near her. The trouble is that what I translate as "a member of her former household" is far more ambiguous in Latin (*Epitaphium Sanctae Paulae* 20. 3): "si qua erat nobilis, non permittebatur de domo sua habere comitem." St. Jerome does not explain clearly the principle of the organization of each group, and the reference by modern commentators to Pachomius who, following the order of an angel, divided his monks into twenty-four τάγματα or companies does not help much either (*Vita III Pachomii* 31, ed. Halkin).

As for the direct utterances of Gregory of Nyssa in his biography, he does not even remotely attempt to disguise that he is proud of his ancestry, proud of the Great Basil, proud of the Great Macrina. More than that, when in the last section of his biography he comes to speak of how they decided on the appropriate form for the funeral (and Macrina, incidentally, was buried in the family tomb, which seems to have been either in or near the family estate), his main adviser appears to have been the most aristocratic member of Macrina's monastery, a woman high in rank, wealth, and beauty called Vetiana, who belonged to a senatorial family. When even later the moment comes to say something about Macrina's miracles (and Gregory is aristocratically reticent on this subject) the principal witness is a high-ranking officer who goes to greet Gregory on his way back after Macrina's funeral.

The relation between Macrina, Gregory of Nyssa, and Basil of Caesarea is evidently exceptional. It presupposes a combination of high birth, high intellectual power, and, what is rarest even among aristocrats, extraordinary discretion. Gregory knows how to describe a life which is to him both exemplary and indicative of disturbing realities without ever falling into the wrong word. The question which is more difficult to answer is how far this movement of aristocratic women went—and how affected it was by the decline in Roman power which made itself felt at the turn of the century, especially in the West. The presupposition for this aristocratic movement was the ability to move oneself and one's own wealth from one part of the Empire to the other. Support from and alliance with certain ecclesiastical personalities—men like St. John Chrysostom, St. Jerome, St. Basil—was another precondition. But perhaps no less important was the support of the governors of the provinces, who with other high-ranking officers allowed, helped, and protected the new settlements. One consequence might well be direct involvement in ecclesiastic and theological battles: Macrina seems to have been alone in avoiding the lot of Paula, Olympias, and Melania, who had to take sides in theological controversies. All that of course required cultural sophistication. But on the whole, one has the impression that rhetorical learning and philosophic competence were left by these women to their pagan counterparts, the philosophic ladies such as Hypatia. Christian women leaders had to know the Bible, and perhaps had to know how to sing in tune. The rest could not be taught.

When we say that Christian women such as Macrina, Paula, and Olympias seem less well trained than their counterparts Sosipatra and Hypatia, I think we are telling the truth. But there were people who compared Macrina to Theano, the legendary pupil and (in one version) wife of Pythagoras. At least we know that in the fourteenth century a collection of letters including those of both Theano and Macrina was still in circulation. Whether Macrina's letters were forgeries, as Theano's letters certainly were, we cannot tell, because the man who gives us this information, the scribe of the ms. Vaticanus Graecus 578/II (f. 189), decided that he would copy only Theano's letters, not Macrina's. The reason he gives is that too many centuries separated Macrina from Theano. The scribe obviously respected antiquity more than anything else. Yet he himself adds that, though both women were wise and a credit to womanhood, only Macrina was *theosophos*, that is, she alone had the wisdom which comes from God.

Select Bibliography

There would be no purpose in giving here a general bibliography either on Gregory of Nyssa or on late Roman biography. The best bibliography on Gregory is probably in M. Canévet, *Dictionnaire de Spiritualité* 6 (1967), 971–1011; but cf. also H. Dörries in *Reallexikon für Antike und Christentum* 12 (1983), 863–95. J. Daniélou summarized best his research on Gregory in *Enciclopedia Cattolica*.

G. May, "Die Chronologie des Lebens und der Werke des G. v. N." in M. Harl, ed., *Écriture et culture philosophique dans la pensée de G. de Nysse* (Leiden, 1971), 217–30 is helpful. J. Bernardi, *La prédication des Perés Cappadociens* (Paris, 1964) is indispensable.

The most useful edition with commentary of the life of St. Macrina is by P. Maraval, *Sources Chrétiennes* (Paris, 1971). Cf. also the critical edition by V. Woods Callahan, 1959; the orations for Meletius, Pulcheria, and Flacilla ed. by A. Spira, 1967; the dialogue *De anima* ed. by J. G. Krabinger, 1840; and the oration on St. Basil ed. by J. A. Stein (Washington, 1925). A good Italian introduction to it is by S. Lilla (Rome, 1981). The life of Moses is also edited by H. Masurillo, 1964. For general background it will be enough to refer to P. Brown, *The Cult of the Saints* (Chicago, 1981); P. Brown, *Society and the Holy in Late Antiquity* (Berkeley, 1982); P. Hadot, *Exercises spirituels et philosophie antique* (Paris, 1981); E. Giannarelli, *La Tipologia femminile nella biografia e nell'autobiografia cristiana del IV secolo* (Rome, 1980); A. Rousselle, *Porneia* (Paris, 1983); G. Fowden, "The Pagan Holy Man in Late Antique Society," *Journ. Hell. Studies* 102 (1982), 33–59; F. E. Consolino, "Modelli di santità femminile nelle più antiche passioni romane," *Augustinianum* 24 (1984), 83–113. J. Gribomont in *Rev. Ascet. et Myst.* 43 (1967), 249–66 helps to situate the treatise on Virginity in Gregory's development. For details cf. J. Daniélou, "Moïse exemple et figure chez Grégoire de Nysse," *Cahiers sioniens* 8 (1954), 385–400; J. Daniélou, ed., "Grégoire de Nysse a travers les lettres de S. Basile et de S. Grégoire de Nazianze," *Vig. Christ.* 19 (1965), 31–41; P. Maraval, "Encore les frères et les soeurs de Grégoire de Nysse," *Rev. Hist. Phil. Rel.* 60 (1980), 161–66; A. Quacquarelli, "L'antropologia del martire nel panegirico del Nisseno a san Teodoro di Amasea," *Archè e telos, L'antropologia di Gregorio di Nissa* (Milan, 1981), 217–30. H. Crouzel has proved in *Gregorianum* 60 (1979), 312–19 that Gregory of Nyssa knew the Thaumaturgus's speech on Origen. On late ancient biography in general cf. P. Cox, *Biography in Late Antiquity* (Berkeley, 1983). But L. Bieler, *Theios Aner* (Vienna, 1935) is still indispensable. Two other important recent works are by E. A. Clark, *Jerome, Chrysostom, and Friends* (New York and Toronto, 1979); and *The Life of Melania the Younger*, ibid., 1984.

14

A Medieval Jewish Autobiography

HUGH TREVOR-ROPER and I have for a long time shared interests both in Jewish history and in the history of historiography. An unusual text by a German Jew has attracted my attention on both accounts. I would like to offer some remarks on it to Hugh Trevor-Roper as a token of gratitude for all that I have learned from him.

Medieval autobiographies are a relatively rare commodity, and this one—by a German Jew telling of his conversion to Christianity (and of becoming a White Canon)—is in no danger of being forgotten. The *Opusculum de conversione sua* by Hermannus quondam Judaeus, who lived from c. 1107 to c. 1181, was written about the middle of the twelfth century. The text was reedited with great care on behalf of the *Monumenta Germaniae Historica* by Gerlinde Niemeyer as recently as 1963. A few years earlier it had been given eighteen pages in the *Geschichte der Autobiographie* by G. Misch (III [2], 1 [1959], 505–22). Even better, it has been placed in its Jewish-Christian context with unique authority by B. Blumenkranz in his paper "Jüdische und christliche Konvertiten im jüdisch-christlichen Religionsgespräch des Mittelalters," which is included in the collective volume *Judentum im Mittelalter* (ed. P. Wilpert, Berlin 1966).

As the Middle Ages are admittedly *terra incognita* to me, my readers may well ask what I am doing there. The answer is that one needs help precisely when one is *in terra incognita*. Having

History and Imagination: Essays in Honour of H. R. Trevor-Roper, London, 1981, pp. 30–37.

read this text on more than one occasion as evidence for the history of Jewish institutions and for the history of biography, I have been left with two or three puzzles, none of which seems to have been solved—or even noticed—by the modern scholars whom I have consulted. In any case, the text as a whole provides food for thought to anyone concerned with the modes and limits of the expression of individuality in autobiography.[1]

The basic facts are well-known and easy to summarize. At the age of twenty Judas Levi, son of David, acting as the representative of his father, lent a large sum of money to Bishop Ekbert of Münster without asking for security. The father, alarmed, sent Judas back from Cologne to Münster with instructions to remain there until the loan had been repaid. It took Judas twenty weeks to recover the money, and he filled the time in friendly contacts with the bishop's retinue and apparently with the bishop himself. He explored local churches and had the opportunity of accompanying the bishop on a visit to the recent Premonstratensian foundation of Cappenberg. He was not reluctant to dispute with Christians, but above all he was impressed by what he saw. He began to think of the possibility of conversion. Months of doubts and of family tension followed. His inclinations had not escaped notice in his Jewish circle. He tried to postpone marriage with the girl to whom he was engaged. The marriage, however, took place: later it appeared to the writer as the devil's supreme trick. "Decursis autem tribus mensibus, ex quo letargico hoc anime mee morbo ceperam laborare" (ch. 11), young Judas was again ready to contact Christian priests, monks, and nuns, both in Cologne and in the neighborhood. He soon decided to run away from home and to kidnap a seven-year-old stepbrother who for unknown reasons lived with his mother in Mainz. Having succeeded in both operations, he took refuge in an Augustinian establishment near Mainz. There he left his stepbrother, who was more or less forcibly baptized and consequently never returned to the family. Judas himself entered as a catechumen another Augustinian foundation at Ravengiersburg. He was solemnly baptized in Cologne in November 1129 under the name of Hermannus and soon afterward was admitted as a novice at Cappenberg, the Premonstratensian place he had visited and loved not long before. There he learned Latin. He took holy orders perhaps about 1137, as apparently he had to be thirty years old before he could be ordained. The autobiography ends at this point, but we know from documentary evidence that Hermannus quondam Judaeus was Provost of Scheda in 1170. Two years later he moved to a canonry in the Church of Maria ad Gradus in Cologne. He was still alive in 1181. The title "primus abbas ecclesiae Scheidensis" given to him by some recent manuscripts of the *Opusculum* seems to be due to confusion. What happened to Hermannus's wife after he left her is of course no part of his story: this "vita nuova" was without a Beatrice.

Hermannus's autobiography, like all autobiographies by converts, raises the problem of the way in which conversion affected the perception of pre-conversion events. A man who changes his own name because he has become another man has to define the borders between his present and his previous self. Hermannus makes it clear that he writes for Christians, not for Jews. At the same time, he projects back into his Jewish past his activities as a controversialist on behalf both of the Jewish and of the Christian faiths. In other words, he recognizes that these activities did not lead to anything. This point—which has already been duly emphasized by B. Blumenkranz—deserves some further clarification because it is central to Hermannus's view of his own conversion. Born in an age of religious controversies, young Judas Levi had obviously been trained to dispute and, as I have already mentioned, had relished open disputations. In that journey to Münster which proved decisive for his future life, the twenty-year-old moneylender had managed to enter into a (public?) debate with no less a person than the redoubtable Abbot Rupert of Deutz, whose *Annulus sive Dialogus inter Christianum et Judaeum* was written just in those years between 1126 and 1128. During the following months, while still searching for an answer, Judas had numerous discussions "opportune importune" with Christian clergymen (ch. 9). On his own showing he had never yielded his ground: in fact he had come out of these disputations rather well, especially in that with Rupert of Deutz. Seen from the Christian point of view, these controversies had contributed nothing to his conversion. By implication his Christian opponents were involved in the failure: they had been unable to enlighten a man who wanted to be enlightened. What is more remarkable, almost on the eve of his conversion Hermannus attempted a disputation inside a synagogue—this time as the champion of Christianity. But he ended by disavowing what he had said. To be more precise, when he was already on his way to being converted he visited an older brother in Worms and went to synagogue with him. As an opportunity was offered, he produced arguments in support of Christianity. As soon as his brother and other listeners began to be alarmed, he blandly assured them that he had intended only to show to the Jews which arguments they should expect from Christian controversialists: "quam illi responsionem gratanter acceperunt" (ch. 16). Perhaps he had no choice but retreat, as he wanted to conceal his intention to become a convert himself. All the same, objectively, he had failed as a champion of Christianity, while before, he had succeeded only too well as a Jewish apologist against his Christian opponents.

Hermannus, therefore, pointedly opposes the barrenness of his controversy with Rupert of Deutz (which is also the barrenness of Rupert's controversy with him) to the spiritual fruitfulness of the kind concern shown to him by a domestic of Bishop Ekbert. If the bishop had allowed it, that domestic would have submitted himself to an ordeal for the sake of the Jew's soul.

In the sole digression in his story, which he appends to this episode, Hermannus emphasizes that love is the only way to convert the Jews: "Confirment igitur ad illos caritatem eorum, quantum valent, necessitatibus communicando ac totius eis forma pietatis existendo, quatenus quos verbo non possunt, lucrentur exemplo" (ch. 5). Hermannus must have known that his famous older contemporary and fellow-convert Petrus Alfonsi (alias Moses Sephardi from Huesca) had championed a more aggressive controversial style with Jews and exploited his knowledge of rabbinical literature to reinforce traditional Christian arguments against Judaism. Whether Hermannus had Petrus Alfonsi in mind or not, his words by implication declared disagreement. He had been converted, not by such arguments, but by the benevolence and affection with which he had been received in the bishop's palace, by the discovery of claustral life at Cappenberg, and finally by the prayers of two ascetic women, Berta and Glismut, to whom he had recommended himself (cf. especially ch. 5 and ch. 12). These women had procured for him that gift of grace which he had been unable to obtain by commending himself to St. Paul and then to

the Cross ("frequenter cor meum signo eiusdem crucis consig-
nabam")—no mean steps for a man who was still a Jew (cf. 6 and
11). Paradoxically, but coherently, the only time in which Hermannus presents himself as successful for the right cause in a
dispute is on the very eve of baptism, but this happens in a dream,
and his defeated opponents are apparently already dead. He dreams
of meeting two relatives in the other world and reproaches them
for not having understood that Isaiah 9: 6 had alluded to the cross.
The poor relatives can produce no objection. They know by now
for themselves that they are damned: "eterne destinati sumus
gehenne" (ch. 18).

In the language of the Psalms, with which he had been familiar
since his early childhood, Hermannus could claim that God "de
stercore pauperem erexit et eum cum principus populi sui col-
locavit" (cf. Ps. 112:7–8). In this perspective a dream he had had
in his thirteenth year acquired capital importance in his eyes. It
determined the structure of his biography and, in some sense,
constitutes the first of my puzzles.

The account of the conversion which I have so far summarized
and commented upon is sandwiched between the description of
this dream and its true interpretation. In other words, the autobiography is presented as the evidence required to explain the dream.
The thirteen-year-old boy dreamt that he received a visit from the
Emperor Henry V who gave him a white horse and a purse with
seven coins in it, hanging from a glamorous belt: futhermore, the
emperor promised to give him the entire property of a prince who
had just died. The boy was then asked to accompany the emperor
to his palace and to take part in a banquet. Apparently Jewish
dietary rules were observed at the feast, for the emperor shared
with him a dish of herbs. The boy had more or less dreamt of
himself as a new Mordecai after the death of Haman. A learned
relative to whom he turned for the interpretation of the dream
confirmed him in his expectations of honors and wealth: he speci-
fied that the white horse was the promise of a beautiful and noble
wife (cf. Babyl. Talmud, *Berakot* 56b; *Sanhedrin*, 93a). But, to use
Dante's language which is here relevant, "lo verace giudicio del
detto sogno non fue veduto allora per alcuno, ma ora è mani-
festissimo a li più semplici." Reflecting on this dream after his
conversion, Hermannus was in a position to give its true explana-

tion: the emperor stood for God; the horse, perhaps less conventionally, for baptism; the seven coins for the seven gifts of the Spirit; and so on.

What I do not know—and should like to know—is whether there are other (medieval) autobiographies so neatly constructed to explain a dream. Hermannus places the whole of his autobiographical data between the account of the dream and its interpretation. Dreams of course play an important part in autobiographies, though it does not seem to have occurred to any of the commentators of Dante's *Vita Nuova* whom I have consulted that the *Opusculum* by Hermannus Judaeus might be a useful text to compare.[2] Dreams occur prominently in documents of two conversions of Christians to Judaism in the late eleventh and early twelfth centuries, though even these do not offer the exact parallel I am seeking. The Cairo Geniza has preserved at least two autobiographical accounts in Hebrew by converts to Judaism; one is anonymous (but by a former priest), the other is by a Norman aristocrat of Southern Italy (almost certainly also a former priest), Johannes of Oppido, who in 1102 on conversion took the name of Obadiah.[3] The anonymous account has been attributed by B. Blumenkranz to Andreas, the Archbishop of Bari, whom we know from Obadiah to have preceded him in the conversion by several decades; but the attribution is not cogent, and the story of Andreas's conversion is a problem in itself into which I do not intend to enter. The anonymous writer who speaks in the first person tells in a letter of a dream which persuaded one of his gaolers to allow him to escape. More relevant to Hermannus's story is the account by the other convert. Johannes-Obadiah, who speaks in the third person in a fairly lengthy personal memoir of which several fragments are preserved, states that he was inspired to become a convert not only by the example of Andreas, but also by a dream which he had had in his youth when he was still in the house of his father and in some situation of impurity. He dreamt of being in a cathedral and of receiving some message or warning from a man (angel?) who stood near him by the altar. A probable interpretation of the text is as follows: "Now in the first year in which Johannes was initially defiled in the night in the house of Dreux, his father, in that year he had a dream. He was officiating in the Cathedral of Oppido . . . when he looked up and beheld a man standing to his right, opposite the altar. The man said to him: Johannes." The content of the message is not preserved, and the situation of impurity in which the dream developed is obscurely described and has been variously interpreted (as its meaning is irrelevant to my argument I refrain from comment).[4]

Obadiah wrote his autobiography after 1121; Hermannus, as I said, became a Christian in 1129. The fragments we have of Obadiah's autobiography come from more than one copy of the text; some are vocalized. A Bible quotation from Joel (3:4) is in Latin, though written in Hebrew characters. The text was therefore meant for wide diffusion, even to those who needed vocalized Hebrew and could appreciate a biblical text in the Vulgate. Obadiah was by then in Eastern, Islamic countries where he met at least one self-proclaimed Messiah, but needed to maintain contacts with the West—if for no other reason, at least to produce evidence for his previous life. In any case, his text would be in demand among Jews; it was of obvious interest. One wonders whether Hermannus knew Obadiah's text. It contained a decisive dream in a decisive situation which seems to be the nearest parallel to Hermannus's dream at the age of thirteen. Both converts considered themselves summoned to conversion in a dream which they had had in adolescence.

The natural assumption is that Hermannus had his dream at thirteen, when a Bar Mizvah. The assumption, however natural, is not without difficulties. The age of thirteen is recognized in Talmudic texts as the beginning of full religious duty and responsibility. Though difficult to date, these texts ae unambiguous in their contents. A "Saying of the Fathers" (5. 21) attributes to either Samuel the Small (first century A.D.) or the perhaps later R. Jehudah ben Tema a definition of the fourteen stages of human life: one of the stages is "at thirteen for the commandments [Mizvot]." A minor Talmudic treatise, Masseket Soferim, which is usually dated in the eighth century, is even more definite (18. 5): "There was likewise a beautiful custom in Jerusalem to train the young sons and daughters to afflict themselves on a fast day . . . and at the age of thirteen [the boy] was taken round and presented to every elder to bless him and to pray for him that he may be worthy to study the Torah and engage in good deeds" (trans. A. Cohen). Furthermore, Bereshit Rabbah, a homiletic commentary on Genesis, usually dated in the fifth century, attributes (63. 10) to R. Eleazar b. Simeon, the controversial rabbi of the second century A.D., a saying destined to great fortune in later Judaism: "A man is responsible for his son until the age of thirteen; thereafter he must say: 'Blessed is He who has now freed me from the responsibility of this boy'" (transl. H. Freedman). Notwithstanding these and other pieces of evidence (for which cf. *Jewish Encyclopaedia*, s.v. Bar Mizvah), specialists, as far as I know, still seem to accept as valid the demonstration given in 1875 by Leopold Löw in his classic book *Die Lebensalter in der jüdischen Literatur* (210–17) that the Bar Mizvah ritual as we know it originated in Germany about the fourteenth century. S. B. Freehof ("Ceremonial Creativity among the Ashkenazim," *Jewish Quarterly Review*, 75 [1967], 217–21) substantially confirms this date and origin. Indeed, the use of the expression Bar Mizvah, to indicate a boy exactly at the stage of initiation, does not seem to occur earlier. According to Löw's account, in the fourteenth century it became a custom among Ashkenazi Jews that a boy should be called for the first time to read at least a chapter from the weekly portion of the Law on the first Sabbath after he has entered his fourteenth year. On that occasion his father recites the blessing attributed to R. Eleazar b. Simeon. The festivity included, and still includes, presents to the Bar Mizvah, a banquet, and, if the child is gifted, a learned speech by him to the guests. Concurrently he assumes the duty of wearing phylacteries, *Tefillin*, at least during morning prayers except on Sabbaths and holy days.

Now if we go back to the dream which Hermannus had at the age of thirteen we find the banquet, the presents and, maybe, even the speech ("tum ego regali munificentiae debitas rependens gratias"), though admittedly before the banquet. The boy's age and the nature of the dream invite the conclusion that as early as 1120 the Ashkenazim of Cologne had already something like a Bar Mizvah ceremonial. The Mordecai pattern of the dream as a whole would not represent an objection. But how legitimate is the conclusion itself?

Whether the *Opusculum de conversione sua* by Hermannus quondam Judaeus offers a unique example of autobiography inserted between the account of a dream and its explanation; whether the *Opusculum* was written with some knowledge of

Obadiah's autobiography, and whether this initial dream is the earliest evidence for the Bar Mizvah ceremony in Germany—these are the questions I ask but cannot answer. The text remains a very telling document of conversion in an age of controversy, because the man who loved controversies before conversion virtually recognized their inanity after it. The relation between this autobiography and the spirituality of the Premonstratensian order to which Hermannus belonged would deserve special study. But if we want to know too much about Hermannus's identity we shall of course end by knowing nothing.[5]

15

A Note on Max Weber's Definition of Judaism as a Pariah-Religion

I

REFERENCES TO JEWS AS pariahs can be found early in the nine-teenth century. In 1823 Michael Beer, the brother of the composer Giacomo Meyerbeer, wrote and produced a tragedy, *Der Paria*, about a Hindu outcast who is not permitted to fight for his coun-try: a transparent allegory of the modern German Jew.[1] Toward the end of the century, Theodor Herzl and Bernard Lazare used the word *pariah* in reference to modern Jews.[2] More recently, Hannah Arendt has given wider circulation to this word in America.[3] Though she used it in her own sense, she specifically borrowed it from Max Weber, who first introduced the term *pariah* into the scientific study of Judaism.[4]

For Arendt, the pariah is one Jewish type, incarnated by Heine, Kafka, Sholom Aleichem, and Charlie Chaplin, to be opposed (and preferred) to another Jewish type, the parvenu. According to Arendt, the pariah self-consciously brings his Jewish existence into the Gentile, unsympathetic world in which he lives; he nei-ther denies nor idealizes his Jewish heritage, while the parvenu does either.

Weber had something else in mind. He starts his monograph on Judaism by stating that "sociologically speaking the Jews were a

History and Theory, XIX, 3, 1980, pp. 313–18.

pariah people, which means, as we know from India, that they were a guest people who were ritually separated, formally or *de facto*, from their surroundings."[5] His question, therefore, is: "How did Jewry develop into a pariah people with highly specific peculiarities?"[6] Weber of course knows that the Jews were never inserted into a system of castes and never shared the religion of those who avoided them. The accent is therefore on the quality of "guest people" (*Gastvolk*), of Jews living on foreign soil. He emphasizes that the Jews deliberately chose to become pariahs— a choice arising from definite religious and moral beliefs and expressed by voluntary ritual segregation. As Weber says, the Jews segregated "voluntarily and not under pressure of external rejection."[7]

II

Clarity, however, ceases at this point. What Weber means by "guest people" is not self-evident. In the section on the sociology of religion in *Economics and Society* (*Wirtschaft und Gesellschaft*) he seems to clarify the issue by giving a slightly different version of his definition of the Jews as pariahs. He writes: "In our usage, 'pariah people' denotes a distinctive hereditary social group lacking autonomous political organization and characterized by prohibitions against commensality and intermarriage originally founded upon magical, tabooistic, and ritual injunctions. Two additional traits of a pariah people are political and social disprivilege and a far-reaching distinctiveness in economic functioning."[8] Weber does not make here any explicit mention of "guest people"; instead he refers to a "group lacking autonomous political organization." This is certainly clearer than the formulation in *Ancient Judaism*, but does not yet explain why and in what sense a guest people necessarily lacks an autonomous political organization or vice versa.

Secondly, Weber seems to suggest that an ethic of resentment (*Ressentiment*) is characteristic of the Jews as pariahs. Always a student and admirer of Nietzsche, he uses in both *Ancient Judaism* and the pertinent section of *Economics and Society* the notion of resentment to characterize Jewish ethics. The trouble is that, following Nietzsche, he extends the term to Christian ethics. In *Ancient Judaism* he even suggests that resentment meant less to the Jews than to the early Christians: the rabbis fought against the religious internalization of revenge while "the less sophisticated early Christians" ("das durch Reflexion ungebrochenere alte Christentum") indulged more openly in it.[9] As, according to Weber himself, Paul freed the Christians from the pariah status of the Jews, the unavoidable conclusion is that there is no necessary connection between pariah status and ethics of resentment.[10]

The connotations of the pariah status are made still more obscure by uncertainties about the time and circumstances in which, according to Weber, the Jews became pariahs. At one point he seems to imply that even the Patriarchs had been pariahs; at another point he connects the pariah status with the combination of prophecy and traditional ritualism which he describes as characteristic of Judaea at the end of the seventh century B.C. before the destruction of the first Temple.[11] More precisely he states: "This place as a guest people was established through ritualistic closure which, in Deuteronomic times, as we saw, was diffused, and during the time of the Exile, was carried through by Ezra's and Nehemiah's enactments."[12] At other points Weber seems to connect generically the transformation of the Jews into pariahs with their exile and dispersion—though, again, it is not clear whether he means the first exile or the destruction of the second Temple.[13]

These and similar difficulties of interpretation would not be lessened by the hypothesis that Weber's thinking on the matter evolved. The sections on religion of *Economics and Society*, though published after his death in 1920, are said to have been written about 1911–1913. The monograph on Judaism was published in Weber's lifetime, 1917–1919 (with the exception of the appendix on Pharisaism). Both works belong substantially to the same period of his activity. The differences in formulation between the texts under consideration are more likely to be due to his feverish style of composition than to the evolution of his ideas.

III

Given these elements of obscurity, the best we can do is to outline the attitude of the Jews toward political power, remaining as it does fairly constant throughout the centuries. We want to see whether it is compatible with that feature of a pariah nation which emerges more clearly from Weber's pages, namely the voluntary segregation and renunciation of political power with its implication of an ethic of resentment.

I shall leave out the Patriarchs. Hebrew historical tradition (as distinct from certain rabbinic speculation) has always maintained that the Patriarchs lived before the Hebrews received their God-given law and God-given land. The status of the Patriarchs cannot be used to define the status of the Jews subjectively attributed to themselves as a consequence of the revelation on Sinai and of the conquest of the Promised Land. The whole Jewish religious tradition from the older strata of the Bible to the present day presupposes that the Jews are committed by pact to obey a divine law and are entitled under certain conditions to own a territory granted to them by God. The loss of political independence and dispersion have never changed this situation in the eyes of believing Jews. The restoration of the Land has merely been deferred to a Messianic age. Believing Jews have never concealed from themselves that there are serious questions about the ways of reconciling their religious views on legislation and territorial claims with the obligations imposed by foreign rule and dispersion. But, interestingly enough, they themselves have legislated (or interpreted divine law) about these conflicts of obligation. The presupposition of Talmudic reasoning and of the later legal developments culminating in the system of Maimonides is that loss of political independence does not entail renunciation of self-government—or rather, that the interpretation of the Law given by God must go on under any circumstances. Indeed, Talmudic and post-Talmudic legal thought is notorious for not taking any notice of faits accomplis. Maimonides goes on talking about the constitution of the Sanhedrin, the supreme court of law, as if the King and the

High Priest were still walking on the hills of Judaea. Believing Jews never gave up their sovereign rights and never admitted to being without political institutions of their own. This excludes that subjective acceptance of an inferior, nonpolitical status which seems to be essential to Weber's definition of the Jews as pariahs.

The only way of saving Weber's identification of the Jews with a pariah nation would be to argue that although they never considered themselves a landless nation without rights, they were treated as such by the political powers under which they successively lived. Lack of "territoriality" would thus become the reason for the pariah status of the Jews. This interpretation, however, would involve a complete transformation of Weber's thesis—and not one to be commended, either. Weber's primary contention is that the Jews themselves chose to be pariahs because of their religious attitude. In the new interpretation, the position of pariah would be imposed on the Jews, not developed by the Jews themselves. It would not throw any light on their religious orientation and its consequences for social life. It would not, therefore, explain what after all Weber wanted to explain when he labeled the Jews as pariahs: their inability to contribute to the modern forms of advanced capitalism, as the Calvinists did. It would also involve us in awkward comparative questions. Would Weber ever have referred to the Germans settled on Roman territory in the Late Empire as pariahs?

One could of course develop compromise interpretations trying to combine voluntary and involuntary factors of the pariah status of the Jews. For instance, one could argue that the Jews remained permanent foreigners in the countries in which they settled by refusing to give up their original land; or one could argue (with some support from Weber himself) that they were reduced to the status of pariahs by a mixture of subjective decisions about commensality and intermarriage and objective deprivations of territory and political rights. These compromise interpretations would certainly be nearer (almost by definition!) to the realities of Jewish "exile." But would they bring us nearer to the Indian model which was Weber's starting point? What would *we* mean if we called the Jews pariahs?

In common-sense terms, one does not see how the different legal statutes under which the Jews have lived since Hellenistic times could be unified by this definition. The Roman period would have to be excluded in any case. The status of the Jews in Islamic law would again not be amenable to a reduction to the pariah-type. The "regimen Iudaeorum" in Christian countries up to the emancipation would, no doubt, be nearer to this description of Jews as guest people. But the definitions formulated by Christian lawyers and theologians at different times characterize far more precisely the status of the Jews at any given moment and place. The term *pariah* has neither law nor theology in its favor.

There is an obvious problem about what discrimination against the Jews meant to the Jews themselves and what it made of them. But this problem is not to be confused with Weber's problem, which was dictated by the conviction that the Jews organized their own ghetto and went into it of their own choice. If the word *pariah* indicates a people who accept their position as inferiors in an alien social system, and work out their own salvation through this acceptance, the Jews were no pariahs. The Jews went on giving laws to themselves and treated their pact with God as their own legal title to the future recovery of their own land in the Messianic age. Their morality encompassed rebellion against injustice and martyrdom—attitudes one does not normally associate with pariahs.

IV

It seems possible that Weber confused ritual separation as willed by a sovereign nation (which is what we find in the Bible, in the Talmud, and in later legal treatises) with pariah status. The ritual separation, presupposing sovereign rights, is no indication of statelessness or of guest status. It is not equivalent to segregation and ghetto life. It may not be reasonable, but it is not intrinsically hostile to ordinary human relations. It goes together with proselytism.

Much of what Weber said on ancient Judaism remains valid even if we eliminate his definition of it as a pariah-religion. He saw that the biblical writers (whether priests or prophets) and their rabbinic successors had a rational, nonmagic approach to social relations, which identified injustice and oppression as such. He duly appreciated the whole Messianic dimension as a promise of future rectification of present injustice: an effort to save the rationality of this world by finding a complement to it in a world to come. The sympathetic understanding of the rabbis, against the entire tradition of German scholarship, is perhaps the most remarkable feature of Weber's interpretation of Judaism. Even his interpretation of the Jewish attitude toward capitalism contains valid elements, though it pays too little attention to the legal constraints on the Jews during the decisive stage of the industrialization of Europe. Proclivity to Messianic hopes may indeed encourage anticapitalistic trends.

There remains a curious basic contradiction in Weber's analysis of Judaism. More perhaps than anybody else he gave importance to its juridical structure—the pact between God and the Jewish nation. On the other hand, he did not appreciate the consequence. Throughout the centuries this pact remained the foundation of the self-regulation of the Jewish communities and therefore saved the Jews from whatever self-abasement can be associated with the word *pariah*.[14]

16

The Jews of Italy [1]

I

ITALIAN HISTORY is always a difficult subject. Behind it and inside it there is the extraordinary variety of regional and urban units: the history of Florence is not the history of Pisa, or even that of Arezzo or Siena or Volterra. Where the Jews are involved, the differences in local traditions are increased by substantial local differences in the past treatment of Jews. Much of Southern Italy and Sicily—splendid Jewish centers in the Middle Ages— lost their Jews in the sixteenth century during the Spanish rule. It is sometimes forgotten that Jews were kept out of most of Lombardy for more than a century until the Austrians replaced the Spaniards in 1714.

In addition, there are the differences of origins of the Jews themselves. Some of us are descendants of the Jews who lived in Italy during the Roman Empire. Some are Ashkenazi Jews who, especially in the fourteenth century, left Germany and came to Italy. French Jews had to leave France in the same century, and there was the Sephardi immigration and the return of Marranos of Spanish origin to Judaism at the end of the fifteenth and during the sixteenth century. Contacts with the East always existed, especially in Venice and Southern Italy, as long as Jews were allowed to remain there. Other Jews from Muslim countries were attracted by

The New York Review of Books, 32, 16, October 24, 1985, pp. 22–26.

the new *porto franco* of Leghorn (Livorno) after the middle of the
sixteenth century.

Leghorn remained the easiest Italian town for Jews to live in
during at least two centuries and developed that Jewish style of its
own which is preserved in the books of Elia Benamozegh and of
which perhaps the paintings of Amedeo Modigliani show traces.
The differences of origins were of course reflected in the differences of rituals and melodies, and in their turn the differences of
rituals were preserved by separate synagogues. Three synagogues—
la scola italiana, la scola tedesca, la scola spagnola—were frequently to be found in the same town; in Rome not long ago, there
were still five synagogues preserving an interesting distinction between *scola catalano-aragonese* and *scola spagnola*.

We in Piedmont, together with Italian, Sephardi, and Ashkenazi
synagogues, had that curious *minhag apam*—the three rather
small congregations of Asti, Fossano, and Moncalvo—which preserved the fossil of a French medieval ritual with its peculiar
mahzor, or prayer book. That the Jews were tolerated in one of the
states of Italy, however, did not mean that they were tolerated in
all parts of the same state. That the Popes allowed the Jews to live
in Rome and Ancona, where we find the Volterras, does not imply
that they were allowed to live in Bologna. It fell to one of my
grandfather's brothers, the rabbi Marco Mordechai Momigliano,
to be sent in 1866 to rebuild the Jewish community of Bologna.
This community, where Obadiah Sforno, Azaria de' Rossi, and
Samuel Archevolti had worked and thought, had been closed
down in 1593 and had not existed, at least officially, for more than
250 years. On the other hand, the Jews prospered at Ferrara under
the same papal rule and preserved some of the brilliance characteristic of their culture under the house of Este, which ended in
1597. The explanation is partly in the agrarian situation of the
region, which helped to form the pro-Fascist attitudes of the Jews
of Ferrara centuries later.

Differing in rituals and often with conflicting interests among
themselves, the Jews of Italy were not, however, beset by more
linguistic differences than their Christian counterparts. The linguistic situation of Italy was already complicated enough in itself.
What we call Italian remained basically a written language to the

end of the nineteenth century. Ordinary people spoke what we call dialects, and the Jews spoke the same dialect as the other inhabitants of the place. Venetian Jews spoke and speak Venetian, and we Piedmontese Jews spoke Piedmontese. My parents spoke Piedmontese between themselves and Italian with us children. So my sisters and I were the only native Italian speakers of our little Piedmontese town and much admired for our linguistic accomplishments. When I grew up I returned to the Piedmontese dialect in conversations at home with my parents—though not with my sisters.

No doubt, ghetto life favored some peculiarity. The dialect of the Roman Jews is known to have remained considerably more archaic than that of the Roman Christians, and of course Hebrew words and sentences were inserted into the local dialect. In the Piedmontese jargon of the Jews there were some Yiddish words imported into Piedmont by Jews of Ashkenazi provenance—the Ottolenghi, Treves, and Diena, who were destined to play such an important part in recent Italian history. So it was usual to speak of the *Becher* for kiddush, or of the *Orzai* for *Jahrzeit*, the anniversary of a death.

The other element that has to be kept in mind concerning the Italian Jews is that we have been so few—so few especially in the last centuries. There were at most perhaps 30,000 Jews at the beginning of the nineteenth century, including the Jews of Trieste, which was technically in Austria, and those of Nice, which became French in 1859. This represented about one per thousand in the population of Italy. Before the last war there were about 50,000. Ten thousand of us were murdered by the Fascists and the Nazis in alliance, and this included eleven members of my family, among whom were my father and mother. About six thousand emigrated, never to return. Others were lost during the period of the persecution when the rate of conversion was higher than average. Among the converts, as is well known, was the chief rabbi of Rome, Israel Zoller, baptized in Santa Maria degli Angeli at Rome on February 13, 1945. If there are now between 30,000 and 35,000 Jews, it is because emigration from Libya, and to a lesser extent from Eastern countries, has swollen the native Jewish population. This figure represents one person for each two thousand of the entire population of Italy. Most of the Jews are now concentrated in a few

large towns. Most of the old synagogues are empty, if they still
exist.

II

Every time I am in an Italian town, I try to figure out whether
and how Jews fared in it. Some of these cities I know well enough.
I have passed many summers in the peace of the beautiful town of
Spoleto in Umbria. Going around the city, I can easily reconstruct
the history of Spoleto since the time of Hannibal. But when I enter the little medieval street which is at present called Via San
Gregorio della Sinagoga I am baffled. When did the synagogue
there stop being a synagogue? Does the name of the street imply
that the San Gregorio church was superimposed on the synagogue? And where are the descendants of the famous Renaissance
Jewish doctors of Spoleto, one of whom was David De' Pomis, the
author of the Hebrew-Latin-Italian dictionary *Zemah David*,
"the offshoot of David," which I used daily as a child? At the moment there is in Spoleto one Jewish family that moved from
Rome. Perhaps I ought to add that two or three years ago I discovered that a couple of American Jewish artists were trying to make
a living by opening a sandwich bar in Spoleto. I hope they are
successful.

The disappearance of the small Jewish communities makes it
difficult to follow up family histories and, even more, local cultural traditions. I wish I could explain how the Volterra family left
Tuscany, where they appear well established in the Renaissance,
to go to Ancona. There is, as we know, more than one version of
the transfer of Disraeli's grandfather to England in 1748: some
have him depart from the small but learned community of Cento,
others from Venice. Research now in progress at Tel Aviv by
Shelomo Simonsohn and his colleagues will no doubt clarify
many details; and the Jerusalem volume by Robert Bonfil has already told us much that we did not know about the Italian rabbis
of the Renaissance. Research on Jews has become fashionable in
Italy, too.

It still remains difficult to say something precise even about
one's own family. I envy my colleague Vittore Colorni, the re-

markable professor of the history of Italian law at the University of Ferrara, who has been able to produce a neat genealogical tree of his family from 1477 to 1977 in a book dedicated to the memory of Umberto Nahon and published in Jerusalem in 1978. His success was made possible by the unusual fact that his family, the Colorni, remained for more than four centuries in the same place, Mantua. As for my family, I can at least say that about the beginning of the fourteenth century, an ancestor of mine had the prudence to leave the little Jewish community of Montmélian in Savoy for the capital of Savoy, Chambéry, where he was duly registered as Lionel—or, if you prefer, Jehudah—de Montmélian. The *juiverie* of Montmélian virtually disappeared about fifty years later when Jews were thrown into the wells as responsible for the black plague.

The descendants of Lionel de Montmélian, following up the expansion of the dukedom of Savoy into Piedmont, went into trade, moneylending, and rabbinical positions in the small Jewish communities of Piedmont: Busca, Cuneo, Mondovi, Asti, Chieri, Ivrea. There they remained for centuries, terribly poor, pious, and scholarly until Napoleon brought new ideas, new hopes, and—as my grandfather, the last traditional zaddick, or "just man," of Italy, was never tired of repeating—new delusions to the Italian Jews.[2]

How are we to explain the sudden explosion of initiative, creativity, intellectual and political responsibility that characterize the history of Italian Jews after Napoleon and above all after 1848? That was the year in which the King of Piedmont and Sardinia gave to the Jews the equality later to be extended to the other regions of Italy in what ultimately became the unification of Italy; the process took more than twenty years.

No doubt the irrational factor—patriotism—had a decisive influence. I shall only indicate what may seem an absurd fact: the sudden enthusiasm of a basically conservative Jewish scholar, Samuel David Luzzatto—Sadal—in 1848. It is not by chance that the *Giudaismo illustrato* by Luzzatto appeared in 1848. It is self-explanatory in its appeal to the tradition of Italian Jews from the days of Shabbatai Donnolo and of the various members of the Kalonymus family of Lucca and Rome to the present day. It is even more characteristic that Luzzatto was moved by seeing a man of Jewish origin, although baptized, Daniele Manin, become the president of the revolutionary republic of Venice in 1848–1849; Daniele Manin's ancestors had been called Medina until the end of the eighteenth century.

This patriotism, this devotion to the new Italy of the Risorgimento, has been in our blood since the days of our great-grandfathers and fathers, whatever reservations they and we may have about what was happening and is happening in Italy. It explains why my grandmother used to cry every time she listened to the "Marcia Reale"—the royal hymn of the Italian monarchy—and if you can cry at such atrocious music you can cry at anything. More seriously, it explains why during the First World War the three university professors who died in battle were all Jews, and at least two of them were volunteers. One of the best-known heroes of the First World War remains Roberto Sarfatti, the eighteen-year-old student who happened to be the son of Margherita Sarfatti, who was later the mistress and the biographer of Mussolini. Even in the disgraceful Abyssinian and Spanish wars of 1936 the young hero was one of our Jewish students in the University of Turin, Bruno Jesi, who soon found himself confronted by the racial laws.

Interestingly enough, it was not the change in economic conditions that gave a new direction to the lives of Italian Jews. No doubt, there was a new opening of opportunities, and they were taken. The most important was the possibility of becoming farmers and landowners. Italian Jews, especially of Piedmont, Veneto, Emilio, and Tuscany, were indeed strongly inclined to buy land and settle on it or near it. This, incidentally, explains the strong conservative bias of many Italian Jews. But Italian Jews never became leading capitalists and industrialists. None of the few great Italian industries, such as Fiat, has been in the hands of Jews; there was an attempt to import a branch of the Rothschild bank into Italy—in Naples, of all places—but it did not last long. The nearest approximation to Jewish ownership of great industry is to be found in the Olivetti firm with its peculiar tradition of technical sophistication and attention to social problems. Many Jews prospered in the medium-sized industries and in the insurance business; others, like my people, stuck to the traditional Italo-Jewish combination of banking and silk mills (filande) to which first Japanese competition and later artificial silk dealt mortal blows.

But the explanation for the high contribution of the Jews, both in quantity and quality, to the Italian social and intellectual life of the last 150 years is to be found elsewhere. First of all, even before 1848, they had managed to get for themselves a very good modern education, all the legal obstacles notwithstanding. Some Piedmontese Jews like the future secretary of Cavour, Isacco Artom, were sent to study in Milan where, under Austrian rule, Jews were allowed to go to a public school. A banker, who was a member of the Todros family, emigrated from Turin to Paris in about 1835 in order to give a good education to his children. The future mother of Cesare Lombroso put only one condition to her father, a Piedmontese Jew, when he was going to arrange her marriage: the husband should be a subject of Austria where education for Jewish children was better. So it happened that Cesare Lombroso, the erratic genius who revolutionized psychiatry and much else, was born in Verona and there he has his monument. But normally it was by reorganization of the traditional school, the Talmud Torah, that Italian Jews acquired knowledge of modern culture before they were admitted to the state schools. As for the Italian universities, there was limited entry for Jews to some, such as Padua and Ferrara, especially in medicine. Later Italian Jews studied hard both in Italian and foreign schools and were known to go gladly abroad to improve themselves. I believe that Leone Sinigaglia, the exquisite musician who collected the Piedmontese songs, was the only Italian pupil of Mahler in Vienna; Sinigaglia died when the Nazi-Fascists knocked at his door in Turin to capture him.

III

What the contribution of traditional Jewish instruction was to this renovation of Italian-Jewish culture is more difficult to say. One fact is obvious. Both traditional Jewish studies and modern research and education prospered in the places where there was greater liberty and prosperity. In certain cases the continuity from traditional, rabbinical education to ordinary modern humanistic and scientific formation is clearly recognizable. Jewish traditional learning was strongest in places like Trieste, Gorizia, Venice, Padua, and Mantua, especially under Austrian rule, then in Leghorn and in Ferrara. During the eighteenth century Isacco Lampronti, the Talmudic encyclopedist of *Pahad Yizhak*, came from Ferrara; new sections of his *Encyclopaedia* are still being published in Israel. One of the founders of modern Hebrew literature, Moshe Luzzatto, came from Padua. In the nineteenth century Isacco Reggio lived in Gorizia; Sadal, the greatest of all, was born in Trieste and taught in Padua. Elia Benamozegh, the mystically minded adversary of Sadal, lived in Leghorn, where at the beginning of the century David Azulai had ended his legendary life as *"Wunderrabbi."*

Rome, which had the largest Jewish community, was not conspicuous for intellectual activity: there Jews were the most miserable and the most oppressed. It must be generally emphasized that there was in Italy more traditional learning and more use of Hebrew as a learned language than is usually believed, at least among modern-day Italian Jews. We even exported a member of the Artom tribe to become the *Haham*, or rabbi, of the London Sephardi community (1866). He was a poet in Hebrew and in Italian. And of course Sabato Morais came to the United States and became, perhaps to his surprise, one of the founders of the Jewish Theological Seminary of New York.

It is also worth reminding ourselves that the last Italian poet in Hebrew was a woman, Rachele Morpurgo, the cousin and friend of Sadal and a member of that Morpurgo tribe which has contributed so many professors to the Italian universities and several members to the Italian Parliament, and in recent years has produced the first woman professor of comparative philology at the University of Oxford, Anna Morpurgo.

If one looks, then, at the map of the provenance of learned professors, the correspondence between the older Jewish and the newer Italian culture is fairly obvious. The greatest comparative philologist and, in the absolute sense, the greatest Italian philologist in the nineteenth century, Graziadio Isaia Ascoli, came from Gorizia where he had been a pupil of Rabbi Reggio. He remained a close friend, even in his Milan days, of Sadal and of Sadal's son Filosseno Luzzatto, the promising Assyriologist who died prematurely. The great master of Italian studies, Alessandro D'Ancona, who was a director of the Scuola Normale of Pisa, grew up in Tuscany. From Venice and Trieste came the families Venezian, Pincherle, and Polacco, to fill the Italian universities and Parliament. The learned rabbi of Mantua, Marco Mortara, whose library was famous, was destined to be the father and grandfather of a dazzling family, the greatest member of which is indisputably Ludovico Mortara (1855–1937), first-class jurist, head of the Supreme Court of Cassazione, minister of justice in 1919, and vice-prime minister.

Examples could easily be multiplied of this continuity of secular and religious Jewish tradition. I shall add only one case which has always seemed to me the most bizarre. The name Mussafia is connected in the seventeenth, eighteenth, and early nineteenth centuries with a series of distinguished rabbinical scholars. The best known is Benjamin ben Immanuel Mussafia, who in the late seventeenth century published in Holland a supplement to what remains the most important Italian contribution to Talmudic studies, the Lexicon *Arukh*. Two other Mussafia, father and son, followed each other as rabbis and Talmudic scholars at Spalato (Split) in Dalmatia at the beginning of the nineteenth century. Their linguistic and hermeneutic abilities were suddenly transferred by their respective grandson and son, Adolfo Mussafia, to the study of the Romance languages. Adolfo Mussafia, the son and grandson of rabbis, became a convert to Catholicism and a professor in Vienna in about 1855, and was later even a member of the Upper House of the Vienna Parliament. He introduced into Romance philology incomparable rigor and subtlety. In later life he felt more and more that he was an Italian, not an Austrian, and toward the end of the century he left Vienna to live and die in Florence. The only devoted pupil he ever had was Elise Richter, a Jewish woman who lived long enough to die in a Nazi torture camp.

This transition from Jewish to secular culture with all its vagaries is striking enough, but what is perhaps characteristic of the Italian Jews is that during the twentieth century they came to play a very important part in the state administration as civil servants, judges, and above all soldiers. Italy must have been the only country in Europe where Jews were welcomed in the army and navy and could reach the highest rank without any difficulty. The Piedmontese Jews became famous at that. General Giuseppe Ottolenghi, as a minister of the war, did much to reorganize the Italian Army at the beginning of the century after the African disasters. General Roberto Segre, as a commander of artillery in the battle of the Piave in June 1918, was the mind behind the strategy that saved Italy. The military profession passed from father to son, as was the case with Roberto Segre and even more conspicuously with two eminent generals, Guido Liuzzi and his son Giorgio.

In 1939, when the Jews were thrown out of the army, the navy, and all other governmental positions, the Italian fleet, which had been rebuilt by the Jewish naval architect General Umberto Pugliese, was commanded by two Jewish admirals, Ascoli and Capon, the latter being the father-in-law of Enrico Fermi. In 1940 the Italian fleet was virtually destroyed by English bombing in the harbor of Taranto, and General Pugliese was called back to save what could be saved of the fleet he had built and the Fascists had lost. Admiral Capon, if I remember correctly, was allowed to fall into Nazi hands.

One should of course dwell on all the branches of the Italian civil service, including the Foreign Office, to give a correct picture. I shall only mention *pietatis causa* the name of Giacomo Malvano, who as an authoritative permanent secretary at the Foreign Office controlled Italian foreign affairs for about thirty years at the turn of the century. Given the close connection between civil service, universities, and politics in Italy, access to the civil service made the entry into universities and politics easier, and vice versa. My impression is that the transition from the ghetto to the upper class happened more frequently in Jewish families through entry into the civil service and the universities than through prospering economic activities.

University professors have made up a very high proportion of the people prominent in Italian politics since at least 1870. During the last decades of the nineteenth century attempts were even made, ultimately to no purpose, to limit the number of university professors who could be members of the House of Deputies at any given time. University professors often became ministers of the crown and even prime ministers. In this sense Luigi Luzzatti, the only Jewish prime minister, conformed to pattern in 1910. He had been both a high civil servant and a university professor of law.

But other factors contributed to the prestige of Jews in politics. One was the advantage some of them had of foreign, especially British, connections. Sidney Sonnino, technically a Protestant but the son of a Jewish landowner from Tuscany, derived advantage from the connections represented by his English mother. He was twice for a short time a prime minister, but above all he is known as the foreign secretary during the entire First World War. He will forever remain associated with the name of his Jewish friend Senator Leopoldo Franchetti, with whom he undertook some of the most penetrating research yet made into Italian social problems. English connections also counted for Ernesto Nathan, a mayor of Rome at the beginning of this century and the head of the Freemasons: the British branch of his family had been the friends of Giuseppe Mazzini during his exile in England.

A second element to be considered is the decisive importance of the Jews of Trieste in the so-called *irredentismo*, the claim of Trieste to be Italian. To the cultural side of the problem I shall return briefly in a moment. As for the political side, Trieste's political *irredentismo* was personified by three Jews: Felice Venezian, Salvatore Barzilai, and Teodoro Mayer. The Italian character of Trieste was and is due to a great extent to Jews who were often of German and Eastern origins but chose Italy—the Italy beyond the border, which seemed to offer an equality for Jews that did not exist in the Austrian Empire.

And finally came socialism. In Italy very few Jewish socialists studied Karl Marx deeply. One exception—the professional economist Achille Loria of the University of Turin—was attacked by Engels and had a bad reputation with the left. He was destined to make a lasting impression in America on Frederick Jackson Turner and his frontier hypothesis. But socialism as a messianic movement appealed to Jews in Italy as elsewhere. It gave them an alternative faith. Emanuele Modigliani, Claudio Treves, and Rodolfo Mondolfo are perhaps the most important of the early Italian Jewish socialists.

As a member of a family that has a permanent place in the history of the Italian socialist movement, I have always had the feeling that somehow the messianism did not quite fit. In fact the most original thinker among my socialist relatives, Felice Momigliano, a professor of philosophy in the University of Rome, tried to combine socialism, Mazzini, and the Hebrew prophets, but found himself thrown out of the Socialist party when the war came in 1915. About the enigmatic and tragic character of this religious thinker, who was basically a reformed Jew like his friend Claude Montefiore—in a country where there has never been any organized reform Judaism—there is much to be said, if we want to understand why the Jews were less a part of Italian life than they thought they were. I felt the same even for the other conspicuous name in my family, Attilio Momigliano, the interpreter of Dante, Ariosto, and Manzoni, of the last of whom he profoundly understood the Catholic inspiration. Though he had many devoted pupils in the universities of Pisa and Florence, Attilio was deeply alone.

It will be enough here to say that this is in effect the question lying behind those Jewish Italian writers whom Stuart Hughes has recently put together under the suggestive title, *Prisoners of Hope*. What perhaps my friend Stuart Hughes ought to have made clearer is that writers of Jewish origin existed, of course, and were respected in the nineteenth century. Tullo Massarani and Giuseppe Revere, two friends who did the most to introduce Heine into Italy, were widely read and respected. They were consciously and explicitly Jewish; so were other, less-read writers—such as David Levi, the author of poems on Jewish themes, or Enrico Castelnuovo, the author of a novel on Italian Jews, *I Moncalvo*, and, incidentally, the father of the mathematician Guido Castelnuovo.

Younger generations of writers, for example the half-English Jewish poet Annie Vivanti—whom Carducci loved—never explicitly admitted their Jewishness until 1939. Three of the greatest writers came from Trieste or nearby, Italo Svevo, Umberto Saba, and Carlo Michelstaedter, the last an extraordinary thinker who committed suicide at the age of twenty-three. A fourth, Alberto Moravia, lives in Rome but is of Venetian origin.

Characteristically, Svevo, Saba, and Moravia used pseudonyms, but while Italo Svevo and Alberto Moravia were concealing the non-Italian names of Schmitz and Pincherle, Saba, whose real family name was Poli, was trying to convey cryptically his allegiance to his Jewish mother rather than to his Christian father. Even when the persecution of Jews made it absurd to deny the Jewish experience—and Carlo Levi, Giorgio Bassani, and Natalia Levi Ginzburg did not deny it—a deeper problem remained: what could Judaism mean for these writers? Primo Levi is of course the exception: he really has a sense of Jewish tradition, but he had to acquire it by surviving in a Nazi extermination camp.

IV

Jewish Italian society developed on its own lines—realistic, connected with business, comparatively open to foreign ideas, but fundamentally introspective, concerned with social justice and yet suspicious of too much novelty. Music, painting, literature, socialism, and science became intense preoccupations of the Italian Jews. Profane music had been one of their interests since at least the Renaissance. Now we have composers such as Vittorio Rieti, Alberto Franchetti, Mario Castelnuovo-Tedesco, and Leone Sinigaglia. Painting was more of a novelty. Perhaps it is no chance that the socialist leader Emanuele Modigliani and the painter Amedeo Modigliani were brothers. Jewish scientists showed uncommon methodological preoccupations: two Jews, Eugenio Rignano and Federico Enriquez, created that important international forum for scientific methodology, the periodical *Scientia*.

How much this brooding, introspective mood contributed to the greatness of Italian mathematicians, physicists, and chemists I can only guess, thinking as I do of some who were my relatives and friends. Where were the roots of the legendary mathematical imagination of Tullio Levi-Civita? Fascism was bound to exclude most of those Jews who had solid liberal or socialist traditions behind them, while economic interests led some Jews to direct involvement with Fascism. One of the most honest Fascists was Gino Olivetti, the representative of industrial interests inside Fascism. Fascist ideological sympathies were also to be found among jurists like Gino Arias and Giorgio del Vecchio, who wanted a reform of the Italian state on corporate lines. I have already mentioned the special situation of Ferrara, where the Fascist mayor was a Jew with a prestigious Jewish name, Ravenna.

But most of the Jews were clearly out. And men like Vito Volterra, a teacher and a senator of immense prestige, spoke clearly and fearlessly for the majority of Jews. To the name of Vito Volterra I would like to add at least the name of my Roman teacher, Giorgio Levi della Vida, the Orientalist of rare distinction who was for some years during the war a professor at the University of Pennsylvania. Max Ascoli, who in 1924 had published a book on Judaism and Christianity (*Le Vie dalla Croce*), came to the U.S. in 1931; Piero Sraffa, the economist, left Italy for England (Cambridge) even earlier. Active opposition was personified by the two brothers Carlo and Nello Rosselli, in whose ancestral house at Pisa Mazzini had died. They were both assassinated on Mussolini's order. The repugnance toward Fascism was repugnance toward Mussolini. During his career he had been helped by Jews, both men and women. He had exploited them ruthlessly, above all the women—and he had betrayed them. He betrayed his Jewish mistress Margherita Sarfatti and his old comrade Angelica Balabanoff and innumerable friends from the early years. When the hour of rebellion came, Jews went into the resistance movement, led it, died for it.

Umberto Terracini, the Jewish Communist leader who had survived about twenty years of confinement in a Fascist prison, was the president of the constituent assembly following the referendum in 1946. Guido Castelnuovo emerged from persecution to become the first president of the revived Accademia dei Lincei in 1946. But a whole generation had been deprived of its best members: men like Eugenio Colorni, the philosopher, Leone Ginzburg, the critic, Emanuele Artom, the young historian of Judaism, and Sergio Diena, a smiling hero full of intelligence and determination. The deaths in the resistance compounded by the deaths in the Nazi-Fascist torture camps created an empty space which has not yet been filled. It made more questionable the existence of a Jewish variety of Italians.

The problem had existed before. It is obvious in a great writer like Italo Svevo, so charged with Jewish Central European culture, and yet so ignorant of traditional Jewish culture and so reluctant to admit his Jewish past. For a few Jews there was a straight choice in favor of a return to Judaism via Zionism and emigration to Palestine. But those who, like myself, have still been fortunate enough to know the older generation of the Italian Zionists—Dante Lattes, Alfonso Pacifici—and to be friends of Enzo Sereni, know also that their choice was not so simple. It was not by chance that Enzo Sereni came back to Italy during the 1940s to fight and die for what he, in private conversation, had always recognized as not dissociable ideals, Zionism and anti-Fascism.

Talmudism had practically ceased to interest Italian Jews at the end of the eighteenth century. Even Sadal was no longer interested in the Talmud. Reform Judaism, as I said, had no roots in Italy. Mystical and cabalistic trends persisted longer, well after Moshe Luzzatto had removed his *Maggid*—the "angel" who accompanied him—from Padua to Amsterdam. My grandfather found consolation in his old age in reading the Zohar every evening and sang Simeon Labi's Hebrew hymn, "Happy are you, Bar Yohai! He anointed you," on Lag Ba 'Omer, the anniversary of the death of Simeon bar Yohai, who is believed by cabalists to be the author of the Zohar. But in fact Jewish culture was seldom transmitted in the sense we Jews intend it to be transmitted. If the Jews themselves know so little about their own Judaism, they can hardly complain that their neighbors understand it even less. Even Benedetto Croce, who was so near to us during the years of persecution, could only recommend that the Jews try to eliminate their peculiarities. It would be foolish to close on a note of optimism when a Jewish child can be assassinated in the synagogue of Rome, as one was in 1982, without an outcry of public opinion. The lines of Nahman Bialik on the murder of children come back to my mind, but I shall not repeat them. And unlike Immanuel of Rome, our old friend who, if not the friend of Dante, was at least the friend of Cino da Pistoia, I do not intend to give any advice to the Messiah. I shall therefore *not* say: "But if you mean to ride on an ass, my Lord, go back to sleep."

I shall rather seek some consolation in the words of my earliest predecessor, the chronicler Ahimaaz of Oria in Southern Italy, who wrote his book of genealogies in the year 4814 of the creation of the world (A.D. 1054)—the first Jewish historian of the Jews of Italy:

I will set down in order the traditions of my fathers, who were brought on a ship over the Pishon, the first river of Eden, with the captives that Titus took from the Holy City, crowned with beauty. They came to Oria; they settled there and prospered through remarkable achievements; they grew in number and in strength and continued to thrive. Among their descendants there arose a man eminent in learning . . . master of the knowledge of God's Law, distinguished for wisdom among his people. His name was . . .[3]

Ahimaaz says "Rabbi Amittai." But he might as well have put another name, "Vito Volterra."

17

Gershom Scholem's Autobiography

IN SEPTEMBER 1923 two young German Jews embarked together at Trieste on their way to settle in Palestine. One, Gerhard (Gershom) Scholem, born in 1897, was soon to become the greatest Jewish historian in our century. The other, Fritz (Shlomo Dov) Goitein, born in 1900,was perhaps slower in developing, from a conventional Arabist into a student of the Jewish-Arabic symbiosis of the Middle Ages and beyond. Yet the volumes of *A Mediterranean Society*, which Goitein started to publish in 1967, amount to a revolutionary picture founded upon new sources (mainly from the repository of documents of the old synagogue of Cairo) that bears comparison with Scholem's achievements.

Such was the beginning of the second science of Judaism, no longer in Germany, where the first *"Wissenschaft des Judentums"* had developed a century before, but in the land of the Fathers—yet still through the agency of Jews born and educated in Germany. The new *Wissenschaft*, like the old one, is characterized by the exploration of recondite texts with all the resources of a rigorous philological method. It has, however, disclosed aspects of Judaism overlooked by the old *Wissenschaft*. Scholem has recovered the gnostic and cabalistic trends of thought and action never absent from Judaism since the Hellenistic age. Goitein has changed our knowledge of the intricate economic and social relations between Arabs and Jews.

The New York Review of Books, 27, 20, December 18, 1980, pp. 37–39.

The comparison between Scholem and Goitein could be continued at length, for both similarities and differences. Scholem came from an assimilated Berlin family where Hebrew had been forgotten: he started as a mathematician and acquired either on his own or with the help of traditional Jewish scholars the mastery of languages and techniques of analysis which was necessary for his success. Goitein, the scion of a rabbinical family, apparently learned Hebrew in his Bavarian home and Arabic at the University of Frankfurt. Scholem has not overlooked Islam (how could he, as the biographer of a Messiah converted to Islam?), nor has Goitein overlooked Christianity. But Scholem remains the historian of the European Jews living within the boundaries of Christendom, while Goitein's special attention is reserved for the Yemenite Jews and for the contacts between Jews and Arabs through the ages, which gave the title to the most popular of his books (1955).

While we can only hope that Goitein will develop the short autobiographical sketch published as an introduction to *A Bibliography of the Writings of Professor Sh. D. Goitein* by R. Attal (Jerusalem, 1975), we can now actually read Professor Scholem's autobiography for the years from 1897 to 1925. The original German text, *Von Berlin nach Jerusalem*, published by Suhrkamp in 1977, has now been translated into English by Harry Zohn (*From Berlin to Jerusalem: Memories of My Youth*).

There is no nostalgia or forgiveness in this book. Now, as fifty years ago, Scholem is determined to speak out. Now, as then, he is primarily concerned with the Jewish assimilated society with which he broke violently—and he broke, first of all, with his father, a Berlin printer. Secondly, he reiterates, at every step, that there was no place for a Jew qua Jew in German society and culture when he decided to leave, though Hitler was still for him nonexistent. Scholem remains Scholem, not a nationalist, not even a religious Jew, but a man who is certain that the beginning of truth for a Jew is to admit his Jewishness, to learn Hebrew, and to draw the consequences—whatever they may be (which is the problem).

Yet in this book he returns from Jerusalem to Berlin, to the parental house and to the maternal language, the tone of which, in its specific Berlin variety, is still unmistakable today in whichever language Scholem chooses to speak. Scholem is a great writer in German. Emigration has saved him from the distortions of German vocabulary and syntax which Hitlerian racism and the post-Hitlerian disorientation produced. The book is therefore untranslatable, in the precise sense in which Scholem declared Franz Rosenzweig's *Der Stern der Erlösung* (The Star of Redemption) to be untranslatable until the day when the text will require interpretation for those who are able to read the original.[1] It would be ungenerous to find fault with a translation which is competent and helpful but was doomed to be insensitive. When Scholem says, "Die Tora wurde seit jeher in 53, in Schaltjahren 54 Abschnitte geteilt" (p. 128), he cannot mean "The Torah has *always* been divided in fifty-three sections—fifty-four in leap years" (p. 98). Professor Scholem can be expected to know that according to academic opinion the division of the Torah into sections does not go back to Moses our Master.

The book ends with Scholem's appointment to a lectureship in Jewish Mysticism at the Hebrew University of Jerusalem on the strength of the recommendation of Immanuel Löw, the author of a five-volume work on the *Flora der Juden* who had found in Scholem's first book two excellent pages on the bisexuality of the palm tree in cabalistic literature. Scholem's concluding remark is pure Wilhelm Busch: "So kam Lenchen auf das Land." The translation substitutes, "Thus began my academic career."

If there is no nostalgia, there are tenderness and gentleness in this book, and a remarkable avoidance of the most acute controversies and crises in which the author was involved. The book is full of friends rather than enemies. Ambivalent feelings are given a positive twist, as in the case of Franz Rosenzweig, who, if he had lived longer, would have been the only scholar capable of challenging Scholem's interpretation of Judaism. Scholem's brief account of his relations with Rosenzweig is a good sample of his writing in this book:

> Every encounter with [Rosenzweig] furnished evidence that he was a man of genius (I regard the abolition of this category, which is popular today, as altogether foolish and the "reasons" adduced for it as valueless) and also that he had equally marked dictatorial inclinations.
> Our decisions took us in entirely different directions. He sought to reform (or perhaps I should say revolutionize) German Jewry from within. I, on the other hand, no longer had any hopes for the amalgam known as

"Deutschjudentum," i.e., a Jewish community that considered itself German, and expected a renewal of Jewry only from its rebirth in Eretz Yisrael. Certainly we found each other of interest. Never before or since have I seen such an intense Jewish orientation as that displayed by this man, who was midway in age between Buber and me. What I did not know was that he regarded me as a nihilist. My second visit, which involved a long conversation one night about the very German Jewishness that I rejected, was the occasion for a complete break between us. I would never have broached this delicate topic, which stirred such emotions in us both, if I had known that Rosenzweig was then already in the first stages of his fatal disease, a lateral sclerosis. He had had an attack which had not yet been definitely diagnosed, but I was told that he was on the mend, and the only thing left was a certain difficulty in speaking. Thus I had one of the stormiest and most irreparable arguments of my youth.

Scholem's father and Martin Buber (whose interpretation of Hasidism it was one of the life tasks of Scholem to repudiate) are not spared, but he has no harsh words for them. The book deliberately avoids entering into the details of the story of how Scholem freed himself from military service during World War I. Readers can turn to his interview with Muki Tsur, published some years ago, where he describes how, to avoid military service, "I put on an act without knowing what I was acting."[2]

Scholem also avoids any deeper probing into his relations with Walter Benjamin and his wife, Dora. The fact that Scholem had previously written a book and many papers on his friendship with Benjamin would not have made it superfluous to say something more definite in his autobiographical account, if the tone of the book in general had allowed it.

The book as it is can give us some first impressions about the wealth of emotional and intellectual stimuli Scholem collected in Germany before going to Jerusalem for good. It is not, however, an account of his intellectual formation, and therefore it cannot help to define the presuppositions of his work which were to remain constant throughout the next sixty years or so.

There is no question that Scholem left Germany at the age of twenty-six as a mature man with a program, a method, and a system of references which remained fundamental to his future activity. He may not have known that himself when he left Germany. He says that he then intended to devote only a few years to the study of Jewish mysticism; he expected to earn his living by teaching mathematics. But it turned out that the method for the study of

Jewish mysticism he had expounded in his first articles on the subject in Buber's journal *Der Jude* in 1920 and 1921[3] and in his dissertation of 1923 (a critical edition of the mysterious gnostic text *Bahir*)[4] would guide all his lifework. More precisely, his concern with language in relation to mysticism, with analytical commentary in relation to sacred texts, and with *anomia*, or lawlessness, in relation to Torah, developed, in foreseeable directions, from these early studies.

Scholem tells us that he abandoned an earlier project of a dissertation on the linguistic theories of the cabala because he realized that he had first to bring cabalistic writings under philological control through critical texts and commentaries. What he did not do as a research student, however, he accomplished fifty years later in his essay on the name of God and the linguistic theory of the cabala (it is included in *Judaica* III, 1975).

Scholem's book concludes with his appointment to a job in Jerusalem in 1925. He thus says nothing about the explorations he made in European libraries, especially during his momentous travels of 1927 (which was also the last time in which he had weeks of direct conversation with Benjamin: in 1938 it was only a question of days). In 1927 Benjamin was the first to be told about his discoveries in the manuscripts of the British Museum and of the Bodleian at Oxford about the antinomian trends of the theology of Sabbatai Zevi's followers. But he did all this with the tools of interpretation he had brought with him from Germany. Nothing indicates more clearly the continuity of his method and the gradual clarification of the issues than a comparison between his prodigiously precocious article on the cabala in the German *Encyclopaedia Judaica* Vol. X, written in 1931, and the article on the same subject about forty years later for the new *Encyclopaedia Judaica*, written in English and published in Jerusalem.

I doubt whether there is anyone now writing who can analyze Scholem's debt to German thought except Scholem himself. David Biale's recent *Gershom Scholem, Kabbalah and Counter-History*,[5] meritorious as it is in other respects, only confirms how remote most American Jews now are from nienteenth-century trends of German thought. For someone like myself who in the late twenties and early thirties read German books and talked to German friends in Italy, it is less difficult to overhear in the prose of Scholem and Benjamin the echoes of those German Romantics—Hamann, Humboldt, and von Baader—who were coming back into fashion. We often heard the dictum "Religion is a vowel and History a consonant," which I later discovered to be a silly remark made in a letter by Rahel Varnhagen.

Not by chance, Rahel Varnhagen early caught the attention of Hannah Arendt for her mixture of Jewish guilt feelings and German metaphysical "*Sehnsucht.*" Another Jewess, Eva Fiesel (neé Lehmann), the extraordinarily able Etruscan scholar, summarized such Romantic tendencies in her book *Die Sprachphilosophie der deutschen Romantik* in 1927. Esotericism was in the air. Followers of Stefan George were multiplying among the younger generation of German Jews.

I was mildly amused when, in his by now famous review of the book by L. W. Schwartz on *Wolfson of Harvard* in the *TLS* of November 23, 1979, Scholem seemed to be surprised that Wolfson should boast to him of having delivered a little sermon for Harvard Chapel in which it was impossible to discover what, if any, religious belief he held. Was this so unprecedented in the circles in which Scholem moved in his youth? In his later American days, Leo Strauss, another great German Jew of the same generation, interpreted esoteric attitudes and double meanings as integral to the art of writing in an age of persecution. That persecution has something to do with esotericism is obvious; but the case of Leo Strauss himself—an addict of esotericism if ever there was one, as those who have read the introduction to the English translation of his book on Spinoza (1965) must know—shows that persecution is not the whole of the matter.

Reticence, allusiveness, and ambiguity were characteristic of Walter Benjamin. Scholem for his part has excluded, even hunted down, any ambiguity or esotericism in the practice of scholarship, politics, or daily life. But he has fully endorsed esotericism as central to the ultimate objects of his lifework. In "Towards an Understanding of the Messianic Idea" (1959), he wrote: "It is one of those enigmas of Jewish religious history that have not been solved by any of the many attempts at exploration just what the real reason is for this metamorphosis which makes knowledge of the Messianic End, where it oversteps the prophetic framework of the biblical text, into an exoteric form of knowledge." Even more uncompromisingly he wrote, in the "Ten Unhistorical Statements about Kabbalah" (never translated into English?): "The true language cannot be spoken."

Such comments, however, do no more than suggest that "spirit of the age" which an older reader can recognize in Scholem's writings. We are perhaps nearer to a real problem in the following observation. Scholem has always been an open, though respectful, opponent of the established German-Jewish science of Judaism, the influence of which went well beyond German Jews, as is evident in the work of Italian Jewish scholars from S. D. Luzzatto to Umberto Cassuto—the biblical scholar for a while a colleague of Scholem's in Jerusalem. What Scholem found wrong with this scientific approach is that it used categories of German Romantic thought without realizing that their creators (Herder, Humboldt, Savigny, etc.) were laying the foundation of a German nationalism that was incompatible with any autonomous Jewish culture inside the German nation.

He also reproached the Jewish scholars of the previous generations for being apologists, that is, for expounding only those sides of Jewish life which the non-Jews were expected to like. Not only Cabala and Hasidism, but also the less decorous aspects of ghetto life were kept out of sight. Not unnaturally, Scholem has reserved his more negative judgments for the more recent offshoots of the old science: "Anyone who wants to become melancholy about the science of Judaism need only read the last twenty volumes of the *Jewish Quarterly Review*" (1959).

But one wonders whether Scholem's reaction against that science is not itself rooted in other aspects of German Romantic thought that emphasized the magical and mystical potentialities of language and myth and indulged in negative dialectics. Nor were the German Romantics unaware of the rough and sordid sides of life. The hypothesis that both the old science of Judaism and the new science of Jewish Mysticism, which is identified with the very name of Scholem, reflect contrasting trends of German Romantic thought—one decisively Protestant, the other nearer to Catholicism—may help to establish the point in Scholem's development where he turned his back on German thought and began to speak on behalf of a new Judaism.

Scholem has said more than once that if he had believed in

metempsychosis he would have considered himself a reincarnation of Johannes Reuchlin, the Christian German humanist who in 1517 published *De arte cabalistica*, the main source of which Scholem himself discovered in the library of the Jewish Theological Seminary of New York in 1938. He has also constantly pointed out that his only predecessor in the study of the cabala to have lived in nineteenth-century Germany was the Catholic Joseph Franz Molitor. These are not casual remarks.

Yet there is indeed a point beyond which Scholem becomes unclassifiable according to any school or any category of German thought. That point is where his Zionist and his cabalistic pursuits intersect. For Scholem the primary meaning of Zionism, so far as intellectual life is concerned, is to make it possible for the Jews to recover all their past history and consequently to call into question all the aspects of their heritage. It is this freedom of movement into the past of the Jewish people that characterizes for Scholem the movement into the future called Zionism.

This radical and total reckoning with the past is obviously far more dramatic and painful in relation to recent times than to the Middle Ages. Scholem becomes correspondingly more drawn to value judgments when he turns his attention from the origins of the cabala to Sabbatai Zevi, the Polish-Jewish adventurer Jacob Frank, and Hasidism, not to speak of his comments about the "German-Jewish dialogue which never took place." A book like *Ursprung und Anfänge der Kabbala* (1962) basically belongs to the history of ideas. Other books by contemporary German scholars— say Aloys Dempf's *Sacrum Imperium* (1927) or H. Grundmann's *Religiöse Bewegungen im Mittelalter* (1935)—can be compared with it in method, though not in depth of analysis. But all the researches leading to his great book on Sabbatai Zevi (published in English translation) are without any precedent in Germany.

There Scholem faces the entire destiny of modern Jews, and more particularly of himself. The sudden mad convergence of cabalistic speculations and Messianic hopes in Sabbatai Zevi and his prophet Nathan of Gaza attracted vast numbers of educated Jews who were longing for liberation and a new start within the Jewish tradition itself. In what is perhaps one of his greatest essays, "Redemption through Sin" (1937), Scholem went so far as to argue that the movement which led to the collective conversion of

Frank's followers to Catholicism in 1759 had its place within Judaism: "One can hardly deny that a great deal that is authentically Jewish was embodied in these paradoxical individuals, too, in their desire to start afresh and in their realization of the fact that negating the exile meant negating its religious and institutional forms as well as returning to the original fountainheads of the Jewish faith."

There are pages of Scholem's writing which give the impression that he recognized something of himself in the destructive and anomic personalities of Sabbatai Zevi and Jacob Frank and drew back from the abyss. As a collective phenomenon, Zionism has therefore become for Scholem the constructive answer to the purely negative conversions to Islam and to Catholicism of Zevi and Frank and many of their followers. Just because Zionism means to Scholem the opening of all the gates of the Jewish past, it is absurd to expect a specific religious message from him. Part of his case against Buber is that Buber misused scholarship in his religious message. The substantial correctness of Scholem's exegesis of Buber is confirmed by Buber's autobiographical fragments,[6] which show that his discovery of the "I-Thou" religion is independent of his interpretation of the Hasidic tradition.

Nor can I see any evolution in Scholem's thought. On the contrary, he seems to me remarkably constant in his intellectual attitudes, as he is in his political reactions to the daily problems of Israel. But it also seems to me that only as long as he tries to understand the cabala is he justified in considering himself a reincarnation of Reuchlin. When the cabalists turn into apostates or illuminists or, finally, Zionists—and then gather in the streets to march into a promised land—no model and no tradition can serve Scholem. He is left on his own, the first Jewish historian able to take full cognizance of the new situation. It is indeed possible that his precocious development prevented him in later years from grasping the full implications of what the Nazis have done to the Jews. Who, after all, is sure even now of what these implications are—or will be?

Other limits of his historical thought, easier to define, are suggested by the symbolic departure from Germany in the company of Shlomo Goitein. For it was Goitein, the more traditionally minded Jew, who penetrated the complexities of social relations between Jews and Arabs and entered into the mentality of the Jews of the Islamic world who, as Scholem is the first to acknowledge, were far from the center of Zionist attention. Even Fritz (Yitzhak) Baer, Scholem's colleague and friend, who has given us so much original research and thought on many fields of Jewish history, never went beyond the Jews of *Christian* Spain during the Middle Ages.

On the other hand, it is difficult to appreciate adequately all the patience that Scholem, who is not famous for patience, has put into understanding his own relation to Christian thought, and especially to modern Germany. This is inseparable from his effort to understand his friend Walter Benjamin, who in his attempt to preserve his links with Germany and German culture finally chose Marxism or what he believed to be Marxism. It is no consolation to anyone to recognize that by carrying on his dialogue with Scholem to the end (and we have just now been given by Scholem their correspondence of the years 1933–1940) Walter Benjamin, that sad and noble victim of Nazism, contributed in ways he perhaps never suspected to securing for Israel and for the world one of the most remarkable historians of our century.

18

How to Reconcile Greeks and Trojans

I

I OWE TO MY LATE colleague of Pisa, Marino Barchiesi—a Latinist of rare intelligence (*I Moderni alla ricerca di Enea*, Bulzoni, Rome, 1981)—my first awareness that Aeneas has a place of his own in American literature as a prototype of the immigrant. "Aeneas at Washington" by Allen Tate, most conspicuously, and, less so, Robert Lowell's "Falling Asleep over the Aeneid" are only the most recent links in a chain which goes back through Thornton Wilder's *The Cabala* to Longfellow's *Evangeline*, which contains the line "bearing a nation with all its household into exile." That Hermann Broch should give its final form to "Der Tod des Vergil" in his American exile, and that one of the most penetrating recent evaluations of the *Aeneid* should come from the American Brooks Otis under the characteristic title *Virgil: A Study in Civilized Poetry* (1963) is perhaps part of the same story. And there is of course the admiration of T. S. Eliot for Virgil. As for myself, I can testify to having read in the University of Chicago library a tragedy *Aeneas* published in 1885 by Charles Gildehaus and republished in Saint Louis in 1888 together with two other tragedies, *Sibyl* and *Telemachus*—the whole being dedicated to William Shakespeare. Toward the end of the tragedy Aeneas leaves no doubt about his ideal destination:

Mededelingen der Koninklijke Nederlandse Akademie van Wetenschappen, Afd. Letterkunde, N.R. 45, 9, 1982, pp. 231–54.

The humblest member of our commonwealth
shall own a passport ampler than a king's
to make condition. Let us, gentle friends,
be most exact and proper with ourselves,
and staff our virgin law so full of justice . . .

That even beyond the borders of America our time, which has
seen so many exiles and emigrants, should altogether be very sensitive to the poem of Aeneas is not surprising. What is surprising
is that not enough recognition has yet been given to the fact that
Dido too was an emigrant—a more unfortunate emigrant that
Aeneas just because she was a woman. The troubles which Aeneas
could inflict upon those with whom he came into contact multiplied after his arrival in Italy. It was the task of Virgil to sort out
the various traditions about the ambiguous events surrounding
Aeneas and to produce his own version.

If by reflecting on Aeneas as an immigrant we can begin to per-
ceive some of the universal implications of the Aeneas myth, Virgil's care for it, just in the time of Augustus, may indeed indicate
some of the more specific reasons why this myth was central to
Roman ideology and served Augustus well.

The Greeks had known migrations throughout their history. No
stigma attached to them. That idealized nation of the *Odyssey*,
the Phaeacians, had retired to Scheria under the guidance of Nau-
sithoos to escape the Cyclops (6. 4–12). Who would have blamed
them? But in classical Greece to be *autochthones* was more respectable than being *epeludes*, emigrants. The Athenians took
pride in their autochthony, which they contrasted with the migrations of the Dorians. As Albrecht Dieterich showed in *Mutter
Erde*, autochthony was the precondition for claiming to have been
procreated by Mother Earth herself. Autochthony did not necessarily imply civilization. The Ethiopians had the reputation of
having been generated by the Earth, but were not on the same
level as the Athenians. Yet the Athenians succeeded well enough
in linking their own superior merits with autochthony. As there is
no time and no place in which the Romans were free from Greek
influences, the appreciation of autochthony spread to Rome. Let
me quote this Greek conceit in Livy's words (38. 17): "generosius
in sua quidquid sede gignitur." It is therefore the more remarkable
that when the Romans came to speak about themselves, they sel-

dom made any effort to claim autochthony. What the Romans had to say about themselves was centered on Romulus and Aeneas. We may take it for granted that the two stories were originally independent and only later were connected by artificial genealogies which made Romulus a descendant of Aeneas. According to the Romulus legend, the twins Romulus and Remus started out as leaders of rather disreputable robber bands; the foundation of the city they envisaged was marred by fratricide; the killer Romulus went on collecting refugees from the neighborhood whom he provided with sanctuary. The primitive institutions, such as the three tribes allegedly corresponding to three main groups of settlers—Latins, Sabines, and Etruscans—and some of the religious fraternities, such as the Luperci ("fera quaedam sodalitas," as Cicero says, *Pro Caelio* 26), would reflect the conditions in which the new robber state was founded. Even Livy, who does his best to make the founders of Rome respectable, has to describe them as "a miscellaneous rabble without distinction of bond or free [sine discrimine liber an servus esset] eager for new conditions" (1. 8, trans. B. O. Foster, Loeb). Some sensitive scholars have chosen to believe that this cannot be a native tradition and therefore must be the invention of enemies of Rome. This thesis has been developed, with the erudition and the logical rigor we would expect of him, by one of the best contemporary students of ancient historiography, H. Strasburger (*Sitzungsb. Heidelberg. Ak.* 1968, 5). Unfortunately, such a suggestion is entirely incredible. It does not explain why the Romans, having been accused by some enemies of having started their collective life with fratricide and robbery, declared themselves delighted and turned the accusation into a sacred national tradition. Nor does it explain why other Latin cities, most clearly Praeneste, claimed to have been founded by a leader of robbers (Servius *Aeneas* 7. 678). Secondly, and even more decisively, this solution is incompatible with all we know about the development of the legend of Romulus. In the fifth and fourth centuries B.C. the Greeks imagined that Rome was founded by one man, or even by one woman, whose name, Rome, would have been given to the city. They did not think of twin brothers and fratricide. But in 296 B.C. the legend of the twins was consecrated by a public monument in Rome (Livy 10. 23. 12), and in 269 the wolf and the twins appear on the coins of Rome. We must assume that the story of Romulus and Remus was current in Rome in the fourth century B.C., when the Greeks apparently did not yet know it. One is left to wonder which enemies of Rome had managed to persuade the Romans in the fourth century B.C. or earlier that Romulus had murdered his brother. Twins who become rivals fill the chronicles of gods and men, and the archetype of brother killing brother has its place in familiar sacred history. Juvenile robber bands certainly played their part in real history during the monarchic period of Rome. The Romans took in their stride the idea that they were the descendants of robbers and had a fratricide in the foundation ritual of their city. They did their best to inform the Greeks about their own version of the foundation of Rome. The story of the twins was told by the first Roman historian in the Greek language, Fabius Pictor, about the end of the third century. If Diocles of Peparethos, as Plutarch seems to suggest, preceded Fabius in telling the same story (*Romulus* 3), Diocles must have learned it from Roman oral tradition. We now know that, to please the Romans, the Greeks of Chios put up a piece of sculpture representing the twin brothers, in a public place, about 200 B.C. An inscription the text of which had been circulating privately for about thirty years was finally published in the not very accessible *Chiakà Chronikà* of 1975, pp. 14–27, and has been made more accessible, with a first attempt at a commentary, by M. Moretti in *Riv. Fil. Class.* 108, 1980, 33–54. From about 200 B.C., the story of Romulus and Remus, including the murder of the latter, was evidently the orthodox explanation of the origins of Rome and the symbol of Roman power offered to the friends and the subjects of Rome. The Greeks, to all appearances, learned about the twins and the fratricide from the Romans themselves. At the same time, more or less, the story of Aeneas reaching the shores of Latium with his companions, not exactly in splendor, was put into Latin verse by Naevius and into Greek prose by Fabius Pictor. In other words, it was definitely consecrated by the earliest monuments of Roman literature under Hellenistic influence. Here again, a recent discovery has added some new elements to our scanty information. A catalogue of a library of the second century B.C. found painted on the walls of a house of Tauromenium (modern Taormina) in Sicily has given us some details of the account Fabius Pictor provided of Aeneas's wanderings, including his special alliance with the founder of the Latin city of Lavinium.[1]

I shall soon return to an examination of the development of the Aeneas legend. What I want to emphasize for the moment is the obvious cumulative effect of these two stories of Romulus and Aeneas. They presented the Romans as the descendants of the Trojan immigrants and the foundation of Rome as a further occasion for collecting stragglers of dubious reputation. The personal connection of Aeneas and Romulus was envisaged in different ways. Here it may be enough to register the oldest version known to us, perhaps to be dated about 350 B.C., by a Sicilian writer Alcimus (*FGrH* 560, F. 4), who made Romulus the only son of Aeneas by Tyrrhenia. Romulus in his turn was for Alcimus the father of Alba, whose son Rhodios (a strange name almost certainly to be emended to Rhomos) became the founder of Rome. Here a Greek writer evidently tried to combine Greek and Roman stories: though he did not make Romulus the founder of Rome, he treated him as the son of Aeneas. As such, Alcimus's version is no evidence for Roman genealogical thinking about 350 B.C. But it confirms that while the Greeks, and more precisely the Athenians, claimed autochthony as a reason for pride, the Romans were ready to be seen and received as *epeludes*, as migrants, of a very strange, and un-Greek, kind.

Whatever one may think of the character and progressive evolution of Roman imperialism, we must not separate the character it took and the evolution it achieved from this early indifference of the Romans toward racial purity and stability. The Romans, who thought their city to be originally populated by individuals of different extraction, were also ready to extend their citizenship to foreigners. The specific development of Roman imperialism which first extended Roman citizenship to the whole of the Italian peninsula and then to the greatest part of the populations of the provinces is not separable from this very early attitude of the Romans toward their own humble and mixed origins. On the other hand, whatever we may say of the details of the attitudes (I must emphasize the plural *attitudes*) of the Greeks toward their own origins, the pride in autochthony and purity prevailed: it characterized the severe restrictions limiting citizenship inside the individual *poleis* and the basic unwillingness to turn from the city-state to

the territorial state. The stories of Aeneas and Romulus are therefore very relevant to any attempt to understand the nature of Roman political mentality.

II

With this in mind, we may return to the story of Aeneas with
the three specific purposes of seeing: first, how, contrary to its
premises, it paradoxically made Aeneas a migrant hero; second,
what chances this story had of being acceptable to the Greeks as
an invitation to like the Romans and to collaborate with them;
and third, how the Romans, and more specifically Virgil, managed
to turn the image of the Trojan Aeneas into a symbol of friendship
between Greeks and Romans. It may help the understanding of my
argument if I add here a point which I shall repeat later, namely
that Aeneas remained specifically the symbol of reconciliation between Greeks and Romans, and never became a generic symbol of
friendship between the various peoples of the Roman Empire. For
instance, to the best of my knowledge, the story of Aeneas was
never used to say a nice word about the Carthaginians, though
Dido was after all the founder of Carthage.

Aeneas had been provided with a perfect genealogical tree in
the *Iliad*, Book XX, 215ff. Thus Aeneas belonged to a cadet branch
of the royal family of Troy. As a good cadet he had reasons for
complaining against the ruling branch, which did not show him
sufficient respect (13. 46off., 20. 179). At the outbreak of the war
he was, like his father, Anchises, a sort of shepherd king near
Mount Ida. Homer is not very clear about his status. During the
war he was next to Hector in valor among the Trojans, but had to
be saved by his divine protectors more than once. In the fight
against Diomedes, he was saved by his mother, Aphrodite, and
Apollo. In the struggle with Achilles, he was rescued by Poseidon,
who told him that he should leave Achilles alone: once Achilles is
dead, no Greek warrior will be able to kill Aeneas. Indeed, Poseidon promises that Aeneas will reign among the Trojans, and his
children's children after him. Thus Poseidon repeats on the battlefield the promise Aphrodite had made to Anchises on parting after
their brief love interlude: "and you shall have a dear son who shall

reign among the Trojans, and his children's children after him, springing up continually" (Homeric *Hymns* V. 195–97, trans. H. E. White, Loeb). Whether Book XX of the *Iliad* here echoes the Hymn to Aphrodite or vice versa, both texts reflect a historical situation: the poet implies that a dynasty claiming descent from Aeneas reigned in the Troad after the destruction of Troy. Apparently, some tradition had developed that Aeneas had survived the destruction of Troy by the Greeks and had established a new kingdom in the same region. Some later texts, most notably Demetrius of Scepsis quoted by Strabo 13. 1. 52–53, presuppose the existence of a degraded royal family claiming such a descent from Aeneas in the fourth or third century B.C. This of course does not prove that the poet of the Homeric Hymn to Aphrodite composed his poem for a member of a dynasty allegedly deriving from Anchises. Whatever the true historical background, the message of the Homeric poetry was unambiguous: Aeneas had *not* left the Troad, had *not* left Asia; he had established there a monarchy for generations to come. This excluded emigration both for Aeneas and for his direct descendants.

How then did it happen that Aeneas was sent out of the Troad and became a sort of Trojan competitor to the Greek Odysseus both in his peregrinations and in his love adventures? Place names which seemed to allude either to Aeneas himself or to his father may have helped to turn the sedentary Aeneas into a vagabond. The place Aineia in Macedonia was certainly considered rather early to have been founded by him: local coins with the image of Aeneas carrying his father on his shoulders go back to the sixth century B.C. The name of Mount Anchisia in Arcadia encouraged the idea that Aeneas and his old father had traveled there. Modern scholars have also toyed with the idea that Aeneas was made to travel in order to explain the foundation of sanctuaries dedicated to his mother, Aphrodite: at least it is a fact that ancient tradition associates many cult places of Aphrodite with the pilgrimages of Aeneas. But the obvious truth is that we simply do not know why, against the authority of Homer, Aeneas and his Trojan companions were made to abandon the region of Troy and to find a new place to settle in the West. In the fifty century, Aeneas had made himself at home in Sicily among the Elymi, as Thucydides knew (6. 2). At the end of the century, Hellanicus said that Aeneas had founded Rome. Hellanicus's text is known to us only second-hand through Dionysius of Halicarnassus, who wrote in the first century B.C. The manuscripts of Dionysius leave us in doubt whether Hellanicus had said that Aeneas founded Rome *with* Odysseus or *after* Odysseus. As "after Odysseus" does not make much sense, it would seem that, according to Hellanicus, Odysseus and Aeneas had combined forces in founding Rome. Another tradition which seems to go back to the end of the sixth century B.C. (Hecataeus, 1. F. 62 Jacoby) is that the city of Capua in Campania owed its name to the Trojan Capys: evidently Aeneas was not the only Trojan to have been credited with the foundation of a city in southern Italy.

This reinforces the claim of the Tabula Iliaca, a relief of the first century A.D.—and admittedly a garbled and composite source—when it attributes to Stesichorus, a Greek poet active in Italy about 550 B.C., the story that Aeneas reached Campania. Such evidence as we have seems to point to the conclusion that the wanderings of Aeneas in Italy were already registered in cold historical prose a century later. In joining the name of Odysseus to that of Aeneas in the foundation of Rome, Hellanicus reminds us that Odysseus had already been linked with the Latin race. In Hesiod's *Theogony* Odysseus appears as the father of Latinus. No other Greek source makes Aeneas the direct founder of Rome, but the tradition reappears in a difficult passage of Sallust, *Catilinarian Conspiracy*, 6. 1–2; and there are plenty of other texts which in one way or in another relate Aeneas to the direct founder or founders of Rome.[2]

The number of Attic vases representing Aeneas which have been found in Etruria has led to the conclusion that in the sixth century B.C. the Etruscans had taken a special interest in the story of Aeneas and had transmitted it to their Latin neighbors. This is by no means unlikely; but we must remember that Greek vases arrived in Etruria in the thousands, and we simply do not know whether the relatively high number of representations of Aeneas reflects the preference for Aeneas of the Attic vase-painters or of the Etruscan buyers. Three vases made by Etruscans with Aeneas as a subject might in themselves be interpreted as an imitation of Greek themes: one of them is the Munich amphora depicting Creusa carrying an earthenware jar with sacred objects.

There is only one original Etruscan piece, of about 500 B.C.—a scarab of the de Luynes collection in Paris which represents Aeneas carrying Anchises and the Penates—to testify that the Etruscans had a genuine interest of their own in Aeneas (*JHS* 99, 1979, plate IIIb): not very much. Statuettes of Aeneas carrying his father have been found in a temple of Veii. They would be of decisive importance if we could date them in the sixth or fifth century B.C., as was suggested by the first archaeologists who published them. The very crude manufacture of these statuettes makes it very difficult to date them on stylistic grounds: even if we discount extreme dates, such as 200 B.C., we cannot exclude the possibility that they reflect the prestige of Aeneas in Latium and neighboring territories after he had been accepted as an ancestor in Latium in the fifth or fourth century B.C.[3]

There was in fact at least one other place in Latium which claimed Aeneas and contributed to shape the legend of his settling in central Italy. In the early third century B.C., the Sicilian historian Timaeus learned from natives of Latium that Aeneas had brought sacred objects of his own to Lavinium, where they were preserved (566 F. 59 Jac.). These domestic sacred objects must be identical with the domestic gods of the Roman people, the *Penates populi Romani*, whom the Roman consuls used to visit ceremonially in Lavinium once a year. The poem *Alexandra* attributed to Lycophron is the first to state (or rather to imply) that Aeneas founded Lavinium (l. 1259). Modern scholars dispute whether the *Alexandra* was written about 270 B.C. or about 190 B.C.: I have repeatedly taken a position for the earlier date, but a date of about 190 B.C. would not detract from the importance of this evidence. Lycophron depends on earlier and good authors for his statements, and he is confirmed by Dionysius of Halicarnassus (I. 64), who speaks of a sanctuary dedicated to Aeneas—more precisely of a *heroon*—existing in Lavinium in his own days (late first century B.C.) and seems to have visited it. The literary evidence has received powerful support from archaeology in the last twenty years. The excavations on the site of ancient Lavinium by P. Sommella brought to light a sacred building of the fourth century B.C. which includes a tomb of the seventh century B.C. This has been identified as the sanctuary of Aeneas mentioned by Dionysius of Halicarnassus. If this identification is correct, a tomb of the seventh century would have been regarded in the fourth century, for whatever reason, as the tomb of Aeneas and surrounded by a sanctuary: a *heroon* normally implies a tomb in it.[4] There are, however, complications. We hear from the second-century-B.C. annalist Cassius Hemina (fr. 7 Peter) that Aeneas was worshiped as *pater indiges*, while Livy asserts that Aeneas died by drowning in the river Numicus and received a cult under the name of Iuppiter Indiges (1. 2. 6). The Numicus flowed near Lavinium. An inscription discovered at Tor Tignosa, not very far from Lavinium, reads, according to M. Guarducci: "Lare Aenia d(ono)"—that is, "gift to Lar Aeneas." The question raised by this much debated inscription is whether Lar Aeneas means "god Aeneas" and therefore confirms the existence of a cult of Aeneas, as a god, in Lavinium.[5] Even if we take Lar Aeneas to be equivalent to "god Aeneas," we have still to explain why Aeneas was considered in Lavinium either a full god (in the Latin way) or a hero (in the Greek way) and why he was called either *pater indiges* or even simply *indiges* (the variants are collected by A. Schwegler, *Römische Geschichte*, I, 1853, 287–88).

Underlying these specific questions is a more general and important question: whether and how Aeneas came to be connected with Lavinium. In the present state of the evidence, it is equally conceivable that early, say in the sixth or fifth century B.C., the citizens of Lavinium directly imported Aeneas from Greek legend or that later, in the fourth century B.C., they received Aeneas from Rome. Correspondingly we do not know whether in his story that Aeneas founded Rome *with* Odysseus (or less probably *after* Odysseus) Hellanicus was simply imposing a Greek pattern on Roman origins or somehow reflecting an active Latin interest in being colonized by a Trojan. To have been founded by Aeneas meant, for Latins, not to be Greeks, while keeping some of the glory of being related to the Trojan War. It was a proclamation of noble origins combined with the recognition of diversity from the Greeks. In Rome, the Trojan idea had to be reconciled with a tradition attributing the foundation of the city to one or two indigenous beings. In Lavinium the competition of a native founder was apparently not so strong.

Whatever the details, if the Romans toyed with the idea of their city having been directly founded by Aeneas—a notion which we have found repeated by Sallust—they settled for a compromise. Aeneas was left to Lavinium, but his descendants founded Rome. Chronological difficulties in placing the foundation of Rome immediately after the destruction of Troy helped to reinforce this compromise when chronology became a serious consideration, but we may doubt that in the fifth or fourth century B.C. the Latins worried about it.

What we can learn from combining literary evidence and archaeological exploration is that Aeneas was important to Lavinium at least from the fourth century B.C. onward. He was considered the founder of the city. On the other hand, archaeology confirms that Lavinium was an important religious center for archaic Latium. Somebody has called the city a little Italian Delphi. It must have appeared suitable to its situation that Aeneas should be its founder. As after all Rome was known to have been founded by Romulus, the Greek legend that Aeneas was the founder of Rome could be modified to the extent that Aeneas was considered the ancestor of Romulus. This process allowed the insertion of a third Latin city into the process, Alba Longa. Alba Longa had been destroyed by Rome very early, and its aristocracy had been transferred to Rome. At a certain point some of these aristocratic clans from Alba Longa claimed Trojan descent. By crediting Aeneas's son Ascanius with the foundation of Alba Longa, their claims were both justified and used to increase the prestige of Rome. We know that the Aemilii and the Julii were among the clans which claimed such Trojan ancestry. For our purpose they are less interesting than the clans of the Geganii, the Nautii, and perhaps the Decii which disappeared in the fourth and third centuries B.C. but are known to have boasted of their Trojan ancestors. Whatever theory we ultimately prefer, the Trojan legend appears to have taken root in Rome and in the rest of Latium not later than the early fourth century B.C.[6]

III

If our account is roughly correct, the Greeks imagined Aeneas traveling to the West not later than the sixth century B.C. In the late fifth century, Aeneas was already considered by some Greeks to be the founder or co-founder of Rome. The Romans did not completely accept these stories about Aeneas, because they had their own founder—Romulus. But they adapted their own foundation legend to accommodate Aeneas and harmonized it with the claims of other Latin cities, especially Lavinium and Alba Longa, to Trojan ancestry. As there were authoritative Greek writers who declared the Romans to be Trojan descendants of Aeneas, the Romans could go round the Mediterranean claiming acknowledgment of this descent and exploiting it diplomatically. I shall soon mention some cases of this exploitation. But the Romans were bound to find in certain quarters unwelcome reactions to their claims. Some Greeks might think that the Romans, as Trojans, were the natural enemies of the Greeks. Some others might think that Aeneas was not quite the good Trojan he was reputed to be: if he really left Troy, had he not been a traitor to his side? And finally there was the simple but old and formidable objection that, according to Homer, Aeneas and his descendants had been fated to rule the Troad, not Latium. Were not the Romans cheating in claiming that they were the descendants of Aeneas?

All three types of objections are documented in our tradition. They confirm that after all it was not so easy for the Romans to be acceptable as Trojans in the Greek world, even if some writers had presented Aeneas as a good Trojan and the Romans as the descendants of this good Trojan.

We start with the most dangerous consequence the Romans had to face in their claim to be Trojans. It was the probability of being told by unsympathetic Greeks: "So if you are Trojans, never mind Aeneas; you are the enemies of the Greeks." We know that this is what happened about 281 B.C. when Pyrrhus, King of Epirus, landed in southern Italy to help the Tarentines. As Pausanias tells us, obviously using a good source (1. 12. 1): "Pyrrhus remembered the sack of Troy, and he had the same hopes for his success in the war, as he, a descendant of Achilles, was waging war against a colony of the Trojans." This statement, the authenticity of which can hardly be doubted, has perhaps not the world-shaking significance that Jean Perret tried to attribute to it in his *thèse* of 1942, *Les origines de la légende troyenne de Rome*, where he suggested that Pyrrhus in fact invented the Trojan origins of the Romans in order to have an excuse, as a descendant of Achilles, for attacking them. We do not have to argue now that his theory goes against both evidence and common sense. But the simple notion that the Romans *qua* Trojans were enemies of the Greeks could hardly be alien to the adventurous king who claimed descent from Achilles. It was a notion bound to have some reverberations even later. We have a papyrus containing a strange forgery—a letter allegedly sent by Hannibal to the Athenians after the battle of Cannae (R. Merkelbach, in B. Snell, *Griechische Papyri der Hamburger Staats- und Universitätsbibliothek*, 1954, no. 129, l. 106). In this letter Hannibal promises to deal with the Romans in the way in which the Greeks of old had dealt with the Trojans. We are not certain about the date of this forgery (perhaps the late second century B.C.), but it clearly reflects the exploitation of the Trojan legend in ideological warfare against the Romans (E. Candiloro, *Studi Classici e Orientali* 14, 1965, 171–76).

The second obstacle the Romans had to surmount was, as I have said, the rumor that Aeneas had been a traitor to his own side. After all, Homer had left it entirely unclear how Aeneas would survive the destruction of Troy and get his new kingdom. Aeneas was not alone among the Trojan heroes in being suspected of treason. Antenor is treated by Homer as one of the worthiest Trojans: seven of his eleven sons are said to have died for their country. Before the war, we are told, he had had as guests in his house both Odysseus and Menelaus. Later traditions credited him with having survived and emigrated to Italy with the Eneti, whom Homer knew to be allies of the Trojans (*Il.* 2. 851). As there were Veneti in northern Italy, it was easy to conjecture that Antenor had brought his Eneti there and founded Patavium, the present Padova, on Venetian ground. But Antenor became a traitor in the tradition preserved by Lycophron (l. 340) and after him by Dictys and Dares. If Antenor had been a traitor, why not the other emigrant to Italy, Aeneas? Menecrates of Xanthos is quoted by Dionysius of Halicarnassus (1. 48) as a historian who said that Aeneas betrayed Troy out of hatred for Paris and because he was allowed by the Greeks to save his household. We have no sure way of dating Menecrates, but the language and style of the few fragments is not incompatible with a date in the fourth century B.C. (Jacoby *FGrH* 769). The accusation of treason was repeated by a Roman historian,

Q. Lutatius Catulus, consul in 102 B.C., in his *Communes Histo-riae*. He is quoted by the author of the *Origo gentis romanae*, who wrote perhaps about A.D. 360. I have argued in the *Journal of Roman Studies* of 1958 that the quotations from archaic authors in the *Origo* are, as a rule, authentic.[7] In imperial times the treachery of Aeneas was alluded to by numerous authors, such as Dictys and Dares, and was exploited by Tertullian, *Ad nationes* 2. 9. 12, in an antipagan argument. Servius, the commentator of Virgil, came to believe, we do not know why, that even Livy had considered Aeneas a traitor (*Aeneas* 1. 242). The tradition that Aeneas had become acceptable to the Greeks only by turning traitor to the Trojans was not necessarily created to embarrass the Romans, but certainly became embarrassing. One recognizes the embarrassment in Dionysius of Halicarnassus and perhaps in Virgil.

Finally, the Romans had to face the objection that, according to the oldest and most authoritative sources, Aeneas had never left the Troad. The distinguished antiquarian Demetrius of Scepsis, himself a native of the Troad, emphasized this fact in the second century B.C. He was taken seriously by Strabo, who used him as his main source for his description of the region around ancient Troy. Demetrius thought he knew that Aeneas remained in that region and that his son Ascanius, jointly with a son of Hector, moved to a new Scepsis, which by a lucky coincidence happened to be the birthplace of Demetrius. We must assume that in Demetrius's account Aeneas moved from the city of Troy to the city of Old Scepsis in the neighborhood and there established his kingdom (Strabo 13. 1. 53). Emilio Gabba showed in a fundamental study that Demetrius, who witnessed the Roman intervention in Asia and the use which the Romans made of their Trojan ancestry, was not an innocent erudite oblivious of contemporary issues (cf. M. Sordi ed., *I canali della propaganda nel mondo antico*, 1976, 84–101). He knew perfectly well that by denying the reality of Aeneas's immigration into Latium he was by implication inviting the Romans to leave alone the descendants of Aeneas in the Troad. In simpler words, Demetrius of Scepsis was hostile to the Romans before the Romans permanently established themselves in Asia Minor and made it dangerous for any local writer to say the things Demetrius was saying. One must add that in that crucial second century B.C. several Greek writers supported the Roman claim that Aeneas had migrated to Latium. Thus Demetrius of Scepsis was a minority voice in an extended polemic.

We must see the use the Romans made of the legend of Aeneas in the third and second centuries B.C. in relation to this barrage of criticisms. In the mythologically oriented world of Greek culture, the Romans could not expect not to be challenged when they presented their credentials as the descendants of one of the best of the Trojans and his companions. It shows their strength that they were soon able to operate with some success on the assumption that they could speak on behalf of the Trojans and their descendants. About 237 B.C. the Romans took the Greek inhabitants of Acarnania under their protection against the Aetolians, because the Acarnanians had not taken part in the war against Troy: they were the good Greeks (Just. 28. 1. 5; Strabo 10. 2. 25). It seems that the special relation between Rome and the new Ilion in the Troad (which was taken to be the continuation of the old Troy) goes back approximately to the same time. Suetonius, *Claudius* 25. 3, relates that the Romans asked a king of Syria called Seleucus to free the inhabitants of the Troad from all taxation. If the document was not a forgery, the most likely Seleucus to have been involved seems to be Seleucus II Callinicus of about 240 B.C. At that date the Romans would have been feeling strong enough to interfere with the internal affairs of the Seleucid State and to parade as the protectors of their remote cousins left behind in Troy. Again, in 205 B.C. the introduction of the cult of Cybele into Rome was justified by reference to the Phrygian origins of Aeneas (the most explicit evidence is, however, Ovid, *Fasti* 4. 251ff.). It is unnecessary here to add that consanguinity (*syggeneia*) was recognized as an argument in Hellenistic diplomacy.[8] The Romans by using it showed that they were learning how to play the game. Nearer home we are told that in 263 B.C. at the beginning of the first Punic War the inhabitants of Sicilian Segesta killed the Carthaginian garrison and joined the Romans because of their common descent from Aeneas (Zonaras 8. 9): a fact which Cicero, *In Verrem* 4. 72, and Diodorus 23. 5 remembered. Later, as a very interesting inscription published by G. Manganaro in 1963 shows (reproduced with textual improvements in A. Alföldi, *Röm. Frühgeschichte,* 88; cf. J. et L. Robert, *Rev. Ét. Grec.* 1965, 499), the

citizens of another Sicilian town, Centuripae, were anxious to remind the citizens of Rome and Lavinium about their connections
with Latium going back to Aeneas. In 217 B.C. the Romans themselves erected a temple to Venus of Eryx, another Sicilian town,
because Aeneas was supposed to have founded Eryx: they were
then in a difficult stage of the second Punic War. About 196 B.C.
the city of Lampsacus in Asia Minor sent requests to the Roman
Senate in the name of the old Trojan brotherhood (Ditt.³ 591).⁹
When the Romans finally managed to get a hold in Asia a few
years later, the Trojans of course became especially useful (Livy
37. 9. 7; 37. 37. 2; 38. 39. 10). In general, one can say that Aeneas
helped the claims of Rome over Sicily and her interventions in the
Greek East.

IV

These claims, though very important in providing the Romans
with pretexts for interventions abroad, did not, however, contribute greatly to what by and by became a necessity to the Romans,
apart from being an ambition: to be acceptable to the Greek
world, even while keeping outside it. By the middle of the second
century B.C., and of course even more so later, the Romans controlled the whole of metropolitan Greece and were extending their
grip over the Asiatic Greeks, not to speak of the Greeks of Italy.
They needed the cooperation of the Greek upper classes to govern
the territories they controlled, and, above all, they needed the intelligence and the knowledge of the Greeks to make the Empire
work as a whole. The exploitation of Western Europe and Punic
Africa was partly conditioned by the cooperation of the Greeks.
Thus the Aeneas myth had to be turned into a myth of real collaboration between Greeks and Romans if it was to be really useful in
the new situation. What is interesting in this new stage is the
reshaping of the myth, the stressing of selected features of it, in
order to present it as a myth of reconciliation between the two
races. I should like to leave out of my picture an element which is
indeed very curious and mysterious in itself and has attracted a
great deal of attention from modern scholars, but which seems to
be irrelevant to our quest. We know that in historical times the

ancient Romans performed a strange ceremony on May 14. Twenty-seven straw puppets were thrown by the Vestal Virgins into the Tiber from the bridge Sublicius. These puppets had the name of Argei. What was the origin of the ceremony and what is the original meaning of the name Argei are important questions in themselves.[10] Though the etymology of Argei from the city of Argos was current in ancient Rome and give rise to various explanations (for instance, that Heracles when in Latium threw these puppets into the Tiber in memory of dead Argive companions), I am not aware that anybody in antiquity connected this ritual with the enmity between Trojans or Romans *and* Greeks or Argives. This connection, as far as I know, was first proposed by H. Diels and accepted with modifications by G. Wissowa at the end of the last century (cf. K. Latte, *Röm. Religionsgeschichte*, 1960, 412–14). Such a modern idea played no part in the meaning of the Trojan legend in Roman minds. On the contrary, the Romans liked to think that Greek heroes such as Euander and Heracles had come to the site of future Rome before the Trojan Aeneas. A tradition which was already to be found in the earliest of the Roman historians, Fabius Pictor, maintained that sixty years before Aeneas the Arcadian Euander had come to Latium, had settled on the Palatine with his followers, and had organized a little independent Greek colony with all the best attributes of Greek civilization: knowledge of the alphabet, which Euander passed on to the other inhabitants of Latium, knowledge of musical instruments, cult of the rustic god Pan (from which cult the Roman festival of the Lupercalia would have developed), and altogether that enviable idyllic peace and simplicity we still call Arcadian. How this legend of Euander came into being remains something of a mystery. We can say fairly safely that there is no historical foundation for it, if by historical foundation we mean an authentic settlement of Greeks on the Palatine. Giambattista Vico had already understood this. In recent years, Professor Emilio Peruzzi has tried to refurbish the old legend of a Greek settlement by turning it into a Mycenaean settlement, to which some Mycenaean shards found near by would lend credibility (for instance, in *La Parola del Passato* 1974, 309). But Arcadian heroes are different from Mycenaean tradesmen, and Mycenaean shards, even when they exist (which is very doubtful in our case), are rather witnesses for trade than for settlements.[11] Some Greek, we may suspect, noticed the similarities between the name of the Palatine and the Arcadian name Pallanteum and between the Lupercalia and the Arcadian ritual of the Lycaea: he deduced that somebody must have brought such Arcadian features to Latium and attributed the operation to the fabulous Euander. Euander had something in common with a god or hero of Latium called Faunus with whom he could be identified and this would explain why the Latins wrote in the Greek alphabet. The Romans accepted Euander gladly.

Euander was closely followed by no less a hero than Heracles, another Greek. Heracles had been worshiped in Rome since time immemorial in the *ara maxima* of the Forum Boarium not far from the Palatine. It was said that Euander had organized this cult in the presence of Heracles himself and had placed it in the hands of two *gentes*, the Potitii and the Pinarii, who transmitted it to their descendants for some centuries. Furthermore, when he went away from Latium for other adventures, Heracles left behind on the Capitoline hill some of his followers of Peloponnesian origin. Thus at least two of the future Roman hills had been occupied by Greeks before Aeneas arrived.

All would depend, of course, on Aeneas's behavior after his arrival. But we are perhaps already in a position to forecast that it was not the intention of those historians and poets who took charge of the arrival of Aeneas to make him an enemy of the Greeks he found on the spot. We cannot say much about those early Roman historians and poets, such as Fabius Pictor and Naevius, who first gave literary shape to the story of Aeneas in Latium. But we have the full text of the two writers of the Augustan age who reshaped the story for their time, Dionysius of Halicarnassus and Virgil, and we can see with our own eyes that they wanted the story to mean reconciliation and friendship between Greeks and Trojans. It is also fairly evident that though they innovate many important elements in the tradition (and disagree among themselves about the innovations), they did not transform an anti-Greek story into a pro-Greek one. The philhellenism preexisted.

Dionysius of Halicarnassus had only one serious ambition. He wanted the Romans to be Greeks—not pure Greeks, which was impossible, but as Greek as possible in the circumstances. He was

convinced that the Latin language was a sort of Greek dialect of
the Aeolian variety, and he was not the first to think so. This is
less strange than believing that Welsh is the Hebrew of the lost
tribes. In Book VII Dionysius has an elaborate comparison of the
Roman games *(ludi Romani)* with the Greek games and assumes a
very close imitation of Greek institutions in Rome. The explanation of these institutional similarities was sought by Dionysius in
the early strata of the population of Latium: the Aborigines, notwithstanding their name which points to autochthony, had come
from Arcadia; the Pelasgians were Greek, and Greeks of course
were Euander, Heracles, and their followers. What is more, the
Trojans themselves had been (he says) a nation as truly Greek as
any and had come from the Peloponnese to Asia (I. 61). Aeneas
was ultimately a Greek. In Dionysius's story, King Latinus had
decided to make war against Aeneas and his band. But after an
interview with Aeneas he was convinced that he should share
power and land with the newcomer. He declared to Aeneas: "I
cherish a kindly feeling towards the Greek nation" (I. 58). As we
can see, Dionysius was in no need to make Euander a prominent
link between Aeneas and Latinus. Euander provided a prominent
background of Hellenism for Rome; but Aeneas, in Dionysius's
opinion, was Greek in his own right.[12]

The more sophisticated Virgil—not being a Greek himself, like
Dionysius—was not so optimistic. He knew that there were differences between Greeks and Romans. Aeneas himself, by descending "imas Erebi . . . ad umbras," had learned that the struggles
between Romans and Greeks were bound to be long and bloody.
The destruction of Corinth would be the revenge for the destruction of Troy. Yet when he reaches Latium, Aeneas finds his
staunchest ally in the Greek king Euander. Old family bonds, the
recollection of a visit of father Anchises to frozen Arcadia, and the
common enemies on the land in which they are both immigrants
undoubtedly helped; but what Virgil wants us to feel is that Euander, "Romanae conditor arcis," is the man who really introduces Aeneas to what is best in Roman ancestral virtues and
beliefs and gives him the support he needs. King Latinus is well-
meaning, but weak and at the mercy of those who surround him.
He knows that Aeneas's ancestor Dardanus went from Italy to
Asia (7. 205, 240): he admits that Aeneas was really returning to

the land of his ancestors. This does not help Aeneas much. Altogether the Greek notion of autochthony is characteristically picked up by Virgil only to be dropped again. The Trojan Penates are never explicitly declared to be of Italian origin, not even in 3. 147–71 (cf. 3. 94, 167). The connection between Rome and the recently founded Nicopolis (3. 503), of which we were reminded by V. Buchheit, is never central to the *Aeneid*.[13] It is due to the Greek Euander, who apparently does not care for Dardanus, that the Trojan Aeneas can settle in Latium and rule the Latins. Next to Euander, Diomedes himself—the old contender with Aeneas—gives him decisive negative help by refusing to help the Latins and warning them that the best they can do is to make peace with Aeneas. He, Diomedes, had seen too much of the consequences of the destruction of Troy for the Greeks to want another duel with Aeneas.

The *Aeneid* is not a poem of general reconciliation. Poor Dido spells out the future tragedy of the Punic Wars, which, ending as they did in the total destruction of the Carthaginian nation, were beyond redemption. Nor is Virgil entirely certain that civil wars, such as those prefigured in the war between Turnus and Rome, will not happen again. The Etruscan Virgil, who is a friend of the Etruscan Maecenas, is ambivalent about his Etruscans: some fight for, some fight against Aeneas. Where Virgil seems unequivocal is about the Greeks. Their common interests with the Trojans go back to the arrival of Aeneas in Latium. Euander sealed the pact. For Homer, the Trojan War started the wanderings of the Greeks. For Virgil, the *Odyssey* precedes the *Iliad*. Aeneas's wanderings are earlier than Aeneas's war, and the war leads to Aeneas's permanent settlement in Latium. Aeneas built cities, he did not destroy them. It is the Greek Euander, with the implicit blessing of Diomedes, who makes this reversal possible.

If I were a student of Virgil, I should worry less about the relations between the figure of Aeneas and the personality of Augustus, and a bit more about the *Aeneid*, as the poem of the reconciliation between Greeks and Romans. This was after all the teaching of Eduard Norden in his memorable essay on the *Aeneid* of 1901 (now in *Kleine Schriften* 1966, 358–421).

When it reached Rome, the story of Aeneas gave the Romans the chance to decide whether they wanted to be Trojans rather than Greeks. By preferring this option, the Romans declared themselves the opponents of the Greeks, but left open the possibility of reconciliation. In any case, through Aeneas, the Romans put themselves into the sphere of the Greeks without considering themselves Greeks.

The story of Aeneas is a story of self-definition which is less tragic than the story of Romulus. It is at the root of the unusual symbiosis of Greeks and Romans. It provided a model for the medieval legends of Trojan desent. In its second stage, during the last centuries of the Republic, it helped, and therefore occasionally hampered, the imperialistic ambitions of the Romans. It this secondary development Aeneas became important to the upper class which controlled the policy of conquest. The *gentes* which claimed Trojan origin were classified by Varro. One of them supplied the first emperors. As the shade of Virgil said to Thornton Wilder, or at least to his hero in *The Cabala*: "The secret is to make a city, not to rest in it."

Select Bibliography

R. H. Klausen, *Aeneas und die Penaten*, Hamburg, 1839–1840.

A. W. Zumpt, *De Lavinio et Laurentibus Lavinatibus commentatio epigraphica*, Berlin, 1845.

A. Schwegler, *Römische Geschichte* I, Tübingen, 1853.

J. A. Hild, "La légende d'Enée avant Virgile," *Rev. Hist. Rel.* 6, 1882, 41–79; 144–77; 293–314.

E. Wörner, "Aineias" in *Roscher's Lexikon* I, 1884, 157–91.

E. Pais, *Ancient Legends of Roman History*, London, 1906.

W. W. Fowler, *Aeneas at the Site of Rome*, Oxford, 1917.

J. Carcopino, *Virgile et les origines d'Ostie*, Paris, 1919.

J. Gagé, "Les Étrusques dans l'Énéide," *Mél. Éc. Fr. Rome* 46, 1929, 115–44.

L. Malten, "Aineias," *Arch. Religionsw.* 29, 1931, 33–59.

C. Koch, *Gestirnverehrung im alten Italien*, Frankfurt, 1933.

E. Wikén, *Die Kunde der Hellenen von dem Lande und den Völkern der Apenninenhalbinsel bis 300 v. Chr.*, Lund, 1937.

H. Boas, *Aeneas' Arrival in Latium*, Amsterdam, 1938.

A. Momigliano, "Thybris Pater" (1938), now in *Terzo Contributo*, Roma, 1966, 609–39.

J. Perret, *Les origines de la légende troyenne de Rome*, Paris, 1942.

E. Goldmann, "Di Novensides and Di Indigetes," *Class. Quart.* 36, 1942, 43–53.

F. Bömer, *Ahnenkult und Ahnenglaube im alten Rom*, Leipzig, 1943.

P. Boyancé, "Les origines de la légende troyenne de Rome," *Rev. Ét. Anc.*

How to Reconcile Greeks and Trojans 285

45, 1943, 275–90 (= *Études sur la religion romaine*, Rome, 1972, 153–70).

J. Bérard, "Nouvelles notes sur la légende de la diaspora troyenne," *Rev. Ét. Grecques* 57, 1944, 71–86.

V. Ussani Jr., "Enea traditore," *St. Ital. Fil. Class.* N.S. 22, 1947, 109–23.

B. Tilly, *Vergil's Latium*, Oxford, 1947.

W. Ehlers, "Die Gründungsprodigien von Lavinium und Alba Longa," *Mus. Helvet.* 6, 1949, 166–75.

P. Grimal, "Enée à Rome et le triomphe d'Octave," *Rev. Ét. Lat.* 53, 1951, 51–61.

F. Bömer, *Rom und Troja*, Baden-Baden, 1951.

E. Bickermann, "Origines gentium," *Class. Phil.* 47, 1952, 65–81.

E. D. Philipps, "Odysseus in Italy," *J.H.S.* 73, 1953, 53–67.

E. Vetter, "Di Novensides, Di Indigetes," *Indogerm. Forsch.*, 62, 1955, 1–32.

A. Alföldi, *Die trojanischen Urahnen der Römer*, Basel, 1957 (cf. S. Weinstock, *J.R.S.* 49, 1959, 170–71).

K. Schauenburg, "Aeneas und Rom," *Gymnasium* 67, 1960, 176–91.

R. Merkelbach, "Aeneas in Cumae," *Mus. Helvet.* 18, 1961, 83–99.

J. Gagé, "Enée, Faunus et le culte de Silvain Pélasge," *Mél. Éc. Fr. Rome* 73, 1961, 69–138.

G. Pugliese Carratelli, "Achei nell'Etruria e nel Lazio?" *Parola del Passato* 17, 1962, 5–25.

P. Boyancé, *La religion de Virgile*, Paris, 1963.

V. Buchheit, *Vergil über die Sendung Roms*, Heidelberg, 1963.

C. J. Classen, "Zur Herkunft der Sage von Romulus und Remus," *Historia* 12, 1963, 447–57.

Id., "Gottmenschentum in der römischen Republik," *Gymnasium* 70, 1963, 312–38.

J. Gagé, "A propos des origines et du cheminement de la légende troyenne de Rome," *Rev. Hist.* 229, 1963, 305–34, and 230, 1963, 1–24.

A. Alföldi, *Early Rome and the Latins*, Ann Arbor, 1963.

L. Lacroix, "Sur les traces d'Enée en Sicile," *Bull. Fac. Lettres Strasbourg* 42, 1964, 265–70.

A. Sadurska, *Les tables iliaques*, Warsaw, 1964.

E. Heitsch, *Aphroditehymnos, Aeneas und Homer*, Göttingen, 1965.

J. Heurgon, "Lars, Largus et Lare Aineia," *Mél. A. Piganiol*, II, Paris, 1966, 655–64.

J. Cl. Richard, "Enée, Romulus, César et les funérailles impériales," *Mél. Éc. Fr. Rome* 78, 1966, 67–78.

A. G. McKay, "Aeneas' Landfalls in Hesperia," *Greece and Rome* 14, 1967, 3–11.

D. van Berchem, "Rome et le monde grec au VIᵉ siècle a.n.e.," *Mél. A. Piganiol*, II, Paris, 1966, 739–48.

S. Mazzarino, *Il pensiero storico classico*. I-III, Bari 1966–1967.

G. Pugliese Carratelli, "Lazio, Roma e Magna Grecia prima del secolo IV a.C.," *Parola del Passato* 23, 1968, 321–47.

H. Strasburger, "Zur Sage von der Gründung Roms," *Sitzungsb. Heidelberg. Akad.*, 1968.

K. Schefold, "Die römische Wölfin und der Ursprung der Romsagen," *Festschrift für R. Laur-Belart,* Basel, 1968, 428–39.

G. K. Galinsky, *Aeneas, Sicily and Rome,* Princeton, 1969.

J. Heurgon, "Inscriptions étrusques de Tunisie," *CR Ac. Inscr.* 1969, 526–51 (cf. *Rev. Ét. Lat.* 47, 1969, 284–94).

H. G. Kolbe, "Lare Aineia?" *Mitt. Deutsch. Arch. Inst. Rom* 77, 1970, 1–9.

W. A. Schröder, *Cato, Origines I,* Meisenheim am Glan, 1971.

M. Guarducci, "Enea e Vesta," *Mitt. Deutsch. Arch. Inst. Rom* 78, 1971, 73–118.

A. Alföldi, "Die Penaten, Aeneas und Latinus," *Mitt. Deutsch. Arch. Inst. Rom* 78, 1971, 1–57.

J. Perret, "Rome et les Troyens," *Rev. Ét. Lat.* 49, 1971, 39–52.

G. Binder, *Aeneas und Augustus,* Meisenheim am Glan, 1971.

V. I. Georgiev, "Troer und Etrusker. Der historische Kern der Aeneas-Sage," *Philologus* 116, 1972, 93–97.

F. Della Corte, *La mappa dell'Eneide,* Firenze, 1972.

F. Castagnoli, *Lavinium,* I, Roma, 1972.

P. Sommella, "Heroon di Enea a Lavinium," *Rend. Pont. Acc. Archeol.* 44, 1971–1972, 47–74.

E. Weber, "Die trojanische Abstammung der Römer als politisches Argument," *Wiener Studien* 6, 1972, 213–25.

W. Wimmel, *Hirtenkrieg und arkadisches Rom,* München, 1973.

W. Fuchs, "Die Bildgeschichte der Flucht des Aeneas," *Aufstieg und Niedergang d. Römischen Welt* I, 4, Berlin 1973, 615–32.

N. Horsfall, "Corythus: the Return of Aeneas in Virgil and his Sources," *Journ. Rom. St.* 63, 1973, 68–79.

K. W. Weber, "Troiae Lusus," *Ancient Society* 5, 1974, 171–96.

P. Sommella, "Das Heroon des Aeneas und die Topographie des antiken Lavinium," *Gymnasium* 81, 1974, 273–97.

A. Alföldi, *Die Struktur des voretruskischen Römerstaates,* Heidelberg, 1974.

I. Cazzaniga, "Il frammento 61 degli Annali di Ennio: Quirinus Indiges," *Parola del Passato* 29, 1974, 362–81.

G. K. Galinsky, "Troiae qui primus ab oris . . . ," *Gymnasium* 81, 1974, 182–200.

Id., "The Tomb of Aeneas at Lavinium," *Vergilius* 20, 1974, 2–11.

T. N. Gantz, "Lapis Niger: the Tomb of Romulus," *Parola del Passato* 29, 1974, 350–61.

E. Peruzzi, "I Micenei sul Palatino," *Parola del Passato* 29, 1974, 309–49.

R. E. A. Palmer, *Roman Religion and Roman Empire,* Philadelphia, 1974.

T. J. Cornell, "Aeneas and the Twins: the Development of the Roman Foundation Legend," *Proceed. Cambridge Philol. Soc.* 201, 1975, 1–32.

E. Gabba, "Mirsilo di Metimma, Dionigi e i Tirreni," *Rend. Accad. Lincei* 8, 30, 1975, 35–49.

P. M. Martin, "Dans le sillage d'Enée," *Athenaeum* 53, 1975, 212–44.

R. Schilling, "Les Lares Grundiles," *Mél. J. Heurgon,* II, Rome 1976, 947–60.

J. Perret, "Athènes et les légendes troyennes d'Occident," *Mél. J. Heurgon,* II, Rome 1976, 791–803.

G. Dumézil, "Virgile, Mézence et les Vinalia," *Mél. J. Heurgon*, I, Rome, 1976, 253–63.

G. D'Anna, *Problemi di letteratura latina arcaica*, Roma, 1976.

D. Briquel, "Les jumeaux à la louve," *Recherches sur les religions de l'Italie antique* (ed. R. Bloch), Genève, 1976, 72–97.

A. Alföldi, *Römische Frühgeschichte*, Heidelberg, 1976.

Civiltà del Lazio Primitivo, Roma, 1976.

E. Gabba, "Sulla valorizzazione politica della leggenda delle origini troiane di Roma fra III e II sec. a.C" in M. Sordi (ed.), *I Canali della propaganda nel mondo antico*, Milano, 1976, 84–101.

J. Gagé, "Comment Enée est devenu l'ancêtre des Silvii Albains," *Mél. Éc. Fr. Rome* 88, 1, 1976, 7–30.

O. Carruba, "Nuova lettura dell'iscrizione etrusca dei cippi di Tunisia," *Athenaeum* 54, 1976, 163–73.

T. J. Cornell, "Aeneas' Arrival in Italy," *Liverpool Classical Monthly* 2, 1977, 77–83.

J. Heurgon, "La thèse de Jérome Carcopino et les fouilles actuelles dans le territoire des Laurentes," *Hommage à la mémoire de J. Carcopino*, Paris, 1977, 169–74.

J. Gagé, "Bases de migration 'dardanienne' et escales 'troyennes' dans la mer Ionienne," *Rev. Ét. Lat.* 55, 1977, 84–112.

R. Scuderi, "Il mito eneico in età augustea," *Aevum* 52, 1978, 88–99.

J. Poucet, "Le Latium protohistorique et archaïque," II, *Ant. Class.* 48, 1979, 177–90.

F. Castagnoli, "Il culto di Minerva e Lavinium," *Quaderni Lincei*, 246, 1979.

R. Schilling, "Le culte de l'indiges à Lavinium," *Rev. Ét. Lat.* 57, 1979, 49–68.

N. Horsfall, "Some Problems in the Aeneas Legend," *Class. Quart.* 29, 1979, 372–90.

Id., "Stesichorus at Bovillae?" *J.H.S.* 99, 1979, 26–48.

G. Elftmann, "Aeneas in His Prime," *Arethusa* 12, 1979, 175–202.

B. Liou-Gille, *Cultes héroiques romains. Les fondateurs*, Paris, 1980.

W. Suerbaum, "Hundert Jahre Vergil-Forschung," *Aufstieg und Niedergang der Römischen Welt* II, 31, 1, Berlin, 1980, 99–110 (bibl. on Vergil).

R. Schilling, "La déification a Rome: tradition latine et interférence grecque," *Rev. Ét. Lat.* 58, 1980, 137–52.

G. Dury-Moyaers, *Enée et Lavinium*, Bruxelles, 1981.

F. Zevi, "Note sulla leggenda di Enea in Italia," in *Gli Etruschi e Roma. Incontro di studio in onore di M. Pallottino*, Roma, 1981, 145–58.

Enea nel Lazio, archeologia e mito, Roma, 1981.

"Virgil: 2000 Years," *Arethusa* 14, 1, 1981.

P. M. Smith, "Aineiadai as Patrons of Iliad XX and the Homeric Hymn to Aphrodite," *Harvard Studies in Class. Philol.* 85, 1981, 17–58 (to which I refer especially for literature on Homer).

F. Castagnoli, "La leggenda di Enea nel Lazio," *Studi Romani* 30, 1982, 1–15.

M. Sordi, "Lavinio, Roma e il Palladio," in M. Sordi (ed.), *Politica e religione nel primo scontro tra Roma e l'Oriente*, Milano, 1982, 64–78.

C. Cogrossi, "Atena Iliaca e il culto degli eroi," ibid., 79–98.

D. Quint, "Painful Memories: *Aeneid* 3 and the Problem of the Past," *Classical Journal* 78, 1982, 30–38.

D. Asheri, "Il millennio di Troia," *Saggi di Letteratura e Storiografia antiche*, Como, 1983, 53–98.

19

Georges Dumézil and the Trifunctional
Approach to Roman Civilization

I

LET US START by paying homage to the immense work which
Georges Dumézil, who was born in 1898, has done over an immense territory, inside and outside the cultures we call Indo-
European. A formidable linguist, Dumézil, as is well known, has
produced enough work on the Caucasian language to ensure for
himself a permanent place in that field. He has virtually saved
the evidence of a dying language, Ubykh, which about ten years
ago was still being spoken in Turkish villages near the Sea of Mar-
mara by a few dozen elderly people, the descendants of refugees
from the Russian occupation of their native country. He has
furthermore contributed to the comparative grammar of the
northwestern group of Caucasian languages and has edited and
translated texts in some of them. It is also known that Dumézil
extended his linguistic and cultural interests to Chinese and to
the Indian languages of America. We also owe to him most of what
we know about the heroic traditions of the Ossetes, the Indo-
European-speakers of the Caucasus, who have a claim to be considered the survivors of the ancient Scythian nation. While his
first book on the Ossetes, *Les légendes sur les Nartes*, goes back
to 1930, the most recent one, at least to my knowledge, is *Ro-*

History and Theory, XXIII, 3, 1984, pp. 312–30.

mans de Scythie et d'alentour which appeared in 1978. There is practically no Indo-European language with which Dumézil has not worked. Sanskrit, Old Persian, Icelandic, and Irish texts have been interpreted by him in an original way which is simply enviable. The stature of the scholar Dumézil is beyond question.

But I think we have to ask ourselves whether his method is legitimate. Dumézil's extraordinary career and success are understandable only if placed where they belong: with the contrasting and not always conherent trends of French sociological and political thought from the end of the First World War to the present day. In more than sixty years Dumézil has had time to support successively the ideology of Indo-European supremacy, the school of Durkheim—or rather of Durkheim's nephew Marcel Mauss—the linguistics of Benveniste, and the structuralism of Lévi-Strauss—and occasionally he has been supported by them. The latest paradox is that Dumézil, while remaining the darling of the extreme right, to which he may originally have belonged, has persuaded left-wing sociologists and anthropologists, such as J.-P. Vernant, and was received among the Immortals of the Académie Française by the very leader of the structuralist revolution, Lévi-Strauss himself.

The beginnings of Dumézil (about which he and his friends tell us little) are in the military and intellectual class which, after having contributed to the victory of 1918 and to the French hegemony in the twenties, found itself challenged by the rebirth of Germany and by communism. Dumézil is a son of the intellectual general Jean-Anatole Dumézil (1857–1929), who ended the First World War as inspector-general of the French artillery. While still a pupil at the elitist *lycée* Louis-le-Grand, young Dumézil was introduced by one of his schoolmates to his grandfather, who happened to be the octogenarian Michel Bréal, the great master of Indo-European linguistics and mythology. Bréal in his turn introduced Dumézil, who already knew some Sanskrit, to the scientific study of languages. No wonder that after the war, in which Dumézil proved himself worthy of his father, he chose to work with Antoine Meillet, the successor of Bréal in the chair of Indo-European linguistics at the Collège de France.

But what attracted Dumézil to the Indo-European world in those years, and later, was not so much language as myth, heroic tradition, and folklore. His two *thèses* of 1924 are both on the borderline between myth and folklore: the *Festin d'immortalité* and the *Crime des Lemniennes*. The *Festin* studies in a very original way various legends to be found in the Indo-European world about a special drink—"ambrosia" to the Greeks—which is either reserved to the immortal gods or confers immortality: as such it is the cause of fights either between gods and men or between rival groups of gods. The *Crime des Lemniennes* is an investigation which starts from a famous chapter of Herodotus (6. 138) on crimes by women which explains rituals both inside and outside the Indo-European sphere. What is evident from these two volumes and from the immediately succeeding one of 1929 on the Centaurs is that young Dumézil's methodology was still uncertain. Linguistic problems in the classic Meillet style were not absent; though, as I have said, they were relatively secondary.

The book on the Centaurs is only mildly concerned with proving the linguistic identity of the name of the Greek Centaurs with the Indian Gandharvas. If anything, the book tends to prove that Centaurs, Gandharvas, and similar beings (to which the Latin Luperci are assimilated) are either monsters or human imitations of monsters of the New Year, for which they provide rituals. J. Cuthbert Lawson, who in 1910 had tried to show that the *Kallikántzaroi* of modern Greek folklore, the demons who control the days between Christmas and Epiphany, were the descendants of the ancient Centaurs, pleased Dumézil and provided him with his best argument. One can well see that behind Dumézil, just as behind Lawson, there is the English school of folklore—perhaps James Frazer rather than Jane Harrison. James Frazer was a more persuasive model to young Dumézil than was his teacher Meillet. Dumézil did not share the more philosophical preoccupations of Frazer about the succession of magic, religion, and science, but was attracted by the wide horizon of Frazer's research and by his constant interest in the interrelation among magic, religion, and power.

No doubt Dumézil had men nearer home who understood problems of magic and religion more profoundly than did Frazer. He had followed their courses and was in a sense their pupil. After all, there was a constant exchange between Meillet and these men who were continuing and developing Durkheim's study of religion. Those two exemplary friends, Marcel Mauss and Henri Hubert, were still collaborating, though Hubert's death was approaching. Marcel Granet, the Chinese scholar, and—more remote because he was teaching at Strasbourg—Maurice Halbwachs were in their most creative years. P. Fauconnet had ushered in the revival of the Durkheim school after the master's death and the loss in the war of some of his best pupils. Fauconnet's book on *La responsabilité* appeared in 1920; it was followed by a classic, G. Davy's *La foi jurée*, in 1922. Even earlier, in 1919, Marcel Granet had started with *Fêtes et chansons anciennes de la Chine*, that series of masterpieces on early China which opened up new vistas on the analysis of literary texts for sociological and anthropological enquiry. We may now suspect that Marcel Granet was, next to Marc Bloch, the most original French historian of the period between the two world wars. He died in 1940, not killed by the Germans like Bloch, but simply terrified by them. Then in 1924 Joseph Vendryes published his book on language, where the cross-fertilization between Meillet's linguistics and Durkheim's sociology is most evident. Let me add that Meillet himself went beyond his usual limits with his lectures on the *Gathas* of the Avesta, which appeared in 1925. The year 1925 was the *annus mirabilis* of the school. Maurice Halbwachs published *Les cadres sociaux de la mémoire*, Marcel Mauss his revolutionary *Essai sur le don*, and Henri Hubert gave those lectures on the Germans which were to be posthumously published only in 1952.

Dumézil was not only aware of all this, but shows in his book on the Centaurs that he was trying to use for his own purpose Marcel Granet's approach to the Chinese festivals. His later work on Celts and Germans confirms Hubert's presence in his mind. Yet it is common knowledge that in his early stages Dumézil had serious difficulties with the group of the *Année Sociologique* and more specifically with Hubert and Granet themselves. He had to spend about fourteen years abroad before obtaining his first position in France at the École des Hautes Études in 1933, which may well be owing to his strained relations with his Paris teachers. Ultimately it was a blessing for him to have to teach history of religions in Istanbul from 1925 to 1931, when he got to know his Ubykhs, and then to be a simple *lecteur* of French at Uppsala from 1931 to 1933, when he established precious connections with Swedish students of German and Indian antiquities, above all Stig Wikander. But on his own admission, there was then a danger that he might find himself isolated in France.

The precise difficulties have never been explained. One can see that Dumézil's early work, and even his enthusiasm for James Frazer, might give offense to the Durkheimian group. As early as 1899 in the joint essay on sacrifice, which was programmatically reprinted in *Mélanges d'histoire des religions* of 1909, Hubert and Mauss had criticized what they described as the analogical method of Frazer and had opposed to it their request that individual ceremonies and beliefs should be analyzed in the context of the whole ritual system of an ethnic group. As young Dumézil had as yet no system and gave no clear indication of looking for one, the criticism affected him, too.

It is impossible, however, to avoid the suspicion that men like Mauss, Hubert, and perhaps Granet were not insensitive to the fact that in political matters of the highest importance Dumézil appeared to have too much *esprit de système*. One of his closest friends was Pierre Gaxotte, to whom he dedicated his first book on *Le festin d'immortalité*. Gaxotte was in those years the secretary of Charles Maurras and the editor-in-chief of *Candide*, the right-wing organ. For Gaxotte's activity in those years it will be enough to refer to Eugen Weber's book on the *Action Française* (1962). Any unbiased reader of the first edition of the book by Dumézil, *Mythes et dieux des Germains*, which appeared in 1939, is bound to find in it sympathy with Nazi ideologies. As such the book was explicitly critized by Albert Grenier in the *Revue des Études Anciennes* 14 (1939), 378–79. This book was rewritten by Dumézil about 1958, and the American version, with the title *Gods of the Ancient Northmen* (1973), is of course based on the modified postwar text. Idealization of the warrior habits of the Indo-Europeans in fact goes back to Dumézil's first book, *Le festin d'immortalité* (p. 264). In the *Mythes et dieux des Germains* the sympathy was more precisely for the "type de société magico-militaire spécifiquement Germanique" (p. 155). Political differences may therefore have contributed to the disagreements between Dumézil and the group of the *Année Sociologique* which was committed to the Third Republic.

But those who come to write Dumézil's biography will not find the matter so simple. Just when political contrasts were becoming sharper in France about 1936, and Dumézil was getting nearer to defining his Indo-European ideology, his relations with the Durkheimians improved. About 1935 there happened the famous encounter between Granet and Dumézil in which Granet told Dumézil: "Allons! Vous n'avez dit jusqu'à maintenant que des bêtises, mais c'étaient des bêtises intelligentes." The result was that Dumézil learned Chinese and followed Granet's courses for three years. Even before making himself a mature pupil in a new subject, he had already indicated his greater awareness of, or his warmer sympathy with, the Durkheimian methodology by his two little books of 1934–1935, *Ouranos-Varuna* and *Flamen-Brahman*, where two aspects of Indo-European society are analyzed very much in agreement with the methods of the *Année Sociologique*. In *Ouranos-Varuna* Dumézil studies the god of sovereignty, and in *Flamen-Brahman* he tackles the relation between priest and sacrifice at that precise point in which the priest acts in support of sovereignty. These two books incidentally contain the nucleus of some of the most original ideas which Dumézil was to develop later.

The years of association with Granet ended about 1938 when Dumézil outlined the first sketch of his general theory on the social structure of the Indo-Europeans. There is some irony in observing that Dumézil made himself the apostle of an Indo-European trifunctional society by wandering in the wilderness of sinology for three years.

II

It was in 1938 that Dumézil reported in an article of the *Revue d'Histoire des Religions* (118 [1938], 188–200) on "La préhistoire des flamines majeurs" that the Aryan fathers had sharply separated the function of the sovereign-priest from that of the soldier, and the function of the soldier from that of the producer (artisan or peasant). He was then extending to the whole Indo-European world an organization by castes which in an earlier article ("La préhistoire indo-iranienne des castes," *Journal Asiatique* 216 [1930], 109–30) he had taken to be characteristic of the stage when Indians and Iranians still formed one community. In the paper of 1938 the Indian structure by castes not only appeared to be the most characteristic feature of primitive Indo-European society, but was declared to be particularly well preserved in the West by the Romans. According to Dumézil, in Rome Jupiter, Mars, and Quirinus were the specific gods of the three castes (priests, warriors, and producers). By a further step, taken in the volume *Jupiter Mars Quirinus* I (1941), the three Romulean tribes of Ramnes, Luceres, and Tities were respectively identified with the three castes of priests (and possibly of kings), of warriors, and of producers. By 1941 it was clear to Dumézil that the Indo-European spirit survives where societies keep alive this original Indo-European discovery: the functional tripartition of priests, warriors, and producers. In its turn this theory implied the researcher's ability to pass from the institutions, the traditions, and more generally the ways of thinking of nations speaking an Indo-European language to the institutions, the traditions, and more generally the ways of thinking of the original Indo-European nation. By these criteria the Greeks appear to have been rather poor Indo-Europeans: not much of the original tripartition survived among them. Next in faithfulness to the Romans were the Germans and the Celts (as the Irish medieval evidence seemed to show).

By 1948 Dumézil had seen a capital difficulty in the straight identification of Ramnes, Tities, and Luceres respectively with priests, agriculturalists, and warriors. This identification implied that Rome had as many priests as it had warriors and peasants. But Rome, after all, was not Israel; and Israel had one tribe of Levites out of twelve. To avoid this difficulty Dumézil suggested what amounted to a compromise. In the fourth volume of his series *Jupiter Mars Quirinus* and in *L'héritage indo-européen à Rome* (1949) he proposed to take only the aristocrats of each tribe as the authentic priests, warriors, and peasants. The mass of the people distributed among the three tribes would have been undifferentiated. Dumézil never explained what he meant by taking the aristocrats of the Tities as the only real producers or agriculturalists. His compromise made less sense than the original trifunctional partition of the tribes. There have been moments in his later works in which Dumézil has indeed seemed to give up entirely the idea that at any stage the Indo-Europeans had actually been divided into the three corporations of priests, warriors, and producers. In such moments Dumézil has declared that the trifunctional partition was to be understood as a mentality or ideology or principle of organization of the mental world of the Indo-Europeans rather than as a formula describing the three sections of an Indo-European society. One of the most radical statements by Dumézil in this sense is also one of his most recent. In an interview published in the *Nouvel Observateur* of 14 January 1983 Dumézil reached the point of saying:

The question of the incarnation of the three functions in the social reality is an insoluble problem. This is a question which I am not asking and which cannot be scientifically asked. . . . On the contrary, thanks to the discovery and the comparison of homologous facts in India, Rome, Scandinavia, etc. we can understand the system of thought which organizes the different accounts. The trifunctional vision of the world is found in the texts in the condition of a fossil, as a compulsory mental scheme.

In fact, however, much of even the most recent research by Dumézil implies the existence of a real tripartition in Indo-European societies. It would seem to me that on the whole a declaration by him of 1958 is still the fairest expression of the presuppositions of his actual research: "Il se peut que la société ait été entièrement, exhaustivement repartie entre prêtres, guerriers et pasteurs. On peut aussi penser que la distinction avait seulement abouti à mettre en vedette quelques clans ou quelques familles spécialisés" (*L'idéologie tripartie des Indo-Européens* [1958], 18).

Dumézil's increasing emphasis on mentality rather than institutions undoubtedly produces epistemological problems which we shall have to consider briefly at the end of this paper. For the moment, two points must be clarified in this connection.

First, one text has played quite an extraordinary role in persuading Dumézil that the Romans were aware of the trifunctional partition of their archaic society. Since the early 1940s he has taken Propertius IV. 1. 9–32 to mean that the Ramnes exercised a ruling and priestly function, the Luceres fulfilled military tasks, and the Tities produced wealth. Propertius in his turn would be supported by the end of Virgil's second *Georgic,* if properly interpreted. But the really decisive text was Propertius. As far as I know, Dumézil has never abandoned his interpretation of it even though he has abandoned the hope of providing adequate demonstration for the existence of three castes in early Rome. Yet anyone can satisfy himself, as the Latin of Propertius is not too difficult, that Propertius tells a different story. Propertius emphasizes the rustic simplicity of the primitive Romans and describes them as peasants and warriors. He then adds that the Etruscans, or rather the Etruscan Lygmon, and Titus Tatius introduced some sophistication into this primitive simplicity, the former by his more professional military style, and the latter by his greater pastoral wealth. There is no suggestion in Propertius that the primitive Romans (or Ramnes) were denied an army or economic activities and were therefore only interested in the cult of the gods. Propertius is no evidence for the existence of castes.

Second, the question whether one could prove the existence of castes in early Rome was not the only one which exercised Dumézil about 1949 or immediately after. In 1949 Dumézil published his book on *Le troisième souverain,* one of his most controversial books, which provoked polemics with specialists on ancient India such as P. Thieme. What interests us in this book is that Dumézil was becoming less certain that sovereignty could be confined to the first two layers of society—even if the first function was divided into the two sectors of magic and law (that is, according to Dumézil's Indian prototypes, into the sectors of Varuna and Mitra). Dumézil was now trying to show that the third function of production and prosperity contributed directly to sovereignty. The evidence he adduced was mainly Indian and Irish, but he duly reminded us of the story that the gods Iuventas and Terminus had refused to leave the Capitol when Tarquinius decided to build the shrine to Jupiter (Livy 1. 55; Ovid, *Fasti* 2. 667ff; Livy 5. 54, and so on). The two gods avoided eviction, according to Dumézil, because they were auxiliary gods of sovereignty, though they came from the sphere of fertility and wealth.

The subject was taken up in a different form in the book *La saga de Hadingus* (1953) which is available in English in a revised edition as *From Myth to Fiction* (1973). In studying the Hadingus saga, as reported by the thirteenth-century Danish chronicler Saxo Grammaticus, Dumézil was concerned both with the general transposition from myth to saga which he had encountered in Rome and with the more specific transition of a hero from the third to the first function. After association with a god of the third function, Hadingus became a protégé of Odinus and passed to the first, royal and priestly, function. So did Romulus in Rome. After all, he had been a shepherd before being promoted to the first function. There was now a new social mobility in Dumézil's functions. Gods and heroes were jumping over the barriers of the once well-ordered society which some of us had suspected of smacking of fascism. Dumézil had always admitted some collusion between priests and warriors in the making of kings, but he now also explored more thoroughly the relations between monarchy and army in another volume, *Aspects de la fonction guerrière* (1956). He recognized closer links between military prowess and sovereignty and incidentally made some penetrating contributions to the study of the guilt psychology of the warrior class. He took up Tullus Hostilius, whom he considered to be the typical Roman representative of the warrior class. Tullus Hostilius is a king who allows three other warriors, the Horatii, to fight his war against Alba. Yet he has to cope with the guilt of the third of the Horatii, who after winning the battle kills his sister. Even more directly he is the schemer of the trick which allows the Romans to seize unarmed the Alban chief Mettius Fufetius and to execute him cruelly. Tullus Hostilius shares the guilt of his class.

No wonder that during such a revision of old notions Dumézil felt the need of defining more precisely what was still valid in his system in comparison with the school of thought of those whom at that time he considered to be his main competitors in the interpretation of Roman religion: those whom he called the "primitivists." In the late 1940s and early 1950s Dumézil was repeatedly engaged in discussions with H. J. Rose and H. Wagenvoort. Rose, whose *Primitive Culture in Italy* appeared in 1926 and was later supplemented by *Ancient Roman Religion* in 1948, thought that the Melanesian notion of *mana*—an impersonal supernatural force—had its exact equivalent in the Latin word *numen* and could explain many of the features of Roman religion. The Utrecht professor Wagenvoort was, if not the first, the most systematic to develop this point of view in a book which was originally published in Dutch under the Latin title of *Imperium* in 1941 and which reappeared in an English translation supervised by Rose in

1947 under the title *Roman Dynamism*.[1] Though at least Rose never denied that the Romans had preserved some Indo-European gods—Jupiter being one—he and Wagenvoort were inclined to see most Roman personal gods of the late Republic as developments of primitve impersonal *numina* or *mana*. In a sense they were rejoining the old Varro, who maintained that the early Romans had not known gods in human form (Augustine, *De civitate Dei* 4. 31).

In his search for the Indo-Europeans in Rome, Dumézil could hardly sympathize with such primitivism. The best exposition of his point of view is in chapter IV, "Quelques caractères des dieux romains" of the book *Les Dieux des Indo-Européens* (1952). Dumézil insisted on the personal character of the Roman gods and tried to explain why, before the identification with the Greek gods, the Roman gods seem to have been endowed with so few personal stories and even less with a family life (no old Roman god appears as the son or the brother of another god). His answer was complex: partly he believed that the Romans turned myths about gods into stories about Roman kings and heroes, partly he suspected that the Romans forgot their mythology rather late in the last centuries of the Republic. This raises problems in its turn. The first is why Dumézil, while worrying so much about the primitivism of Rose and Wagenvoort, never gave adequate attention to a far more elaborate and profound "primitivist" approach to Roman religion: that formulated by H. Usener in *Götternamen* of 1896, where he identified and classified two categories of momentary or impersonal gods of Roman religion (among other religions) under the names of "Augenblicksgötter" and "Sondergötter." The consequences we shall soon see in the great synthesis of 1966, *La Religion romaine archaïque*. But one must immediately add that Dumézil was instinctively right in being suspicious of the identification of *numen* with *mana* which played such a part in Rose's ideas. It was left to Stefan Weinstock (no sympathizer of Dumézil's either) to deprive the identification of *numen* with *mana* of its main chronological support. In half a page of the *Journal of Roman Studies* 39 (1949), 167 he simply observed that the word "numen," originally meaning "motion," became a religious term in Rome only in the first century B.C.,

probably under the influence of the new theology and as a corresponding term to "daimon." "Numen" was thus proved to be a
late, not a "primitive," notion.[2]

III

Dumézil arrived at his synthesis *La Religion romaine archaïque* (2 ed. 1973, which is substantially identical with the English
translation, *Archaic Roman Religion* [Chicago, 1970]) with two
basic uncertainties: the extent to which he would go in treating
archaic Roman society as founded upon the three-castes system,
and the meaning he would attribute to those elements of Roman
religion which looked archaic, but not obviously Indo-European.
It is not my impression that Dumézil succeeded in clarifying
these two points in either of the two editions of his book.

Dumézil had to face the replacement of the trinity Jupiter-
Mars-Quirinus (to which he continued to attribute a trifunctional
character) by the so-called Capitoline triad of Jupiter, Juno, and
Minerva. He recognized that this event—which coincided with
the building of the temple of Jupiter Capitolinus of about 500
B.C.—interrupted at a vital point the continuity of the Indo-
European ideology in Rome because the new trinity cannot easily
be interpreted in trifunctional terms: neither Juno nor Minerva is
a likely candidate for the military function. Dumézil had no satisfactory explanation for this change. The same difficulty is observ-
able in Dumézil's interpretation of the position of the pontiffs.
They are less amenable to Indo-European interpretations than the
flamines. Unlike the *flamines*, the *pontifices* were not associated
with individual gods and therefore could not be easily interpreted
as functional priests of functional gods. Dumézil has a long polemical chapter against K. Latte, who had tried to explain the rise
of the pontiffs against the *flamines* as "a pontifical revolution."
But the fact remains that Dumézil does not provide an alternative
model for explaining how a group of ordinary aristocrats came to
control so much of Roman religion under the name of *pontifices*.

On the other hand, Dumézil found himself faced by a variety of
Roman gods and rituals which dangerously resembled Usener's
"Augenblicksgötter" and "Sondergötter," but for which he had no

place in his trifunctional world. He registered them under the names of "forces et éléments" without explaining the relations between them and the trifunctional Indo-European mentality. The whole apparatus of communication with the world of the dead, to which the *mundus* belongs, is left unexplained. If anything, the *mundus*, a zone of contact between the living and the dead, indicates that the Romans had other preoccupations than that of keeping society tripartite.

IV

All the work done by Dumézil on Roman religion after his *Archaic Roman Religion* seems to me to confirm that he has not been able to overcome these two basic difficulties in his system: the vagueness of what is the Indo-European heritage in Rome and the lack of relation between the Indo-European element and the mass of beliefs, ceremonies, and institutions which have nothing to do with castes and three functions. It would also seem to me that in his work after 1966 Dumézil has been more interested in reconfirming the existence of a trifunctional mentality in Rome (and even of the tripartition of the Roman people into priests, warriors, and producers) than in pursuing the attempt to give a balanced view of Roman society—or at least of Roman religion. In a series of books, of which the three volumes on *Mythe et épopée* (1968–1973) are perhaps the most important, and *Les dieux souverains des Indo-Européens* (1977) the most systematic, Dumézil has reiterated and developed his old thesis about trifunctional mentality and castes. A considerable part of these books represents a reelaboration of old papers and of sections of old books, but much is new. In both the old and the new sections, Dumézil reasserts and develops what we have already recognized as his two strongest approaches to trifunctionality: trifunctionality in cults and trifunctionality in the pseudohistory of Rome (and of other nations), which is presented by Dumézil as being modeled on ancient trifunctional myths. An important new feature of this analysis of pseudohistory is that it has now been expanded to include the personal creations of Virgil. Virgil's *Aeneid*, especially in *Mythe et épopée*, I, is treated as a product of the trifunctional mentality of the Romans and therefore as evidence of its effective presence in the time of Augustus.

But an even more important novelty of the latest researches by Dumézil, in which he was encouraged by his pupil Lucien Gerschel, is the extension of trifunctional interpretation to juridical institutions, such as marriage and testament. In *Mariages indo-européens* of 1979 Dumézil argues that the three forms of marriage *cum manu* and the three more ancient forms of testament correspond to the three functions. This is a surprise. While previously Dumézil gave us to think, in various declarations, that he had abandoned the hope of finding institutions controlled by the rule of tripartition, he now argues that there are institutions like marriage and testament to which tripartition applies. Dumézil seems to recapture by way of private Roman law what he had given up when he admitted the impossibility of proving that the Ramnes, Tities, and Luceres were three different social groups. Indeed, it would seem obvious that an interpretation of the three forms of marriage and testament in trifunctional terms makes sense only if we attribute each form of marriage and each form of testament to a different social group. I cannot of course discuss in detail all these aspects of Dumézil's latest production. But I must at least give some idea of what I think of his theories about trifunctional cults, trifunctional pseudohistory (including Virgil's poetry), and finally law.

While it was difficult to make out a serious case for the Romulean tribes as castes, it was less difficult to argue that Jupiter, Mars, and Quirinus were the gods of the three dominant social groups. Jupiter after all had always been the king of the gods, and Mars was the god of war. Two of the three functions were there for the asking. Dumézil had only to prove that Quirinus was the god of production; and arguments were not lacking. For instance, the priest of Quirinus, the *flamen Quirinalis*, used to have a conspicuous role in the agrarian cults of Consualia and Robigalia. Furthermore, the festival of Quirinus, the Quirinalia, was considered to be a legitimate substitute for the festival of Fornacalia, a rather rustic occasion to which only those who still knew to which curia they belonged were admitted. What Dumézil forgot, however, is that it is easier to prove that Quirinus was a god of fertility than to disprove that Jupiter is also a god of war and Mars is also a god of fertility. The connection of Jupiter with war and victory needs no demonstration. The same must be said about Mars as a god of the fields: one need not go beyond the famous prayer to Mars in Cato's *De re rustica* 141. A good case can also be made for Quirinus as the god of the *Quirites*, of the Roman citizens in general: as such he was identified with Romulus at an uncertain date. In other words, Jupiter, Mars, and Quirinus never show the exclusive functional specialization Dumézil requires. On reflection, that specialization could hardly have existed in a city where the peasants were soldiers, and the soldiers filled the priesthoods.

The successive history of the triads in Rome confirms their lack of specialization, in the Dumézilian sense. We have already seen that even Dumézil does not claim that the Capitoline triad was trifunctional. We have good reason to suspect that the Capitoline triad was not only introduced by an Etruscan king, but reflected some Etruscan doctrine. We are told by Servius in his commentary on Virgil (*ad Aen.* I. 422) that the specialists in Etruscan doctrine did not consider a city properly founded unless Jupiter, Juno, and Minerva each had a temple, a gate, and a street in it. This is not the same as having a tripartite temple, as the Capitoline temple was. But it shows that the triad Jupiter, Juno, and Minerva was considered Etruscan. A few years after the foundation of the triple temple of Jupiter Capitolinus, the plebeians of Rome found it necessary to have their own trinitarian sanctuary, and built one to the triad Ceres, Liber, and Libera in 493 B.C. It is interesting to note that the plebeians accepted the principle of having a trinity with two goddesses and one god, but gave pride of place to the goddess Ceres, who best suited their preoccupations. Again, the three Indo-European functions are not involved. Outside the triads trifunctionality is of course even less likely to appear. Trifunctionality is altogether alien to the Roman pantheon.

Dumézil makes out a more convincing case for the mythical stories turned into legendary history. But we must remember that it is one thing to argue that archaic Roman history incorporates older myths and quite another thing to prove that either the older myths or the later legends or both have a trifunctional meaning.

Dumézil is certainly right in suggesting that Romulus and Numa supplement each other as sovereigns, more or less as Varuna and Mitra supplemented each other as gods. But that does not make Romulus and Numa into decayed gods. There are serious reasons for concluding that Romulus and Numa are fictitious, but these reasons appear unconnected with the alleged trifunctional structure of their stories. As for myself, I would even like to draw a distinction between Romulus, whose name reminds me too much of Rome, and Numa Pompilius, who seems to carry a plausible human name and may have been a real person to whom legends were attached.

Things become even more difficult when Romulus is opposed as the magician-king to Tullus Hostilius as the warrior-king, or when Ancus Marcius is assigned the role of representing the third function of productivity and fertility. Tullus Hostilius is traditionally connected with the destruction of Alba Longa and with a building later known as Curia Hostilia. Ancus Marcius is said to have built the Sublician bridge, to have occupied Politorium and other territories, and to have planted a colony at Ostia. All these traditions have their problems. Alba Longa is not exactly well known archaeologically; Ostia does not seem to have been occupied before the fourth century B.C.; and we are entitled to have our own doubts about the date of the Sublician bridge or of the Curia Hostilia. But these doubts neither affect the existence of the kings Tullus Hostilius and Ancus Marcius as such, nor can they be justified by reference to the three functions. Is there anything surprising in a king being chiefly a warrior, like Tullus Hostilius? And why should a conquerer and a colonizer like Ancus Marcius be deemed to represent the third function?

It is of course more probable that some myth or at least some old legend should be behind the duel between the Horatii and Curiatii, though I doubt that the Indian story of the victory of Trita over a monster with three heads is the prototype we are seeking. What is really questionable is the interpretation of such stories as trifunctional myths. There is nothing trifunctional in the three Horatii or in their Curiatii opponents.

One of the most ingenious suggestions ever made by Dumézil concerns Horatius Cocles and Mucius Scaevola, the two heroes who together with the young woman Cloelia persuade the Etruscan Porsenna to leave the Romans alone after they have thrown out Tarquinius. Horatius is nicknamed Cocles—which must be the Greek name Kyklops, perhaps through an Etruscan intermediary. Cocles was thus supposed to be one-eyed. As for Mucius Scaevola, he becomes Scaevola, left-handed, by burning his right hand. One-eyed or left-handed heroes are not scarce in folklore, but Dumézil produces a splendid parallel from German mythology. The god Odin gives one of his eyes to buy magic science, and the god Tyr sacrifices one of his hands to save the other gods from the mythical Wolf. Can we say that this parallel shows Horatius Cocles and Mucius Scaevola to be decayed gods—perhaps respectively of the first and of the third function to be compared with Odinus and Tyr? There are many obstacles to this solution, and I shall indicate only one. In the German myth, the gods each lose one organ of their body in the act of performing in the story. The same applies to Scaevola who becomes left-handed by burning his right hand during the story. But we simply do not know why and how Horatius came to be called Cocles, one-eyed. Livy can tell his story without any reference to this peculiarity of Cocles. There may of course have been other stories about Horatius Cocles to explain why he was Cocles: if so, they are lost. At present we do not know, I repeat, why Cocles should be Cocles. In explaining myths or legends, what counts is the validity of the terms of comparison: there is no real comparison between Odin and Cocles. We are better placed with Mucius Scaevola, who burned his right hand and as such can be compared with the god Tyr. But what Mucius and Tyr have in common is that they are prepared to sacrifice their hand to save their comrades. They have in common a spirit of sacrifice. I therefore also doubt that Dumézil has produced the right kind of comparison for the rape of the Sabines. He thought that the whole story of the war between Latins and Sabines repeated the mythical pattern of the Scandinavian myth about the war between the *Aesir*, the god-magicians, and the *Vanir*, the wealth-gods. But the Scandinavian myth lacks what is so prominent in the Roman story: the acquisition of wives by rape.[3]

The danger of this mythological approach to the origins of Rome was revealed in a particularly acute form when in 1943 Dumézil devoted a whole book to the tradition of Servius Tullius, the sixth king of Rome. The figure of Servius is certainly not without legendary elements, as the stories about his birth and his

death show. But the attempt to make him a mythical king whose
prototypes would be the Celtic god Lug or the Indian Pṛthu seems
rather far-fetched. A comparison with Solon and other Greek legislators is more to the point. I have the impression that Dumézil
himself would not now defend his case.

In his latest stage, Dumézil attributes more importance to
the legends of Camillus and Coriolanus, in both of which he
recognizes the preservation of the trifunctional Indo-European
mentality. Camillus and Coriolanus would be antithetic heroes:
Camillus saves Rome, Coriolanus betrays Rome. In the episode of
the siege of Rome by the Gauls, in which Camillus is ultimately
involved as the savior, three episodes discourage the Gauls and
give courage to the Romans. The geese repel the Gauls; the Romans throw bread from the besieged Capitol to show that they
have plenty to eat; and a member of the Fabian *gens* goes down
from the Capitol to fulfill religious duties and is not molested,
which may be a miracle. In the attempt to persuade Coriolanus
not to attack Rome, there is a sequence of three embassies: the
first by Roman notables; the second by priests; the third by ladies,
including Coriolanus's mother: needless to say, the success is
with the Roman ladies, "matronae." Dumézil has no particular
difficulty in showing that in the Camillus story the geese may
represent the military function, the bread is evidently third function, and the godly Fabius who performs a sacrifice is first function par excellence. Things are not so simple for Dumézil in the
story of Coriolanus because Dumézil is not prepared to admit that
the first embassy of the notables represents the Roman army, that
is, the second function, while of course the priests and women of
the other delegations easily fit the roles of the first and of the
third function. Dumézil prefers to believe that both the first and
the second embassy represent the first function in its bipartition
of magic and law. Why then is the second function missing?
Dumézil has a wonderful solution to his own difficulty. If the second function does not appear in the embassies, it is because the
second function was embodied in Coriolanus, and Coriolanus is
now, so to speak, on the other side. Those who composed the legend of Coriolanus knew so much about the three functions that
they could intentionally eliminate the second function from the
embassies.

For once I would like to improve on Dumézil rather than criticize him. It seems to me that Coriolanus's story must be compared with Porsenna's story rather than with Camillus's story. Both Porsenna and Coriolanus want to conquer Rome and are persuaded to retreat: Porsenna, it will be remembered, by the succession of the feats of Horatius Cocles, Mucius Scaevola, and Cloelia, while Coriolanus is pressed by three embassies. Can it be chance that in both cases the decisive result is achieved by women? It is really Cloelia, as we can read in Livy, who persuades Porsenna to give up the siege of Rome, and it is Veturia, Coriolanus's mother, who induces her son to renounce the fight against Rome. Both stories show that what men cannot do women achieve.

Whether these stories are trifunctional, as Dumézil would like to make them, is another matter. I confess that I do not see much trifunctionalism in the tripartition of these stories. What attracts the narrator is first the crescendo of the first two acts, then the anticlimax of the victory of a woman in the third act. In any case, even if we admit an allusion to priesthood, army, and reproduction, I do not see what we gain. Life was made up of them, and any story was likely to allude to them. The real test for the presence of a trifunctional system would be a sharp separation of the three elements. But even in the privileged case of the siege of the Capitol at the time of Camillus, all we have is a miracle by geese which can hardly be a real military feat, a discharge of pieces of bread which may look like a mock battle, and finally a real piece of authentic Roman *pietas* performed by a young military leader of the very military clan of the Fabii. Any Roman knew that a good day's work included religious rituals, self-defense, and domestic care.

What we must not do is to generalize occasional allusions to these three aspects of life and assume a system or *Weltanschauung* behind them. The interpretation of the second part of the *Aeneid* by Dumézil is a case in point (as I said, it is to be found in the first volume of *Mythe et Épopée*). Dumézil thinks that when Aeneas appears on the shores of Latium, he represents the first function: he is the king-priest. When he associates himself with Latinus, he incorporates the third function, the producers. And when he allies himself with the Etruscan Tarchon, he annexes the second, military, function. In a sense Dumézil returns here, once again, to the trifunctional interpretation of the Roman tribes that he had previously, but never wholeheartedly, repudiated. The military function of the Etruscans led by Tarchon is identical with the military function of the tribe of the Luceres who were supposed to be Etruscans. There is, however, an interesting change. The Latins who, as the original Ramnes or Ramnenses, used to be the sovereigns and the priests now become the agriculturalists or producers in the place of the Sabines. The role of priests is left to the Trojans. All this is suggested to Dumézil by a few lines of the agreement between Aeneas and Latinus in Book XII of the *Aeneid*. Before the duel with Turnus, Aeneas promises that if he wins, Latinus shall remain the real king with the necessary military power; he, Aeneas, will contribute sacred ceremonies and gods, "sacra deosque dabo; socer arma Latinus habeto" (l. 193). It is not an easy line to interpret. It seems to mean that as long as Latinus is alive, Aeneas will play the role of what in later Rome was known as the *rex sacrificulus*, a king without military power who had a respected, but limited, religious sphere under his control. Whatever the precise meaning may be, there is no trifunctional distribution of tasks here. Latinus—*ex hypothesi* an agriculturalist—is specifically left in control of the weapons, while Tarchon is left out of the bargain.

Virgil is obviously not concerned with the three functions. He wants to steer the story toward its proper end, which is the union of Trojans, Latins, and Etruscans, but in such a way that the Latin name shall prevail. The Trojans must become Latins, not the Latins Trojans. This is after all what Juno requests and obtains from Jupiter as a condition for her own peace with the Trojans. Though the Etruscans are admitted to the league, they have a subordinate position, and there is no question of assimilating them to the Trojans or to the Latins. Hence the unification of power in the hands of Latinus, but with the proviso that Aeneas shall retain some sort of royal dignity near Latinus, until such time as his own family becomes the ruling family of the future Rome. The Etruscans can be satisfied with the position of close and respected allies. In Augustus's Italy this was the position conscious Etruscans like Maecenas, and Virgil himself, could legitimately ask for. In other words, we have in the second part of the *Aeneid* a sort of tripartite story, but it is not a story of priests, warriors, and peasants: it is a story of Trojans, Latins, and Etruscans, in which nobody ever doubted that Aeneas was a warrior. It is significant that Aeneas leaves the control of the weapons to Latinus at that moment in which he has a personal duel with Turnus.

I shall conclude by turning to the recent views of Dumézil on Roman Law, contained in his book on *Mariages indo-européens.* In this work Dumézil partly depends on the late Lucien Gerschel, but has also received help at various stages from specialists of Roman Law of the eminence of the late Pierre Noailles and of André Magdelain. Dumézil argues that the three Roman forms of marriage (by *confarreatio*, by *usus*, and by *coemptio*), the three forms of testament (before the *comitia curiata, in procinctu,* and *per aes et libram*) and finally the three forms of manumission of slaves (*vindicta, censu,* and *testamento*) reflect the trifunctional structure of Roman society with its Indo-European roots. Taken literally, this statement would mean that Roman society was divided into priests, warriors, and peasants and that each group had its own peculiar form of marriage, of testament, and of manumission of slaves. Thus the priests would marry by *confarreatio*, by sharing a sort of cake. They would make their testament at stated dates (perhaps twice a year) before the whole assembly of the *comitia curiata,* and would liberate their slaves by the complex and symbolic ceremony of the *vindicta.* The soldiers in their turn would marry informally by simple cohabitation (*usus*), would make their own testament in the presence of their own comrades just before a battle (*in procinctu*), and would free their slaves by inserting their names into the lists of Roman citizens during a *census.* The workers would buy their wives (*coemptio*), would make their testament in the form of a fictitious sale of their own property (*per aes et libram*), and would free their slaves by testament only. Of course, none of this is true, or almost none. It is possible that the marriage by *confarreatio* was originally confined to patricians; it was certainly not confined to priests. All the rest was anarchically left to individual choice. It was for the individual citizen to choose what form of testament he preferred. It is also obvious that the testament on the battlefield was an emergency measure for those who had not made a testament either before the *comitia curiata* or in the complex form of a fictitious sale. In later periods there were in fact even more than three forms of testament. Societies are apt to provide alternative forms of doing the same thing.

Now the rather comic aspect of the situation is that the tripartition of marriages, testaments, and manumission not only does not work in any trifunctional way, but Dumézil himself is no longer certain about the existence of the three social groups or castes in Rome. Accordingly he interprets this tripartition of juridical institutions as a survival from a previous social order into a society which did not need the tripartition. But these forms of marriage, testament, and manumission are so typically Roman that Dumézil cannot really find any equivalent to them elsewhere. Thus he is compelled to postulate a non-Roman explanation for institutions which are wholly Roman and which (with the possible exception of the marriage by *confarreatio*) were open to all the citizens at their choice. Dumézil basically recognizes that he cannot argue the case for the manumissions, and does not make a conspicuous effort to argue the case for the testaments. But he seems to be encouraged by Indian parallels to postulate an Indo-European origin for the three Roman marriages. On Dumézil's showing, Indian theorists knew eight forms of marriage, including simple cohabitation and rape, which they considered rather suitable for warriors. We shall not be surprised. But rape had been eliminated from Roman customs, as the story of the Sabine women paradigmatically shows: they were duly married to Romans whether by *confarreatio* or otherwise (cf. Dionysius Hal. 2. 30). That leaves cohabitation (*usus*) as the only form of marriage which Indians and Romans have in common. Furthermore, in Rome there is not the slightest indication that *usus* was considered particularly suitable for soldiers: in fact, as we have repeatedly emphasized, nobody, or everybody, was a professional soldier in Rome. *Usus* was not a soldier's marriage. There is no case for a trifunctional interpretation of the tripartition which occurs in marriage just as in other sectors of Roman Law.

Let us admit that tripartition is a peculiarity of much Roman life. But it is not an exclusive and even less a profound feature of Rome. Bipartition was much more decisive: we need only think of patricians and plebeians, or of the two consuls. In any case, tripartition is not equivalent to trifunctionalism. There is little evidence in Rome that priests, warriors, and peasants were three different social classes and even less that they were three different mental categories.

V

The question whether Dumézil is or is not a structuralist has been variously answered—even by Dumézil himself. It is a question of secondary importance for those who realize that no French structuralist is foolish enough to avoid questions of change. It is therefore an element of strength in Dumézil's method that he can deal with structures while emphasizing change.

The real difficulty is another. It is the difficulty Dumézil was bound to encounter in his effort to pass from the individual cultures of each Indo-European group to the culture of the original Indo-European nation. The magnitude of the difficulty can be visualized if we try to reconstruct the Latin culture of, say, 200 B.C. from the data of the various European cultures of the twentieth century A.D. on the assumption that no Latin book, no Latin institution, no reliable archaeological monument has survived. The reconstruction of the Indo-European institutions is infinitely more difficult and doubtful than the reconstruction of the Indo-European language. Even if we assume for linguistic reasons that the original Indo-Europeans had kings, we do not yet know what sort of kings they were. There is an in-built element of prudence in the title of the great work by Émile Benveniste, *Le Vocabulaire des institutions indo-européennes* (1969). To know the vocabulary of the institutions is not equivalent to knowing the institutions. But Dumézil who, interestingly enough, has become rather skeptical about reconstructing the institutions of the Indo-Europeans, asks us to try to do something even more difficult: to discover the basic principles of the Indo-European mentality. He applies to this task the apparently simple rule, with which the linguists have made us familiar, that India and Iran on the one side and Latium, Scandinavia, and Ireland on the other side preserve more of the archaic language of the original Indo-Europeans than the rest of the Indo-European world, especially in religious formulas. Can we equally argue that in these lateral areas more of the authentic Indo-European mentality is preserved? Indeed, if we could really find in such areas a coherent system of thinking based on the trifunctional separation of priests, soldiers, and producers, the inference would be easy. What is common in ideas and emotions to Indo-Iranians on the one hand and to Germans, Celts, and Latins on the other could be deemed to represent an original Indo-European mentality. Unfortunately, there is nothing of the kind anywhere. There is no region of the Indo-European-speaking world where a common mentality—trifunctional or otherwise—is visible. What we have at best is a certain number of texts which may suggest that the Latins or the Scandinavians or the Celts occasionally divided society or the gods into three groups somehow related to priesthood, war, and production. But each Indo-European group preserves innumerable other documents which display complete ignorance of, or indifference to, trifunctional partition. What Dumézil has never tried to do is a statistical survey of all the Roman or Irish or Scandinavian texts which do not concern themselves with trifunctional partition. To confine myself to the area I know best, the texts of the Roman republican period which allude to tripartition are very few in comparison with those which do not. One has only to think of the bipartition of patricians and plebeians, patrons and clients, *ius* and *fas*, senate and people, Romans and Sabines, and so on, to see that bipartition might easily replace tripartition as a scheme of the Roman mentality—if we were ever tempted to look for such a scheme. The existence of priests, warriors, and producers is patent in any society, and it would be surprising to find the Romans un-aware of them. It would, however, be even more surprising to find the Romans obsessed by such division, because in Roman society producers, warriors, and priests were not separate groups.

If there are other Indo-European societies in which the empha-sis on the so-called trifunctional structure is greater than in Rome, then the first question to ask is whether the reason is not to be found inside that society rather than in the Indo-European original society.[4] Feudal society fulfills Dumézil's requirements more obviously than the Roman society. But it fulfills them be-cause of the combination of Christianity with feudalism. I am not

surprised that Professor G. Duby has found the High Middle Ages
a haven of trifunctionalism. Nor am I surprised that Dumézil
should sympathize with what was after all the organization of pre-
revolutionary France, a tripartite state if there ever was one. The
Middle Ages are trifunctional because they are Christian. The Romans were not trifunctional in any serious sense. Who can tell us
that the Indo-Europeans of old had more tripartition in the functional sense than the Romans? By assuming that what is at best a
partial organization in known societies must be explained by a
total organization of the same kind in an unknown, more ancient,
society we are perhaps going beyond the limits of legitimate conjecture. The question we must ask ourselves is: are scattered
traces of trifunctionalism in various Indo-European cultures a sufficient argument for postulating an original all-pervasive Indo-
European trifunctional mentality?

Select Bibliography

The book by C. S. Littleton, *The New Comparative Mythology* (Berkeley, 1966), which must now be read in its third edition (1983—2nd ed.
1973) provides an excellent introduction to Dumézil and a reliable bibliography which I presuppose throughout. Among the French introductions, *Georges Dumézil et les études indo-européenes*, ed. Alain de
Benoist, a special issue of "Nouvelle École" 21–22, 1972; *Georges
Dumézil à la découverte des Indo-Européens*, ed. J. C. Rivière (Paris,
1979); *Georges Dumézil*, by various authors (Paris, 1981). Rivière has a
useful bibliography. Cf. also G. J. Larson and others, *Myth in Indo-
European Antiquity* (Berkeley, 1974) and D. Briquel, "Initiations grecques
et idéologie indo-européenne," *Annales* 37 (1982), 454–64. A series of
papers on Dumézil read at my seminar in the Scuola Normale Superiore
of Pisa in February 1983 has been published by the periodical *Opus* 2,
1983. Among the critiques of Dumézil cf. J. Brough in *Bulletin of the
School of Oriental and African Studies London* 23 (1959), 69–85; P.
Smith and D. Sperber in *Annales* 26 (1971), 559–86; and also by Brough
the review-article in *Times Literary Supplement*, 3 January 1975.

Of more than historical interest are H. J. Rose in *Journal of Roman
Studies* 37 (1947), 183–86; J. Gonda, *Mnemosyne* 4, 13 (1960), 1–15 and
"Triads in the Veda," *Verh. Kon. Nederlandse Akademie*, N.R. 91, 1976.
See also A. Brelich, *Studi Mater. Storia Religioni* 28 (1957), 113–23; 29
(1958), 109–12; F. Jesi, introduction to Dumézil, *Ventura e Sventura del
guerriero* (Turin, 1974).

The best study on M. Granet, Dumézil's teacher, is perhaps M. Freedman's introduction to Granet's *The Religion of the Chinese People* (Oxford, 1975), 1–29. On the academic situation in France, see T. N. Clark,

Prophets and Patrons: The French University and the Emergence of the Social Sciences (Cambridge, Mass., 1973). For some developments of Dumézil's theories see for instance: *Hommages à Georges Dumézil* (Brussels, 1960); *Myth and Law among the Indo-Europeans*, ed. J. Puhvel (Berkeley, 1970); G. Duby, *Les trois ordres ou l'imaginaire du féodalisme* (Paris, 1978); O. Niccoli, *I sacerdoti, i guerrieri e i contadini: Storia di una immagine della società* (Torino, 1979); J. H. Grisward, *Archéologie de l'épopée médiévale* (Paris, 1981).

NOTES

4. The Theological Efforts of the Roman Upper Classes in the First Century B.C.

1. It is the sole purpose of this paper (one of my lectures in the University of Chicago in the spring of 1983) to contribute some points of view to a general reinterpretation of the religious situation of the first century B.C. The paper was written before I could read the very valuable article by J. Linderski, "Cicero and Roman Divination," *PP* 36 (1982), 12–38, with which I am glad to find myself often in agreement. It would make no sense to give here any bibliography on Cicero's religious thought. But I must declare some old debts. First, to J. Vogt, *Ciceros Glaube an Rom* (Stuttgart, 1935; repr. Darmstadt, 1963); P. Boyancé, *Étude sur le Songe de Scipion* (Paris, 1936); M. van den Bruwaene, *La théologie de Cicéron* (Louvain, 1937); W. Süss, *Cicero: Eine Einführung in seine philosophischen Schriften,* Abh. Akad. Mainz 1965, no. 5; M. Gelzer, *Cicero* (Wiesbaden, 1969); P. Boyancé, *Études sur l'humanisme cicéronien* (Brussels, 1970); R. J. Goar, *Cicero and the State Religion* (Amsterdam, 1972); *Ciceroniana: Hommages à K. Kumaniecki* (Leyden, 1975), and especially to the two papers in it by J.-M. André (pp. 11–21) and J. Kroymann (pp. 116–28); A. Heuss, *Ciceros Theorie vom römischen Staat,* Nachr. Akad. Göttingen 1975, no. 8; K. Büchner, *Somnium Scipionis,* Hermes Einzelschr. 36 (Wiesbaden, 1976). Among more recent studies, cf. J. Glucker, *Antiochus and the Late Academy* (Göttingen, 1978); E. A. Schmidt, "Die ursprüngliche Gliederung von Ciceros Dialog *De natura deorum,*" *Philologus* 122 (1978), 59–67; J.-P. Martin, *Providentia deorum* (Rome, 1982); K. M. Girardet, *Die Ordnung der Welt,* Historia Einzelschr. 42 (Wiesbaden, 1983), on the *De legibus.* See also K. Büchner (ed.), *Das neue Cicerobild* (Darmstadt, 1971).
2. Review of Weinstock, *JRS* 65 (1975), 171–77. Cf. the discussion of Weinstock by A. Alföldi, *Gnomon* 47 (1975), 154–79, and Alföldi's review of *Die Vergottung Caesars* (Kallmünz, 1968), by H. Gesche, *Phoenix* 24 (1970), 166–76; and in general the two recent monographs by Z. Yavetz, *Caesar in der öffentlichen Meinung* (Düsseldorf, 1979; Eng. trans. London, 1983), and Chr. Meier, *Caesar²* (Berlin, 1982).
3. On Nigidius Figulus, cf. L. A. El'nickij, "Social'no-Političeskie Aspekty Brontoskopičeskogo Kalendarja P. Nigidija Figula," *Vestnik Dr. Istorii* 116 (1971), 107–16; B. Gallotta, "Nuovi Contributi alla conoscenza della cultura romano-italica," *Centro Studi e Documentazione sull'Italia romana* 6 (1974–75), 139–54.
4. "Die Theologia Tripartita in Forschung und Bezeugung," *ANRW* 1. 4 (1973), pp. 63–115; cf. J. Pépin, "La théologie tripartite de Varron," *Rev. Ét. Aug.* 2 (1956), 265–94.

5. For the details I must refer to the paper by E. Norden, who apparently was the first to draw attention to Lydus's passage in 1921, now in *Kleine Schriften* (Berlin, 1966), 282–85.
6. "Cicerone e Varrone. Storia di una conoscenza," *Athenaeum* 40 (1962), 221–43.
7. "Varro's *Antiquitates Rerum Divinarum* and Religious Affairs in the late Roman Republic," *BJRL* 65 (1982), 148–205. Cf. the papers on Varro by P. Boyancé collected in *Études sur la religion romaine* (Rome, 1972); A. Dihle, "Zwei Vermutungen zu Varro," *Rh M* 108 (1965): 170–83; N. Horsfall, "Varro and Caesar," *BICS* 19 (1972), 120–28; P. Boyancé, "Les implications philosophiques des écrits de Varron sur la religion romaine," *Atti . . . Congresso Studi Varroniani* (Rieti, 1976), 137–61. References to the *Antiquitates Rerum Divinarum* are collected in B. Cardauns, *M. T. Varro "Antiquitates Rerum Divinarum" I–II*, Abh. Akad. Mainz (Wiesbaden, 1976); cf. idem, "Varro und die römische Religion," *ANRW* 2. 16. 1 (1978), 80–103.
8. Cf. P. L. Schmidt, *Die Abfassungszeit von Ciceros Schrift über die Gesetze* (Rome, 1965); E. Rawson, "The Interpretation of Cicero's *De Legibus*," *ANRW* 1. 4 (1973), 334–56. My views on Cicero can be considered an independent confirmation of ideas put forward by C. Koch in papers posthumously collected in the volume *Religio* (Nürnberg, 1960), esp. 187–204.
9. It will be enough to refer to the three commentaries on *De natura deorum* by A. S. Pease (1955–58), M. van den Bruwaene (1970–81), and W. Gerlach and K. Bayer (1978); for *De divinatione*, see Pease's commentary (1920–23). I am aware that W. Jaeger took the appeal to the authority of tradition at the beginning of Book 3 as the essential section of *De natura deorum* and considered it an anticipation of the Christian argument from authority; but the Christian basis for authority was revelation. Cf. W. Jaeger, "The Problem of Authority and the Crisis of the Greek Spirit," *Authority and the Individual*, Harvard Tercentenary Conference (Cambridge, Mass., 1937), 240–50, summarized by Jaeger himself in *Early Christianity and Greek Paideia* (Cambridge, Mass., 1962), 42 and 122.
10. On Ovid, cf. R. Schilling, "Ovide interprète de la religion romaine," *REL* 46 (1968), 222–35 (= *Rites, cultes, dieux de Rome* [Paris, 1979], 11–22; cf. also pp. 1–10); W. R. Johnson, "The Desolation of the Fasti," *CJ* 74 (1978), 7–18. For the background, see G. P. Goold, "The Cause of Ovid's Exile," *ICS* 8 (1982), 94–107. Cf. W. Fauth, "Römische Religion im Spiegel der *Fasti* des Ovid," *ANRW* 2. 16. 1 (1978), 104–86, esp. for the bibliography, and T. Gesztelyi, "Ianus bei Ovid: Bemerkungen zur Komposition der *Fasti*," *ACD* 16 (1980), 53–59.
11. In A. Guarino (ed.), *La rivoluzione romana* (Naples, 1982), 222–35. Cf. P. Jal, "Les dieux et les guerres civiles," *REL* 40 (1962), 170–200; H. Pavis d'Escurac, "La pratique augurale romaine à la fin de la république," in *Religion et culture dans la cité italienne* (Strasbourg, 1981), 27–35.
12. It is worth mentioning C. B. Schmitt, *Cicero Scepticus: A Study of the Influence of the "Accademia" in the Renaissance* (The Hague, 1972). For *De natura deorum* in the Renaissance, cf. D. P. Walker, *The Ancient Theology* (London, 1972).

5. Religion in Athens, Rome, and Jerusalem in the First Century B.C.

1. A lecture at the University of Chicago in a course on Roman religion, April–May 1983..The purpose was to call attention to what is seldom observed—the obvious. Bibliography is added only to clarify some controversial points. General works, such as the recent volumes II, 16; 17; 19 of *Aufstieg und Niedergang der römischen Welt* and vol. II of Schürer-Vermes-Millar (*The History of the Jewish People*) are presupposed.

2. See S. Calderone, *Pistis-Fides*, Messina, n.d. (but 1964). I must here express partial disagreement with the interesting remarks on Fides by G. Piccaluga, *Aufstieg und Niedergang* 17, 2 (1981), 703–35. Tacitus, *Ann.*, 2, 49 is misinterpreted by her. For a thorough analysis of the political side cf. E. S. Gruen, *Athenaeum* 50, 1982, 50–68 (with bibl.); P. Grimal, *CRAcad. Inscr.* 1984, 472.

3. See the very pertinent remarks by E. Stein, "Gute Hoffnung," *Monatsschrift Gesch. Wiss. Judent.* 82, 1938, 376–81. I am generally indebted to R. J. Z. Werblowsky, *Faith, Hope and Trust: a Study in the Concept of Bittahon*, Papers Inst. Jewish Studies, London, ed. by J. G. Weiss, I, Jerusalem 1964, 96–139. Cf. F. Van Menxel, *Elpis, Espoir, Espérance*, Berne, 1983.

4. It will be enough to refer to the bibliography of S. Holm-Nielsen, *Die Psalmen Salomos* in *Jüd. Schriften aus hell.-röm. Zeit* IV, 2, 1977 and of J. Schüpphaus, *Die Psalmen Salomos*, Leiden, 1977. But neither quotes A. Büchler, *Types of Jewish-Palestinian Piety*, London, 1922, a penetrating analysis of part of the Psalms. I cannot agree with the Essenian interpretation of them supported, among others, by E.-M. Laperrousaz, *L'attente du Messie en Palestine à la veille et au début de l'ère chrétienne*, Paris, 1982, 259–84. Such labels (even the Pharisaic one) mean little anyway: G. W. E. Nickelsburg, *Jewish Literature between the Bible and the Mishnah*, Philadelphia 1981, 203–12. Cf. G. Stemberger, *Die römische Herrschaft im Urteil der Juden*, Darmstadt, 1983.

5. There is still much to learn from P. Graindors's books, especially *Athènes sous Auguste*, Le Caire, 1927. Cf. also E. Kadletz, *AJA*, 86, 1982, 444–46.

6. Specific research on Homeric *scholia* in relation to late Greek religion would be desirable. In addition to H.-I. Marrou (*Histoire de l'éducation dans l'Antiquité* which I use in the sixth ed. 1965) and M. P. Nilsson (*Die hellenistische Schule*, München, 1955) I should like to refer to the volume ed. by M. Vegetti, *Oralità, scrittura, spettacolo*, Torino, 1983, especially to 187–209 by M. A. Manacorda. Notice the remark by U. Wilamowitz, *Sappho und Simonides*, Berlin, 1913, 312.

7. On the world of Ovid see some indications in Chapter 4, "The Theological Efforts of the Roman Upper Classes in the First Century B.C.," pp. 58–73 above.

8. Cf. Chr. Ulf, *Das römische Lupercalienfest*, Darmstadt, 1982.

9. It will be enough to refer to J. N. Sevenster, *Do you know Greek?*, Leiden, 1968; to J. Guttmann, ed., *The Synagogue*, New York 1975, and especially to the papers in it by M. Hengel (by Hengel cf. also *Between Jesus and Paul*, London, 1983, 1–29) and to the relevant chapters in *Aufstieg und Niedergang* 19, 1. For the Palestinian evidence, F. Hüttenmeister, *Die antiken Synagogen in Israel*, Wiesbaden, 1977, I. Cf. also the relevant chapters by S. Safrai, in *The Jewish People in the First Century*, Assen, 1976, II, and J. Guttmann, *Ancient Synagogues. The State of Research*, Chicago, 1981.

10. A. D. Nock, *Conversion*, Oxford, 1933, 26; M. Nilsson, *Gesch. d. griech. Religion*², München, 1961, II, 244; *Jewish and Christian Self-Definition*, III, ed. by B. F. Meyer and E. P. Sanders, London, 1982, especially 137–60; U. Bianchi and M. J. Vermaseren (eds.), *La soteriologia dei Culti Orientali nell'impero romano*, Leiden, 1982. But the evidence is poor. See by contrast the Jewish evidence on the Mysteries of God in J. J. Collins, *Between Athens and Jerusalem*, New York, 1983, 195–243.

6. How Roman Emperors Became Gods

1. Cf. on this controversial point E. J. Bickerman, *Athenaeum* 41, 1964, 70–85 = *Religions and Politics in the Hellenistic and Roman Periods*, 1985, 473–88; E. Badian in H. J. Dell (ed.), *Ancient Macedonian Studies in Honor of Ch. F. Edson*, 1981, 28–67; id., *Cambridge History of Iran* II, 1985, 488 n. 1. I am in agreement with P. A. Brunt, *Greece and Rome* II, 12, 1965, 210.

7. What Josephus Did Not See

1. P. Vidal-Naquet, "Économie et société dans la Grèce ancienne: l'oeuvre de M. I. Finley," in *Archives Européenes de Sociologie* 6, 1965, 111–48; introduction to the French translation of *Democracy Ancient and Modern* (*Tradition de la démocratie grecque*), Paris, 1976. For his work with J.-P. Vernant, it is sufficient to refer to their book, *Mythe et tragédie en Grèce ancienne*, Paris, 1972. It is not possible to produce here the requisite list of even the most important writings of Vidal-Naquet due to the difficulty in tracing his numerous contributions to volumes of collected articles and his own introductions to the works of others. Mention should at least be made of the excellent and well-chosen selection of annotated texts which he brought out with M. Austin, *Économies et sociétés en Grèce ancienne*, 1972, of which there is an enlarged English edition (*Economic and Social History of Ancient Greece*, London, 1977).
2. See, e.g., V. Di Benedetto, in *Belfagor*, 33, 1978, 191–207, which contains valid objections, and also the curious piece by B. Hemmerdinger, *Belfagor*, 31, 1976, 353–58.
3. Cf. J. Guttmann (ed.), *The Synagogue*, New York, 1975. Three different approaches to the study of Judaism of the first century A.D. may be seen in S. Safrai and M. Stern (eds.), *The Jewish People in the First Century*, I–II (so far published), Leiden, 1974–76; E. Rivkin, *A Hidden Revolution: The Pharisees' Search for the Kingdom Within*, Abingdon, 1978; W. S. Green (ed.), *Approaches to Ancient Judaism: Theory and Practice*, Missoula, 1978. On the educational system, J. Goldin in *Ex Orbe Religionum. Studia G. Widengren*, I, Leiden, 1972, 176–91. It may be interesting to compare these with a sociological study of the modern American synagogue, S. C. Heilman, *Synagogue Life*, Chicago, 1973.
4. On the legend of Nero, A. Yabro Collins, *The Combat Myth in the Book of Revelation*, Missoula, 1976, 170–206. Certain points are filled by J. J. Collins, *The Sibylline Oracles of Egyptian Judaism*, Missoula, 1974, 73–90.
5. Among the better commentaries to the Apocalypse are: W. Bousset (1906); R. H. Charles (1920); B. M. Allo, 3rd ed. (1933); G. B. Caird (1966); H. Kraft (1974). The commentary of J. Massyngberde Ford (1976) who basically sees the Apocalypse as a pre-Christian work seems more subtle than correct. For guidance on the social and religious background, Sh. E. Johnson, "Unsolved Questions about Early Christianity in Anatolia," *Studies in New Testament and Early Christian Literature* [. . .] *in Honour of A. P. Wikgren*, Leiden, 1972, 181–93.
6. The dating of the Apocalypse to the time of Nero (which I accepted in *Cambridge Ancient History* X, 1934, 726) is defended point by point by J. A. T. Robinson, *Redating the New Testament*, London, 1976, 221–53. For the situation of the Jews and Christian in the Flavian era, cf., e.g., Bo Reicke, *The New Testament Era* (2nd English ed. of *Neutestamentliche Zeitgeschichte*, 1964), London, 1969; P. Keresztes, "The Jews, the Christians and Emperor Domitian," *Vigiliae Christianae*, 27, 1973, 1–28. H. Kreissig, "Rom und die Entwicklung der judäischen Kultur," *Atti Ce. R.D.A.C.*, 10, Milan, 1978, 83–97, seems unfocused.
7. This point was developed by me in the essay "The Origins of Universal History" which was presented at the University of Chicago and in the Chr. Gauss Seminars in Criticism at Princeton University (1979), pp. 31–57 above.
8. Verses 155ff. allude to a comet of A.D. c. 74 which should probably be identified with the comet dated 76 by Pliny (*Nat. Hist.* 2. 89).
9. G. Mussies, *The Morphology of Koine Greek as Used in the Apocalypse of St. John*, Leiden, 1971.
10. The passage in Josephus, *Ant.* 10, 276 is mutilated, but it is cited in what is clearly a more complete form (although not necessarily completely correct) by

John Chrysostomus, *Adv. Judaeos* (*P.G.*, 48, 897). The attempt by J. Braverman, *Jerome's Commentary on Daniel*, Washington, 1978, 109–10, to uphold the reading of the manuscripts of Josephus does not work in my opinion. On Flavius Josephus and Daniel, apart from V. Nikiprowetzky, *Hommages à André Dupont-Sommer*, Paris 1971, 461–90, and A. Paul, *Recherches de science religieuse*, 63, 1975, 367–84, cited by Vidal-Naquet, cf. U. Fischer, *Eschatologie und Jenseitserwartung im hellenistischen Diaspora-Judentum*, Berlin, 1978.

11. Cf. my article "Flavius Josephus and Alexander's Visit to Jerusalem," *Athenaeum* 57, 1979. See also W. C. van Unnik, *Flavius Josephus als historischer Schriftsteller*, Heidelberg, 1978, and the earlier observations by M. I. Finley in the introduction to Flavius Josephus, *The Jewish War and Other Selections*, London, 1966, which though brief is one of the best evaluations of the historian.

12. Cf. my observations on the *Contra Apionem* (1931) now in *Terzo Contributo*, 1966, 513–22, which I still hold to be substantially correct.

13. For the problematic reconstruction of the figure of Johanan ben Zakkai cf. J. Neusner, *Journal of Jewish Studies* 24, 1973, 65–73, where he corrects his earlier writings on the subject.

14. Cf. H. Schreckenberg, *Die Flavius-Josephus-Tradition in Antike und Mittelalter*, Leiden, 1972.

15. The French title of Vidal-Naquet's book, *Flavius Josèphe ou du bon usage de trahison*, suggests Pascal's *Prière pour demander à Dieu le bon usage des maladies*, which the reader would do well to keep in mind.

12. The New Letter by "Anna" to "Seneca"

1. Ms. 17 Erzbischöfliche Bibliothek in Köln.
2. I am indebted to Carlotta Dionisotti for discussion.

Additional Note: At a meeting on March 1, 1985, of the American Academy in Rome, where I spoke about this letter, my friend Professor G. N. Knauer rightly raised the question of the relation between the letter by Anna to Seneca and the letter by "Mardocheus Iudeorum minimus" to Alexander the Great which circulated in isolation and became an appendix to what is known as *Historia de preliis Alexandri Magni*, Rezension J³, edited by Karl Steffens, 1975, 208–17. The similarity is obvious in the sense that Mardocheus, too, was making propaganda for monotheism.

But the individual arguments are different (notice Mardocheus's preoccupation with astral polytheism). As far as I know, Mardocheus's letter has been dated around the twelfth century (F. Pfister, *Kleine Schriften zum Alexanderroman*, Meisenheim a.G. 1976, 344). It will have to be studied again in relation to Anna's letter, but it does not appear to have been a model for it.

14. A Medieval Jewish Autobiography

1. G. Niemeyer's edition of Hermannus's *Opusculum* was reviewed by F. J. Schmale, *Hist. Zeitsch.* CC, 1965, 114–20. Previous bibliography in P. Browe, S. J., *Die Judenmission im Mittelalter und die Päpste*, Roma, 1973, 62. The text, it seems to me, is basically misunderstood by W. P. Eckert, in *Monumenta Judaica. 2000 Jahre Geschichte und Kultur der Juden am Rhein*, ed. K. Schilling, Köln, 1963, 150–51. For background see in the same *Monumenta Judaica* the section by E. Roth, 60–130. Cf. furthermore G. Kisch, *The Jews in Medieval Germany*, Chicago, 1949, second ed., New York, 1970, and the two papers by H. Liebeschütz, *Journal of Jewish Studies* 10, 1959, 97–111; 16, 1965, 35–46. For medieval biography in general see K. J. Weintraub, *The Value of the Individual*, Chicago, 1978,

18–114 (on Hermannus and the Premonstratensians, p. 63). Cf. also Pl. F. Lefèvre and W. M. Grawen, *Les statuts de Prémontré au milieu du XIIᵉ siècle*, Averbode, 1978. (W. Goez, *Gestalten des Hochmittelalters*, 1983, 238–53).

2. Cf. M. Pazzaglia in *Enciclopedia Dantesca* V, 1976, 1086–96. For medieval theories on dreams, F. X. Newman, *Somnium*, Princeton, 1962. Cf. also A. Löwinger, *Der Traum in der jüdischen Literatur*, Leipzig, 1908.

3. A critical edition was published under the title "Megillat Obadiah hager" with a discussion in Hebrew by N. Golb in *S. D. Goitein Festschrift*, Jerusalem, 1980, making all these fragments available together. The bibliography provided by *Encyclopaedia Judaica*, s.v. "Obadiah the Norman Proselyte," 12, 1971, 1306–8, is supplemented by A. Scheiber, "Der Lebenslauf des Johannes-Obadja aus Oppido," in P. Borraro (ed.), *Antiche Civiltà Lucane*, Galatina, 1975, 240–44. The most recent contribution, of great importance, is by J. Prawer, *Studies in Medieval Jewish History and Literature*, ed. I. Twersky, Cambridge, Mass., 1979, 110–34. I indicate here only the previous editions of texts and the discussions relevant to my argument. The anonymous text published by S. Assaf in *Zion* 5, 1940, 118–19 (and also in the volume *Meqoroth u-mehqarim*, Jerusalem, 1946, 143; corrections to this edition by N. Golb, *Journ. Jewish Studies* 16, 1965, 71) was attributed to Andreas, archbishop of Bari, by B. Blumenkranz, *Journ. Jewish Studies* 14, 1963, 33–36, whereas S. D. Goitein, *Journ. Jewish Studies* 4, 1953, 74–84 had preferred the identification, already hinted at by Assaf, with Obadiah. Neither suggestion is cogent, as N. Golb remarks, *Journ. Jewish Studies* 16, 1965, 69–74. The main fragments of Obadiah's autobiographical text in the third person were published by E.-N. Adler, *Rev. Ét. Juives* 69, 1919, 129–34; J. Mann, *Rev. Ét. Juives* 89, 1930, 245–59; S. D. Goitein, *Journ. Jewish Studies* 4, 1953, 74–84 (English trans. only); A. Scheiber, *Acta Orientalia Hungarica* 4, 1954, 271–96 (basically repeated in *Kiryath Sefer* 30, 1954–55, 73–98 and *Journ. Jewish Studies* 5, 1954, 32–37); A. Scheiber, *Hebrew Union College Annual* 39, 1968, 168–72 (text already translated by Goitein in *Journ. Jewish Studies* 4, 1953, but Scheiber publishes also a letter in verse concerning another convert to Judaism of about 1100). Relevant also is the paper in Hebrew by N. Golb, "A Study of a Proselyte to Judaism who fled to Egypt at the Beginning of the Eleventh Century," *Sefer Zikkaron le-I. Ben Zwi*, Jerusalem, 1964, 87–104 (especially 102–4). Essential for the background is S. D. Goitein, *A Mediterranean Society. The Jewish Communities of the Arab World*, 2, Berkeley 1971, especially 308–11. It is to be hoped that all the evidence about Obadiah will be translated and commented upon with due consideration of the traditions of Norman historiography.

4. For the more probable interpretation see N. Golb, *Sefer Zikkaron le-I. Ben Zwi*, 102–3 and *Journ. Jewish Studies* 18, 1967, 43–63. For dreams of another convert, A. Scheiber, *Tarbiz* 34, 1964–65, 367.

5. I am deeply indebted to my colleague Professor N. Golb of the University of Chicago who allowed me to use his critical text of Obadiah's fragments before publication and discussed with me their interpretation. I owe further information to Dr. B. Smalley, to my daughter A. L. Lepschy, to Rabbi L. Jacobs, and to Joanna Weinberg.

15. A Note on Max Weber's Definition of Judaism as a Pariah-Religion

1. Efr. Shmueli, "The 'Pariah-People' and Its 'Charismatic Leadership.' A Revaluation of Max Weber's *Ancient Judaism*" in *Proceedings of the American Academy of Jewish Research* 36, 1968, 167–247 at 170.

2. See Hannah Arendt, *The Jew as Pariah*, ed. R. H. Feldman, New York, 1978, 126.
3. *Ibid.*, 68; but for her special usage of the term compare more especially her biography *Rahel Varnhagen* [1957], New York, 1974, 199–215, "Between Pariah and Parvenu." For German terminology about the Jews cf. A. Bein, "The Jewish Parasite," *Year Book* of the Leo Baeck Institute 9, 1964, 3–40.
4. See Max Weber, *Ancient Judaism*, trans. and ed. H. H. Gerth and Don Martindale, New York, 1967, and Max Weber, *The Sociology of Religion*, trans. Ephraim Fischoff and intr. Talcott Parsons, Boston, 1963. "Das antike Judentum" appeared first in the *Archiv für Sozialwissenschaft und Sozialforschung*, 1917–19, and was reprinted with the addition of a supplement on the Pharisees in *Gesammelte Aufsätze zur Religionssoziologie* III, Tübingen 1921. *The Sociology of Religion* is a section of *Wirtschaft und Gesellschaft* first published in Tübingen in 1922; the English translation follows the revised edition by J. Winckelmann, Tübingen 1956, I, 2, 245–381.

   Among discussions of Weber's texts on Judaism I shall mention only W. Caspari, *Die Gottesgemeinde vom Sinai und das nachmalige Volk Israel. Auseinandersetzungen mit Max Weber*, Gütersloh 1922; I. Schiper, "Max Weber on the Sociological Basis of the Jewish Religion," *Jewish Journal of Sociology* 1, 1959, 250–60 (originally published in Polish in 1924); J. Guttmann, "Max Weber's Soziologie des antiken Judentums," *Monatsschrift für Geschichte und Wissenschaft des Judentums* 69, 1925, 195–223; J. Taubes, "Die Entstehung des jüdischen Pariavolkes" in *Max Weber, Gedächtnisschrift*, ed. K. Engisch and others, Berlin, 1966, 185–94; J. Freund, "L'éthique économique et les religions mondiales selon Max Weber," *Arch. Sociol. des Religions* 26, 1968, 3–25; Fr. Raphaël, "Max Weber et le Judaïsme antique," *Arch. Européennes de Sociologie* 11, 1970, 297–336; F. Parente, "Max Weber e la storia dell'antico Israele," *Annali Scuola Normale Superiore di Pisa* 3, 1978, 1365–96. But the most important work is H. Liebeschütz, *Das Judentum im deutschen Geschichtsbild von Hegel bis Max Weber*, Tübingen, 1967: cf. his previous essay "Max Weber's Historical Interpretation of Judaism," *Year Book* of the Leo Baeck Institute 9, 1964, 41–68. A critique of Weber from points of view ultimately going back to Durkheim is in A. Causse, *Du Groupe ethnique à la communauté religieuse*, Paris, 1937. For other criticism: J. A. Holstein, "Max Weber and Biblical Scholarship," *Hebrew Union College Annual* 46, 1975, 159–79. Cf. also P. Bourdieu, "Une interprétation de la théorie de la religion selon Max Weber," *Arch. Europ. Sociol.* 12, 1971, 3–21.
5. Weber, *Ancient Judaism*, 3. "Das antike Judentum," 2: "Denn was waren soziologisch angesehen, die Juden? Ein Pariavolk. Das heisst, wie wir aus Indien wissen: ein rituell, formell oder faktisch, von der sozialen Umwelt geschiedenes Gastvolk."
6. *Ibid.*, 8: "Das Problem ist also: wie sind die Juden zu einem Pariavolk mit dieser höchst spezifischen Eigenart geworden?"
7. Weber, *Ancient Judaism*, 417. "Das antike Judentum," 434: "Und zwar freiwillig von sich aus, nicht etwa unter dem Zwang äusserer Ablehnung."
8. Weber, *Sociology of Religion*, 108–9. *Wirtschaft und Gesellschaft*, 2 ed. 1925, I, 282 = 4 ed. 1956, II, 2, 300: "eine, durch (ursprünglich) magische, tabuistische und rituelle Schranken der Tisch- und Konnubialvergemeinschaftung nach aussen einerseits, durch politische und sozial negative Privilegierung, verbunden mit weitgehender ökonomischer Sondergebarung andererseits, zu einer erblichen Sondergemeinschaft zusammengeschlossene Gruppe ohne autonomen politischen Verband."
9. Weber says more precisely (*Ancient Judaism*, 404): "the struggle of the rabbis against the religious internationalization [sic] of revenge is ethically impressive and indicates, indeed, a strong sublimation of ethical feeling." Cf. "Das antike Judentum," 422: "der Kampf der Rabbiner gegen die religiöse Verinnerlichung der Rache."

10. Weber, *Sociology of Religion*, 260.
11. Weber, *Ancient Judaism*, 51, 336ff.
12. *Ibid.*, 345. "Das antike Judentum," 360: "Diese Gastvolksstellung nun wurde durch die rituelle Abschliessung begründet, welche, in der deuteronomischen Zeit wie wir sahen, verbreitet, in der Exilszeit und durch die Gesetzgebung des Esra und Nehemia durchgeführt wurde."
13. In *Sociology of Religion*, 108: "Since the Exile, as a matter of actual fact, and formally since the destruction of the Temple, the Jews became a pariah people." Cf. *Wirtschaft und Gesellschaft* I, 282 = I, 2, 300: "Seit dem Exil tatsächlich und auch formell seit der Zerstörung des Tempels waren die Juden ein 'Pariavolk'." Weber's allusion to the pariah status of the Jews in the conclusion of *Politik als Beruf* belongs to another context.
14. I am much indebted to Professor E. Shils for discussing the topic of this paper in our joint seminar on Weber's *Judaism* at the University of Chicago in the autumn of 1979. I owe other critical remarks to Professor J. Ben-David, to S. C. Humphreys, and to Rabbi L. Jacobs.

16. The Jews of Italy

1. This essay was prepared for a meeting at Brandeis University last year in honor of Vito Volterra, the great Italian mathematician who died in 1940. Volterra had been a professor at three Italian universities—Turin, Pisa, and Rome—where I also taught. He was elected by the king to the Italian senate in 1905 and later spoke out strongly against Fascism. Two distinguished mathematicians of my own family, Eugenio Elia and Beppo Levi, were inspired in their work by him. My friendship with his sons, especially with Edoardo, a student of Roman law, goes back to 1929, when I had just moved to Rome from Turin.
2. Yet though I am not the first trained historian of my family to be interested in our history—I have been preceded by a better man than myself, my late cousin and friend Arturo Carlo Jemolo, a Momigliano on his mother's side, a Sicilian Catholic on his father's side—there are too many facts we do not know. I wish I knew more of Giuseppe Vita Momigliano of Ivrea who was one of the representatives of the Piedmontese Jews in the Napoleonic Sanhedrin of 1806. Another Piedmontese Jew of the Segre (my wife's) family, Salvatore Segre, was the *av-bet-din*, the chairman of the same Sanhedrin. I wish I knew more also of Isacco Momigliano, who pestered eminent men with his questions on religion and literature; it was to him that Sadal—Samuel David Luzzatto—wrote his famous letter on Judaism and Christianity, arguing, of course, for the right to exist of the former.
3. *The Chronicle of Ahimaaz*, translated by M. Salzman (Columbia University Press, 1924).

17. Gershom Scholem's Autobiography

1. See his letter in M. Buber, *Briefwechsel* II, 367–68.
2. In *On Jews and Judaism in Crisis*, Schocken, 1976.
3. *Der Jude* 5, 1920, 363–91; 6, 1921, 55–69 (cf. his letter to Buber in the latter's *Briefwechsel* II, 86–88).
4. In its published form (*Das Buch Bahir*, Leipzig, 1923) the dissertation contains only the German translation of the text and a commentary.
5. Harvard University Press, 1979.
6. *Begegnung*, 1960, 36–38.

18. How to Reconcile Greeks and Trojans

1. The text edited by G. Manganaro in A. Alföldi, *Römische Frühgeschichte*, 1976, 83–96.

2. N. Horsfall, *JHS* 99, 1979, 26–48 has a better case in denying that the Roman Tabula Iliaca reflects Stesichorus than in disputing the credibility of Dionysius about Hellanicus (cf. his article in *CQ* n.s. 29, 1979, 372–90). The captions of the Tabula Iliaca raise two problems: whether the author of the captions intended to establish a connection between Stesichorus and Aeneas's migration to the West and whether this connection, if any, was correct. In the case of Dionysius there is only one problem: whether Dionysius is reliable in reporting Hellanicus. I still believe that the author (Isidore?) of the Tabula Iliaca intended to establish a connection between Stesichorus and Aeneas's journey to the West and was correct in doing so. But obviously I attribute less probability to this opinion than to the opinion that Dionysius read and understood his Hellanicus. Cf. F. Prinz, *Gründungsmythen und Sagenchronologie*, 1979, 155; D. Ambaglio, *L'opera storiografica di Ellanico di Lesbo*, 1980, 124–26, and my own remarks in *La storiografia greca*, 1982, 353–56.

3. It will be enough to refer to the bibl. in L. Vagnetti, *Il deposito votivo di Campetti a Veio*, 1971, 88, but for the lower date cf. M. Torelli, *Dialoghi d' Archeol.* 7, 1973, 399–400. The historical implications of the oinochoe 179 of the Bibl. Nationale of Paris (*C.V.A. France*, 7, pl. 12)—if it represents a scene of the destruction of Troy—are obscure to me. I cannot quite follow F. Zevi's conjectures in *Gli Etruschi e Roma* (Colloquio M. Pallottino), 1981, 148.

4. Cf. F. Castagnoli, *La Parola del Passato* 32, 1977, 355; C. F. Giuliani and P. Sommella, ibid. 367. Though I consider it probable that the *heroon* was built for Aeneas in the fourth century B.C., the objections by T. J. Cornell, *Liverpool Classical Monthly* 2, April 1977, 79–80 remain serious: the inscription of the *heroon* did not mention the name of Aeneas, and the place of the *heroon* is rather far from the Numicus. The answer by F. Castagnoli, *Studi Romani* 30, 1981, 13 does not entirely solve these doubts. C. Cogrossi in M. Sordi (ed.), *Politica e religione nel primo scontro tra Roma e l'Oriente*, 1982, 79–98 is speculative.

5. M. Guarducci's reading of the text, as represented in *Mitt. Deutsch. Arch. Inst. Rom.* 78, 1971, 73–118, seems on the whole plausible: it was confirmed by A. Degrassi, *I.L.L.R.* 1271, in 1963. But notice the doubts by T. J. Cornell, *Liverpool Classical Monthly* cit. in note 4, 79. For the interpretation of Lar see the acute remarks by J. Heurgon, *Mél. Piganiol*, 2, 1966, 655–64.

6. The evidence on the Decii is ambiguous; it depends on the interpretation of the title of L. Accius's tragedy *Aeneades sive Decius* (I, 281, Ribbeck²). But the evidence of the Nautii (Dionys. 6, 69; Verg. *Aen.* 5, 704; Serv. *Aen.* 2, 166) and on the Greganii (Serv. *Aen.* 5, 117) is unambiguous. See P. T. Wiseman, *Greece and Rome* 2 s., 21, 1974, 153–60.

7. On Menecrates cf. P. M. Smith, *Harv. St. Class. Phil.* 85, 1981, 33 who sees anti-Greek, not anti-Roman bias. My friend D. Asheri allowed me to see a chapter on Menecrates of a yet unpublished book. He plausibly treats Menecrates as a neutral observer of previous (fifth-century-B.C.) politically tinged debates on Greco-Trojan (= Persian) relations. On the attribution of the *Communis historia* or *communes historiae* to the consul of 102 cf. A. La Penna, *Scritti in onore di B. Riposati*, Rieti 1979, 229–40.

8. Cf. D. Musti, *Ann. Scuola Normale Pisa* 2, 32, 1963, 225.

9. The reference to Troy in Ennius's Annals ll. 358–59 may be connected with this

event, as E. Badian acutely suggested in *Ennius*, Entretiens Fondation Hardt, 1971, 178–79.

10. A heterodox interpretation in G. Maddoli, *Parola del Passato* 26, 1971, 153–66.

11. E. Peruzzi's latest book, *Mycenaeans in Early Latium*, Rome, 1980, includes with exemplary honesty its own refutation in the archaeological appendix by L. Vagnetti (see especially p. 164). See also the authoritative statement by R. Perone, in *Enea nel Lazio, Bimillenario Virgiliano*, 1981, 87–88.

12. For all this I simply refer to E. Gabba, *Miscellanea di Studi Alessandrini in memoria di A. Rostagni*, 1963, 188–94; D. Musti, *Tendenze nella storiografia romana e greca su Roma arcaica*, 1970; id., *Gli Etruschi e Roma*, quoted, 23–44.

13. We do not know, for lack of evidence, whether Virgil invented the Italian origins of Dardanus. For the two opposite views V. Buchheit, *Vergil über die Sendung Roms*, 1963, 151–72; N. Horsfall, *Journ. Rom. St.* 63, 1973, 68–79.

19. Georges Dumézil and the Trifunctional Approach to Roman Civilization

1. Cf. also by H. J. Rose, "Mana in Greece and Rome," *Harvard Theological Review* 42 (1949), 155–74 and by H. Wagenvoort, *Studies in Roman Literature, Culture and Religion* (Leiden, 1956) and *Pietas, Selected Studies in Roman Religion* (Leiden, 1980).

2. On H. Usener I should like to refer to *Aspetti di H. Usener filologo della religione*, ed. A. Momigliano (Pisa, 1983).

3. Much of the recent work purporting to develop Dumézil's ideas on Roman legends is on very shaky ground. Cf. for instance J. Puhvel, "Remus et frater," *History of Religions* 15 (1975), 146–57; G. Camassa, *L'occhio e il metallo* (Genoa, 1983). But see as an example of more persuasive analysis in the same direction R. Schilling, "Romulus l'élu et Rémus le réprouvé," *Revue des Études Latines* 38 (1961), 182–99 (*Rites, cultes, dieux de Rome* [Paris, 1979], 103–20).

4. The absence of a priestly class in Germany noticed by Caesar is a notorious example. A short poem of the Edda, the *Rigsthula*, which is often quoted as evidence for consistent trifunctional thinking among the Scandinavians, is interesting evidence for the division into slaves, freemen, and noblemen, not for the three functions. The king is chosen from among the warriors, but to be king he must have a modicum of magic, of runes. One god creates the three classes: the poem does not presuppose functional gods for each class. The findings by the Japanese disciples of Dumézil, Atsuhito Yoshida and Taryo Obayashi, of which we are informed by two articles in *Diogenes* 98 (1977), 93–116 and 117–32 and in the collective volume *Georges Dumézil* (Paris, 1981), 319–24, are bound to raise problems about the character of the so-called trifunctional Indo-European system altogether. (Dumézil's *La Courtisane et les seigneurs colorés* [Paris, 1983] appeared too late for discussion in this article; cf. above all pp. 161–80.)

INDEX

Diognetus, 136
Diomedes, 269, 283
Dionysius of Halicarnassus, 8, 46, 87,
    272, 276, 277, 281–282, 310,
    323*n*
Dionysos, 192
Dio of Syracusé, 97
divination, 60, 61, 69–70, 71, 72, 124,
    181
    astrology and, 103
    see also oracles; prophecies
Divine Antiquities (Varro), 16–17
Divus Julius (Weinstock), 59
Domitian, Roman Emperor, 99, 105,
    114, 186
Dorians, 265
Dörner, F. K., 184
dreams, in biographies and
    autobiographies, 169, 226–230
Droysen, Johann Gustav, 6
Druids, 121, 122, 124–126, 179,
    196–197
Drusilla, 184
Duby, Georges, 313
Dugdale, William, 23
Dumézil, Georges, 108, 123, 160,
    289–313
    see also trifunctional approach
Dumézil, Jean-Anatole, 290
Dupuis, C. F., 26
Durkheim, Émile, 28, 29, 290,
    291–292, 293, 294

Ecclesiastes, 51
ecclesiastical history, 19–20, 23
Economics and Society (Weber),
    232–233
Edom, 132
Egypt, 14, 25, 27, 35, 42–43, 45, 58,
    100, 101, 112, 121, 123, 149,
    154, 158, 171, 184, 186, 196,
    197, 198
    prophecy in, 127–129
    proseuche in, 89–90
Ekbert, Bishop of Münster, 223, 225
Elagabalus, Roman Emperor, 126, 183
Eleazar (Masada defender), 118
Eleazar ben Simeon, 229
Eleusis, 82, 168
Elijah, 212
Eliot, T. S., 264
Elpis, 75, 79, 80
Elymi, 270
emperors, cults of, *see* imperial cults
Eneti, 276

Engels, Friedrich, 28, 248
Enlightenment, 25–26, 27
Ennius, Quintus, 15
Enriquez, Federico, 250
ephebes, 84
Ephialtes, 9
Ephorus, 40, 44
Ephraim, Saint, 176
Ephrem the Syrian, 215
Epictetus, 77
Epicureanism, 17, 37, 51, 68, 69, 75,
    80, 148, 163, 207
Epicurus, 14, 37, 85, 97, 168–169,
    170, 172, 195
epigraphy, 4
Epitaphium Sanctae Paulae, 208
Eratosthenes of Cyrene, 15
Eros, 75
Eryx, 279
esotericism, 259
Estienne, Henri, 23
ethnography, 44
Etruria, Etruscans, 123, 183, 266,
    271–272, 283, 297, 303, 307–309
Euander, 280, 281, 282, 283
Eudoxus of Cnidus, 174
euhemerism, 15–16, 21, 22, 26
Euhemerus, 15, 18
Eunapius, 165, 175–176, 177, 193,
    207, 209
Eunus, 122
Euripides, 75, 77
Eusebius of Caesarea, 19, 61–62, 114,
    135, 136, 151, 152, 153, 156,
    170, 194, 207
Eustathius, 176
Eustochium, 208, 210
Euthymius, Saint, 208
evidence:
    as basis of history, 7
    in Renaissance historiography, 23
Evocatio, 178
evolution, 28
Ezekiel, 46, 117
Ezra, 131, 233
Ezur Vedam, 25

Fabii, 306, 307
Fabius Pictor, Quintus, 267–268, 280,
    281
Fabricius, J. A., 23
Faith, 75–81, 191
    in Jerusalem, 79–81
    as *pistis* vs. *fides*, 77–79
Fascism, 239, 240, 244, 250–252

About the Author

Arnaldo Momigliano held university chairs in three countries; at the time of his death in 1987, he was professor emeritus of University College London, Alexander White Professor at the University of Chicago, and Professore Emerito di Storia Antica, Scuola Normale Superiore, Pisa. He had lectured at numerous other universities and colleges, among them Oxford, Cambridge, Harvard, Princeton, and the universities of California, Michigan, Rome, and Turin. His books include *Essays in Ancient and Modern Historiography* (Wesleyan, 1977) and *New Paths of Classicism in the Nineteenth Century*. Momigliano has received the Feltrinelli Prize of the Accademia Lincei, the Kaplun Prize of the University of Jerusalem, and the Kenyon Medal for Classical Studies of the British Academy. In 1987 he was appointed a MacArthur Fellow.

About the Book

On Pagans, Jews, and Christians was composed in Trump Medieval, a contemporary typeface based on classical letter proportions issued in 1954. Trump Medieval was designed by the German graphic artist and type designer Georg Trump (1895–1986).